DATE DUE

		PRINTED IN U.S.A.

Business Plans Handbook

Business Plans

A COMPILATION
OF BUSINESS
PLANS DEVELOPED
BY INDIVIDUALS
THROUGHOUT
NORTH AMERICA

Handbook

VOLUME

35

**Kristin B. Mallegg,
Project Editor**

GALE
CENGAGE Learning·

Farmington Hills, Mich • San Francisco • New York • Waterville, Maine
Meriden, Conn • Mason, Ohio • Chicago

GALE
CENGAGE Learning

Business Plans Handbook, Volume 35

Project Editor: Kristin B. Mallegg

Content Developer: Michele P. LaMeau

Product Design: Jennifer Wahi

Composition and Electronic Prepress: Evi Seoud

Manufacturing: Rita Wimberley

For product information and technology assistance, contact us at
Gale Customer Support, 1-800-877-4253.
For permission to use material from this text or product,
submit all requests online at **www.cengage.com/permissions.**
Further permissions questions can be emailed to
permissionrequest@cengage.com

Gale, a part of Cengage Learning
27500 Drake Rd.
Farmington Hills, MI 48331-3535

ISBN-13: 978-1-4103-1107-8
1084-4473

Printed in Mexico
1 2 3 4 5 6 7 19 18 17 16

Contents

BUSINESS PLANS

CONTENTS

Highlights

Business Plans Handbook, Volume 35 (BPH-35) is a collection of business plans compiled by entrepreneurs seeking funding for small businesses throughout North America. For those looking for examples of how to approach, structure, and compose their own business plans, *BPH-35* presents 20 sample plans, including plans for the following businesses:

- Agritourism Attraction
- Auto Detailing Business
- Children's Art, Dance, and Play Space
- Commercial Cleaning Business
- Commercial Pool Cleaning and Maintenance
- Craft Glass Jewelry Business
- Ghostwriting Business
- Gift Box Business
- Homeless Shelter
- Homemade Candle Company
- Housesitting and Property Management Business
- Ice Cream Retail and Manufacturing Business
- Land Clearing
- Mentally Disabled Care Facility
- Painting Contractor
- Scrap Metal Salvage Business
- Self-Published Author Business
- Seminar Retreat Business
- Senior Citizen Yoga Instructor
- Tree Removal and Stump Grinding Service

FEATURES AND BENEFITS

BPH-35 offers many features not provided by other business planning references including:

- Twenty business plans, each of which represent an attempt at clarifying (for themselves and others) the reasons that the business should exist or expand and why a lender should fund the enterprise.
- Two fictional plans that are used by business counselors at a prominent small business development organization as examples for their clients. (You will find these in the Business Plan Template Appendix.)

- A directory section that includes listings for venture capital and finance companies, which specialize in funding start-up and second-stage small business ventures, and a comprehensive listing of Service Corps of Retired Executives (SCORE) offices. In addition, the Appendix also contains updated listings of all Small Business Development Centers (SBDCs); associations of interest to entrepreneurs; Small Business Administration (SBA) Regional Offices; and consultants specializing in small business planning and advice. It is strongly advised that you consult supporting organizations while planning your business, as they can provide a wealth of useful information.

- A Small Business Term Glossary to help you decipher the sometimes confusing terminology used by lenders and others in the financial and small business communities.

- A cumulative index, outlining each plan profiled in the complete Business Plans Handbook series.

- A Business Plan Template which serves as a model to help you construct your own business plan. This generic outline lists all the essential elements of a complete business plan and their components, including the Summary, Business History and Industry Outlook, Market Examination, Competition, Marketing, Administration and Management, Financial Information, and other key sections. Use this guide as a starting point for compiling your plan.

- Extensive financial documentation required to solicit funding from small business lenders. You will find examples of Cash Flows, Balance Sheets, Income Projections, and other financial information included with the textual portions of the plan.

Introduction

Perhaps the most important aspect of business planning is simply doing it. More and more business owners are beginning to compile business plans even if they don't need a bank loan. Others discover the value of planning when they must provide a business plan for the bank. The sheer act of putting thoughts on paper seems to clarify priorities and provide focus. Sometimes business owners completely change strategies when compiling their plan, deciding on a different product mix or advertising scheme after finding that their assumptions were incorrect. This kind of healthy thinking and re-thinking via business planning is becoming the norm. The editors of *Business Plans Handbook, Volume 35 (BPH-35)* sincerely hope that this latest addition to the series is a helpful tool in the successful completion of your business plan, no matter what the reason for creating it.

This thirty-fifth volume, like each volume in the series, offers business plans created by real people. *BPH-33* provides 20 business plans. The business and personal names and addresses and general locations have been changed to protect the privacy of the plan authors.

NEW BUSINESS OPPORTUNITIES

As in other volumes in the series, *BPH-35* finds entrepreneurs engaged in a wide variety of creative endeavors. Examples include an agritourism attraction, an auto detailing business, and a children's art, dance, and play space. In addition, several other plans are provided, including a commercial cleaning business, a craft glass jewelry business, a homemade candle company, and a scrap metal salvage business, among others.

Comprehensive financial documentation has become increasingly important as today's entrepreneurs compete for the finite resources of business lenders. Our plans illustrate the financial data generally required of loan applicants, including Income Statements, Financial Projections, Cash Flows, and Balance Sheets.

ENHANCED APPENDIXES

In an effort to provide the most relevant and valuable information for our readers, we have updated the coverage of small business resources. For instance, you will find a directory section, which includes listings of all of the Service Corps of Retired Executives (SCORE) offices; an informative glossary, which includes small business terms; and a cumulative index, outlining each plan profiled in the complete *Business Plans Handbook* series. In addition we have updated the list of Small Business Development Centers (SBDCs); Small Business Administration Regional Offices; venture capital and finance companies, which specialize in funding start-up and second-stage small business enterprises; associations of interest to entrepreneurs; and consultants, specializing in small business advice and planning. For your reference, we have also reprinted the business plan template, which provides a comprehensive overview of the essential components of a business plan and two fictional plans used by small business counselors.

SERIES INFORMATION

If you already have the first thirty-four volumes of *BPH*, with this thirty-fifth volume, you will now have a collection of over 650 business plans (not including the updated plans); contact information for hundreds of organizations and agencies offering business expertise; a helpful business plan template; more than 1,500 citations to valuable small business development material; and a comprehensive glossary of terms to help the business planner navigate the sometimes confusing language of entrepreneurship.

ACKNOWLEDGEMENTS

The Editors wish to sincerely thank the contributors to *BPH-35*, including:

- Fran Fletcher
- Paul Greenland
- Claire Moore
- Zuzu Enterprises

COMMENTS WELCOME

Your comments on *Business Plans Handbook* are appreciated. Please direct all correspondence, suggestions for future volumes of *BPH*, and other recommendations to the following:

Managing Editor, Business Product
Business Plans Handbook
Gale, a part of Cengage Learning
27500 Drake Rd.
Farmington Hills, MI 48331-3535
Phone: (248)699-4253
Fax: (248)699-8052
Toll-Free: 800-357-GALE
E-mail: BusinessProducts@gale.com

Agritourism Attraction
Hummingbird Farm

1776 Fletcher Falls Road
Colquitt, Georgia 39837

Fran Fletcher

Hummingbird Farm is a Georgia Agritourism business owned by the Houston family. Hummingbird Farm will offer season-specific activities for the whole family.

EXECUTIVE SUMMARY

Hummingbird Farm is a Georgia Agritourism business owned by the Houston family. Hummingbird Farm will offer season-specific activities for the whole family.

Mr. Houston, a fourth generation South Georgia farmer, has 25 years of experience working on the family farm. After growing corn, peanuts, cotton, and soybeans for many years, Mr. Houston and his wife have decided that they want to share the farm experience with area families by providing:

- A strawberry patch
- A pumpkin patch
- A petting zoo
- Fresh seasonal vegetables

According to the Georgia Department of Tourism, Agritourism is continuing to rise in popularity and is getting an increasing portion of tourism dollars. It is currently a multi-million dollar industry in Georgia, with no signs of slowing down. The farm is located on a major road between the towns of Colquitt and Donalsonville, Georgia. The farm's entrance is highly visible and the road is heavily traveled by beachgoers, especially in the spring and summer months.

There are a couple of similar businesses in the area, but Hummingbird Farm will be unique because it will include:

- A petting zoo
- A fall festival in November
- A glow-in-the-dark corn maze

The overall growth strategy of the company is to offer activities that appeal to families and to add new attractions and make changes as needed each year to keep things fresh and new. Hummingbird Farm hopes to make a modest profit during the first year of operation.

At this time, Mr. Houston wishes to purchase trailers (for hayrides), picnic tables, benches, and a metal building to use as a small country store. Mr. Houston will also need facilities in the metal building to make pies and other desserts.

The owners would like to obtain a business line of credit in the amount of $49,450 to cover the start-up costs and operating expenses for the first three months. The owners will make monthly payments on the loan and will also contribute 10 percent of the annual profits to pay extra on the loan at the end of each year. The owners will use the land and building as collateral for the line of credit and plan to repay the line of credit in the sixth year of operation.

COMPANY DESCRIPTION

Location

Hummingbird Farm is a thirty-acre farm in rural Miller County, Georgia. The entrance to the farm is located on GA Hwy 91 South, a paved two-lane road between Colquitt and the neighboring town of Donalsonville. People traveling to Florida beaches heavily travel this road from March to September.

Hours of Operation

Spring (March 1–May 31)	Summer (June 1–Sept 30)	Fall (Oct 1–Nov 30)	Winter (Dec 1–Feb 28)
Strawberry garden	**Fresh vegetables**	**Pumpkin patch**	**Fresh vegetables**
M–F 8:30–6:00	Call for availability	M–F 8:30–6:00	Call for availability
Sat 9:00–6:00		Sat 9:00–6:00	
Sun 2:00–6:00		Sun 2:00–6:00	
		Glow in the dark corn maze	
	Country store	Fri/Sat	**Country store**
		8:00 pm–11:00 pm	
Groups/parties	M–F 2:00–6:00	**Groups/parties**	M–F 10:00–6:00
Call for appointment	Sat 9:00–6:00	Call for appointment	Sat 9:00–6:00
Country store		**Country store**	
Same as strawberry garden		Same as pumpkin patch	

Personnel

Dave Houston (Owner)
Mr. Houston is a fourth generation farmer. He has twenty-five years of experience working in agriculture. He has successfully grown many crops, including corn, cotton, peanuts, and soybeans. Mr. Houston will oversee/perform most of the planting, harvesting, and maintenance at Hummingbird Farm.

Faith Houston (Owner)
Ms. Houston is relatively new to farming, but has ten years of experience working at a local family entertainment establishment. She will oversee/perform all of the group and party activities. Additionally, she will oversee the General Store and will manage all customer activities.

General Store Helper
A part-time helper will be hired to work in the general store and to coordinate parties and groups.

Farm Helper
A full-time farm helper will be hired to assist with planting, harvesting, and maintenance activities at the farm.

Products and Services

Products (Farm)

- Strawberries

- Fresh Vegetables

- Pumpkins

Products (General Store)

- Salsa

- Relish

- Pickles

- Jellies/Jams

- Boiled Peanuts

- Pie

- Ice cream

- Drinks

- Cotton Angels

- Gift baskets

Services

Groups or individuals may visit Hummingbird Farm and enjoy the following activities:

- Strawberry Patch

- Pumpkin Patch

- Hayride

- Corn Maze

- Kiddie Corn Maze

- Petting Zoo

- Play area

- Flower/Butterfly garden

- Family Fall Festival

- Birthday parties

MARKET ANALYSIS

Industry Overview

According to the Georgia Department of Tourism, agritourism is continuing to rise in popularity and is claiming an increasing portion of tourism dollars. It is currently a multi-million dollar industry in Georgia, with no signs of slowing down. Some farms specialize in one area, while others, like Hummingbird Farm, offer a wide range of activities spanning several seasons.

Hummingbird Farm is located in Miller County, a rural county in Southwest Georgia. The current population of Miller County and its neighboring counties is 52,000, which will provide a large customer base for the business.

Target Market

The target market for Hummingbird Farm is families and school groups in a 30-mile radius. An additional market during the spring and summer months is people traveling to and from the beach.

Competition

There are currently two similar businesses in the surrounding area.

1. Topp's Tree Farm, 100 Tree Farm Road, Climax, Georgia. Christmas trees, petting zoo, parties with covered party area, hayrides. Open October 1- December 23 for Christmas trees; party facilities available all year.

2. Knight's Strawberries, 500 Strawberry Lane, Colquitt, Georgia. Strawberry Patch, General Store. Open spring for strawberries, General store open all year.

GROWTH STRATEGY

The overall strategy of the company is to offer activities that attract families and school groups, to add new things, and to make changes as needed each year to keep things fresh and new.

In addition to strawberry and pumpkin patches and related activities, the owners are going to offer a glow in the dark corn maze to attract older kids and young adults on weekends during the fall. The farm will also host a fall festival in November featuring food, crafts, contests, and hayrides. The owners are already planning to add a haunted hayride during the second year of operation.

While planning this business venture, the owners noticed that the winter months are lacking in activities, and thus profits. The owners are interested in finding some fun activities for the winter and are thinking of adding a snow machine the second year. Another idea includes planting Christmas trees so that they could sell Christmas trees in approximately five to six years.

The owners wish to make a living doing what they love and as long as they can make even a modest profit, they will consider the business a success.

Sales and Marketing

The owners plan to grow their business by providing an enjoyable experience for customers. Hummingbird Farm will be a place where families can gather and experience spring and fall activities. According to the Small Business Development Center, word-of-mouth and referrals serve as the main advertising method for most small businesses, and referrals will be important to the marketing strategy of Hummingbird Farm. Additionally, the owners have identified key advertising avenues and tactics to support Hummingbird Farm's growth strategy.

Hummingbird Farm will market the fact that it is a Georgia agritourism site offering farm fun for the whole family. There is a big, colorful sign at the entrance to the farm that is visible to people traveling in either direction.

Advertising

Hummingbird Farm will advertise through:

*   Social Media
*   *Georgia Tourism Magazine*
*   *The Rural Electrical Membership Corporation Magazine*
*   *The Miller County Liberal*

- *The Donalsonville News*
- *The Early County News*
- *The Post Searchlight*
- Fliers sent to local schools, daycare facilities, and churches

The owners believe these advertising methods will reach most everyone in their target market.

FINANCIAL ANALYSIS

Start-up costs

Estimated start-up costs

Metal building	$10,000
Business license	$ 250
Trailer	$ 500
Play set	$ 1,500
Picnic tables	$ 1,000
Fencing	$ 2,500
Strawberry plants	$ 2,000
Supplies (buckets, boxes)	$ 1,000
Advertising	$ 500
Total	**$19,250**

Estimated Monthly Income

Prices for products—general store

Relish	$ 5
Jam/jelly	$ 5
Pickles	$ 5
Salsa	$ 5
Boiled peanuts	$ 4
Strawberry pie	$12
Pumpkin pie	$12
Peanut brittle	$10
Canned soda	$ 1
Bottled water	$ 1
Gift basket	$12 + Cost of items
Animal food	$2–$5

Prices for Activities

Prices for activities are listed in the chart below. Groups of 10 or more will receive a $2 discount per person if their visit is scheduled in advance.

Strawberry patch	Pumpkin patch	Parties*	Special events
Pick strawberries	Hay ride	Train ride	Glow in the dark corn maze
Face painting	Corn maze	Picnic tables	**$20 per person**
Train ride	Corn pile	Play area	
Strawberry ice cream	Pick small pumpkin	Face painting	
Play area	Play area	Petting zoo	Fall festival
Petting zoo	Petting zoo		2nd Saturday in Nov
$10 per person	**$12 per person**	**$100 for 10 guests** **$8 each additional**	**$12 per person**

Parties held during strawberry or pumpkin season have the option of including related activities.

Prices for Services

Hummingbird Farm will offer picked produce in addition to pick-your-own strawberries.

Strawberries	$10 per bucket
Pumpkins	$5–$25 depends on size
Vegetables	Varies $5–$25 a bushel/bucket
Tomatoes	$10 bucket
Cucumbers	$ 6 bucket
Zucchini	$ 6 bucket
Sweet corn	$ 5 bucket
Peas	$25 bushel shelled
Broccoli	$ 5 per bunch
Cauliflower	$ 5 per bunch
Mustard greens	$10 bucket
Collard greens	$10 bucket

Estimated Monthly Expenses

The owners estimate that employee wages will be the largest monthly expense. They expect expenses to remain steady.

Estimated monthly expenses

Bank loan	$ 200
Electricity	$ 400
Diesel	$ 300
Phone/Internet	$ 100
Liability insurance	$ 300
Advertising	$ 50
Wages (est.)	$ 7,800
Property taxes	$ 500
General store supplies	$ 250
Farm supplies	$ 500
Total	**$10,400**

Profit/Loss

Hummingbird Farm hopes to make a modest profit during the first year of operation. The owners conservatively estimate that there will be some months during the winter when no income will be made. It is their hope that spring, summer, and fall will generate enough income to pay the monthly expenses during the winter.

Estimated profits are based on making approximately $16,640 during the spring months, $15,400 during the summer months, and $33,540 during the fall months. This increase in the fall is due to the projections for the glow in the dark corn maze.

Estimated profits months 1–6

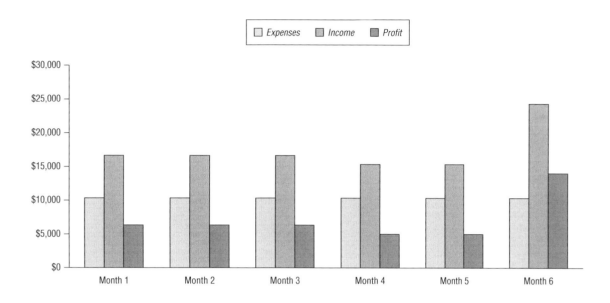

Estimated profits months 7–12

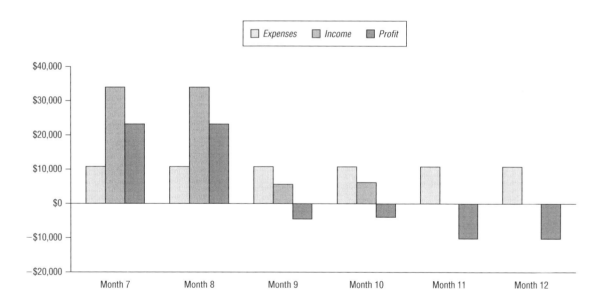

Estimated profits year 1

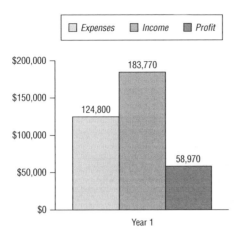

Financing

Mr. And Ms. Houston would like to obtain a business line of credit for $49,450, the amount needed to cover the start-up costs and operating expenses for the first three months. The owners will make monthly payments on the loan and will contribute 10 percent of the annual profits to pay extra on the loan. The owners will use the land and building as collateral for the line of credit and plan to repay the line of credit in the sixth year of operation.

Loan repayment plan

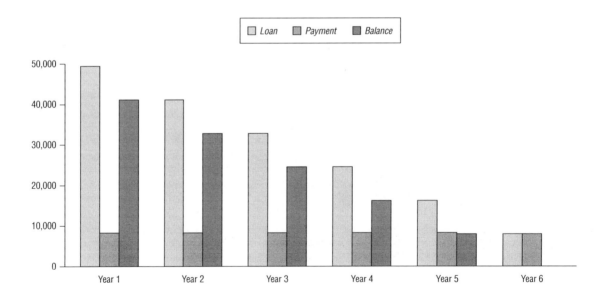

Auto Detailing Business

Star Shine Mobile Auto Detailing, Inc.

223 Vernon Street
Roseville, CA 95661

Claire Moore MBA

EXECUTIVE SUMMARY

Star Shine Mobile Auto Detailing (SSMAD) is a mobile automobile detailing service for owners of autos, SUVs, vans and motorcycles in Northern California. SSMAD detailers travel to the customer's location and provide detailing services on site. Service calls are set in advance by appointment.

Depending on the services chosen, detailing can take from a half hour up to four hours. Prices range from $35 to $315 with the average service call generating $150.

SSMAD is a corporation and is forecasted to reach profitability by the end of its first nine months of operation. It is projected that annual gross revenues will reach or exceed $90,000 by the end of year three.

Objectives

The objectives for the first three years of operation include:

- To create a service-based company whose primary goal is to exceed customer's expectations.

- To increase the customer base by at least 12% per year.

- To develop a scalable business that can grow and increase services and geographic areas covered.

Services

Our vision for SSMAD is to provide auto detailing services to individuals and businesses at their location. We will be a mobile service using our trailer, equipment and supplies to create customer satisfaction in maintaining the appearance and value of their vehicles. We will service automobiles of all sizes, commercial vehicles and trucks, and motorcycles.

A thorough explanation of our services appears later in this plan.

Financing

Ben Stillman will be providing the startup financing of $23,900 out of his own funds. The business does not require any outside financing at this time.

Mission Statement

Star Shine Mobile Auto Detailing (SSMAD) will provide auto owners quality auto detailing services in a timely fashion and at competitive prices. We aim to make the detailing experience as pleasant and convenient as possible and the results beyond expectations.

Management Team

The Company was founded by Ben Stillman. Mr. Stillman has more than 25 years of experience in auto repair and detailing services. Through his expertise, he will be able to bring the business operations to profitability by its second year of operation.

Sales Forecasts

Mr. Stillman expects a steady rate of growth during the first three years of operation. As he is an employee of the corporation, net profits reflected in these projections are calculated after payment of his salary and payroll taxes.

	Year 1	Year 2	Year 3
Sales	$50,000	$75,000	$90,000
Operating costs	$ 4,000	$ 6,000	$ 7,200
EBITDA	($ 2,795)	$ 7,300	$11,270
Taxes, interest, and depreciation	$ 1,435	$ 2,315	$ 2,910
Net profit	($ 4,230)	$ 4,985	$ 8,360

Mr. Stillman's salary is projected as follows:

	Year 1	Year 2	Year 3
Payroll	$30,000	$42,000	$50,000

COMPANY AND FINANCING SUMMARY

Star Shine Mobile Auto Detailing (SSMAD) is a mobile automobile detailing service for owners of autos, SUVs, vans and motorcycles in Northern California. SSMAD detailers travel to the customer's location and provide detailing services on site. Service calls are set in advance by appointment.

Registered Name and Corporate Structure

The company is registered as a corporation in the State of California. The office will be located in the home of Ben Stillman at 223 Vernon Street in Roseville, CA 95661.

Required Funds

Mr. Stillman is not seeking an investment from a third party at this time.

Management Equity

Mr. Stillman owns 100% of Star Shine Mobile Auto Detailing.

Exit Strategy

If the business is very successful, Mr. Stillman may seek to sell the business to a third party for a significant earnings multiple. At the time a qualified business broker will be hired to sell the business on Mr. Stillman's behalf.

STARTUP SUMMARY

Star Shine Mobile Auto Detailing (SSMAD) will incur costs for the items needed to start the business.

The list of equipment and supplies needed includes:

- Wet/dry vacuum

- Air compressor: to run pneumatic tools and for blowing out vents

- Pressure washers and vapor steamer

- Buffer and polishers

- Brushes

- Wash tools, brushes, towels, applicators

- Extractor for carpet/upholstery

- Ozone generator

- Chemicals: shampoo, vinyl/rubber dressing, leather conditioner, glass cleaner, penetrating oil, tar remover, concentrated tire/wheel cleaner, odor neutralizer, rubber & trim restorer, polish, detailing clay, spot remover, carnauba wax, leather/vinyl cleaner

Ben Stillman plans to purchase an auto detailing trailer that will come equipped with the following items:

- 2000-psi pressure washer

- 50-foot hose reel

- 90-gallon water tank

- 3,500-watt generator

- 150-psi air compressor

- Two chemical storage racks

- 50-foot air line with storage bracket

The trailer will have a full custom graphic wrap that includes our name, logo and contact information. The trailer will be attached to our company van which is being rented.

Projected startup costs

Startup costs

Incorporation fees	$ 1,200
Licenses	$ 500
Work uniforms	$ 450
Chemicals & supplies	$ 400
Merchant fee setup	$ 300
Misc tools	$ 400
Misc supplies	$ 700
Accounting fees	$ 400
Cell phone	$ 200
Startup assets	
Equipment	$ 1,500
Laptop & mobile printer	$ 850
Detailing trailer	$12,000
Total startup costs	**$18,900**

SERVICES OFFERED

Services

Star Shine Mobile Auto Detailing will offer the following auto detailing services.

Basic Services:

- Exterior wash & dry: prices range from $35 to $45

- Exterior wash/dry & interior vacuum & wipe down: prices range from $50 to 75

Packages

One Star Service

Compact $65; Two/FourDoor $75; SUV $95; MiniVan/Mid SUV $105; Extra large $125

- 1 to 1 1/2 hours

- Exterior hand wash & microfiber towel dry

- Interior vacuum

- Clean wheels and tires

- Dust interior dash and console

- Clean interior windows

Two Star Service

Compact $125; Two/Four Door $145; SUV $160; MiniVan/Mid SUV $190; Extra large $215

- 1 1/2 to 2 hours

- Exterior hand wash & chamois dry

- Interior vacuum

- Deep clean & treat rims, wheels and tires

- Clean and polish interior dash and console

- Clean interior/exterior windows

- One coat of Carnuba spray wax

Three Star Service

Compact $205; Two/Four Door $245; SUV $250; MiniVan/Mid SUV $265; Extra large $315

- 3 to 4 hours

- Exterior hand wash & chamois dry

- Deep clean/treat rims, wheels and tires

- Interior vacuum

- Dress tires

- Clean and polish complete interior surfaces

- Clean interior/exterior windows

- Premium machine sealant/wax application

- Shampoo all upholstery and carpets

- Vehicle jambs cleansed & degreased

Additional Services

Interior Deep Clean

Small $135; Medium $145; Large $155; Extra large $165

- 2 to 3 hours

- Vacuum

- Shampoo and deep clean all upholstery and carpet

- Clean and condition leather/vinyl

- Clean and polish interior dash and console

- Blow out all pockets, gauges and vents

- Clean and polish all interior/exterior mirrors, windows, gauges

Odor eliminating ozone treatment
- 1/2 to 2 hours

- from $60 to $120

Clean and Protection for leather and upholstery
- 1/2 to 2 hours

- from $50 to $100

Windshield repair
- 1/2 to 2 hours

- filling of small chips and cracks

- from $45 to $75

Headlight restoration & protective coating
- 1/2 to 2 hours

- $75

Motorcycle detailing
- 2 to 3 hours

- prices start at $150

Service areas include: Natomas Davis, Woodland, Elk Grove, Citrus Heights, North Highlands, Orangevale, Fair Oaks, Rancho Cordova, Folsom, El Dorado Hills, Roseville, Rocklin, and Granite Bay.

MARKET ANALYSIS

The market for auto detailing services includes anyone who owns an automobile. We expect that the newer the vehicle, the more the owner will be interested in keeping up its appearance. We also assume that companies are committed to keeping company cars in both working order and their appearance in excellent condition.

According to Kelly Blue Book (KBB), maintaining a car can make a difference in value of as much as $1,000 after just a few years of ownership. KBB stated that a "top factor in determining a vehicle's worth is the interior and exterior condition."

The cost of auto detail runs anywhere from $25 to about $300 depending on the size of the vehicle and the services desired. The time involved in auto detailing ranges from a half hour up to 4 hours.

Car owners can companies will be targeted with a marketing message that emphasizes the benefits of regular auto detailing as part of an auto maintenance program.

Star Shine Mobile Auto Detailing's target customer will be the following groups:

- an individual car owner whose car is five-years-old or newer

- a company that owns a vehicle that is five-years-old or newer

- collectors of vintage cars

While other car owners may be potential customers, we believe that the newer the car, the more likely it is that the customer will consider auto detailing services.

According to Edmunds.com, in 2014 the average person kept his car for about six years before trading it in. We aim to emphasize how auto detailing can help to maintain a car's value at trade-in time.

Target Market Strategy

Our sales and marketing strategy will be based on communicating Ben Stillman's expertise and experience, his participation in the vintage car community, and SSMAD's primary service area in the Placer County area.

Our target market may not easily differentiate us from our competition in terms of the services that we offer so we will stress our customer service. Marketing materials will communicate our ability to travel to the customer and provide detailing services at their home or place of work. We will stress that our service is professional yet friendly.

Methods used in our marketing efforts will include:

- Direct bulk mail by zip code

- Direct mail to new car purchasers in our service area

- Flyer stuffers in local newspapers

- Web site

- Yellow pages

Direct mail to new car purchasers in our service area can be accomplished by purchasing a targeted mailing list. The base price for such a service is $100 per thousand names with a minimum purchase of $500.

In addition, Ben Stillman will increase his visibility at vintage car shows by sponsoring events at local shows.

Social media efforts will include a Facebook page that offers car care tips and coupons for detailing services.

COMPETITION

A study of the greater Sacramento area revealed that there are 27 auto detailing services within the Sacramento area. Most are located within 20 miles of the city's center. Only five offer mobile services. They all state in their advertising material that they travel throughout Sacramento and surrounding cities.

We believe that our location in Roseville may work to our advantage against this Sacramento-centric competition. Roseville is located in Placer County and is 26 miles from the center of Sacramento. Cities within 20 miles include Rocklin, Lincoln and Auburn. These areas are growing at increased pace thanks to the continued expansions in its transportation infrastructure and the location of prominent businesses such as Hewlett Packard, Oracle Corporation, Ace Hardware and PRIDE Industries.

Competitive Edge

Placer County's population grew 26 percent in the 2003 to 2013 period, making Placer the fastest-growing county in the Sacramento Region and exceeding average growth rates of the Bay Area and

California. Lincoln's population showed the greatest increase of Placer County cities almost 115 percent growth in this ten-year period. Both Roseville and Rocklin also experienced high ten-year increases with respective growth rates of approximately 31 percent and 27 percent.

We believe that when car owners seek a detailing service they will be more likely to contact one that is conveniently located to them. We will take advantage of the growth in Placer County cities by focusing our advertising efforts to residents and businesses in those cities.

Star Shine Mobile Auto Detailing's competitive edge is also the experience and expertise of Ben Stillman. Ben holds a Master Automotive Technician Certificate and has 25 years experience in automobile repair and maintenance. His certification and experience has given him the knowledge and expertise to provide high quality auto detailing services.

MANAGEMENT SUMMARY

Star Shine Mobile Auto Detailing (SSMAD) was developed by Ben Stillman in order to fulfill his desire for premier auto detailing for his vintage car collection. After years of dealing with professional detail companies, Stillman took on the role of professional detailer himself.

Stillman is a graduate of the Automotive Technology Program at Sierra College in Rocklin, California. The program is certified by the National Automotive Educational Technician Foundation (NATEF) and is a member of the Professional Automotive Training Centers (PATC).

After earning his Master Automotive Technician Certificate in 1990, Stillman went to work as an automotive technician for a local car dealership. Over the years Stillman developed his skills in automotive repairs and added auto restoration and detailing to his skills set.

A lover of vintage cars from the 1950s, Stillman gradually built up his personal collection of restored cars. He enjoys showing them off at such events as Hot August Nights and Classics on the Green.

Milestones

Star Shine Mobile Auto Detailing will meet the following milestones:

Milestone	End date	Budget
Business plan completion	1/5/2016	$ 0
Set up of mobile detailing trailer	11/30/2015	$7,000
Completion of web site and social media campaign	1/21/2016	$ 800

PERSONNEL PLAN

SSMAD will be a one person operation. Using his cell phone and mobile detailing trailer, Ben Stillman will be able to connect with customers, complete sales and billing procedures, and service customers in the field.

Personnel plan	Year 1	Year 2	Year 3
Owner	$30,000	$42,000	$50,000
Other	$ 0	$ 0	$ 0
Total people	**0**	**0**	**0**
Total payroll	**$30,000**	**$42,000**	**$50,000**

FINANCIAL PLAN

Star Shine Mobile Auto Detailing has based its proforma financial statements on the following:

- SSMAD will have an average growth rate of 20% per year after the first year.

- The company will initially be funded with $23,900 of investment capital by Ben Stillman.

Start-up assets

Cash required	$ 5,000.00
Other current assets	$ 0
Long-term assets	$14,350.00
Total assets required	**$19,350.00**
Total start-up expenses	**$ 4,550.00**
Total requirements	**$23,900.00**

Start-up funding

Start-up expenses	$ 4,550.00
Start-up assets	$19,350.00
Total funding required	**$23,900.00**

Use of funds

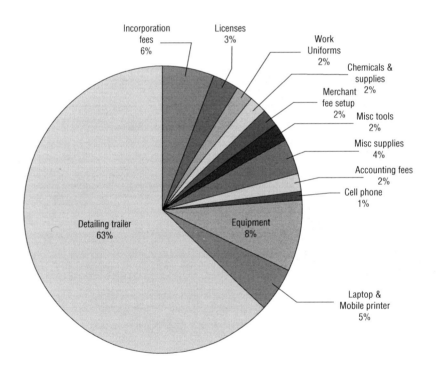

Financing

Equity contributions	
Initial investment	$23,900
Total equity financing	**$23,900**
Banks and lenders	
Total debt financing	**$ 0**
Total financing	**$23,900**

Pro forma profit and loss

	Year 1	Year 2	Year 3
Sales	**$50,000**	**$75,000**	**$90,000**
Expenses			
Payroll	$30,000	$42,000	$50,000
Depreciation	($ 1,435)	($ 1,435)	($ 1,435)
Merchant fees	$ 865	$ 1,420	$ 1,800
Phone/Internet	$ 2,400	$ 2,600	$ 2,600
Insurance: liability life/disability	$ 550	$ 550	$ 550
Payroll taxes	$ 3,000	$ 4,200	$ 5,000
Professional dues/memberships	$ 300	$ 300	$ 350
Advertising	$ 1,800	$ 1,800	$ 1,800
Office supplies	$ 200	$ 250	$ 300
Van lease	$ 4,200	$ 4,200	$ 4,200
Van insurance	$ 3,000	$ 3,000	$ 3,000
QuickBooks online	$ 500	$ 500	$ 500
Chemicals	$ 4,000	$ 6,000	$ 7,200
Telephone/Internet	$ 2,200	$ 2,400	$ 2,400
Other expenses	$ 400	$ 600	$ 800
Repairs & maintenance	$ 550	$ 750	$ 1,100
Legal fees	$ 1,700		
Total operating expenses	**$54,230**	**$69,135**	**$80,165**
Profit before interest and taxes	($ 4,230)	$ 5,865	$ 9,835
Taxes incurred	$ 0	$ 880	$ 1,475
Net profit after corporate tax	**($ 4,230)**	**$ 4,985**	**$ 8,360**
Net profit/sales	**−8%**	**7%**	**9%**

Projected balance sheet

	Year 1	Year 2	Year 3
Assets			
Cash in bank	$ 5,000	$ 9,985	$18,345
Other current assets			
Total current assets	**$ 5,000**	**$ 9,985**	**$18,345**
Fixed assets			
Trailer	$12,000	$12,000	$12,000
Laptop/printer	$ 850	$ 850	$ 850
Misc equipment	$ 1,500	$ 1,500	$ 1,500
Less: depreciation	($ 1,435)	($ 1,435)	($ 1,435)
Total assets	**$17,915**	**$22,900**	**$31,260**
Liabilities			
Current liabilities	$ —	$ —	$ —
Accounts payable	$ —	$ —	$ —
Current maturities loan	$ —	$ —	$ —
Total current liabilities	**$ —**	**$ —**	**$ —**
Long term liabilities loan	$ 0	$ 0	$ 0
Total liabilities	**$ —**	**$ —**	**$ —**
Ben Stillman, paid in capital	$23,900	$23,900	$ 23,900
Retained earnings	($ 1,755)	($ 5,985)	($ 1,000)
Earnings	($ 4,230)	($ 4,985)	$ 8,360
Total capital	**$17,915**	**$22,900**	**$31,260**
Total liabilities & capital	**$17,915**	**$22,900**	**$31,260**

Children's Art, Dance and Play Space
Imagination Station

315 E. Randolph St.
Chicago, IL 60601

Zuzu Enterprises

Imagination Station is a drop-in arts space for children to explore the many facets of creative play. It features classes, open play spaces dedicated to different themes, and an open studio to create one's own masterpiece! Though all children are welcome to visit Imagination Station, special focus is given to creating an environment for children five and under.

EXECUTIVE SUMMARY

Imagination Station is a drop-in arts space for children to explore the many facets of creative play. It features classes, open play spaces dedicated to different themes, and an open studio to create one's own masterpiece! Though all children are welcome to visit Imagination Station, special focus is given to creating an environment for children five and under.

The open studio features tables, easels, and clay mounds where young artists can work. Surrounding shelves are stocked with everything you need to encourage your genius, including paint, paper, glue, crayons, pencils, glitter, scissors, brushes, and even objects from nature and recycled tidbits. Children develop confidence in expressing and messing as they create art pieces that convey their sense of the world.

In addition to the open studio, there are several dedicated play rooms to explore the dramatic arts, music, and dance and movement. The dance space is outfitted with mirrors, bars, and a sound system. Tutus, tap shoes, bells, and streamers allow dancers to explore movement and the joy of dancing.

Dramatic play spaces changes monthly so children can explore the creation of story lines with ever changing scenery, props, costumes, and puppets. The space features puppets and puppet theaters, sets, dress-up costumes, and a stage for young performers to sing and bring to life stories of their own creation or to retell ones they already know.

Adjacent to the dramatic play space is the fort room. All supplies needed to create your own fort are included, using fabric, boxes, pillows, and props ready for young hands.

A music exploration space offers instruments from around the world so that budding musicians can strum, form drum circles, or form a band for the afternoon. Bang walls and full-sized instruments are mounted to walls for children to create music without having to manage weight and size.

The courtyard provides the space where the wildest messes occur as children enjoy a painting wall, paper mache, water play, and gravel, mud, and sand exploration.

The nest is reserved for those babies still finding their feet. The nest offers a tactile wall, a soft play river walk, and tummy time space where parents and care providers can introduce their babies to a variety of adventures.

The building room features all kind of building blocks, from a Duplo table and pieces to wooden blocks, as well as large cardboard "bricks" used to make life-size structures.

Classes are another component to Imagination Station. Scheduled throughout each day, classes are offered for guided exploration of various arts, not for mimicry or mastery. They target specific age groups so that, no matter what the activity, the class can be made safe and fun for all involved. Class offerings include: Clay Work, Painting, Mixed Media, Ballet, Tap, Hip Hop, Singing, Rhythm Sessions, Drama, and Acting. Storytelling, puppet shows, and sing-alongs invigorate each day. The large classroom offers plenty of room and comfortable seating for parents to watch and connect with one another.

Parents or caregivers stay on-site with each child to promote their comfort in exploration.

Imagination Station uses a gym membership model. Visitors can choose to drop-in or select a monthly membership. Like a gym membership for adults, a child is free to choose from a variety of courses offered and has the freedom to explore.

Imagination Station will also offer parents the opportunity to enjoy an evening out as their children explore arts in our care on periodic weekend nights. In the future, Imagination Station will offer summer and holiday camps for children.

IMAGINATION STATION PHILOSOPHY

The philosophy of Imagination Station is simple: let kids be kids! Kids should be allowed to be messy and loud as they learn through play. They don't need constant guidance and structured activities–they need the space and freedom to explore and play. We should guide them and provide them with opportunities to do so instead of demanding specialization and excellence at an early age and despite all costs. Imagination Station promotes a free range childhood and helps parents provide it for their children.

Our guiding principles include:

- Art can never come from precut circles and step-by-step directions.

- Children deserve space to explore every art before choosing one to master.

- If you fill a child's life with stories and opportunities to build and play and discovery, you will not be able to hold them back from reading and science and learning.

- Children must know stories of beauty and truth before they learn the letters that record them.

- The act of creating is more important than the art piece created.

- Children would rather tell people about their painting than have it proclaimed "nice" or "good".

- The look on a child's face when they are concentrated on creation is sacred.

Each day at Imagination Station, we strive to provide the space and opportunity for children to play, explore, and learn.

OPERATIONS

Hours of Operation

Imagination Station Studio is open daily from 9am to 6pm.

Location

Imagination Station is located in a converted warehouse and features 5,000 square feet over three stories. Each level features a small unisex bathroom in addition to the specialized play places.

Equipment

Imagination Station features a wide variety of equipment, including:

- Child-size tables and chairs
- Easels
- Ribbon sticks, scarves, and streamers
- Bookcases
- Selection of books
- Drying racks
- Musical instruments, including keyboards, egg shakers, drums, rain sticks, bells, rhythm sticks, and more
- Costumes, scenery, and props
- Sound system
- Puppets and puppet theaters
- Tutus and tap shoes
- Fabric and pillows
- Water table
- Sand table
- Various cookie cutters, sand rollers, scoops, cups, and other tools
- Duplo table and blocks
- Wooden blocks
- Cardboard "bricks"
- Storytime rug
- Large stuffed book characters
- Felt wall and story sets
- Storytelling sets (Three Little Pigs, Goldilocks, etc.)
- Parachute
- "Crawl and Explore Climber"
- Waterproof smocks
- Play cubes
- Light table

PERSONNEL

Co-Owners/Operators

The co-owners of Imagination Station are Elizabeth Pierce and Jillian Nowakowski. Elizabeth and Jillian have been great friends since kindergarten; their friendship has survived the trials of growing up as well as time apart as each attended university in separate cities. Eventually, the close-knit pair found themselves back in the Chicago area, married with small children. They faced the task of raising smart, well-rounded children in a predominantly urban setting where space was at a premium. They longed for places to take the children where they could just "play" in a safe, encouraging atmosphere; they longed for a place where their kids could use the latest "big" toys that they didn't want to purchase and didn't have the space to put them even if they did. They wanted their kids to explore and try new things without the constraints of being "good" at them.

What Elizabeth and Jillian decided to do was open the place they always wanted for their own children. Imagination Station was born.

Elizabeth brings her dance background and love of art to the operation. Having taken 16+ years of tap, ballet, and jazz, Elizabeth has worked as a part-time dance instructor for the youngest dancers in the past, and she is reprising this role at Imagination Station. Rather than teaching a year-long class geared specifically to the recital, however, Elizabeth is trying to instill a love of movement and expressing oneself through dance. Specific moves will be taught, but focus will also be on feeling the beat and the rhythm of the music and being inspired to move in certain ways because of how the music makes you feel.

Art is another passion of Elizabeth's. She took private art lessons since she was a small child as well as every art class she could take in school. She majored in art history in college with minors in painting and sculpture. At Imagination Station, this will translate into process art classes with an emphasis on color, technique, and expression rather than creating an end product that looks exactly like a provided sample. Kids will be allowed to paint, work with clay, use found objects to create sculpture, and other, similar projects.

Jillian brings her love of drama, music, and literature to the mix. She has been in numerous plays, starting as an Oompa Loompa in third grade and including such other plays as Annie, Shrek, Into the Woods, Suessical, The Lion, the Witch, and the Wardrobe, the Wizard of Oz, and even The Taming of the Shrew, to name but a few. Lead roles were earned in community theater, high school productions, and even college shows. While still in college, she began helping in junior productions working with children as young as five. She will continue the tradition here by teaching a basic drama workshop and doing younger versions of readers' theater. Drama will also be encouraged with puppets, a puppet theater, a dress-up/costume collection, a shadow puppet theater, as well as making one's own puppets to act out stories.

Music, especially singing, piano, and guitar are other passions of Jillian. More than half of her acting career has been in musicals, and she has also participated in state competitions for solo and ensemble for both singing and piano. She was thrice named to the State Chorale and participated in concerts held in downtown Chicago theaters. Music classes will be held to explore different types of music, various musical instruments, as well as sing.

Finally, Jillian loves to read. Her mother is a librarian and she grew up surrounded by books and stories. She knows the transformative powers of books and wants to share her love of stories with future generations. She will hold weekly storytimes and maintain a collection of books to be used on-site. A giant felt board with characters and props will be changed out monthly to also encourage original storytelling and retelling of books. A giant fort of sheets and pillows will be constructed to encourage reading.

Support Staff

Other support staff will be added as necessary. A receptionist will be stationed at the door at all times to greet visitors and process admissions as well as answer questions, field phone calls, and schedule birthday parties. He or she may be tasked with preparing materials, accepting deliveries, and other tasks as needed.

"Roamers" will also be on staff, especially when Elizabeth and Jillian are leading classes. They will roam throughout the spaces to interact with and encourage the kids as well as clean up any messes, refresh supplies, and the like.

The role of party host may be filled by a roamer or either of the co-owners, depending on availability.

Professional and Advisory Support

A merchant account has been established with U.S. Bank so that we can accept both one-time payments as well as monthly, recurring payments. Bookkeeping and tax services are provided by A&L Services. Insurance is purchased through a national carrier.

MARKET ANALYSIS

Competition

There are several direct competitors to Imagination Station. These include:

- Purple Monkey Playroom, 2040 N. Western Ave.
- The Sod Room, 1454 S. Michigan Ave.
- Kid City, 1837 W. Grand Ave.
- Explore & Much More, 3827 N. Southport Ave.

All of these businesses offer similar services. Imagination sets itself apart, however, because of its focus on the arts and its location. Realistically, there is enough target population and traffic to support all five businesses. Some will choose Imagination Station over the others merely due to convenience of the location, and others will choose Imagination Station because of its focus on art, dance, music, and the dramatic arts.

PRICING

Daily admission to Imagination Station is $8 per person, including parents. Children under 1 and one extra adult in same family are free.

Imagination Station also offers monthly memberships.

For the same price you'll pay monthly for a one-time-a-week, 45 minute children's art class at many studios, you can join Imagination Station. As an Imagination Station member, you enjoy:

- Unlimited open studio time on YOUR child's schedule.
- Unlimited use of Imagination Station's play spaces.
- Four free classes each month per child.
- Connection to the Imagination Station community through playgroups and member events.
- Heavily discounted family memberships so multiple children can access the arts.

Our memberships allow children to sample the arts affordably so that they needn't pick a single discipline or limit exploration to 45 minutes a week. At Imagination Station, children have free range!

The **Adult and Child Monthly Pass** is available for $38 a month with annual contract, or $60 a month without. This pass admits one child accompanied by an adult. Multiple adults can use the pass to accompany the same child.

The **Family Monthly Pass** is available for $48 a month with annual contract, or $75 a month without. This pass admits one family's children and accompanying adults. Imagination Station is designed for children under 6, but older children are welcome to join younger siblings in the Open Studio.

Another membership option is the **Annual Pass.** For $350 (for child and adult) or $475 (family), you receive free admission for one year AND 4 classes a month for each child under 6. Also included in this membership package is 10% discount on birthday parties and special events.

SERVICES

Open Studio

The open studio features tables, easels, and clay mounds where young artists can work. Surrounding shelves are stocked with everything you need to encourage your genius, including paint, paper, glue, crayons, pencils, glitter, scissors, brushes, and even objects from nature and recycled tidbits. Children develop confidence in expression as they create art pieces that convey their sense of the world.

Play Spaces

In addition to the open studio, there are several dedicated play spaced to explore the dramatic arts, music, and dance and movement.

Dance Studio: The dance space is outfitted with mirrors, bars, and a sound system. Tutus, tap shoes, bells, and streamers allow dancers to explore movement and the joy of dancing.

Dramatic Play: The dramatic play spaces changes monthly so children can explore the creation of story lines with ever changing scenery, props, costumes, and puppets. The space features puppets and puppet theaters, sets, dress-up costumes, and a stage for young performers to sing and bring to life stories of their own creation or to retell ones they already know.

Fort Room: Adjacent to the dramatic play space is the fort room. All supplies needed to create your own fort are included, using fabric, boxes, pillows, and props ready for young hands.

Music Studio: A music exploration space offers instruments from around the world so that budding musicians can strum, form drum circles, or form a band for the afternoon. Bang walls and full sized instruments are mounted to walls for children to create music without having to manage weight and size.

Courtyard: The courtyard provides the space where the wildest messes occur as children enjoy a painting wall, paper mache, water play, and gravel, mud, and sand exploration.

The Nest: The nest is reserved for those babies still finding their feet. The nest offers a tactile wall, a soft play river walk, and tummy time space where parents and care providers can introduce their babies to a variety of adventures.

Building Room: The building room features all kind of building blocks, from a Duplo table and pieces to wooden blocks, as well as large cardboard "bricks" used to make life-size structures.

Classes

Classes are another component to Imagination Station. Scheduled throughout each day, classes are offered for guided exploration of various arts, not for mimicry or mastery. They target specific age groups so that, no matter what the activity, the class can be made safe and fun for all involved. Class offerings include: Clay Work, Painting, Mixed Media, Ballet, Tap, Hip Hop, Singing, Rhythm Sessions, Drama, and Acting. Storytelling, puppet shows, and sing-alongs invigorate each day. The large classroom offers plenty of room and comfortable seating for parents to watch and connect with one another.

Classes are capped at 15 children for most classes. Parents are always welcome to stay close during the class, and many classes invite and encourage parent participation. All classes can be explored without committing to the full series. However, we encourage families to consider trying a class for 4 to 8 weeks so that children get the opportunity to explore the art, build a relationship with the teacher, and develop rapport with their classmates. Monthly memberships include 4 classes a month and annual memberships include 52 classes a year for each child under 7. Drop-in visitors to Imagination Station can join a class on any visit. Most days there will be plenty of room! Only Imagination Station members can reserve a space in advance.

Our memberships allow children to sample the arts affordably so that they needn't pick a single discipline or limit exploration to 45 minutes a week. Drop-in visitors can join a class if the class is not full. Classes are included with drop-in admission.

What makes Imagination Station different from other studios?

- Our classes are designed specifically for kids 5 and under

- Our classes emphasize process over product

- You can take a class AND play for hours afterward in our play spaces

- Parents can join many of the classes or easily watch from the comfortable, roomy seating area

- While one child takes a class, you have a building of play spaces to explore with your other children

- Classes beat other studios prices AND include far more than a 45 minute session

- Your child does not need to commit to an 8 week session. They can dabble and try out various classes to find a good fit.

CLASS SCHEDULE

A sample schedule is included below.

Monday

10:15 Art Explorers (3 to 6)
Children will explore the art elements and design principles used in the creation of art. By using a variety of materials, we will investigate lines, shapes, colors, textures as well as space and pattern.

12:30 Little Kids Sing, Dance & Play! (0 to 6)
A mixed-age class for babies, toddlers & preschoolers. Older siblings welcome too as space permits! This class is designed for anyone looking to spend 30 minutes singing, dancing, listening to a short book and just having fun! Similar in format to the Baby & Me and Little Kids class but without an art or sensory activity, this class was created to be flexible and accommodating for families with children of various ages or who wish to attend an afternoon class. Families are invited to come join us after lunch to sing, move their bodies, share a story and play together!

Tuesday

9:30 Baby and Me Music & Sensory Play! (0 to 2)

Connect with your baby through songs, books, and sensory activities. Relying heavily on repetition and close adult/child interaction, the carefully selected components of this class are designed to get you and the little one on your lap engaged with each other as well as the teacher and the other babies in class. A very short, age appropriate art or sensory activity will follow 15-20 minutes of circle time fun. Both parts of the class will take place on the floor where babies and caregivers can comfortably explore this engaging experience together. The process oriented art/sensory portion will usually be finger painting or some other simple, open ended, activity for you and your little one to engage in together. This is a quieter, less stimulating class for those who prefer that type of environment.

11:00 Little Kids Sing, Dance, and Create! (2-5)

This fun and highly engaging class is designed for little kids who have outgrown our baby class. The art portion of this class will be up on tables and children should be able to sit safely in a chair to explore a simple, thematic art project on their own but with the support of their caregiver. Similar in format to the Baby & Me class but with more variation, more independent movement activities and a lot more energy, this class offers a comfortable transition from baby to big kid by encouraging young spirits to move their bodies, sing along with the teacher, and explore art making. Music, books, movement games, creativity and social interaction with peers and teachers are all part of this dynamic class for toddlers and preschoolers. This class is designed to help young children become comfortable with playing and interacting with one another and participating in a group in a comfortable and age appropriate setting. Children are invited but not pressured to join the teacher in singing, dancing, playing movement games, making music, creating art, and most importantly-having fun!

Wednesday

11:00 Hand Building and Exploring Texture with Clay (All Ages)

In this fun process art class we will explore clay techniques using various tools. Children of all ages are welcome to roll, score, pinch and squish clay all while experiencing the process of creating.

2:00 Messy Science (4 to 5)

Children will dive right into the messy part of science as we explore a new theme each session. Children will be encouraged to stretch their brains, creativity, bodies, and imagination as we investigate science. Working together we'll use our silly ideas, playfulness, and curiosity to hypothesize and experiment. Whether making alien goo, rubber bones, or tornadoes in a jar, children are certain to leave filled with wonder.

Thursday

9:30 Move and Dance (2 to 5)

This high-energy class is designed for children who need to move! Children will dance to various songs and well as explore different type of dance, including tap.

2:00 Little Actors Studio (3 to 5)

Calling all drama queens (and kings)! This class is for those who want to explore storytelling using scenery, costumes, and props. Each week a new story will be introduced and then re-enacted by the "players." Stories include The Three Little Pigs, Goldilocks and the Three Bears, Little Red Riding Hood, The Little Old Lady Who Swallowed a Fly, and more.

Friday

10 Art Workshops for Big and Little Kids (All Ages)

Each Friday features a new workshop to explore the arts. Imagination Station provides the supplies and guidance as grownups and children explore an art together.

OTHER SERVICES

Concessions

Beverages are available, including tea, coffee, and water. Vending machines are also available to purchase small snack items.

Birthday Parties

Invite your child's friends to a creative, cozy birthday party at Imagination Station! Your party includes admission for up to 15 children and 15 adults, exclusive use of our party studio, and open-ended fun in all the play spaces at Imagination Station!

Your friends and family will participate in a sweet birthday celebration where a host is available to lead a craft and help you run your party. You and your guests will enjoy the homey feel and relaxed environment of Imagination Station while the children have free-range to create art, put on a show, move their bodies, and travel wherever their imaginations will carry them. Guests can come any time before the party and stay afterward to explore all the playrooms at Imagination Station.

The party studio is decorated with festive paper lanterns. Tables are set up with table clothes, real plates, cloth napkins, real flatware, glasses and vases. (Paper waste is kept at a minimum to reduce environmental impact.) Children make a craft to celebrate the day. Once the party ends, we take care of the cleanup.

Birthday Party Package: $275

- Available for groups of up to 15 children (fee includes one adult per child)
- 2 hours private use of the Birthday Room
- Shared use of the Imagination Station Studio and Play Rooms all day long
- Host helps with running the party and guides craft
- Craft table set up with choice of craft
- Tables beautifully set with real plates, glasses, and flatware to reduce paper waste
- Free Admit 5 Pass for future visit to Imagination Station
- White Imagination Station t-shirt for Birthday Girl or Boy
- Birthday Invitations

Imagination Station members receive a 10% discount on all birthday party packages.

Party Times:

- Saturday from 10-12, 1-3 or 4-6
- Sunday from 10-12, 1-3, or 4-6
- Weekdays and after hours may be available upon request.

Party Add-Ons:

- White Imagination Station t-shirts for all children: $10 per child
- Private Class: $50.00
- Additional Craft: $40.00
- Additional Hour in Studio: $100

Commercial Cleaning Business

Anderson Cleaning Inc.

58 Weathervane St.
Centerville, PA 15350

Paul Greenland

Anderson Cleaning Inc. is a cleaning services provider specializing in the commercial market.

EXECUTIVE SUMMARY

Anderson Cleaning Inc. is a cleaning services provider specializing in the commercial market. Specifically, the business focuses on cleaning offices between 500 and 3,000 square feet in size. Anderson Cleaning is being established by Mary Anderson, who has been independently cleaning houses on a part-time basis for the last five years. Recently, one of her clients asked if she would be interested in providing regular housekeeping services for his small law firm. Several other business owners in the community also have inquired about her availability to provide similar services. Because she prefers to work evening hours and has no family commitments, Anderson has decided to specialize in this type of work. She is fortunate to begin a new business with two clients, and has developed the following business plan, which outlines her strategy for growing the business from the ground up.

INDUSTRY ANALYSIS

According to the U.S. Bureau of Labor Statistics, janitors and building cleaners are projected to experience employment growth of approximately 12 percent between 2012 and 2022. One factor driving growth is the increasing number of companies looking to outsource cleaning services, which bodes well for Anderson Cleaning Inc.

Commercial cleaning services are represented by several leading trade organizations, including ISSA-The Worldwide Cleaning Industry Association and the IEHA (International Executive Housekeepers Association).

With more than 7,000 members, Northbrook, Illinois-based ISSA offers members benefits such as educational products, publications, business tools, and legislative/regulatory services. ISSA also offers conventions and exhibitions and the Cleaning Industry Management Standard (CIMS), a "consensus-based management standard that outlines the primary characteristics of a successful, quality cleaning organization." More information is available at: http://www.issa.com.

Westerville, Ohio-based IEHA is a professional association for management level housekeeping professionals. Formed in 1930, the organization includes more than 3,500 members. Its members benefit from resource materials and education programs, as well as an employment referral service and a technical question hotline. Additionally, IEHA hosts an annual convention and publishes the bimonthly electronic trade publication, *Executive Housekeeping Today*. Finally, IEHA offers two certification opportunities: REH (Registered Executive Housekeeper) and CEH (Certified Executive Housekeeper).

MARKET ANALYSIS

Overview

Anderson Cleaning is located in Centerville, Pennsylvania, which has a thriving service economy and numerous office facilities. Specifically, the community included 2,251 business establishments in 2015. The owner has classified prospective customers as follows:

- Advertising Agencies (7)

- Health & Medical Service Providers (42)

- Legal Services (44)

- Membership Organizations (86)

- Professional Services (22)

In particular, Mary Anderson has identified the following organizations as top prospects, and will make them a special focus of Anderson Cleaning's sales and marketing efforts:

- Centerville Chiropractic Care

- Centerville Manufacturing Co.

- Fairfield Financial Services LLC

- Hess Insurance

- Johnson Sign Co.

- Law Offices of Johnson and McKinney

- Lewis Enterprises Inc.

- McWilliams & Allerton LP

- Orange Creative

- West Safety Consulting Inc.

- Weston Engineering Services Inc.

- Worchester Inc.

Competition

The majority of Anderson Cleaning's prospects in Centerville already have a cleaning services provider. Mary Anderson will concentrate on identifying local companies who are unhappy with their current service, from a cost and/or quality standpoint. Although she will not market the business as the lowest-cost provider, Anderson Cleaning will be cost competitive and will emphasize satisfaction and quality service.

Although there are a number of other commercial cleaning service providers in the Centerville market, Mary Anderson has identified the following primary competitors, which also specialize in serving small and medium-sized businesses:

- B & B Maintenance Co.

- Bill McCreary Janitorial Enterprises

- City Janitorial Services

- Prime Building Services Inc.

- Servicemaster

- Sunshine Janitorial Inc.

SERVICES

Anderson Cleaning will provide the following housekeeping services to small and medium-sized businesses:

- Changing Light Bulbs

- Cleaning Bathrooms/Restrooms (e.g., toilets, sinks, mirrors, etc.)

- Cleaning Break Room/Kitchenette Areas

- Dusting

- Emptying Trash

- Light Pickup (e.g., magazine racks, etc.)

- Mopping

- Restocking Supplies (e.g., paper towel dispensers, soap dispensers, etc.)

- Sweeping

- Vacuuming

- Washing Walls

- Washing Windows (indoors only)

Although some commercial cleaning businesses provide minor repair services, exterior window washing, lawn maintenance, snow removal, and floor stripping/waxing, Anderson Cleaning will not provide these services.

Process

Mary Anderson will provide free consultation to prospective clients, which includes an assessment to understand their specific needs. She will use this information to develop a detailed time and cost estimate, so that she can calculate Anderson Cleaning's fees.

In addition to overall square footage, Anderson will consider a number of other factors during the estimation process, including, but not limited to:

- Cleaning frequency (e.g., daily/twice-weekly/weekly, etc.)

- Cleaning supplies (required or provided by client)

- Floor surface types (e.g., hard surface vs. carpet)

- Number of bathrooms

- Number of individual offices

- Number of kitchenettes/break room areas

- Stairs/no stairs

PERSONNEL

Mary Anderson (owner)

Anderson Cleaning is being established by Mary Anderson, who has been independently cleaning houses on a part-time basis for the last five years. Recently, one of her clients asked if she would be interested in providing regular housekeeping services for his small law firm. Several other business owners in the community also have inquired about her availability to provide similar services. Because she prefers to work evening hours, and has no family commitments, Anderson has decided to specialize in this type of work.

Mary Anderson possesses a number of key attributes that enable her to be successful as a housekeeper and small business owner. These include good interpersonal skills that enable her to successfully interact with a wide range of individuals; physical health/stamina, enabling her to work long hours on her feet; physical strength for moving cleaning equipment and supplies/trash receptacles; and excellent time management/organizational skills, which are critical for keeping on-schedule and maintaining client satisfaction.

Mary is a graduate of Centerville High School and has completed one year of junior college, including some classes and small business management. She currently attends Centerville Community College on a part-time basis.

Professional and Advisory Support

Anderson Cleaning will use popular off-the-shelf software for bookkeeping and tax preparation. A popular online legal document service has been used to incorporate the business cost-effectively. The same service also provided Mary with contracts (which are easily customizable) that she can use with her customers. Additionally, a commercial checking account has been established with Centerville Community Bank, along with a merchant account for accepting credit card and debit card payments from customers. Liability insurance has been obtained from a reputable national provider. Finally, several dependable independent contractors have been identified who can assist Mary with cleaning projects as the business grows, enabling her to increase capacity without hiring employees.

GROWTH STRATEGY

Anderson Cleaning Inc. will commence operations with two clients. Building upon this initial customer base, the business has established the following three-year growth strategy:

Year One: Secure four new clients and generate net profit of $9,044 on annual sales of $66,000.

Year Two: Gradually transition to clients with larger facilities and generate net profit of $12,976 on annual sales of $91,200.

Year Three: Increase client base to include 16 customers, continuing to gradually add larger facilities. Generate net profit of $18,307 on annual sales of $128,400.

The following table details Anderson Cleaning's strategy for growing the business' customer base:

Customer category	2015	2016	2017
500–1,000 SF	6	5	8
1,001–2,000 SF	2	4	5
2,001–3,000 SF	1	1	3
Total	**9**	**10**	**16**

The following pie charts illustrate how Anderson Cleaning plans to gradually transition to a business that serves clients with larger facilities:

2015

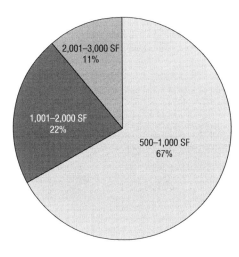

2016

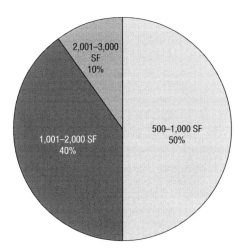

2017

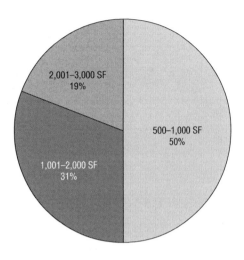

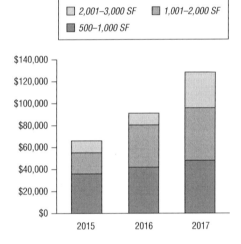

	2015	2016	2017
Sales			
500–1,000 SF	$36,000	$42,000	$ 48,000
1,001–2,000 SF	$19,200	$38,400	$ 48,000
2,001–3,000 SF	$10,800	$10,800	$ 32,400
Total	**$66,000**	**$91,200**	**$128,400**
Expenses			
Direct costs			
Salaries	$33,000	$45,600	$ 64,200
Contract labor	$10,250	$13,700	$ 19,250
Supplies	$ 6,600	$ 9,120	$ 12,840
Indirect costs			
Marketing	$ 2,970	$ 4,104	$ 5,778
Insurance	$ 3,300	$ 4,560	$ 6,420
Telecommunications	$ 825	$ 1,140	$ 1,605
Total	**$56,945**	**$78,224**	**$110,093**
Net profit/loss	**$ 9,044**	**$12,976**	**$ 18,307**

Commercial Pool Cleaning and Maintenance

Pristine Pool Services, LLC

3552 Fishtail Blvd.
Panama City Beach, Florida 32407

Fran Fletcher

BUSINESS OVERVIEW

Pristine Pool Services, LLC is a pool cleaning and maintenance service in Panama City Beach, Florida. It is owned and operated by Miguel Coronado, a recent graduate of Gulf Coast Community College and lifetime resident of the Florida panhandle. Hanging out at the pool is a favorite pastime for people living in the Sunshine State. However, maintaining pools in accordance with regulatory requirements can be a daunting task. Mr. Coronado is familiar with these requirements and also has the know-how to maintain crystal clear water for his clients.

Mr. Coronado got the idea for Pristine Pool Services when he was working as a maintenance worker at Pelican Point Condominiums while also attending high school and college. During his tenure at Pelican Point, he learned about pool and spa systems and how to properly maintain them according to local health department regulations. Now that Mr. Coronado has completed college, he has decided to put his business idea into action by starting Pristine Pool Services.

Mr. Coronado has been maintaining pools and spas for five years. Additionally, he has taken several courses on the subject, and feels confident in all areas of pool and spa maintenance. He will use his experience and extensive knowledge to provide pool service and maintenance for area hotels and condominiums. Pristine Pool Services will offer several maintenance schedules and a variety of services for its customers including:

- Pool opening and closing services

- Chemical application

- Chemical monitoring

- System maintenance

Data collected by the pool industry estimates that pool cleaning and maintenance is a multi-billion dollar industry. Panama City Beach has more than one hundred hotels and condos with one or more pools, which will serve as a large customer base.

There are currently five other businesses in the area offering commercial and residential pool cleaning and maintenance. Mr. Coronado will promote his services by approaching hotels and condos directly. His customer service and attention to detail will set his pool business apart from the rest.

Mr. Coronado and his helper will be able to maintain eight pools. Income projections reveal that Pristine Pool Services should start making a profit after two months of operation. Conservatively, the owner hopes to acquire a new customer each month until the eight pool maximum is reached.

Mr. Coronado is not seeking financing at this time. He will use his savings to cover expenses incurred during start-up and the first few months.

COMPANY DESCRIPTION

Location

Pristine Pool Services is located in Panama City Beach, Florida. Mr. Coronado will maintain a small office at his residence.

Hours of Operation

Pristine Pool Services will be available 7 days a week to perform cleaning and maintenance.

Personnel

Miguel Coronado (owner)

Mr. Coronado is the owner of Pristine Pool Services and will perform commercial pool maintenance. He has five years of experience maintaining the swimming pools at Pelican Point Condominiums. He has taken several maintenance courses, including "Maintaining Correct Chemical Balance", "Saltwater System Operation and Maintenance", and "Keeping Your Pool Debris Free" and is knowledgeable in regulatory requirements.

Eduardo Velez (assistant)

Mr. Velez will assist with pool maintenance. He has one year of experience cleaning approximately four pools in his neighborhood.

Products and Services

Services

- Preventive maintenance

- Ongoing maintenance

- Cleaning services

- Chemical monitoring

- Chemical application

- Special services (opening/closing)

Products

- Pool chemicals

- Test kits

MARKET ANALYSIS

Industry Overview

According to the Bureau of Labor Statistics, the pool maintenance and service industry is set to increase by 13% over the next decade.

Swimming pools are a multi-billion dollar industry. There are approximately 4.5 million homeowners in the U.S. with in-ground swimming pools. According to a recent survey by the National Pool Builders Association, Florida is home to six of the top ten cities in the U.S. with the most swimming pools.

The residential sector of the industry is somewhat affected by the economy. Homeowners may choose to clean and maintain their own pools to save money during an economic downturn, only to return to using a cleaning service when the economy is strong. Commercial customers are required to maintain pools according to government regulations. Therefore, the commercial business remains strong even in a failing economy.

Target Market

The target market for Pristine Pool Services will be hotels and condos in Panama City Beach, Florida.

Competition

Mr. Coronado plans to specialize in commercial pools and will offer annual maintenance plans to his customers. There are currently five other area businesses providing the same or similar services as those offered by Pristine Pool Services.

1. The Pool Boy—provides residential pool cleaning services

2. Two Friends Cleaning Service—provides hot tub cleaning for vacation rentals

3. S & S Pools—sells pool products and provides cleaning and maintenance services

4. Clearly Better Pool Cleaning—provides residential and commercial pool cleaning services

5. Homestead Pools—sells pool products and provides cleaning and maintenance services

GROWTH STRATEGY

Mr. Coronado has several contacts at local hotels and condos from his years of working in the industry. He hopes that this will lead to service and maintenance contracts at Pelican Post Condominiums as well as others. Pristine Pool Services will strive to provide excellent customer service so that clients will want to renew their service agreement every year. Mr. Coronado has the know-how and realizes the importance of a good reputation and the benefit of referrals. He believes that providing excellent service will make the business grow and will enable him to expand his staff and number of clients. Mr. Coronado may add residential services in the future or as opportunities arise and time permits.

Sales and Marketing

The company's primary marketing strategy will be direct marketing to hotel and condominium management.

FINANCIAL ANALYSIS

Start-up Costs

Start-up costs will be minimal. The main expenses will be pool cleaning equipment.

Start-up costs

Business license	$ 400
Business cards	$ 50
Cell phone	$ 200
Insurance	$ 300
Cleaning equipment	$1,000
Total	**$1,950**

Estimated Monthly Expenses

Generally, the cost of monthly expenses is fixed. The wages of Mr. Coronado will be $20 per hour worked and the wages of Mr. Velez will be $15 per hour worked. The following chart estimates that each employee will work 40 hours per week during the peak pool season and Mr. Velez's hours will decrease to 20 hours per week during the off-season. This may be more or less, depending on volume of business. Profits will be saved to pay expenses during off-season months, for unexpected expenses, and to purchase new equipment when needed.

Estimated monthly expenses

Expenses	Peak season (6 months)	Off-season (6 months)
Phone/Internet	$ 100	$ 100
Insurance	$ 200	$ 200
Wages (40 hours weekly)	$5,600	$4,400
Test kits and supplies	$ 400	$ 400
Total	**$6,300**	**$5,100**

Estimated Monthly Income

The number of clients and level of service will determine monthly income. Monthly income needs to be at least $700 to pay basic monthly expenses and $6,300 to pay basic expenses plus wages during peak season. Since the employees only get paid for hours worked, there will be a fluctuation in monthly wages and in the estimated total monthly expenses. The owner estimates that he will be able to service eight pools with his current staff.

Price Schedule

Pristine Pool Services will offer two annual maintenance contracts. Clients can make a single payment or can make monthly payments. The price schedule below details what services are included in each plan. Pool chemicals will be billed separately each month.

Annual service contracts	Gold	Silver
Cost (per month)	$910.00	$770.00
Cost (per year)	$10,400	$ 8,800
Preventive maintenance		
Check filter operation	*	+200
Check pump operation	*	+200
Check hoses and connections	*	+150
Check gaskets	*	+150
Chemical application		
Check pH	*	*
Chemical testing	*	*
Chlorine dosing	*	*
Chemical dosing	*	*
Cleaning services		
Vacuuming	*	*
Brushing pool walls and floor	*	+500
Filter backwashing	*	*
Skimming	*	*
Cleaning skimmer basket	*	*
Tile cleaning	*	+500
Special services		
Opening	*	+600
Closing	*	+600

*Included in the annual service agreement.

All maintenance plans include a detailed inspection and cleaning report for record keeping. A 25% discount will be given for additional pools at the same facility. Pools will be inspected three to four times weekly, depending on client need. The owner will work with hotel or condominium maintenance supervisor to schedule services. Each routine visit will take approximately one hour.

Profit/Loss

The following chart details profit/loss projections for the first twelve months. Conservative estimates will be used to forecast profits. Expected profits are calculated based on securing one client with two pools the first month, acquiring an additional client with two pools the second month, and one additional client with one pool each month for the next four months. Profit projections are based on the first two clients using the Silver service plan and the next four clients using the Gold service plan. The business will offer a 60-day trial for its first clients. This gives clients the cheaper yearly rate, but allows them to pay monthly for two months to make sure they are satisfied with Pristine Pool Services. The remaining balance is due at the end of the 60-day trial.

The expenses are expected to remain constant with a fluctuation in wages during the off-season (October—March). This chart is based on both employees working 40 hours a week during peak season (April—September) and Mr. Velez working only 20 hours a week during the off-season. This chart also assumes that clients will receive impeccable customer service and will continue using Pristine Pool Services for a year.

The first two months show a profit loss as a result of start-up and accepting monthly payments for the first 60 days. Enough profit is made in subsequent months to make up for the lack of profit during the first two months and during the off-season.

Profit/loss year 1

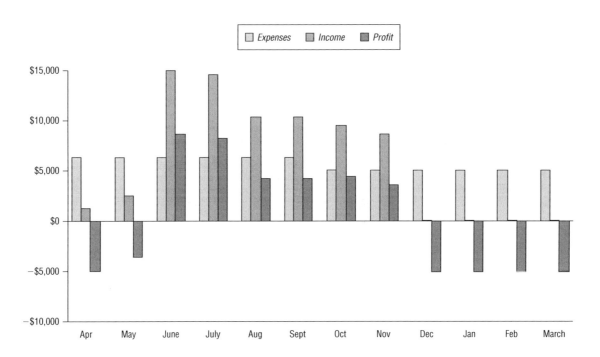

Profit data for the second year of operation estimates that all clients from the first year will be retained in the second year and that each will renew its previous service plan. The graph also indicates one new client paying for a Gold maintenance plan in April.

Profit/loss year 2

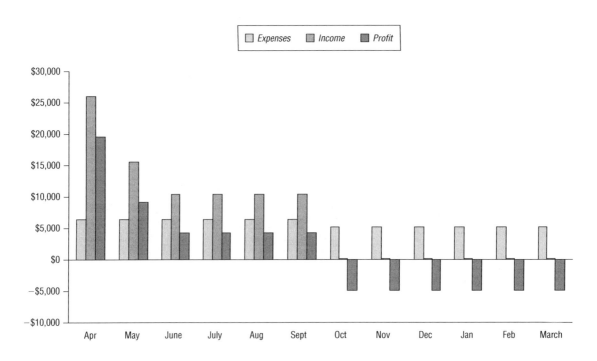

Profit/loss first three years

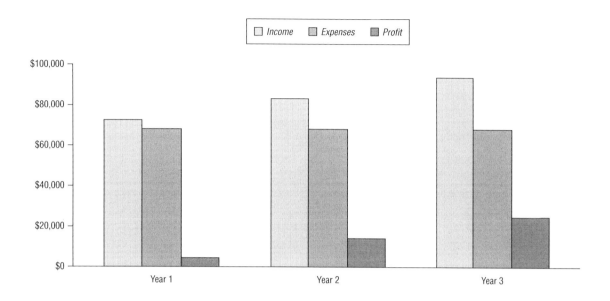

Profit/loss projections for the first three years are based on the expenses staying constant and income increasing each year from the addition of one Gold Service client each year.

Financing

The owner of Pristine Pool Services is not currently seeking financing. He has a truck that he will convert to business use and he has approximately $12,000 in savings to cover start-up and expenses for the first two months.

Craft Glass Jewelry Business
Colorful Creations

445 McCourtney Road
Newcastle, CA 95658

Claire Moore MBA

Colorful Creations is a fused glass studio that produces unique and custom designs in jewelry and home decor. All of the products are designed and created by Jill Baldwin. In order to reach the desired levels of sales and growth within the next three years, the following business plan has been created.

EXECUTIVE SUMMARY

Colorful Creations is a fused glass studio that produces unique and custom designs in jewelry and home decor. All of the products are designed and created by Jill Baldwin. In order to reach the desired levels of sales and growth within the next three years, the following business plan has been created.

Colorful Creations is a sole proprietorship and expects to reach profitability by the end of its first year of operation.

The Products

Colorful Creations creates jewelry and home decor items using dichroic glass that is heated and fused in a kiln. By combining different colors of glass, an infinite number of designs are possible. We will focus on creating a line of jewelry items that includes: earrings and pendants. Our home decor line will include: holiday ornaments, night lights, and platters.

At Colorful Creations we specialize in the use of fused glass as our material of choice. Fused glass is a glass that is layered and heated in a kiln to temperatures ranging from 590 degrees Celsius (1099 F) to 815 degrees Celsius (1501 F). Pieces of dichroic glass are used. This type of glass comes in a multitude of colors and most have a reflective coating that gives off a shiny, rainbow effect.

Sometimes called kiln-formed or kiln-glass, fused glass does not contain the lead lines that are required in stained glass works. Unlike blown glass, fused glass is easy to learn and does not require the same physical strength.

All items will be based on the designs of owner Jill Baldwin. Jill will also perform the manufacturing of product at her studio which is located at her home.

Financing

Jill Baldwin will be providing the startup financing of $8,500.00 out of her own funds. The business does not require any outside financing at this time.

Objectives

The objectives for the next three years include:

- Obtaining display space in three local galleries.

- Increasing web site sales by at least 10 percent each year.

- Increasing sales of higher ticket items from the home decor line.

- Contracting with a sales representative who will increase sales through specialty stores.

Management Team

The Company was founded by Jill Baldwin. Jill has more than 25 years' experience as an artist and art teacher. Through her experience she will be able to bring the operation of the business to profitability by the end of its first year of operation.

To help Jill deal with the business aspects of running the Company, she has contracted with a local CPA and QuickBooks expert to help her set up her books and online payment system.

Jill's husband, Walter, will be helping her to set up and maintain her web site and online store. Walter is a retired network engineer with 30 years' experience in computers, programming and network maintenance.

Sales Forecasts

Ms. Baldwin expects a steady growth rate during the first three years of operation primarily due to her regular use of social media.

	Year 1	Year 2	Year 3
Sales	$45,000	$66,000	$77,000
Net profit	$20,440	$23,100	$25,700

Sales forecast

The Company

Colorful Creations is located in Newcastle, California. The company produces and sells custom jewelry and home decor using fused glass. All pieces are designed and crafted by owner Jill Baldwin. The business is based out of her home located on ten acres. Jill sells her work through local galleries, art tours, online storefronts and her web site.

The Company is owned by Jill Baldwin and operates as a sole proprietorship.

Investor Equity

Ms. Baldwin is not seeking an investment at this time.

The Market

The market for handcrafted jewelry includes a diverse group of artisans and products as well as materials used. Some specialize in the use of metals such as gold and silver while others prefer to work with stones.

The market available to crafters is likewise diverse and includes the following groups:

- Retail stores
- Art tours and craft fairs
- Online stores
- Web site

Our competition includes other artisans and sellers of jewelry.

Colorful Creations will focus its marketing efforts on local galleries and retail customers. We will reach these consumers through the following channels:

- *Local:* galleries and art tours
- *Online:* stores such as Etsy and our own web site

Financial plan

Colorful Creations will be completely financed by the owner, Jill Baldwin. Because we are able to keep overhead costs low, we expect to reach break-even by the end of our first full year of operation.

The location of Ms. Baldwin's studio is in a converted barn on her ten-acre property. Baldwin currently sells from her home and at local shops and galleries. She does not expect to maintain her own retail space in the future.

Through our sales and marketing efforts we expect to grow at a rate of at least 10 percent per year and reach annual gross revenue of $77,000 by the end of year three.

COMPANY SUMMARY

Colorful Creations is located in Newcastle, California at the home of its owner Jill Baldwin. The company's lead product is custom jewelry crafted in fused glass. Our jewelry offerings include earrings and pendants. All pieces are designed and created by owner and crafter Jill Baldwin.

Pieces are sold direct to consumers through art tours, online stores and our web site. We also sell to the public through galleries.

COMPANY OWNERSHIP

Colorful Creations was founded in February 2015 by Jill Baldwin. As an art teacher since 1987, Jill has a wealth of experience in using various media to manifest her artistic vision. The ownership structure of Colorful Creations is as a sole proprietorship. We believe that because there is little liability exposure, other forms of structure such as corporation or LLC are not required at this time.

STARTUP SUMMARY

The following expenditures will be instrumental is setting up the business:

Startup requirements

Business consultant	$ 350
Web site creation	$ 550
Office furnishings	$ 200
Computer equipment	$ 600
Business telephone	$ 200
Studio equipment	$5,000
Office supplies	$ 200
Studio supplies	1,400
Total	**$8,500**

PRODUCTS

Colorful Creations offers its customers a range of custom fused glass jewelry in the following forms:

- Pendants—large and small

- Earrings

- Holiday pins and decorations

- Platters—large and small, including lighted boxes and bowls

While pieces may include metallic elements, the primary feature in each piece is an individually crafted fused glass element. All pieces are created by Jill Baldwin based on her designs.

Dichroic glass is the material used most often in our pieces because of the wide variety of colors available. A key feature in dichroic glass is its ability to reflect multicolors. In fact, the name literally means "two colored." In this respect it is very reminiscent of natural materials such as mother-of-pearl and opals. The iridescent effect is due to the same thin-film physics that produce a rainbow effect in a bubble or a pool of water and oil.

An example of a typical piece is a pendant. A piece such as this would usually be made by layering a piece of colored dichroic glass, a piece of black glass for backing, and jump ring in between. The piece is then fired in a kiln where the heat fuses the glass pieces together.

The piece can be made more interesting by adding other elements such as layering of dichroic glass pieces or using the following methods:

- *Tack fusing:* use special glue to arrange colorful pieces in a design.

- *Acid etching:* after a stencil is applied to the glass piece masking the area that will not be etched, a special acid is applied then rinsed off revealing the shape in dichroic colors. Another version of this technique involves painting the acid product over a dichroic glass piece to create the design.

- *Screen print:* special screen printed enamel artwork is applied to a finished piece and then kiln fired again.

- *Engraving:* by engraving a finished piece of fused artwork, the underlying black glass is revealed in the design.

- *Painting:* special paint is applied to a finished piece to create a design.

- *Molding:* special molds are used to shape the glass during firing. The piece is then cold worked by hand.

- *Wire wrapping:* Adding a precious metal wrap or embellishment to a finished piece adds interest and value.

We are also excited about our home decor line of fused glass products which includes:

- Night lights

- Platters—large and small

Some items, such as the holiday ornaments, are easy to produce in volume and are expected to be popular. These will have a low price point and designs have been created for fall and winter.

Products such as platters require more thought and time to create and their price level will reflect the higher level of materials and craftsmanship. Platters can be shaped into bowl-like objects that can sit on a table or flat like a picture. Flat platters can be displayed upright either in a metal frame stand or incorporated into a box that can be hung from the wall. The addition of a small light illuminates the platter from behind, enhancing the design.

MARKET ANALYSIS

Jewelry is not a commodity like food and clothing. It is more of a luxury purchase and yet jewelry, like clothing, tends to be worn on a regular basis by those who wear jewelry at all. When it comes to choice, there are a myriad of choices in every price range. This is true for commercial jewelry as well as custom, handmade jewelry.

Colorful Creations will focus marketing efforts on three groups of customers: retail specialty shops, galleries and the individual consumer.

MARKET SEGMENTATION

According to the *2014 U.S. Jewelry State of the Market Report*, the biggest spender on fine jewelry is a married person between the ages of 55 and 64 years old who lives in an urban area in the Midwest with a population of 1 to 2.5 million. This person has a bachelor's degree, works as a manager or professional, has a spouse who also works, and their joint income is $150,000 or higher.

That is not our market, however. We are aiming for those who wish to find unique pieces in the $15 to $50 range. The affordability of our pieces allows the consumer to add to their collection with several different items.

Our typical customer is a female between the ages of 20 and 45 who appreciates unique and colorful jewelry. Their income is anywhere from $24,000 per year and up. But our customer base is not limited to this demographic. Also, our line of home decor products can appeal to anyone seeking a new way to express themselves through art and design.

Retail stores: Colorful Creations is located in the heart of Placer County, California. The county, located in the foothills of the Sierras, includes several cities and towns that draw visitors each year. These locations house many specialty art and gift shops where customers know they can find hand-made, unique treasures. Whether sales are contracted through commission or wholesale, our profit margins tend to be less but are offset by the ability to reach a larger audience.

Galleries: The arts community in Placer County is the home of several art galleries, art centers and an artist cooperative. We currently display and sell items at an art gallery in Auburn and we are a member of the Placer Arts Association which sponsors art tours three times a year. Each year we also participate in the Crocker Holiday Art Festival which is sponsored by the Crocker Museum of Sacramento. Because galleries charge a fee as do festivals, our profit margins are less here. However, we gain exposure to a target market of consumers who are interested in crafted works and who are more likely to become loyal customers.

Individuals: Sales directly to individuals bring the largest net profit yet are difficult to achieve in large volume due to time constraints. Efforts to cultivate an audience of faithful customers pay off because a satisfied buyer is likely to not only purchase again, they will spread the word about our products. Individual customer sales are achieved through our participation in art tours, art shows, fairs and online sales.

INDUSTRY ANALYSIS

Thanks in large part to online marketplaces like Etsy, the craft and hobby business reached the $30 billion mark last year in the U.S. alone. Of that figure, jewelry and bead crafts comprised $2.9 billion. Of the top ten craft segments, jewelry making comes in fourth behind woodworking, drawing, and food crafting.

After experiencing a dip following the 2008 recession, jewelry sales are steadily increasing. Buying trends show that while consumers are spending more for jewelry, they are spreading their dollars spent over more purchases rather than concentrating on a few high–value items. We believe that this presents an opportunity for handmade jewelry to compete for consumers in the jewelry market.

According to the *Craft & Hobby Association (CHA) Trends Report for 2015*, design trends for jewelry in 2015 include:

- Cuff bracelets will be popular, especially those made with leather and chain combinations.

- Wide chokers.

- The broach is back and materials to use include rhinestones, metals and Plexiglas.

- Colored resins mimicking gemstones will be a feature in many designs.

- The Art Deco look of geometric earrings and cuff bracelets.

- Crystal collars and broaches.

- Ear jewelry including ear cuffs, ear jackets and faux piercings are making a comeback.

COMPETITION

Competition in the handmade jewelry industry comes from several fronts:

Home crafters who make their own jewelry: Studies show that when the economy tightens people are more likely to engage in making their own products rather than buying them. This holds true for clothing, jewelry and even some food items. When it comes to jewelry, consumers can go to any craft or hobby store and buy individual pieces and kits for making jewelry. The primary investment is their time.

Retail stores: Millions of stores and shops carry jewelry in all price ranges. Consumers can be tempted to buy jewelry anywhere from museum gift shops to the largest retailer.

Other jewelry crafters and sellers: Millions of artisans create jewelry and sell to the public. The Internet makes it possible for consumers to purchase all kinds and all designs from anywhere around the world.

Online stores that sell at deep discount: Online stores such as Ebay regularly offer a large number of jewelry items at rock bottom prices. Most of these items come from China.

Pricing Strategy

Our prices reflect the cost of production and a reasonable profit. We will use our pendants as an example of our pricing philosophy. The average prices of our pendants range from $25 to $35 which is much higher than prices to be found on sites such as Ebay. We believe that price is an important factor in creating the perception of value. Our prices are based on the reality of covering our costs and making a profit as well as communicating to the public the value of our hand-crafted, original designs.

Our target market is not the person who wants to accumulate cheap trinkets. While that type of jewelry has its place, we prefer to cultivate a loyal following of discriminating customers who understand the value of quality handmade items.

Keys to Success

In order to stand out from the crowd, Colorful Creations will emphasize the following attributes in order to build brand loyalty and a customer base.

- *Customer service:* One way to distinguish us from our competition is to treat each customer as if they were our only customer. To this end we strive for continuous improvement in maintaining good customer relations. The design of our web site provides contact information and a widget for sending us an email. We will follow up on emails within 24 hours of receipt six days a week.

- *Design creativity:* We will continue to create unique designs to keep our product line fresh and appealing.

SWOT Analysis

The following SWOT Analysis describes the key strengths and weaknesses of the business and identifies opportunities and threats that challenge our growth.

Strengths	Weaknesses
• Unique designs that can be customized • Variety of color within the materials used means that each item is different from another with the same design. • Strong relationships with local art community • Established relationship with local gallery • Robust web site maintained in house • Techniques used to create pieces require equipment and skills beyond the average home hobbyist	• Large target market • Large number of competitors • Lack of brand awareness by the public • Must split time between marketing and manufacturing
Opportunities	**Threats**
• A rebounding economy means more disposable income • Grow the company to the point of taking on help • Expansion of home décor line to reach a broader target market • Increase exposure through galleries and mentions on popular blog sites • Contract the services of one or more sales reps who can propel wholesale accounts	• Availability and price fluctuations of materials required • Theft of designs and sales for lower prices • Economic downturn that affects consumer spending • Ability of consumers to buy materials and make their own jewelry

SOCIAL MEDIA MARKETING PLAN

Social media is an affordable method for connecting with customers and potential customers. Regular participation allows merchants to create and build relationships with their target audience, receive feedback, deal with questions and complaints, and offer special promotions.

The social media channels that we plan to use include:

- *Email promotions:* We are using Mail Chimp, a free service, to collect the email addresses of our customers so that we can cultivate an ongoing relationship with them. This service also allows us to create a landing page where customers can sign up for exclusive offers.

- *Facebook page:* A Facebook page is another channel for staying connected to our customers. It is a way to drive traffic to our sales site. One advantage of a Facebook page is that customers can find us more easily on their mobile devices. Images posted can generate multiple Likes, Shares and Comments.

- *Twitter:* Regular posts will link to both our Facebook page and our web site.

- *YouTube:* A YouTube channel that contains regularly posted content is another way to reach a broader audience. Videos need only be a few minutes long and can contain links to our web site and other sales sites. Videos can be instructional in informing the viewer about the qualities of dichroic glass and our manufacturing techniques.

- *Pinterest:* One of the most popular social media tools allows users to post visual content related to their products and services with links to sites. Links on our sites invite visitors to Pin our page to their own Pinterest boards where the link can be seen by their subscribers.

- *Instagram:* With an emphasis on the visual, Instagram is the perfect medium for marketing our jewelry. Building rapport with our audience means that we will intersperse photos of our products with pictures from our day, including feeds from our workshop.

We have chosen these social media tools because they are currently the most popular and offer the most exposure in relation to the effort invested.

Marketing Strategies

Another method that we have been pursuing with success is contacting the editors of online sites that we believe appeal to our demographic such as *Huffington Post* and *Girl's Life Magazine*. The approach involves a pitch to the editor along with a sample piece of jewelry. The advantage is that the product appears in an article rather than in an advertisement, giving it more credibility. The bonus is that it only costs time and the jewelry sample, plus postage to ship.

We intend to continue this strategy on a regular basis. In conjunction with this strategy, we added a sales page on our web site where customers can place their orders and pay by credit card. Using this strategy we were able to get a mention in an article on *Girl's Life* and we saw our online orders spike.

Another strategy that we believe will add to the impact of mentions in online magazines is our advertising campaign on blogs. We have located a service that allows us to dictate how much we will spend per day for banner ads that will appear on blogs that serve our target market. The price we pay is not based on clicks but on time spent on a web site. It's still too early to tell how successful this method is but at least we can limit our spending while we test this service.

The bulk of our sales come from customers that we have connected with in person. We believe that it's important to continue to grow our audience of loyal customers. To that end, we aim to gather the emails of all of our customers and to engage in periodic offers through email contact. In order to meet with potential customers, we will continue to participate in local arts events such as arts festivals and art tours.

Galleries: We will continue to build relationships with galleries that would be appropriate venues for our product lines.

Web site: Our web site will be the hub for all of our marketing efforts. The site address will appear on all of our marketing materials including sales receipts, tags, and packaging. Our site address also appears in articles about our business. The site contains widgets that allow visitors to find us on Facebook, Twitter, Pinterest and Instagram. In addition, our Twitter feed appears on our web page.

We would like to expand our reach to wholesale venues and intend to engage at least one sales representative by the end of year two. To that end we are researching sales representatives who have experience in custom handmade fashion.

MILESTONES

Colorful Creations has outlined the following milestones for our first three years of operations:

Year One
- Completion of the business plan.
- Setup of office and studio.
- Establishment of sales relationships with at least two galleries.

Year Two
- Transition of Jill Baldwin from part-time to full-time.
- Contract with a sales representative.

Year Three
- Addition of two production assistants.
- Installation of our product in five stores.
- Nationwide exposure on a major television program.

MANAGEMENT SUMMARY

Colorful Creations is owned and operated by Jill Baldwin and is structured as a sole proprietorship. Jill earned her Bachelor's of Fine Arts (BFA) from the University of Florida where she found her passion in art education and in visual studies. Jill has been working with glass since the year 2000 and has found it to be a medium that affords endless surprises.

Jill became a teacher in 1985 and taught art to K-6 students for several years. Then she transitioned to high school teaching and continues to this day. In 2014 Jill went to part-time status so that she could devote more time to her business as she moves closer to retirement from teaching.

Jill is looking forward to the day when she can exit the teaching profession and dedicate her time to fully developing her business. Her teacher's pension will help her in the transition.

From the beginning, Jill received the full support of her husband, Walter, a retired network engineer. It was Walter who converted the old barn into a working studio where Jill could produce and display her pieces. Walter also maintains the company web site on the company server.

PERSONNEL PLAN

Jill currently handles all of the tasks associated with the business with the help of her husband. She has contracted with a local freelance accountant to help her maintain her financial and office records and to operate her QuickBooks online accounting for the business. The accountant will prepare the tax return at year end.

	Year 1	Year 2	Year 3
Jill draw	$12,000	$12,000	$ 18,00
Sales rep fees		$ 3,000	$ 7,000
Production assistants wages		$12,000	$18,000
Total people	**1**	**3**	**3**
Total investment	**$12,000**	**$27,000**	**$43,000**

FINANCIAL PLAN

Startup Equipment Required
Studio equipment

MagicFuse	$ 130
Table top kiln	$ 750
Fusing kiln	$ 870
Glass kiln	$ 700
Fusing tools	$ 400
Torches	$ 300
Forms & molds	$ 300
Display stands	$ 550
Saws & grinders	$ 600
Metal stands	$ 400
Total	**$5,000**

The following Pro Forma Profit and Loss projection does not reflect the draw that Jill will take from profits.

Pro forma profit and loss

	Year 1	Year 2	Year 3
Sales			
Web site	$31,500	$46,200	$53,900
Wholesale	$ 6,750	$ 9,900	$11,550
Etsy	$ 1,800	$ 2,640	$ 3,080
Shows & galleries	$ 4,950	$ 7,260	$ 8,470
Total gross sales	**$45,000**	**$66,000**	**$77,000**
Less: direct costs of sales	$ 6,750	$ 9,900	$11,550
Less: shipping	$ 6,750	$ 9,900	$11,550
Total cost of sales	**$13,500**	**$19,800**	**$23,100**
Gross profit	$31,500	$46,200	$53,900
Gross margin %	70%	70%	70%
Expenses			
Depreciation	($ 500)	($ 600)	($ 600)
Payroll	$ 0	$ 9,000	$12,000
Payroll taxes	$ 0	$ 900	$ 1,200
Merchant fees	$ 1,530	$ 2,244	$ 2,618
Phone/Internet	$ 1,800	$ 1,800	$ 2,000
Insurance	$ 485	$ 500	$ 525
Professional dues/memberships	$ 300	$ 300	$ 300
Advertising	$ 4,095	$ 6,006	$ 7,007
Office supplies	$ 450	$ 400	$ 550
QuickBooks online	$ 500	$ 500	$ 500
Other expenses	$ 350	$ 350	$ 400
Repairs & maintenance	$ 250	$ 250	$ 250
Utilities	$ 600	$ 600	$ 600
Legal & accounting fees	$ 1,200	$ 850	$ 850
Total operating expenses	**$11,060**	**$23,100**	**$28,200**
Net profit/sales	**$20,440**	**$23,100**	**$25,700**
Net profit %	**45%**	**35%**	**33%**

Sales by year and category

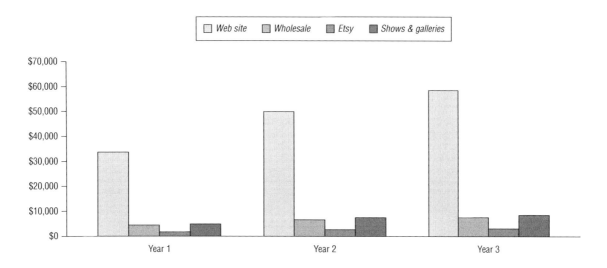

Projected balance sheet

	Year 1	Year 2	Year 3
Assets			
Cash in bank	$3,500	$11,440	$23,140
Other current assets			
Total current assets	**$3,500**	**$11,440**	**$23,140**
Fixed assets			
Misc equipment	$5,000	$ 6,000	$ 6,000
Less: depreciation	($ 500)	($ 600)	($ 600)
Total assets	**$8,000**	**$16,940**	**$28,640**
Liabilities			
Current liabilities			
Accounts payable	$ —	$ —	$ —
Current maturities loan	$ —	$ —	$ —
Total current liabilities	**$ —**	**$ —**	**$ —**
Long term liabilities loan	$ 0	$ 0	$ 0
Total liabilities	**$ —**	**$ —**	**$ —**
Jill Baldwin, capital	$8,000	$16,940	$28,640
Total liabilities & capital	**$8,000**	**$16,940**	**$28,640**

Sales Forecast

This sales forecast is our best projection of sales made and income generated from sales. Many factors can influence these numbers such as availability and prices of materials and the cost of shipping. We are assuming a direct cost of sales equivalent to 30 percent of sales.

These direct costs include materials, sales commission and the costs of shipping finished product to customers.

Sales forecast

	Year 1	Year 2	Year 3
Unit sales			
Small pendants	375	525	600
Large pendants	195	350	410
Holiday items	125	180	200
Nightlights	77	107	116
Small platters	75	115	120
Large platters	55	72	95
Total unit sales			
Unit prices			
Small pendants	$ 25.00	$ 25.00	$ 25.00
Large pendants	$ 35.00	$ 35.00	$ 35.00
Holiday items	$ 15.00	$ 15.00	$ 15.00
Nightlights	$ 25.00	$ 25.00	$ 25.00
Small platters	$150.00	$150.00	$150.00
Large platters	$250.00	$250.00	$250.00
Sales			
Small pendants	$ 9,375	$13,125	$15,000
Large pendants	$ 6,825	$12,250	$14,350
Holiday items	$ 1,875	$ 2,700	$ 3,000
Nightlights	$ 1,925	$ 2,675	$ 2,900
Small platters	$11,250	$17,250	$18,000
Large platters	$13,750	$18,000	$23,750
Total sales	**$45,000**	**$66,000**	**$77,000**
Direct unit costs			
Small pendants	$ 7.50	$ 7.50	$ 7.50
Large pendants	$ 10.50	$ 10.50	$ 10.50
Holiday items	$ 4.50	$ 4.50	$ 4.50
Nightlights	$ 7.50	$ 7.50	$ 7.50
Small platters	$ 45.00	$ 45.00	$ 45.00
Large platters	$ 75.00	$ 75.00	$ 75.00
Direct cost of sales			
Small pendants	$ 2,813	$ 3,938	$ 4,500
Large pendants	$ 2,048	$ 3,675	$ 4,305
Holiday items	$ 563	$ 810	$ 900
Nightlights	$ 578	$ 803	$ 870
Small platters	$ 3,375	$ 5,175	$ 5,400
Large platters	$ 4,125	$ 5,400	$ 7,125
Subtotal direct cost of sales	**$13,500**	**$19,800**	**$23,100**

Ghostwriting Business

John Warner LLC

29 Main St.
Abbington, AZ 85333

Paul Greenland

John Warner will use his corporate experience to start his own company specializing in business writing.

EXECUTIVE SUMMARY

After working in the corporate sector for 15 years, marketing communications professional John Warner has decided to go into business for himself in the specialized field of ghostwriting. Specifically, Warner will use his corporate experience to specialize in business writing. While working for a large, well-known consumer packaged goods company, Warner frequently was called upon to help members of the executive team write white papers, articles for business magazines and trade publications, and more. In addition, the chief executive officer and chief operating officer frequently used him to develop talking points and speeches for various occasions, and Warner had the opportunity to ghostwrite the CEO's autobiography and two other business books. Realizing that there is a lucrative market for individuals with his abilities, and wanting to satisfy his entrepreneurial spirit, Warner has decided to go into business for himself.

INDUSTRY ANALYSIS

The practice of ghostwriting dates back many centuries, especially in areas such as politics and religion. Although the number of writers working in this specialized field is unknown, there are several industry associations to which many ghostwriters belong:

Association of Ghostwriters

Established by Marcia Layton Turner, a veteran ghostwriter, the Association of Ghostwriters (http://associationofghostwriters.org) bills itself as "the leading professional organization for ghostwriters of books, articles, speeches, blogs and social media content." The association provides members with a variety of benefits, including monthly professional development teleseminars, a service that provides job leads, networking opportunities, a member directory, market information, a monthly newsletter, and more. Annual membership dues cost $99 per year in 2015.

American Society of Journalists and Authors

Established in 1948, the American Society of Journalists and Authors (www.asja.org) describes itself as "the nation's professional organization of independent nonfiction writers, " with a membership base of more than 1,000 freelance writers. In addition to books, its members write articles and other types of non-fiction. Membership benefits include networking opportunities, educational offerings such as workshops and seminars, and access to confidential market information. The ASJA "is a primary voice in representing freelancers' interests, serving as spokesman for their right to control and profit from uses of their work in the new media and otherwise. " In 2015 the ASJA charged annual membership dues of $210.

MARKET ANALYSIS

There is a lucrative market for ghostwriting services. However, as with any profession, skill and experience played a key role in determining how much a ghostwriter can charge for his or her services. For example, many beginning ghostwriters who focus on book writing earn between $5,000 and $15,000 per project, while those with more experience may earn between $30,000 and $50,000. A very small percentage (e.g., the industry's very best ghostwriters) earn much more. Demand for talented ghostwriters should always exist, considering that many business executives, politicians, and celebrities have fascinating stories to share, but lack the time or ability to produce books, articles, white papers, and other forms of written communication.

According to Statista Inc., the United States holds a position of global leadership in the publishing industry. Each year, book publishers generate revenues of approximately $29 billion. However, lucrative ghostwriting opportunities also exist beyond book publishing. For example, according a June 11, 2014, article in **Demand Gen Report** (DGR), a publication for business-to-business marketing professionals, some of the most popular types of content professionals use to make business-to-business purchasing decisions include:

- White Papers (78%)

- Case Studies (73%)

- Webinars (67%)

- E-books (58%)

- Blog Posts (56%)

SERVICES

Unlike other forms of writing, where contributors receive credit for their work in the form of a "byline" that identifies them as the author of an article, book, or other publication, ghostwriters work behind the scenes, collaborating with celebrities, business people, scientists, war heroes, politicians, underworld figures, professional athletes, doctors, and others to produce written communications on their behalf. In some cases, ghostwriters work as co-authors and receive credit for writing a book in conjunction with their client.

Ghostwriters may specialize in specific areas. John Warner will specialize in writing white papers, reports, case studies, and other business publications. Additionally, he will work with business executives to develop write articles and biographies for the business market. (Some ghostwriters subspecialize in other areas, such as health & fitness, spirituality, how-two, history, sports, etc.).

Process

Before beginning any project, John Warner will take steps to define exactly what it will entail by determining the following:

1. **Scope:** Some clients may have an idea for a book or article, but nothing more, while others may have a rough manuscript that needs polishing/enhancing/rewriting. Some clients already may have a publishing contract in place for a book, while others may be seeking assistance in developing a strong proposal that can be submitted to literary agents or book publishers. In this phase, Warner will clearly identify what a client's expectations are.

2. **Timeframe:** During this phase, Warner will identify a target completion date for the project. Once this has been identified, he then will work back from that date, developing smaller project milestones. This information will be critical when it comes to ensuring that the project stays on schedule.

3. **Payment Terms:** Most clients desire to pay a flat fee for ghostwriting services. For this reason, it is absolutely critical that the ghostwriter accurately identifies the scope of the project. Ghostwriting projects often involve more time than anticipated, so it is in the best interest of the writer to accurately gauge the amount of time that will be required, so that he or she does not underestimate the amount of work involved (or project fees).

4. **Development:** It is in the best interest of both parties to identify particulars of the working relationship in advance. Perhaps most importantly, Warner will identify how his client wishes to work together. Some clients feel strongly about meeting with a ghostwriter in person on a regular basis. This may involve long-distance travel, which the ghostwriter must account for when estimating the project. Other clients may prefer to communicate via online video chats, telephone conversations, or e-mails. Another important aspect of the development process involves identifying how much material will be provided to the ghostwriter in advance. In some cases, clients can provide a rough manuscript, presentations, notes, articles, videos, or other content. This usually will expedite project development considerably. If no content is available and the ghostwriter must develop an article or book from scratch, this must be considered when developing time and cost estimates. The bottom line is that the writer must identify where the information is to come from, and when it will be provided.

Once the scope, time frame, payment terms, and development particulars have been identified, John Warner will get everything in writing by developing a written contract. In the event that a particular client becomes difficult to work with, Warner will include a clause in the agreement allowing either party to terminate the contract for any reason. Additionally, Warner will agree to sign non-disclosure agreements when necessary, ensuring confidentiality for his client.

Keys to Success

No two ghostwriters (or clients) are alike, and every ghostwriting project is different. However, ghostwriters with the following attributes will be in the strongest position for success:

- Excellent Writing Skills
- Patience
- Accuracy/Attention to Detail
- Flexibility
- Sense of Humor
- Social Intuition
- Strong Interviewing Skills
- Ability to "get inside" a client's thought processes and understand their communication objectives.
- Ability to capture a client's "voice" and write in their particular style.
- A knack for developing/transforming ideas into written communications.
- Strong organizational and time management skills (to keep busy customers on-schedule)

PERSONNEL

After working in the corporate sector for 15 years, marketing communications professional John Warner has decided to go into business for himself in the specialized field of ghostwriting. Specifically, Warner will use his corporate experience to specialize in business writing. While working for a large, well-known consumer packaged goods company, Warner frequently was called upon to help members of the executive team write white papers, articles for business magazines and trade publications, and more. In addition, the chief executive officer and chief operating officer frequently used him to develop talking points and speeches for various occasions, and Warner had the opportunity to ghostwrite the CEO's autobiography and two other business books.

Prior to working for packaged goods company, Warner spent five years working for a leading public relations firm. In that role, he gained valuable experience working with top executives from companies in a number of different industries. In addition, he also sharpened his writing and editing skills.

Warner earned an undergraduate marketing slash communications degree from Central State University, where he also served as a reporter for the school newspaper. Following this, Warner furthered his education by earning a master's in business administration degree from Northern College.

Professional and Advisory Support

Warner will use a local accounting firm for assistance with tax preparation and bookkeeping. In addition, he has identified an attorney who specializes in the publishing field, in the event that related legal services are needed. Finally, Warner has established a business banking account with his local bank and has identified a freelance developmental editor, a proofreader, and two transcriptionists to assist him as needed. These professionals were identified from listings in **Literary Market Place,** a leading directory for the publishing industry.

GROWTH STRATEGY

Based on his knowledge of the business communications and book publishing markets, John Warner projects that he will be able to increase his project volume at a steady pace over the course of his first three years as a full-time ghostwriter, while allowing enough time in his schedule to perform administrative tasks related to the business and take advantage of other revenue-generating opportunities, such as writing his own bylined books and articles for industry and trade publications.

Warner has established the following customer acquisition goals and revenue targets for his first three years:

Customer type	2015	2016	2017
Literary agents	7	9	11
PR firms & speakers bureaus	2	3	4
Companies & organizations	2	2	2
Individuals	1	2	1
Total	**12**	**16**	**18**

Customer type	2015	2016	2017
Literary agents	$36,000	$41,400	$47,610
PR firms & speakers bureaus	$12,000	$13,800	$15,870
Companies & organizations	$9,000	$10,350	$11,903
Individuals	$3,000	$3,450	$3,968
Total	**$60,000**	**$69,000**	**$79,350**

OPERATIONS

Facility & Location

John Warner will operate his ghostwriting business from a home office. He has devoted space within his home exclusively for business purposes. In addition, Warner has installed an Internet-based telephone line for the business, as well as a dedicated broadband Internet connection. He will equip his office with a computer, multi-functional peripheral device (e.g., copy, fax, scanner), and file storage area. Warner also has purchased a smartphone, which will allow him to be accessible via voice, text message, video chat, and e-mail at all times.

Payment & Fees

To some degree, Warner's fees are negotiable. Typically, he will estimate work on a per-project basis. This flat fee is based on a detailed assessment of the project, and an hourly rate of approximately $75 per hour. Warner typically will require clients to pay 25 percent of his fee up front, with two payments due at critical project phases/milestones, and the final payment due upon completion. Warner will not proceed with a given project phase until the appropriate advance payment is received.

MARKETING & SALES

Warner will use the following primary tactics to promote his ghostwriting services:

1. Development of a four-color promotional card (which will fit inside a standard business-sized envelope).

2. A professionally-designed Web site.

3. Regular, highly-targeted direct mailings to public relations firms, speakers' bureaus, book packagers, and literary agents.

4. Prospecting on popular freelance writing job sites (e.g., journalismjobs.com, craigslist.com, freelancedaily.net, etc.)

5. A small online ad in several key regional business magazines.

6. Membership in the Association of Ghostwriters and the American Society of Journalists and Authors, which provides access to online job listings.

7. A subscription to PublishersMarketplace.com, which is valuable for prospecting and listing John Warner's ghostwriting business.

8. An e-mail footer that clearly identifies John Warner as a ghostwriter.

9. Networking at regional and national business events.

10. A listing in *Literary Market Place*, a leading directory for the publishing industry.

FINANCIAL ANALYSIS

John Warner estimates that he will generate about half of his annual revenue from ghostwriting books, with articles accounting for 30 percent, and corporate communications (e.g., white papers, case studies, reports, etc.) making up the remaining 20 percent.

In terms of clients, Warner estimates that 60 percent of his revenue will come from literary agents, followed by public relations firms and speakers bureaus (20%), companies and other organizations (15%), and individuals (5%).

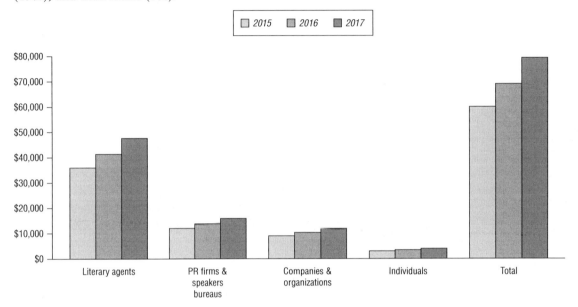

Following are three-year financial projections for John Warner's ghostwriting business, based on his knowledge of the market, skills and ability, and availability:

	2015	2016	2017
Revenue			
Literary agents	$36,000	$41,400	$47,610
PR firms & speakers bureaus	$12,000	$13,800	$15,870
Companies & organizations	$ 9,000	$10,350	$11,903
Individuals	$ 3,000	$ 3,450	$ 3,968
Total	**$60,000**	**$69,000**	**$79,350**
Expenses			
Advertising & marketing	$ 500	$ 500	$ 500
Miscellaneous items	$ 250	$ 300	$ 350
Legal	$ 500	$ 250	$ 250
Accounting	$ 850	$ 500	$ 500
Office supplies	$ 250	$ 250	$ 250
Computers/peripherals	$ 1,500	$ 0	$ 0
Business insurance	$ 500	$ 500	$ 500
Salary	$50,000	$60,000	$70,000
Postage	$ 150	$ 150	$ 150
Telecommunications	$ 750	$ 750	$ 750
Travel	$ 500	$ 600	$ 750
Subscriptions	$ 250	$ 250	$ 250
Total expenses	**$56,000**	**$64,050**	**$74,250**
Net income	**$ 4,000**	**$ 4,950**	**$ 5,100**

Gift Box Business

Reclaimed Treasures Inc.

34750 Orlando Ave.
Detweiler Hills, KY 44887

Paul Greenland

Reclaimed Treasures Inc. makes custom gift and storage boxes from reclaimed wood and metal.

EXECUTIVE SUMMARY

Reclaimed Treasures Inc. makes custom gift and storage boxes from reclaimed wood and metal. Examples include cigar, jewelry, keepsake, and photo boxes. Using a blend of craftsmanship and creativity, business owner Nicholas Owens makes unique and valuable creations from items that others have discarded. Because the majority of materials are obtained at no cost, this business offers strong income potential for the owner, as long as production is managed efficiently.

INDUSTRY ANALYSIS

Reclaimed Treasures is part of the larger retail industry. According to "The Economic Impact of the U.S. Retail Industry," a report from the National Retail Federation (NRF) and PricewaterhouseCoopers LLP, the retail sector ranks as the nation's largest private employer, contributing $2.6 trillion to the United States' gross domestic product every year, and providing employment for some 42 million people. Additionally, the report indicates that most retailers are small businesses like Reclaimed Treasures, accounting for approximately 40 percent of all employees.

NRF, which ranks as the largest retail trade association in the world, includes home goods and specialty retailers such as Reclaimed Treasures among its members. Benefits for Retail Members include access to advocacy initiatives, research (studies, consumer spending surveys, benchmarking reports, economic data, planning guides, etc.), a digital community named Shop.org, news and information (STORES magazine, specialty newsletters, etc.), and educational events/resources such as the NRF Big Show and the Shop.org Digital Summit.

Another leading industry organization is the Gift and Home Trade Association. Established in 2000, the organization "was designed to help and encourage vendors, sales agencies, industry affiliates and retailers to work together, improving relationships and making business better by providing members with the opportunity to exchange ideas and network with industry leaders." Each year, the Gift and Home Trade Association hosts an annual conference and provides members with benefits such as news and industry data.

MARKET ANALYSIS

Although Reclaimed Treasures will sell products at a limited number of local and regional events, Nicholas Owens has decided to adopt an e-commerce model for the business. According to the firm Statista Inc., in the United States, retail e-commerce revenue reached $225.5 billion in 2012, and is projected to nearly double by 2017, reaching $434.2 billion.

Specifically, Reclaimed Treasures will focus on box sales to consumers seeking unique gift items for special occasions such as anniversaries, weddings, promotions, Christmas, Hanukkah, graduations, and birthdays. Owens will appeal to sustainability-minded consumers by emphasizing the fact that his business' products are made from reclaimed/or recycled materials.

PRODUCTS

Most of the boxes that Reclaimed Treasures produces will fall into one of three standard size categories:

Small Boxes ($39.99)

- Cigar Boxes
- Gift Boxes
- Jewelry Boxes
- Keepsake Boxes
- Photo Boxes
- Watch Boxes
- Flag Boxes

Medium Boxes ($49.99)

- Puzzle & Game Boxes
- Tool Boxes
- Wine Boxes

Large Boxes ($69.99)

- Hope Chests
- Foot Lockers

In addition, Reclaimed Treasures will make custom boxes for customers, including items produced from material that has sentimental value. For example, one customer may wish to have a flag box or hope chest made from barn wood from their family's farm.

OPERATIONS

Location

Reclaimed Treasures will operate from Nicholas Owens' residence, which has an extra two-car garage that already has been converted into a workshop space.

Materials

The majority of Reclaimed Treasures' will be made from reclaimed wood and sheet metal, which the owner will obtain at minimal or no cost. Primary sources for materials include, but are not limited to, craigslist, residential curbside pickups, demolition companies, building contractors/remodeling specialists, and businesses in need of material disposal. The owner will provide free pick-up and haul-way services in exchange for the materials. Of particular interest to Reclaimed Treasures are old license plates, sheet metal scraps, appliances, pallets, barn lumber, and construction lumber.

Tools

Reclaimed Treasures already possesses the tools and equipment needed for basic wood and metalworking, including:

Power Tools

- Air Compressor
- Band saw
- Biscuit Joiner
- Combination Disc/Belt Sander
- Compound Double-Bevel Miter Saw
- Cordless Drill
- Drill Press
- Dust Collector
- Grinder
- Jigsaw
- Jointer
- Miter Saw Stand
- Nail Gun
- Orbital Sander
- Palm Sander
- Planer
- Rivet Gun
- Rotary Cutting Tool
- Router
- Router Table
- Table saw
- Workbenches (2)

Hand Tools

- Aviation Snips
- Ball Peen Hammer
- Band Clamps
- Bar Clamps
- Bending Brake
- Carpenters Hammer

- Coping Saw
- Hand Saw
- Mallets
- Marking Tool
- Metal Files
- Nail Sets
- Pliers
- Sanding Block
- Scratch Awl
- Screwdrivers
- Square
- Straightedge
- Tin Snips
- Wood Files

Production

Nicholas Owens has determined that efficiency and scale are important factors in the success of his business. Even though the materials from which he produces boxes will be obtained at no cost, he understands that spending too much time on the production of any one item will hinder his profitability. With this in mind, the business will produce boxes in three standard sizes to maximize efficiency and expedite production. This will allow Nicholas Owens to set up his equipment (e.g., table saw, miter saw, etc.) to pre-cut many pieces of the same size, rather than cutting/bending pieces for individual boxes one at a time. Owens will produce batches of similarly-sized boxes in stages (e.g., cutting, bending, sanding, assembling, finishing, etc.).

By category, about half of the boxes produced by Reclaimed Treasures will be small in size, while medium-sized boxes will account for 35% of production, followed by large boxes (15%).

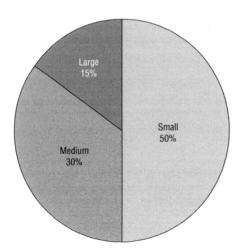

Supplies

Reclaimed Treasures will require the following supplies for production:

- Finishes
- Sandpaper

- Steel Wool

- Glue

- Rivets

- Dowels

- Wood Screws

- Sheet Metal Screws

- Staples

- Finishing Nails

- Hardware (will use reclaimed hardware whenever possible)

- Packaging Materials (e.g., newspaper, bubble wrap, etc.)

Shipping

Unless other arrangements are made per the customer's request, Reclaimed Treasures will utilize U.S. Postal Service Priority Mail to ship all orders, since cardboard shipping containers are available at no cost. Shipping and handling charges will apply to all customer orders. Shipping insurance will be offered for an additional charge.

PERSONNEL

Owens has always had strong industrial arts skills, mainly in woodworking and metalworking. In high school, he took advantage of introductory and advanced classes in both areas. This training provided him with foundational skills that have been useful in his adult years as a homeowner and a hobbyist. However, Owens also is highly creative and possesses an entrepreneurial spirit. After visiting arts and craft shows with his wife, Owens was inspired to use all of his capabilities to produce unique and valuable creations from materials that are available at no cost. The formation of Reclaimed Treasures comes at an ideal time, because Owens has learned that his employer will soon close the manufacturing plant where he works as a machinist. Desiring to remain in his hometown, where there is limited ability in his given field, he will pursue a long-time dream of working for himself. In order to obtain foundational business skills, Owens has read several small business management books from the public library, and also plans to take advantage of courses offered by the non-profit organization, SCORE (www.score.org), whose mission is to "Foster vibrant small business communities through mentoring and education."

Professional & Advisory Support

Reclaimed Treasures has established a business banking account with Detweiler Hills Bank, including a merchant account for accepting credit card payments. Tax advisement is provided by Jones Financial LLC.

GROWTH STRATEGY

Reclaimed Treasures has developed the following projections for the first three years of operations, based on 245 production days per calendar year. Nicholas Owens has determined his daily maximum production capacity. Realizing that he will need to allot a given amount of time for administrative tasks, marketing, and customer service, Owens will establish a goal of producing at 60 percent of his maximum capacity for the first year, 70 percent the second year, and 80 percent the third year.

Category	2015	2016	2017
Small	1,544	1,887	2,058
Medium	343	515	686
Large	172	343	515
Total production	**1,441**	**1,921**	**2,281**

MARKETING & SALES

A local graphic designer has been hired to create a unique brand identity for Reclaimed Treasures (logo and color scheme).

The majority of the business' marketing dollars will be devoted to interactive promotion and search-engine optimization strategies. Owens used the online workplace site, Upwork (formerly oDesk), to evaluate and hire a freelance Web developer/designer to create an engaging Web site for Reclaimed Treasures, which includes mobile functionality and integration with leading social media platforms.

In partnership with the developer, Owens purchased a domain name for his site and identified an ideal hosting solution with a reputable provider that offers guaranteed uptime and robust security features to protect customer data. Specifically, the site's functionality will include essential features such as product profiles, shopping cart, and payment processing. He also has established personal and customer service e-mail accounts featuring his domain name.

As part of its marketing strategy, Reclaimed Treasures will focus on selling products through leading online marketplaces, including Etsy (www.etsy.com), Bonanza (www.bonanza.com), Zibbet (www.zibbet.com), Craft Is Art (www.craftisart.com), and ArtFire (www.artfire.com), as well as social media platforms such as Facebook and Instagam.

FINANCIAL ANALYSIS

The following table shows Reclaimed Treasures' projected gross revenues for the first three years of operations:

Category	2015	2016	2017
Small	$61,725	$75,441	$ 82,299
Medium	$17,147	$25,720	$ 34,293
Large	$12,003	$24,007	$ 36,010
Gross revenue	**$63,612**	**$87,617**	**$106,822**

Even though Reclaimed Treasures will obtain the majority of production materials for free, Nicholas Owens estimates that production costs (e.g., hardware, finishes, etc.) will account for 15 percent of sales:

Category	2015	2016	2017
Small	$52,466	$64,125	$69,955
Medium	$14,575	$21,862	$29,149
Large	$10,203	$20,406	$30,608
Net revenue	**$45,960**	**$63,303**	**$77,179**

The following graph provides a visual depiction of Reclaimed Treasures' gross and net revenues for the first three years of operations:

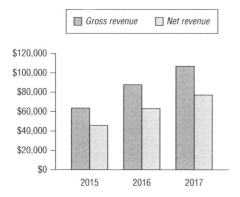

Reclaimed Treasures' sales and expenses for the first three years of operation are projected as follows:

Pro forma profit and loss statement

	2015	2016	2017
Gross revenue	$63,612	$87,617	$106,822
Net revenue	$45,960	$63,303	$ 77,179
Expenses			
Salaries	$30,000	$45,000	$ 55,000
Payroll taxes	$ 4,500	$ 6,750	$ 8,250
Marketing	$ 4,000	$ 5,500	$ 7,000
Business insurance	$ 950	$ 1,050	$ 1,150
Web/interactive costs	$ 1,350	$ 1,350	$ 1,350
Office supplies	$ 1,200	$ 1,200	$ 1,200
Tools & equipment	$ 500	$ 500	$ 500
Misc.	$ 350	$ 350	$ 350
Total expenses	$42,850	$61,700	$ 74,800
Net profit	$ 3,110	$ 1,603	$ 2,379

A complete set of pro forma financial statements has been prepared for the business and is available upon request.

Homeless Shelter

Sister Joan of Arc Center

23 Oak Blvd.
Denver, Colorado 80203

RJ Sak

Sister Joan of Arc Center reduces criminal recidivism and alleviates chronic homelessness by providing short-term shelter that seeks to obtain long-term housing, establish mentoring relationships, and secure stable employment for its clients.

EXECUTIVE SUMMARY

The Saint Patrick Homeless Family Shelter (Patrick House) is an emergency family shelter for women and families in Denver, Colorado. In November 2014, the Saint Patrick Society (SPS) ended its organizational sponsorship of Patrick House because of excessive financial burden. Patrick House and its board of directors became their own unaffiliated 501(c)3 not–for–profit organization. SPS also signed the deed over to Patrick House for the building Patrick House operates from. This severance also resulted in a loss of 25% of Patrick House's total annual funding. In addition, SPS stipulated that the emergency family shelter cease having any reference to "Patrick" in its identity.

The national trend for human service organizations is to consolidate services and programs for the homeless into large centers and consolidated civic plans. The City of Denver is following suit. In December 2014 Denver Mayor Michael Hancock announced that homeless day services would be bolstered in three local emergency shelters. Patrick House is the only emergency shelter not to be directly included in this plan.

Federal grants are rewarding organizations that maintain the national trend of streamlining services. Across the nation organizations that solely offer emergency shelter are both rethinking long-term strategies and making significant changes to stay competitive. To not respond to the trend results in a reduction of services and ultimately ceasing operations due to funding shortages.

It is becoming increasingly difficult for Patrick House to attract funding. During a time of industry transition, stagnation is tantamount to surrender. In order for Patrick House to continue as a viable service provider for the homeless population, honest evaluations must be made, alternatives considered, and proactive forward-thinking decisions made.

The primary demand for homeless services is a constant need. A newly emerging market segment is offender reentry programs. 650,000 people are released from incarceration every year and the statistical rate for recidivism is 66%. Recidivism is over 70% for people who, upon release, are homeless. Homelessness and offender reentry is a significant social issue with costly consequences. To address this issue, the US Government announced a 2013 joint initiative—the Serious and Violent Offender Reentry

Initiative (SVORI). The Colorado Department of Correctional Services implements local SVORI programs. The Colorado Department of Correctional Services has communicated a community demand for a transitional shelter for reentering homeless offenders.

Funding for Patrick House will be pursued through federal grants. Transitional shelter for reentering homeless offenders is of particular interest to the Department of Labor, Department of Justice, and the Housing & Urban Development Committee. Awards are being announced on a regular basis. In addition to $120 million that funds SVORI, an extra $24 million for grant money was announced on April 1, 2015 by the Department of Labor to address offender reentry.

This business plan will detail the steps needed to dissolve Patrick House. The turn around plan is for the creation of the Saint Joan of Arc Center (SJAC)—an organization whose long-term vision is to become the community leader for offender reentry and homeless issues. SJAC's first objective is to establish the Joan of Arc Transitional Living Program (TLP). TLP's mission is to provide shelter for reentering homeless offenders.

BUSINESS OVERVIEW

Organizational Statements

Vision Statement
Saint Joan of Arc Center is a national beacon and the local community standard for serving the homeless with an offender reentry program.

Mission
Saint Joan of Arc Center reduces criminal recidivism and alleviates chronic homelessness by providing short–term shelter that seeks to obtain long–term housing, establish mentoring relationships, and secure stable employment for its clients.

Organizational Name
Saint Joan of Arc Center

Legal Form of Business
Saint Joan of Arc Center is to be a 501(c)3 not–for–profit organization.

COMPANY HISTORY

After twenty years of sponsorship Patrick House became an organization independent from the St. Patrick Society in November 2014. The annual budget for Patrick House had grown to be 25% of the entire budget for the Society. The increasing financial liability for the Society became too heavy of a burden and it was mutually agreed that the Society would be able to best operate separate from Patrick House.

The Society signed over the deed for the building the Patrick House operates from for the cost of $1. The financial result of this separation is a loss of 25% of total funding for Patrick House. Funding loss coupled with a tight environment for funding, has Patrick House surviving financially on a month-to-month basis. Funding and fundraising is the foremost concern for Patrick House. It was additionally agreed that Patrick House would no longer use "Patrick" to identify itself.

In the City of Denver, Patrick House is one of four emergency shelters. In December 2014, Denver Mayor Michael Hancock announced plans to involve three emergency shelters and attempt to create a continuum of care available to Denver's homeless population. Public funding is being used for this project. Patrick House is not included in the plan. It is reasonable to expect that civic attention will be given to the Mayor's plan and, in turn, philanthropists will take interest in seeing this plan succeed. Not being included in the Mayor's proposal will prove to be a significant hurdle that impedes the potential flow for future funding to Patrick House.

Today is April 2015 and Patrick House is in an interim period. The board of directors and staff remain intact and united through the reorganization process with the Society. The critical question at Patrick House today is funding. Patrick House is surviving the short term by tooth and nail financial efforts. Where is it going to come from and how is it going to happen? Now is the time for Patrick House administrators to critically assess Patrick House's role in the Denver community and evaluate the most effective way to both serve the homeless and attract long-term funding.

What follows here is a plan for Patrick House to grow into a financially comfortable and socially valuable organization. The first building block for any not–for–profit organization is to satisfy the demand for a public need.

MARKET ANALYSIS

A national study conducted by the Bureau of Justice Statistics in 2012 revealed that in a three–year window, the recidivism rate for ex–offenders was 67% . Two–thirds of released prisoners are re–arrested and one–half are re–incarcerated within 3 years of release from prison. Over 60% of these offenses were committed with the first year of release. In 2013, researcher Peter Silia observed that "It appears from the available evidence that persons being released from prison today are doing less well than their counterparts released a decade ago in successfully reintegrating into their communities. More of them are being rearrested; these arrests are occurring more quickly; and as a group, ex–convicts are accounting for a growing share of all serious crimes experienced in the United States."

Trends are no different in the State of Colorado. As of March 2013, Colorado's prison population was at 20,135. This figure represents 132% of its capacity.

In a study conducted in 2010, researcher Ali Riker measured the impact that community-based treatment models had upon recidivism for transitioning offenders who are homeless. The key finding of Riker's demonstrates that community-based treatment models that serve the homeless reduce recidivism from 71% down to 44%.

Speaking to the relationship of recidivism and homelessness, Larry Wayne of the Colorado Department of Correctional Services notes: "Recidivism for transitioning offenders is over 70% for those without a non–criminalgenic home environment. In the state of Colorado, there is a chronic shortage of housing for transitioning offenders. There is an absolute need for residential-based, community supportive housing in Denver, Colorado. Stable housing for offender reentry initiatives is an absolute need right now."

In 2013, the United States Departments of Agriculture, Commerce, Education, Health and Human Services, Housing and Urban Development, Justice, Labor and Veterans Affairs came together to produce the Severe and Violent Offender Reentry Initiative (SVORI) . SVORI aims to reduce recidivism rates by funding community-based treatment models. The Colorado Department of Correctional Services is the only organization working with SVORI in the state of Colorado. The Colorado Department of Correctional Services does not have a work plan for a program to provide transitional living services for reentering homeless offenders.

The University of Colorado is currently evaluating SVORI in Colorado. The study is expected to continue for several months before a definitive assessment and recommendation come forth. It is anticipated that this study will highlight a positive correlation between recidivism and homelessness. A need for a transitional living shelter for reentering offenders is expected to be highlighted.

In Denver, the opportunity to enter the offender reentry market is to provide a transitional living program to reenter homeless offenders. The long-term opportunity is for Patrick House is to develop this market segment. An exit strategy for Patrick House is addressed further in the plan. First, the birth of the Saint Joan of Arc Center will be highlighted.

Saint Joan of Arc Center

SJAC is the "turn around" plan for Patrick House. SJAC will work out of the same building (23 Oak Blvd.) as Patrick House did. The board of directors and staff of SJAC are retained from Patrick House. A transition strategy and an overview of SJAC personnel is included later in the plan.

The Saint Joan of Arc Center (SJAC) is a 501(c)3 not–for–profit organization that funds and manages programs that address homelessness and offender reentry. The vision for SJAC is to a nationally recognized and local community leader for services provided to the homeless reentering offenders in Denver, Colorado.

The immediate foundation for SJAC is the establishment of the Saint Joan of Arc Transitional Living Program (TLP). For the short term, SJAC will be indistinguishable from the TLP. The long-term vision is for SJAC to grow into several programs organized under the organizational umbrella of SJAC. The long-term growth vision for SJAC is detailed below.

Saint Joan of Arc Transitional Living Program

Business Strategy

The goal of Saint Joan of Arc Transitional Living Program is to provide individuals with the necessary resources and support they need to gain self–sufficient living in an atmosphere of dignity, integrity and respect. The Saint Joan of Arc Transitional Living Program serves adult (18+) men who, upon being released from prison, are homeless.

Believing all adults have the necessary resources to achieve independent living, we call our guests into high accountability for their actions or inactions. Adults benefit from this philosophy, as does the entire community.

With the increased awareness of the value that community plays in helping to reshape the lives of those in need, we are working to form partnerships and strong relational ties with individuals and community organizations throughout Denver and the surrounding community. We realize that those who need us most belong to the community, and as such, it is the community joining together that is best able to meet their needs. We are hopeful that through the ongoing involvement and support of others, our guests will continue to receive the care and services they need to help enable them to fully participate in the community in which they are a part.

We believe that the community finds value in the services that the Saint Joan of Arc Center provides and that the ongoing support of community organizations, associations and individuals is reflective of the community's means of contributing to the joint effort required to serve the needs of members of the community, and ultimately, of humanity.

The end outcome for TLP is the reduction of offender recidivism. Providing transitional living for reentering homeless offenders pursues this goal. This goal is measured through statistical analysis and is benchmarked by national trends.

Objectives

The work of the Saint Joan of Arc Transitional Living Program is to:

1. Offer short-term transitional shelter for men being served by the Colorado Department of Correctional Services' offender reentry program.

2. Grow to imitate the client services offered by Colorado Department of Correctional Services and provide a long-term homeless offender reentry services without relying on Colorado Department of Correctional Services for resources.

TLP is based on a community treatment model, in that TLP works with the Colorado Department of Correctional Services treatment model. Communication and relationships with potential guests begin while incarcerated and may continue well beyond a guest moving on from the TLP. To encourage the end outcome, the TLP emphasizes security in three areas: housing, mentoring, and employment.

Housing

Short–term transitional housing is located at the building previously known as "Patrick House." The building can comfortably shelter up to 40 people. The standard length of stay is a flexible 30–60 days. Thus, TLP can optimistically serve 480 people each year. A realistic figure is 240 people. A minimum number is 200 people.

All living necessities are provided for guests at no charge. In-house services include: three meals a day, toiletries, clothing, laundry, and basic living expenses as needed.

Long-term housing is explored with staff, social workers, and community organizations to identify available options for either private living or publicly supported housing programs. TLP is a fast track to secure these services and realize "housing first."

Mentoring

Mentoring is the promotion of a person's physical, mental, and emotional health. The basic goal here is to help get a person readjusted and situated within their community. Each person is guided by a social worker to identify personal needs and satisfy personal healing and growth.

While incarcerated, a Colorado Department of Correctional Services social worker establishes a relationship with inmates who may qualify as participants with SVORI. It is here that clients for TLP are identified, their personal needs assessed, and personal goals are established with the inmate. Based on a "community-based treatment model," a care plan for the individual is created by the social worker.

The social worker introduces the client to the staff of TLP. In addition to the Colorado Department of Correctional Services social worker, TLP staff has a significant amount of experience providing a continuum of care for the homeless. Community networking and relationships allow TLP staff to provide entry points for health care, mental health services, support groups, and legal services. The purpose of the mentor is to help the client establish a network of relationships needed to successfully transition from incarceration into reentry.

This mentoring process may or may not be complete by the time a person completes TLP. SJAC will continue to provide community entry points for former guests and be a foundation of support as each person reconstructs a social network and builds core support relationships.

Employment

Employment is the establishment of any sustainable income allowing a person to live a frugal life. For some this may include working a job. For others it may include receiving a disability check. TLP works with the Denver Workforce Development Board to seek employment and cultivate employable skills. Public funding supports other folks. TLP works with all people to identify a means by which to survive.

Exit Strategy

Patrick House receives grants from the Federal Housing and Urban Development Program (HUD), the Federal Emergency Maintenance Act (FEMA), the Colorado Homeless Assistance Trust Fund Act, and other private foundations. Each of these grants requires that Patrick House provide emergency shelter services either for women, children, and/or families. By transitioning into an organization that provides shelter for offenders being released from incarceration, Patrick House breaks the terms of its grants. In order for Patrick House to terminate and for the Saint Joan of Arc Center to be born, several grants will need to be terminated and remaining funding reimbursed to the grantors.

The typical concern for grant termination is loss of funding. Sufficient funding sources for the Saint Joan of Arc Center have been identified and will be addressed in the funding section below.

The transition from old grants into new grants will be both an accounting and a communications matter. Determining the accrual of expenses and the budgeting schedule for each grant will determine how much money needs to be reimbursed to the grantor. The current administrative assistant who has both experience and a background in accounting can handle such facts and details.

The bottom line is that the dissolution of Patrick House will be characterized by communicating a sharpened commitment to serve the homeless population of Denver. The market segment of reentering homeless offenders is developing and it makes economic and social sense to hone services to this population. Communication with grantors and their respective agencies will serve as the ending of Patrick House.

Transitional Period

The legal transition for when Patrick House closes and the Saint Joan of Arc Center opens will be determined by the date of when majority funding begins for SJAC. Given the current grant opportunities and deadlines, an optimistic target date for the end of Patrick House and opening of the SJAC is November 1, 2015. Realistically, the date is flexible and transition will be gradual.

There are two chief concerns for the transition: staff preparedness and community readiness. SJAC will be serving a distinct segment of the homeless population than it has in the past. Reentering offenders all come from the common environment of incarceration and will have unique needs that SJAC staff will need to be sensitive to and prepared to work with.

In the months leading up to the transition, an overview of criminal justice and presentations and conversations with social workers will provide the backbone to equip SJAC staff to be better prepared to address the daily care needs of the people they will be serving. SJAC staff will need to meet with local criminal justice organizations and social workers to be introduced to the population they will be serving. Ongoing invitations to hear presentations from local agencies will not only help share knowledge; it will be an excellent source for networking and building relationships.

Initially, the primary relationship for the SJAC is with the Colorado Department of Correctional Services. Colorado Department of Correctional Services provides community treatment and programming for reentering offenders. Colorado Department of Correctional Services has expressed direct interest to see the establishment of a transitional shelter that would address reentering offenders. Planning the opening of SJAC with the help of Colorado Department of Correctional Services is essential. Colorado Department of Correctional Services is the current beacon for offender reentry and will embrace a relationship with SJAC.

Apart from the community resources, networks, and relationships offered through Colorado Department of Correctional Services, SJAC will maintain relationships with all the local service organizations that Patrick House worked with on a daily basis. To be sure, organizations such as the Greater Denver Workforce Development, Charles Drew Health Services, and Community Alliance have indicated a willingness to support and offer service to programs that address prisoner reentry.

Management Summary

The board of directors and staff of SJAC will remain the same during this period of growth and change. A strong anchor of leadership is needed to see the transition through. In a period of change, maintaining the professional integrity and social fabric of an organization will help stabilize SJAC.

The members on the board of directors are:

Rev. Trent Snow—Spiritual Advisor
Trent is the Pastor of St. Mark's Parish and former Provincial for the Wisconsin Province of the Jesuits. Trent has taught at St. Paul's Preparatory School for 20 years.

Jim Cooper
Jim is the President of Marketing for RBG Service Corp. He has been active in 12 Step Programs for 25 years.

Don Hale
Don served as Executive Director for the Uta Halee Girls Village for 15 years. Today he is retired and does Outreach Ministry for St. Philip Neri Parish.

Bob McCarthey
Bob has been the Director of Human Resources at St. Clair of Montefalco Community College for 10 years. He is a former Chair of the Campfire USA Board and is a Deacon at St. Joseph's Parish.

Donald Oppenmeyer
Donald Oppenmeyer has been the Executive Director of Patrick House for 7 years.

Brett Boyer
Brett teaches Theology at St. Paul's Preparatory School. For 20 years he has served as Director for the school's annual food drive—Operation Others.

Dick Weidlen
Dick has worked as an Investor and Entrepreneur for 15 years and is retired from the Civil Service. He joined the Patrick House board a month ago.

Jane Kitt
Jane taught for 20 years at the University of Colorado. She is a former President of the business community development group Denver Group.

Neal McMurtney—President
Neal has been the Director for the Colorado Community Office of Retardation and Developmental Disabilities for 12 years. He has been involved in community activism for 10 years.

Mike Twiz
Mike is an attorney and a Managing Partner with Twiz PPC. He is active with a variety of community organizations.

Brent Jordan—Treasurer
For 25 years Brent worked as a Comptroller for First Charter Bank. He has also served on the board of New Covenant Center for 6 years.

Lisa Spornon—Vice Chair
Lisa has worked at Denver Methodist Hospital as a Certified Registered Nurse Anesthetist for 20 years and has served on the board of Patrick House for 6 years.

Robert Smith
Robert has been a Managing Director for Smith Investment Company for 15 years. He has also served as the Director of Investments at Girls and Boys Town.

Jack Bruster—Secretary
Jack is a Managing Partner at the Apex Architectural Firm. For 15 years he has worked as an architect for Apex.

Organization

As Patrick House closes, the full-time staff of Patrick House will carry over and form the nucleus for organizing, opening, and operating Saint Joan of Arc Center. In addition to the named staff, two full-time, non–salaried positions will continue to be filled by several part time hourly–wage employees.

Executive Director—Mark Rielle

Mark has a background as both a managerial administrator and as a social servant. In his first career, Mark spent several years as a project manager for an Denver–based financial firm. In the mid 1990s, Mark organized a Denver Catholic Worker house whose ministry was with homeless men. From 2007 until the present, Mark has served as the executive director for the St. Vincent de Paul Homeless Family Shelter. Mark is deeply connected within the Denver community and serves on various boards and committees that address homelessness in Denver. Mark is widely recognized by his peers as being a person who is deeply immersed in the issue of homelessness and is a topical guru for social services.

Administrative Assistant—Daniel Holden

Daniel has served as the Administrative Assistant at the St. Vincent de Paul Homeless Family Shelter for five years. In this position, he oversaw all accounting, budget, and general financial issues for the Family Shelter. Daniel also comes with a background in insurance. Previously, Daniel has spent time as an accountant in the insurance industry.

Community Programmer—Mary Moore

Mary has earned a PhD in occupational therapy and has taught courses at both the University of Colorado and Depauw University. In 2014 she joined Patrick House to focus on the community services available for clients being served by Patrick House.

Funding

A grant-driven financial strategy will stabilize SJAC and orient the organization towards the future. This foundation will build to the vision of establishing SJAC as the organization for reentering offenders and homelessness in Denver, Colorado.

The primary source of funding for Patrick House is a federal grant awarded for offender reentry programs. Conversations with social service professionals, academic researchers, and federal employees are quite optimistic that federal and state funding for offender reentry programs will continue for the next several years. Thus, it is reasonable to expect that SJAC's annual budget of $600,000 can rely on grants for the foreseeable future.

On April 1, 2015 the US Department of Labor (DOL) announced a solicitation for grant application for prisoner re–entry initiatives. DOL seeks faith based and/or community organizations that provide services to prisoners reentering the community. The grant is valued at $790,000 and applications are due July 13, 2015. Grantees must begin services within four months of the award reception. This is a prime grant for SJAC.

Since 2011 the United States Department of Justice (DOJ) has been regularly awarding project grants for offender reentry programs. In recent months, a 2-year grant worth $1 million was announced. The application deadline for this award passed in March. It is anticipated that an identical grant (CFDA 16.202) will be made available in early 2016.

The Severe and Violent Offender Reentry Initiative (SVORI) is a backbone for funding. Between 2013 and 2016, over $100 million is being distributed to sixty–nine grantees to develop offender reentry programs. The Colorado Department of Correctional Services is one of the primary grantees for SVORI and looks to develop and fund such programs in the state. Because current SVORI funding ends in October 2016, relying on Colorado Department of Correctional Services for primary funding is not sustainable. It will be smart to continue to follow SVORI because it is believed that the U.S. Government will continue to sponsor offender reentry programs after SVORI concludes.

The bottom line is that the Saint Joan of Arc Transitional Living Program will provide emergency shelter for people who are both reentering offenders and homeless. There is substantial money available for this market segment. SJAC can pursue grants that are above and beyond offender reentry programs. In addition, The Housing and Urban Development Committee, Federal Emergency Management Agency, and United Way of the Midlands also regularly provide grants, tax credits, and funding opportunities to basic emergency shelters. SJAC is included in this classification. Because SJAC is growing into a center for homeless services, it is reasonable to believe that SJAC can become a player for grant opportunities where Patrick House was losing ground.

Historically, private donations to Patrick House annually exceeded $120,000. In addition, the annual golf fundraiser brought in another $30,000. Although primary care is changing from women and families to reentering offenders, communicating the community need and simultaneously demonstrating the social value of SJAC to past donors should be enough to retain a substantial amount of this private funding. It is realistic to expect that SJAC will be able to secure $600,000 in annual funding.

FINANCIAL ANALYSIS

The 2016 budget is rather loose and is benchmarked by the assumption that SJAC will be realistically able to win a substantial grant with a median value of $600,000.

Patrick House's budget for fiscal year 2015 is $393,840. One full year of operating the Saint Joan of Arc Center is budgeted at $600,000. The largest leap is the salaries being paid to the full time administrators. The figures of $54,000, $48,000, and $42,000 are set to be competitive figures for similar positions in not–for–profit organizations.

SJAC is a forward thinking, growth-oriented organization and its pay scale reflects the caliber of team players involved. Employee benefits have been increased by 55% to encourage workplace unity and ease financial concerns so often associated with social service organizations. If key administrators are shown appreciation, it sets a tone of professionalism and progress throughout the entire organization.

$259,200 is earmarked for two part–time staff members to be at Patrick House every hour of every day. A rate of $14.79/hour for two positions satisfies this figure. Currently, there are several staff members who work part–time at Patrick House. These individuals are the fabric that will encourage continuity throughout the significant change from Patrick House into the Saint Joan of Arc Center. It is important that an appropriate pay scale be used as a vehicle to retain staff members during this transitory period.

Various administrative and operating expenses show slight increases. Professional fees are more than doubled to reflect the potential costs incurred during the legal transition from Patrick House to SJAC. Potential professional fees may also be incurred should SJAC have to engage in legal action to resolve its land threat (see below).

Fundraising expenses reflect the need for SJAC to do basic marketing procedures to establish its identity in Denver. Newsletters, letterheads, basic website, etc. will need to be organized in order to raise awareness about the services of SJAC as well as comfort donors that the transition from Patrick House to SJAC is in fact a smooth and seamless one. Finally, $4,800 is added to building and grounds repairs to reflect changes that the building may need to undergo in order to be up to code with the standards of Colorado Department of Correctional Services as a community partner.

RECOMMENDATIONS AND EVALUATION TOOLS

The University of Colorado's Department of Criminal Justice is currently doing a local study on the Colorado Department of Correctional Services' offender reentry program. This study is expected to be complete in the near future and will deliver program recommendations and insights. It is expected that the report will include correlations for recidivism and homelessness. As SJAC begins to address this very issue, it is in a prime position to seek partnership with criminal justice researchers at the University of Colorado.

SJAC's partnership with the University of Colorado and the Colorado Department of Correctional Services will create a cutting edge synergy that synthesizes experience, research, and implementation. The benefit for SJAC is two–fold. First, being plugged into an active academic body will provide SJAC will progressive social models for service and care. Secondly, SJAC will be able to translate its raw data into meaningful benchmarks and create measuring sticks for success. This information will be able to demonstrate the success and community value of offender reentry programs.

As SJAC seeks to position itself as the leader for recidivism and homelessness, it may be strategically wise to seek research grants and offer employment to the University of Colorado professors and graduate students to strategically work with SJAC. Investing in a smart relationship will encourage local growth, foster national attention, and attract funding oriented towards growth and the improvement of a socially valued service.

GROWTH STRATEGY

As described, the Saint Joan of Arc Transitional Living Shelter is the first program sponsored by the Saint Joan of Arc Center. As the parent organization, the vision for SJAC is to be the recognized community leader for services provided to homeless and returning offenders in Denver. The underpinning of this turn-around plan is building programs poised for long-term organizational growth.

The Transitional Living Program (TLP) is the first step to realize this vision. Over the next one to two years, staff will gain working knowledge for offender reentry programming. In this time, TLP will demonstrate itself as effectively being able to reduce recidivism by alleviating homelessness. The story of Patrick House growing into the Saint Joan of Arc Center will be a modern day benchmark for how emergency shelters grow from surviving into thriving.

In order for SJAC to provide a methodically effective and financially sustainable continuum of care for homeless reentering offenders, SJAC will need to grow and be able to touch society with its message for dignified care in a myriad of ways.

The long-term goal for SJAC is to be the community center for offender reentry in Colorado. Colorado Department of Correctional Services is providing a blueprint for services and SJAC is poised to emulate these services, work with University of Colorado to evaluate successes, and make positive adjustments for long-term effectiveness and growth. Over the next 2–3 years, SJAC can grow vertically to the point of needing to expand into a larger operating space.

Acquiring an additional building would allow SJAC to be able to provide long-term support for reentering offenders living in the community. In the future, the best professionals who deal with offender reentry issues will be employed by SJAC. As a result, it only makes sense to provide a long–term continuum of care for persons needing periodic support and professional consultation.

In order to fund the acquisition of an additional building, it will be necessary to secure tax credits, work with officials from the City of Denver, and seek prospective donors. By now the Transitional Living Program will be having a positive effect on the people it serves and providing a social value for the

Denver community. SJAC will be in position to provide empirical evidence with a goal–based vision for the future, thus attracting the funding needed to acquire a second building for programming and services.

THREATS

SJAC is located at 23 Oak Blvd, Denver, Colorado. SJAC does own the building sitting on this property but does not own the property. Local rumors are suggesting that the current property owner is entertaining proposals to sell the property. Supposedly a major local organization is interested in acquiring and developing the property. The time frame is relatively unknown; as of yet, nothing official has been communicated to SJAC.

It is important for SJAC to take proactive steps to anticipate this proceeding. Crucial steps include developing a bargaining strategy and maintaining a short list for alternative buildings in which to move the SJAC operations. When this issue materializes, it will be imperative for Patrick House to spread the word of the immediacy of its foreclosure and the absolute necessity to secure an alternative site to resume services as soon as possible. Intelligent use of media and public awareness coups will be needed to identify Patrick House as a "champion for the needy."

If and when SJAC is notified of its building foreclosure, instantaneous communication and negotiation with the antagonistic parties will be necessary. Patrick House's priority is to secure an alternative site to continue operations. Cooperation with the Housing and Urban Development Commission and local realtors will swiftly identify potential sites in which to move the guests and operations of Patrick House. Negotiations, public pressure, and emergency private appeals will provide the capital needed for this one–time extraordinary transition.

SEVERE AND VIOLENT OFFENDER REENTRY INITIATIVE

Overview

More than 650,000 people are released from incarceration yearly and arrive on the doorsteps of communities nationwide. The federal government, through the Office of Justice Programs, offers guidance and direction to communities as they prepare for ex–offenders going and staying home. This section presents an overview of this issue and describes OJP's Serious and Violent Offender Reentry Initiative.

The reentry of serious, high–risk offenders into communities across the country has long been the source of violent crime in the United States. As more than 650,000 offenders are released from prison every year, the problem of their recidivism has become a crisis that affects all parts of a community. Fewer than half of all released offenders stay out of trouble for at least 3 years after their release from prison, and many of these offenders commit serious and/or violent offenses while under parole super-vision. This is a significant problem because there were more than 652,000 adult offenders under State parole supervision across the country at yearend 2010 (Hughes, Beck, and Wilson, 2011).

The statistics regarding juvenile offenders present a similar picture. Juveniles were involved in 16 percent of all violent crime arrests and 32 percent of all property crime arrests in 2009. Based on the Office of Juvenile Justice and Delinquency Prevention's (OJJDP's) Census of Juveniles in Residential Placement (Sickmund, 2010), an estimated 100,000 youth are released from secure and residential facilities every year and because the length of incarceration for juveniles is shorter than for adults, a relatively greater percentage of juveniles return to the community each year. In addition, research indicates that a small percentage of juvenile offenders commit the overwhelming majority of juvenile crime.

Some correctional officials—under pressure to cut costs—have curtailed prison programs and services that could ameliorate factors that place inmates at higher risk of recidivism after release. Tougher sentencing laws have, in some cases, removed or limited inmates' incentives to enter available treatment programs. Long, fixed prison terms for serious offenders can sometimes have the perverse effect of returning the most risky offenders to the community with the least control and supervision. There is sometimes little continuity between institutional programs and activities, offenders' reentry plans, and the supervision and services they receive once released.

Communities of law–abiding citizens are victimized by these offenders, making these communities less safe, less desirable places to live. Research has shown that criminal behavior can be predicted for individual offenders on the basis of certain factors. Some factors, such as criminal history, are static and unchangeable. Others, such as substance abuse, antisocial attitudes, and antisocial associates, are dynamic and changeable. With proper assessment of these factors, researchers and practitioners can classify groups of offenders according to their relative likelihood of committing new offenses with as much as 80 percent accuracy. Application of the risk principle requires matching levels or intensity of treatment/supervision with the risk levels of offenders. High–risk offenders require intensive interventions to reduce recidivism (Gendreau and Andrews, 2000). Since the return of these high–risk adult and juvenile offenders is imminent, corrections, law enforcement, and community service agencies should collaborate to monitor offenders while assisting them in the development and implementation of a concrete, specific reentry plan. Unless communities do this, they will continue to be victimized by these offenders.

1. Violent crime includes criminal homicide, sexual assault, robbery, and aggravated assault.

2. Property crime includes burglary, larceny–theft, auto theft, and arson.

3. Such factors could include, but are not limited to, prior convictions for violent offenses or serious offenses that may not be defined by statute as violent; violent, assaultive, predatory, or disruptive in–prison behavior; and other high–risk factors that may include affiliation with gangs or security threat groups.

Serious and Violent Offender Reentry Initiative

The Serious and Violent Offender Reentry Initiative—which was developed by the U.S. Department of Justice, Office of Justice Programs (OJP), in conjunction with the federal partners—is a comprehensive effort that addresses both juvenile and adult populations of serious, high–risk offenders. It provides funding to develop, implement, enhance, and evaluate reentry strategies that will ensure the safety of the community and the reduction of serious, violent crime. This is accomplished by preparing targeted offenders to successfully return to their communities after having served a significant period of secure confinement in a state training school, juvenile or adult correctional facility, or other secure institution.

The Reentry Initiative represents a new way of doing business for federal, state, and local agencies. Instead of focusing the Initiative on a competition for a limited amount of discretionary funds, the federal partners are coming together to help state and local agencies navigate the complex field of existing state formula and block grants and to assist them in accessing, redeploying, and leveraging those resources to support all components of a comprehensive reentry program. The discretionary funding available through this Initiative will be provided only to fill any gaps in existing federal, state, and local resources.

Communities selected to participate in the Reentry Initiative will have the opportunity to develop state–of–the–art reentry strategies and to acquire knowledge that will contribute to the establishment of national models of best practices. The Reentry Initiative allows communities to identify the current gaps in their reentry strategy and present a developmental vision for reentry that seeks to fill those gaps and sustain the overall strategy. Additionally, communities can enhance existing reentry strategies with training and technical assistance that will build community capacity to effectively, safely, and efficiently reintegrate returning offenders.

Federal Partners

The Serious and Violent Offender Reentry Initiative is supported by the U.S. Department of Justice (DOJ), Office of Justice Programs (OJP) and National Institute of Corrections (NIC), and their federal partners: the U.S. Departments of Education (ED), Health and Human Services (HHS), Housing and Urban Development (HUD), Labor (DOL) and Department of Veterans Affairs (VA) and Social Security Administration (SSA).

Three Phases of Reentry

The Reentry Initiative envisions the development of model reentry programs that begin in correctional institutions and continue throughout an offender's transition to and stabilization in the community. These programs will provide for individual reentry plans that address issues confronting offenders as they return to the community. The Initiative will encompass three phases and be implemented through appropriate programs:

* *Phase 1—Protect and Prepare: Institution–Based Programs.* These programs are designed to prepare offenders to reenter society. Services provided in this phase will include education, mental health and substance abuse treatment, job training, mentoring, and full diagnostic and risk assessment.

* *Phase 2—Control and Restore: Community–Based Transition Programs.* These programs will work with offenders prior to and immediately following their release from correctional institutions. Services provided in this phase will include, as appropriate, education, monitoring, mentoring, life skills training, assessment, job skills development, and mental health and substance abuse treatment.

* *Phase 3—Sustain and Support: Community–Based Long–Term Support Programs.* These programs will connect individuals who have left the supervision of the justice system with a network of social services agencies and community–based organizations to provide ongoing services and mentoring relationships.

Examples of potential program elements include institution–based readiness programs, institutional and community assessment centers, reentry courts, supervised or electronically monitored boarding houses, mentoring programs, and community corrections centers.

COLORADO DEPARTMENT OF CORRECTIONAL SERVICES SVORI OVERVIEW

This is an overview of the SVORI–funded Colorado Department of Correctional Services work plan. SJAC is positioned to provide services to phase 2 and phase 3 of the program.

Colorado has one SVORI grantee (Colorado Department of Correctional Services) serving adults returning to four zip codes in metropolitan Denver. The SVORI target population includes individuals who are in need of intensive services upon release. The line chart below provides statistics on adult prison admission and release trends over a 34–year period.

Sentenced state and federal prison admissions and releases and yearend sentenced prison population, 1978–2012

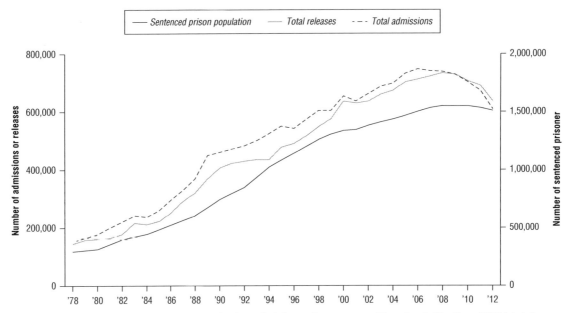

Note: Counts based on prisoners with a sentence of more than 1 year. Excludes transfers, escapes, and those absent without leave (AWOL). Includes other conditional release violators, returns from appeal or bond, and other admissions. Missing data were imputed for Illinois and Nevada (2012) and the Federal Bureau of Prisons (1990–1992). See *Methodology*.

SOURCE: Bureau of Justice Statistics, National Prisoner Statistics Program, 1978–2012.

Data management system

Colorado Department of Correctional Services has a correctional database that can be queried to identify offenders who participate in the Reentry Program. Local evaluation is planned at Denver's College of Public Affairs and Community Services. The University of Colorado is conducting the local evaluation.

Population type: Male adults

Number of targeted prisoners: 201+

Inclusion criteria: Ages 18–35, identified as "violent" by the Colorado Board of Parole, identified as "high risk" on assessment, with tentative release dates equal to or less than 5 years.

Exclusion criteria: Sex offenders, the severely mentally ill, and offenders serving life sentences.

Pre–release facilities: All State prisons

Post–release locations: Four Denver zip codes: 80219, 80204, 80205, and 80207

Participation: Voluntary

Legal release status: Most participants will be under parole supervision, though offenders who are released at expiration of their sentences will not be automatically excluded.

System–level changes

- Increased enthusiasm

- Future expansion of the program throughout the State

Individual–level changes

- Participants are moved to a pre–release facility (Community Correctional Center Colorado) before release, where they receive specialized reentry services.

Phase 1: Institutionally–Based Programs

Duration: At least 1 year

Assessments: Risk assessment designed by the Colorado Board of Parole

Components/services offered within phase:

- Personalized Reentry Program Plan (PREPP), which is designed for each offender at the time of admission

- Participants are moved to a pre–release facility (Community Correctional Center—Denver) before release

- Case management

- Specific targeted services include, as needed, substance abuse treatment, mental health counseling, medical and dental services, life skills training, parenting skills training, domestic violence counseling, employment programs, education, housing assistance, anger management, and faith–based services

Coordination of services:

- One year prior to an offender's parole, the reentry team begins exploring community treatment and programming options. The team is made up of the prisoner, a case manager, law enforcement, the Parole Board, a parole officer, transition manager, treatment providers, community service providers, family and community members, and a representative from victim advocacy groups.

Phase 2: Community–Based Transition

Duration: Variable

Assessments: Ongoing risk assessment

Components/services offered within phase:

- PREPP revised

- Transition plan created

- Supervision program developed

- Specific targeted services include, as needed, substance abuse treatment, mental health counseling, medical and dental services, life skills training, parenting skills training, domestic violence counseling, employment programs, education, housing assistance, anger management, and faith–based services.

Coordination of services:

- Reentry team

Phase 3: Community–Based Long–Term Support

Duration: Up to 2 years

Assessments: Ongoing risk assessment

Components/services offered within phase:

- Revision of Reentry Plan to include services available after release from parole

- Assistance in finding employment

- Specific targeted services include, as needed, substance abuse treatment, mental health counseling, medical and dental services, life skills training, parenting skills training, domestic violence counseling, employment programs, education, housing assistance, anger management, and faith–based services

Coordination of services:

- Reentry team will change to consist of those community programs that have longevity and can provide services to offenders after release from parole.

OFFENDER REENTRY STUDY

The Homeless Release Project is a San Francisco based program that attempts to demonstrate how a continuum of care affects homeless offender reentry. Below is a snap shot of statistical analysis done for the program.

Data Summary Points

While the experimental and comparison groups had similar prior San Francisco arrest histories, the experimental group showed a decrease in recidivism rates after participating in the Homeless Release Project.

The data support an increase in the number of offenders who had no police contact (arrests) after establishing contact with HRP: fifteen (or 37%) for the experimental group and eight (or 20%) for the comparison group.

The data support that the number of arraignments on new misdemeanor and felony cases decreased for HRP participants: eighteen for the experimental group and twenty-nine for the comparison group. We therefore conclude that the re-offense rate for the experimental group was 44%, and 71% for the comparison group.

The data support that re-offenders who participated in HRP were less likely to be arraigned on felonies: eight (or 55%) of the experimental group were arraigned on felonies and twenty-four (or 83%) of the comparison group were arraigned on felonies.

The data support that upon re-arrest, offenders in the experimental group were more likely to have their cases dismissed than the comparison group: seven discharges as compared to three.

GRANT OPPORTUNITIES

SJAC staff members have a long history pursuing grants and federal funding for emergency shelters. Because the TLC qualifies as an emergency shelter, these funding opportunities are not included. The Department of Labor and the Department of Justice have been consistently announcing funding for offender reentry programs and should be noted as primary funding sources.

FINANCIAL INFORMATION

Budget

Revenues	2015	2016
Government grants	$ 79,200	$600,000
Other grants	$ 84,000	$
Unsolicited funds	$ 72,000	$ 24,000
Special events	$ 30,000	$
St. Vincent de Paul Conferences—churches	$ 1,200	$
St. Vincent de Paul Society	$ 0	$
Memorials	$ 3,000	$
Solicited funds	$124,440	$
Total	**$393,840**	**$624,000**

Operating expense

	2015	2016
Salaries		
Executive director	$ 32,400	$ 54,000
Administrator/accountant	$ 36,720	$ 48,000
Community programmer	$ —	$ 42,000
Full-time staff 1	$ 87,600	$129,600
Full-time staff 2	$ 87,600	$129,600
Payroll taxes	$ 21,000	$ 21,120
Employee benefits	$ 10,800	$ 10,800
Continuing education	$ 2,400	$ 3,600
Insurance	$ 14,400	$ 18,000
Vehicle operating expense	$ 6,000	$ 7,200
Professional fees	$ 7,200	$ 13,800
Fundraising expense	$ 18,000	$ 30,000
Administrative expense	$ 7,920	$ 8,400
Non-donated food	$ 3,000	$ 10,800
General family	$ 7,920	$ 10,320
HERO program	$ 9,600	$ 12,960
Buildings and grounds/repairs	$ 18,000	$ 20,400
Insects and rodents	$ 1,440	$ 1,800
Trash removal	$ 1,440	$ 1,800
Furniture and equipment	$ 1,200	$ 2,400
Utilities	$ 18,000	$ 20,400
Security	$ 1,200	$ 3,000
Total	**$393,840**	**$600,000**

Income statement

	2015	2016
Revenue	$393,840	$624,000
Expenses	$393,840	$600,000
Gain/loss	**$ 0**	**$ 24,000**

Current balance sheet

Assets

Current assets

Checking/savings

1000 * Security National Bank—checking	$ 40,225
1025 * Petty cash	$ 360
1040 * Security National Bank—grant	$ 23
1105 * Accounts receivable—EMP	$ 432
Total checking/savings	**$ 41,040**

Other current assets

1056 * Securities—general electric	$ 1,314
Total other current assets	**$ 1,314**
Total current assets	**$ 42,354**

Fixed assets

1205 * Property and equipment	$ 35,293
1210 * Accumulated depreciation	−$ 23,864
1220 * Vehicles	$ 19,080
1230 * Accumulated depreciation—vehicles	−$ 19,080
1240 * Leasehold improvements	$ 30,306
1250 * Accumulated depreciation—leasehold	−$ 9,809
Total fixed assets	**$ 31,926**
Total assets	**$ 74,280**

Liabilities & equity

Current liabilities

Accounts payable

2010 * Accounts payable	−$ 150
Total accounts payable	**−$ 150**
Total current liabilities	**−$ 150**
Total liabilities	**−$ 150**

Equity

2275 * Net assets	$105,286
3000 * Opening balance equity	−$ 350
Net income	−$ 30,506
Total equity	**$ 74,430**
Total liabilities & equity	**$ 74,280**

Homemade Candle Company

Soy Joy Candles

17895 West Rd.
Washington Township, MI 48094

Soy Joy Candles is dedicated to providing its customers with the highest quality soy candles available. Each eight ounce candle is individually hand poured and promises enduring scents with a longer, and cleaner, burn time. Once you burn a Soy Joy Candle, you won't burn anything else!

EXECUTIVE SUMMARY

Soy Joy Candles is dedicated to providing its customers with the highest quality soy candles available. Each eight ounce candle is individually hand poured using 100% soy wax, cotton wicks, and the purest oils available, thus ensuring lasting scents with a longer, and cleaner, burn time. Soy Joy Candles are available in a variety of scents (30+!) and colors to suit every mood and come in an adorable eight ounce jelly jars tied with a cute raffia bow.

SALES STRATEGIES

Candle sales will vary throughout the year, with the highest volumes being purchased in the fall and winter seasons. A main line of scents has been established that will be available throughout the year with a fall and spring line that varies. Summer sales, while lighter overall, may be improved with the addition of these new, seasonal scents including citrus and fruity scents, along with "clean" aromas like laundry and ocean breeze.

A number of different sales avenues have been established. Each is detailed below.

Craft Shows

Craft shows are done throughout the year and include outdoor festivals in the spring, summer, and fall months as well as indoor shows throughout the colder months of fall and winter. Each craft show averages 150-200 candles sold.

Open Houses

The first open house was held in October, 2014 over the course of three hours in my own home. Family, friends, neighbors, and colleagues were invited to stop by to visit and enjoy some snacks while also examining the candles and the various scents available. Over 300 candles were sold during this time, including orders for popular scents that had sold out earlier in the day. Another Open House is planned for October, 2015 and similar sales are expected. This is anticipated to be an annual event.

Local Stores

New, limited displays are being offered at a number of local stores on a trial basis. These stores include an antique/resale shop, two handmade craft stores, and a stationery/card shop. Specific stores include:

- Frontier Town Arts and Craft Mall, Washington Township
- Junktiques, Richmond
- Art-Is-In Market, Clinton Township
- Catching Fireflies, Rochester

All trial periods run for a three-month duration during the fall, 2015 or winter, 2016. Each store offers to stock a limited supply of four to six specific scents, with weekly sales totals being conveyed along with any restock requests. The stores will sell the candles at a marked-up price and keep a percentage of sales as compensation. At the end of three months, the arrangement will be reconsidered based on popularity and customer feedback.

Etsy Shop

A Soy Joy Candles Etsy Shop has just been established and is open for business. With no feedback, sales will be slow to start but should pick up as a good reputation and positive feedback are recognized. It is estimated that sales via Etsy could total 25-40 per month by early 2016.

PRODUCTS

Each eight ounce candles comes in a lidded jelly jar with decorative label and burning/safety instructions. They are priced at $7.00 each, with a multiple purchase discount for every third candle. Specifically, the cost breakdown is:

- 1 candle for $7.00
- 2 candles for $14.00
- 3 candles for $20.00

Additional specials may be made for high-volume purchases, especially during the winter holiday season.

At this time, the eight ounce candle is the only size available, thus making manufacturing and supply ordering as efficient and streamlined as possible. This may be revisited at a future time if demand for additional sizes warrants.

SCENTS

Main Line Scents

- Abercrombie for Men
- Black Raspberry Vanilla
- Butt Naked
- Country Vanilla

- Dream Angel

- Energizing Citrus

- Honeysuckle

- Lavender

- Lemon Poundcake

- Light Blue for Men

- Monkey Farts

- Pink Sugar

- Poppy by Coach

- Strawberries & Champagne

- Sugar Cookie

- White Tea

- Wonderstruck

Spring Scents

- Apples & Berries

- Beachy Coconut

- Blue Skies

- Cherry Lemonade

- French Lilac

- Fresh Fruit Slices

- Fresh Linen

- Honeydew Melon

- Island Nectar

- Kiwi Strawberry

- Mango Papaya

- Memory Lane

- Midnight Pomegranate

- Orange Blossom

- Ocean Breeze

- Peach Schnapps

- Peppermint

- Pure Seduction (like Victoria Secret)

- Red Hot Cinnamon

- Sea Salt & Yuzu

- Spring Rain

- Sundried Cotton (Laundry soap, using Gain scent oil)

- Sweet Pea

- Vanilla Lace

Fall Scents

- Autumn Leaves

- Banana Nut Bread

- Candy Corn

- Caramel Apple

- Christmas Cheer (fruity blend)

- Christmas Past (cinnamon and pine blend)

- Cinnamon Snaps

- Creamy Caramel Apple

- Fall Harvest

- French Vanilla

- Fudge Brownie

- Holiday Scentsation

- Hot Cocoa

- Macintosh Apple

- Midnight Pomegranate

- Mulled Cider

- Oatmeal, Milk, & Honey

- Pumpkin Cheesecake

- Sage & Citrus

- Sandalwood Vanilla

- Southern Apple Pie

- Spiced Pear

- Spiced Cranberry

- Twilight Woods

- Vanilla Sandalwood

- Warm Vanilla Sugar

EQUIPMENT AND MATERIALS

Equipment

Pouring pot, 4 pound

This is a good, low cost, seamless melting pot that has the capacity for holding 4 pounds of wax. Made from aluminum with a pouring spout, it features a plastic handle that stays cool even when the pot is full of hot wax.

Digital Thermometer

Ideal for getting accurate readings of your wax temperature, this thermometer features an easy-to-read digital display and an ON-OFF switch for long battery life. It is made of durable stainless steel and comes with pocket case and extra battery. The measurable temperature ranges from -58 to 302 degrees F.

Digital scale, 55 pound

This larger digital scale has a capacity limit of 55 pounds and measures accuracy up to +/- 0.1 oz. It has a dual range design and has a removable display on a two foot flex-cord for measuring larger items.

Wick Bars

Wick bars keeps your wick perfectly centered and straight. A small groove in the middle of the bar keeps a firm grip on the wick.

Wick Setter Tool

The wick setter tool helps place the wick in the precise center of the candle container.

Additional Supplies

Additional supplies are needed during the candle making process and include such items as:

- Cookie Sheets
- Metal Spoons
- Sauce Pans
- Hot pads
- Trivets

Materials

100% Soy Wax

Soy wax is a hydrogenated vegetable wax derived from soybean oil. The soy wax used in Soy Joy Candles is natural and domestically grown. This candle wax is capable of holding up to 4-5% fragrance and is specifically designed for use in containers. It is manufactured meeting both FDA and Kosher standards.

Soy wax is considered an eco-friendly option because the only limit to soy supply is how much farmers decide to grow. It is therefore renewable and sustainable. Soy wax is known for its clean, slow burn.

Cotton Wicks

Coreless, all cotton braided wicks which are designed to bend at the tip when burning, forcing the tip of the wick into the outermost portion of the flame where it burns hottest. The result is more complete combustion, leaving less carbon buildup behind and less smoking and soot.

Pure Oils

The purest oils available are used when making Soy Joy Candles. The perfume fragrances are 100% concentrates and give candles a lively scent that lasts for the entire life of the candle.

Plant-Based Dyes

Highly concentrated liquid plant-based dyes are used in every Soy Joy Candle. These dyes are 50% stronger than standard liquid dyes and offer excellent color consistency and strength for crisp, clean and bright candles. The dyes disperse well, leaving no dark spots of color. Colors do not separate in storage, so only a minimal shaking is required to be ready to use. The dyes do not contain hazardous solvents or additives such as naphtha or naphthalene.

Lidded Jars

Eight ounce jelly jars with rustic lids are used when making each and every Soy Joy Candle. The look is distinctive and homey, which complements almost any decor.

Labels

Both a product label and burning instructions label are included on each Soy Joy Candle. The product label is a 3.25" x 2" Oval Brown Kraft label that is designed and printed at a local printing company.

The burning instructions/safety labels are preprinted 2" labels that are affixed to the bottom of the jelly jar.

Glue Dots

Glue dots are essential to affixing the wick in the center of the jar prior to pouring.

SAFETY AND CARE

Some people are concerned with the safety of burning candles in the home. As with anything, common sense should prevail and standard precautions should be met. These precautions include:

- Keep burning candles away from children and pets.

- Keep burning candles away from combustibles.

- Never leave burning candles unattended.

Every Soy Joy Candle will feature a safety sticker with these reminders on the bottom of the jar.

Also noted on this sticker will be the care instructions to ensure the soot free and long-lasting burn time. For best results, it is recommended that the wick is trimmed short between burns and any black wick buildup is removed before relighting.

UPCOMING SHOW SCHEDULE

October 3 & 4—Utica Band Booster Craft & Vendor Show

Sunday, October 11—2nd Annual Soy Joy Open House

Saturday, October 18—"Share The Gift" Jury Evaluated show

Saturday, October 24—St Peter's Lutheran Church Bazaar (Macomb Township)

Saturday November 7—St. Margaret of Scotland Women's Club

Saturday November 7—Romeo Ladies Night Out

Saturday, November 14—Memphis Music Booster 29th Annual Craft Show

Saturday, November 14—Golden Hawk Ladies Night Out

Saturday, November 21—Port Huron Elks Arts & Craft Show

Saturday, December 5—Cranberry Christmas Craft Show

SWOT ANALYSIS

Strengths:

- Longer burn time (22 hours!)

- Cleaner burn

- Unique scents

- High concentrations of quality fragrance oils to achieve the strongest smelling products
- Positive testimonies from our repeat buyers
- Little overhead
- Quick manufacturing time
- Welcome feedback of any kind and make changes accordingly
- Eco-friendly—renewable and sustainable
- Locally made

Weaknesses:
- Lack of brand recognition
- Significant competition from big name players including Yankee Candle Company and Bath & Body Works

Opportunities:
- Displays at local stores, including an antique/resale shop, two handmade craft stores, and a stationery/card shop
- Etsy shop

Threats:
- Products are nonessential or "luxury" items that don't fare well during hard economic times.
- Repeat customers can't necessarily just stop by a local store to pick up what they want on a whim.
- Candle sales are lighter in the spring and summer months.

FINANCIAL STATEMENTS

Assets

Item	Cost	Number	Total
Pouring pot	$ 8.75/each	6	$ 52.50
Digital thermometer	$15.95/each	3	$ 47.85
Digital scale	$45.00/each	1	$ 45.00
Wick bars	$ 0.65/each	50	$ 32.50
Wick setter tool	$24.95/each	2	$ 49.90
Additional supplies	Varies	Varies	$200.00
Total			**$427.75**

Consumables

Component	Cost	Unit
Soy wax	$ 50	50-pound case
Cotton wicks	$ 54	1,000 wicks
Pure oils	$14.83	1 pound
Plant-based dyes	$33.31	1 pound
Lidded jars	$ 8.25	12 jars
Labels	$ 1.50	10 product labels
	$17.00	1,000 care and safety labels
Glue dots	$34.95	2,000 dots

Housesitting/Property Management Business

While You Were Away LLC

21 Eastern Pkwy.
Sugar River, WI 69662

Paul Greenland

While You Were Away LLC is a housesitting and property management business with a local/regional focus.

EXECUTIVE SUMMARY

While You Were Away LLC is a housesitting and property management business that is owned and operated by John Bradford, a semi-retired real estate agent, and his wife, Sally. Local ownership is a key differential for While You Were Away. Although there are housesitting Web sites that connect pre-qualified house sitters with property owners, the Bradfords will either provide all of While You Were Away's services directly, or via independent contractors who live directly within the community. The business will begin operations part-time, offering property "check-in" (e.g., non-live-in) services to snowbirds (the business' primary market), and also to traveling executives and busy/vacationing families. Live-in housesitting services will be introduced during the second year of operation, and the Bradfords eventually plan to expand their business to include housesitting services for vacant/for-sale properties.

MARKET ANALYSIS

While You Were Away is located in Sugar River, Wisconsin, an upper-middle-class suburb of Milwaukee. In 2015 the local population consisted of 134,000 people and was home to a substantial over-55 population, including many "snowbirds" who spend the colder winter months living in warmer climates such as Florida and Arizona. Snowbirds will represent While You Were Away's primary target market.

In 2015 individuals over the age of 55 accounted for 40 percent of the population (much higher than the national average of 29 percent). By 2020 the population is projected to reach 132,712, at which time individuals over 55 will account for 42 percent of the population (compared to 31 percent nationally). The following table shows a detailed breakdown of Sugar River's population, with comparisons to the U.S. population for both 2015 and 2020.

	Sugar river	United States
2015		
Age 55−64	15%	14%
Age 65−74	13%	8%
Age 75−84	9%	5%
Age 85+	3%	2%
	40%	**29%**
2020		
Age 55−64	15%	15%
Age 65−74	15%	10%
Age 75−84	9%	5%
Age 85+	3%	2%
	42%	**31%**

As the population ages, the number of snowbirds residing in Sugar River and the surrounding area is expected to increase, providing additional growth opportunities. Beyond Sugar River, significant over-55 populations also exist in the nearby communities of Webster, Pearson Ridge, and Sterling.

Busy executives who travel frequently represent a secondary market for While You Were Away. This demographic has high levels of disposable income. According to an analysis of the Sugar River Market, 19.3 percent of residents in this population category had household incomes between $75,000 and $99,999 in 2015. Those earning between $100,000 and $149,999 accounted for 21.7 percent of the category, while 10.4 percent had household income levels of more than $150,000.

INDUSTRY ANALYSIS

The services provided by While You Were Away fall within the property management industry. According to the Bureau of Labor Statistics, U.S. Department of Labor, employment of property, real estate, and community association managers totaled 297,000 in 2012. By 2022 this figure is expected to increase 12 percent, resulting in the addition of 35,000 new professionals to the workforce. One of the key growth drivers within the industry is the rising number of older individuals, which should result in new opportunities for those managing housing for older adults and the elderly.

The National Association of Residential Property Managers (NARPM) is a key organization that represents the property management industry. With a mission of serving as "the professional, educational, and ethical leader for the residential property management industry," NARPM was established in 1988. The organization's approximately 5,300 members benefit from local chapters, several different levels of membership, and a variety of educational offerings. NARPM keeps its members informed through the magazine, *Residential Resource*. In addition, the association offers several professional certifications, including Residential Property Management Professional, Master Property Manager, Certified Residential Management Company, Certified Support Specialist, and Certified Maintenance Coordinator. More information is available at: www.narpm.org.

PERSONNEL

While You Were Away LLC is a housesitting and property management business that is owned and operated by John Bradford, a semi-retired real estate agent, and his wife, Sally. John Bradford began practicing real estate in the Sugar River area in 1988. Since that time he has sold thousands of homes and is recognized as one of the market's most successful real estate agents. Additionally, John and Sally are active in the community, volunteering their time by serving on the boards of several local charitable organizations. The Bradfords will use their local reputation as a key differential for While You Were Away. Although there are many national and international housesitting Web sites that connect pre-qualified house sitters with property owners, the Bradford's will either provide all of While You Were Away's services directly, or via independent contractors who live directly within the community.

In addition to holding a real estate license, John Bradford is certified as a Residential Property Management Professional by the National Association of Residential Property Managers. Sally, who holds an undergraduate business degree from the University of Wisconsin, recently retired as the office manager for a local general contractor. She will benefit the business with her strong administrative skills and connections with many area contractors.

Professional and Advisory Support

Sally Bradford will utilize off-the-shelf software to perform basic bookkeeping and tax preparation services for While You Were Away. The Bradfords have used the assistance of a local attorney to form their limited liability company and develop standard boilerplate contracts that can be used with their customers. A commercial checking account has been established with Sugar River Community Bank, along with a merchant account for accepting credit card and debit card payments. Liability insurance has been obtained from a reputable national provider. Finally, several dependable independent contractors have been identified who can assist the Bradfords with housesitting commitments, when long-term, "live-in" arrangements are introduced during the second year of operation.

GROWTH STRATEGY

Year One: Establish While You Are Away as a part-time business in the Sugar River community offering basic and deluxe "drop-in" service packages. Begin developing a network of trustworthy, reliable independent contractors who are interested in providing "live-in" housesitting services for occupied residential homes during the business' second year. Focus on developing a reputation for reliability, trustworthiness, and excellent customer service, realizing that word-of-mouth referrals will be essential to growing the business. Become a member of the Better Business Bureau and Sugar River Chamber of Commerce. Achieve gross revenues of $46,800.

Year Two: Begin operating While You Were Away as a full-time operation. Continue to develop the business' reputation in Sugar River. Begin providing "live-in" housesitting services for occupied residential homes, utilizing a network of trustworthy independent contractors who live in the local region. Achieve gross revenues of $90,800.

Year Three: Focus on maintaining While You Were Away's reputation in the community. Increase revenue generation opportunities by offering live-in housesitting services for vacant properties by marketing services to area retailers and property owners. Generate gross revenues of $145,600.

SERVICES

While You Were Away provides housesitting and property management services within a 30-mile radius of Sugar Grove, Wisconsin. During its first year of operation, the business will offer "check-in" (e.g., non-live-in) services to property owners who will be away from their home for a minimum of one week.

Services initially will be provided in two packages:

Basic ($10/day—10-day minimum)

In partnership with the customer, While You Were Away will develop a regular schedule (daily, biweekly, weekly, etc.) for the inspection of the property, grounds, and appliances/equipment (to ensure normal functionality). Additionally, arrangements can be made for routine tasks, such as mail/newspaper pickups. Basic service may include, but is not limited to, the following:

- Air-Conditioner
- Appliances
- Bill Paying
- Carbon Monoxide Detectors
- Door/Window Locks
- Furnace
- Hot Water Heater
- Landscaping
- Light Housekeeping
- Light Timers
- Turning On/Off Lights
- Mail Pickup
- Newspaper Pickup
- Pests
- Pet Care (cats, birds, fish only)
- Showers
- Sinks
- Smoke Alarms
- Sump Pumps
- Toilets
- Vehicle Maintenance (periodic starting)
- Water Softeners

Property owners will be notified immediately if any problems or concerns are discovered. While You Were Away will only take immediate action to resolve issues in the event of an emergency (e.g., shutting off water to a house in the event of a broken pipe, etc.).

Deluxe ($15/day—10-day minimum)

Property owners subscribing to While You Were Away's deluxe package will receive all of the services included in the basic package, plus an additional level of service that includes the management of repairs in the event of an emergency. In the event that a problem is discovered, the Bradfords will serve as project managers, making arrangements with the homeowner's vendor/repair person of choice (or locating a reputable repair person on their behalf). While You Were Away will oversee all repairs, ensuring that contractors do a quality job, and that problems are resolved to the customer's satisfaction. Services will include regular updates to the homeowner via phone, e-mail, or video chat. While You Were Away also will facilitate payment arrangements.

"Live-In" Housesitting Services ($150/month—one-month minimum)

While You Were Away will begin providing "live-in" housesitting services during the second year of operation. This service will provide homeowners with the peace of mind knowing that a trustworthy individual is occupying and caring for their home while they are gone for an extended period of time (minimum one month). While You Were Away will develop a pool of local/regional house sitters who will undergo an extensive background/reference checking process. While You Were Away will then provide homeowners with three to five prospective pre-qualified house sitters to choose from.

Once a house sitter has been selected, While You Were Away will provide management/oversight, serving as an intermediary in the event of any problems and ensuring total customer satisfaction. House sitters will be responsible for paying all utility bills during their stay in the customer's home, and for providing all of the services listed in the basic package. Additionally, the Bradfords will provide customers with the services listed in the Deluxe package in the event that repairs need to be managed.

During the third of operation, While You Were Away will begin marketing live-in housesitting services for vacant properties. These services will be marketed directly to area realtors and property owners. Having a house sitter on-site reduces the likelihood that a vacant property will be vandalized and also helps to increase the property's salability. House sitters for vacant properties typically will be responsible for providing their own furnishings. However, While You Were Away will attempt to partner with home stagers serving the Sugar River market who furnish and decorate vacant homes on behalf of their clients.

MARKETING & SALES

While You Were Away has developed a marketing plan that includes the following primary tactics:

1. A four-color brochure describing the services provided by the business. The brochure will feature lifestyle photos depicting senior citizens relaxing in a warm climate and will tout the benefits and peace of mind associated with using a property management/housesitting service. The brochure also will feature the Better Business Bureau logo, testimonials from satisfied customers, a profile of the owners, and a disclosure that While You Were Away is fully bonded and insured.

2. Membership in the Sugar River Chamber Of Commerce.

3. Periodic presentations to local service clubs/senior citizen groups.

4. Placemat advertising at two local diners frequented by senior citizens.

5. A late summer/early fall advertising campaign on Sugar River's AM talk radio station to reach snowbirds in advance of the cold winter months.

6. Regular direct mailings to households with residents over the age of 65 and reported household income of at least $75,000.

7. A Web site with complete details about While You Were Away and the services provided.

8. A Facebook page.

9. A regular quarter-page print advertisement in *The Sugar River Courier,* a free monthly newspaper serving older adults in the Sugar River region.

OPERATIONS

Location

While You Were Away will operate from dedicated office space within the Bradfords' home. The office, which John Bradford uses for his part-time real estate practice, already is equipped with office furniture, a multi-function printer/fax/copier, and Internet service. However, a dedicated phone line will be established for While You Were Away. The Bradfords will meet with prospective and current customers in their homes, or at a desired public location (e.g., coffee shop, etc.).

Process

When a customer expresses an interest in the services provided by While You Were Away, the Bradfords will provide them with a free consultation. They will make arrangements to meet at a mutually convenient location (preferably the customer's home). During the consultation, an attempt will be made to clearly define the customer's needs. This information will be used to develop a detailed cost estimate/proposal, which will serve as the basis of a formal agreement that specifically addresses what services will be provided, as well as associated costs, payment time frames/arrangements, liability, and dispute resolution. The Bradfords hired a local attorney to develop a standard customer agreement, which they can customize based on the specific needs of their clients. Customers will be provided with information regarding While You Were Away's liability insurance coverage.

FINANCIAL ANALYSIS

While You Were Away's sales and expenses for the first three years of operation are projected as follows:

	2015	2016	2017
Service			
Basic package	$31,200	$41,600	$ 52,000
Deluxe package	$15,600	$31,200	$ 46,800
Live-in housesitting (residential)	$ 0	$18,000	$ 28,800
Live-in housesitting (vacant)	$ 0	$ 0	$ 18,000
	$46,800	**$90,800**	**$145,600**
Expenses			
Salaries	$31,356	$60,836	$ 97,552
Payroll tax	$ 4,703	$ 9,125	$ 14,633
Marketing	$ 4,680	$ 9,080	$ 14,560
Insurance	$ 468	$ 908	$ 1,456
Telecommunications	$ 234	$ 454	$ 728
Professional services	$ 4,680	$ 9,080	$ 14,560
Total	**$46,121**	**$89,483**	**$143,489**
Net profit/loss	**$ 679**	**$ 1,317**	**$ 2,111**

A complete set of pro forma financial statements has been prepared for the business and is available upon request.

Ice Cream Retail & Manufacturing Business

Anna's Homemade Ice Cream Inc.

66939 Knoll Way
Cedar Ridge, WI 53999

Paul Greenland

Anna's Homemade Ice Cream Inc. is an ice cream manufacturing and retail business.

EXECUTIVE SUMMARY

Anna's Homemade Ice Cream Inc. is an ice cream manufacturing and retail business that has been established by Anna McNabb, a retired real estate attorney, and her children, Peter and Sarah. Based on an analysis of the local and regional market, Anna McNabb anticipates that the business will generate gross revenues of nearly $423,000 during its first year of operation, resulting in a net profit of approximately $70,500. McNabb is projecting that gross revenues will grow at a compound annual rate of 4 percent during the first three years of operations.

INDUSTRY ANALYSIS

In the United States, the ice cream and frozen dessert industry produced about 872 million gallons of ice cream in 2014, according to figures from the International Dairy Foods Association (IDFA). The industry includes many family-owned businesses like Anna's Homemade Ice Cream. As of August 2014, industry sales totaled $5.4 billion, up 2.1 percent from the previous year, based on data from the Chicago-based firm, IRI.

Based in Washington, D.C., the IDFA (www.idfa.org) describes itself as "the premier organization for dairy foods processors, manufacturers and marketers." The association provides its members with strategic leadership and expertise, and advocates for their success by influencing government policy at the state, federal, and international levels. Its members enjoy many benefits, including training and education programs and materials. The IDFA includes constituent organizations such as the International Ice Cream Association (IICA), the Milk Industry Foundation (MIF), and the National Cheese Institute (NCI).

The industry also is served by the Elk Grove Village, Illinois-based non-profit National Ice Cream Retailers Association (www.nicra.org), a major trade organization that has operated since 1933. Its mission is "to be the leader in the frozen dessert industry that others look to for help, support, and education." Membership benefits include a training video library; insurance programs; access to information regarding business planning, marketing, promotion, and operations; an annual directory of members, suppliers, and product information; a monthly bulletin; and an annual convention.

MARKET ANALYSIS

According to an IDFA survey, only 16 percent of ice cream and frozen dessert manufacturers market their products nationally. The vast majority (66.7%) market products on a regional basis, as will Anna's Homemade Ice Cream. In terms of market potential, the IDFA reports that, on an annual basis, the typical American consumes approximately 22 pounds of ice cream.

Cedar Ridge, Wisconsin, was home to an estimated 65,347 people in 2015 (21,500 households). By 2019 the population is projected to increase approximately 14 percent, reaching 71,300 (22,200 households). The community is home to a disproportionately high concentration of younger families, which bodes well for Anna's Homemade Ice Cream. Those aged 25 to 34 represent the largest adult population group (32%), followed by those aged 20 to 24 (21%). The next largest categories are those aged 45 to 54 (9%) and 35 to 44 (8%).

Although Cedar Ridge has not been without its challenges, especially during the Great Recession, economic recovery and growth were evident by 2015. Anna's Homemade Ice Cream is located on Knoll Way, one of the city's main thoroughfares. Retail sales will benefit from Anna's Homemade Ice Cream's close geographic proximity to several surrounding residential neighborhoods, providing easy access to the business by foot, bicycle, and car.

The closure of Cedar Ridge Market, an independently-owned grocery store, was a setback for the community in 2013. However, the facility (located directly across the street from the business) has been transformed into a new community center that is highly utilized by both adults and young families engaging in a variety of indoor and outdoor sports. These activities draw local residents, and also families from the surrounding communities of Hampton, Peterborough, and McLean. The community center also features a daycare, as well as preschool and kindergarten programs.

Prior to establishing the business, Anna McNabb utilized her connections to let the community know about her plans to establish Anna's Homemade Ice Cream. She spent six months sharing samples with prospective commercial customers (grocery stores and restaurants), which resulted in initial contracts that will complement direct retail sales and help the business begin on a strong note. Specifically, contracts have been established with the following customers:

Restaurants

- L & L's Family Restaurant
- Nilsson's Cafe
- The Popcorn Hut
- Lucy's Coffee
- The Clubhouse
- The Parkview Hotel

Independent Grocers/Food Markets

- Bob's Supermarket
- Stella's Bakery
- Cedar Ridge IGA
- Market Street Meats

On a percentage basis, Anna McNabb estimates that sales for Anna's Homemade Ice Cream will break down as follows:

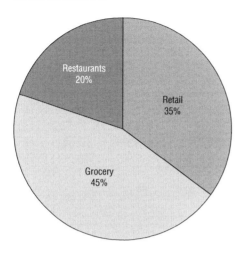

PRODUCTS & SERVICES

Anna' Homemade Ice Cream will sell ice cream to consumers by the scoop (regular, sugar, or waffle cone/dish), pint or quart. Commercial sales will be made in 1 gallon cartons or 2.5 gallon tubs. Anna's Homemade Ice Cream will negotiate commercial prices on a case by case basis.

The business will begin operations with a core selection of ice cream flavors. Based on an International Ice Cream Association survey, vanilla is the most popular ice cream flavor, followed by mint chocolate chip and cookies and cream. With that in mind, Anna's Homemade Ice Cream will include these flavors in its initial grouping of core selections. In addition, the business also will offer a growing selection of specialty flavors, based on financial feasibility and customer interest/demand.

Core Ice Cream Selections

- Vanilla
- Chocolate Chip
- Cookies and Cream
- Chocolate
- Strawberry
- Mint Chocolate Chip
- Strawberry

Specialty Ice Cream Selections

- Oreo Explosion
- Butter Brickle
- Butterscotch
- Mocha
- Black Cherry
- Espresso
- Moose Tracks

- Chocolate Chip Cookie Dough

- Peppermint

Pricing

- Children's Scoop: $1.75

- One Scoop: $2.75

- Two Scoops: $3.75

- Three Scoops: $4.75

- Pint: $4.50

- Quart: $8.00

Waffle cones are an additional $.50.

In addition, the business also will sell the following types of sundaes ($4.75):

- Caramel

- Hot Fudge

- Strawberry

- Butterscotch

Soft drinks will be available from Pepsi, as well as Wisconsin Soda Co., a family-owned soda drink manufacturer. Finally, Anna's Homemade Ice Cream will offer coffee using beans from Cedar Ridge Roasters, a local coffee roaster.

OPERATIONS

Facility and Location

Anna's Homemade Ice Cream will begin operations on a small scale, producing and selling ice cream products from a small location in Cedar Ridge, Wisconsin. The owners have decided to convert a former real estate office they own (located at 66939 Knoll Way) into a space that is ideal for ice cream production and retail. They will accomplish this in partnership with a local architect and builder, who have helped them to develop the appropriate renovation plans, as well as a corresponding time and cost estimate.

Specifically, plans will include space for a small, 300-square-foot seating area with six tables, each capable of seating four guests. Customers can select their desired ice cream from a display case containing large tubs of various flavors. The display case, coupled with a countertop area where the cash register is located, will separate the guest space from a 200-square-foot employee area containing work surfaces, a sink, and access to a 500-square-foot room that will be used for producing, packaging, and storing ice cream. The owners have included plans for a window that gives customers the ability to watch ice cream being made.

Hours

Anna's Homemade Ice Cream will operate from 11 AM-10 PM Monday through Saturday, and 1 PM-6 PM on Sunday.

Suppliers

A number of local, regional, and national food service distributors have been designated to supply the business with ingredients and food/beverage items. This list is available upon request.

Start-up Costs

Anna's Homemade Ice Cream has estimated that renovations will cost $70 per square foot ($70,000). In addition, approximately $30,000 in equipment and furnishings will need to be purchased prior to start-up, including:

Beverage Dispensing Equipment

- Soft Drink Dispenser with Ice Bin (provided by beverage supplier)
- Carbonator with Double Check Valve (provided by beverage supplier)
- Wall Mounted Syrup Pumps (provided by beverage supplier)
- CO-2 Tanks (provided by beverage supplier)
- Automatic Coffee Maker
- Coffee Grinder
- Cup Dispensers
- Lid Organizer
- Commercial Blender
- Ice Machine

Storage Equipment

- 6' x 8' Freezer Storage Shelving Set
- 18" x 36" Storage Shelf Units (4)
- Walk-in Commercial Freezer
- Walk-in Hardening Cabinet
- Electric Can Opener
- Single Door Reach-in Refrigerator
- Reach-in Display Freezer Cases (2)

Sales & Display Equipment

- Cash Register
- Menu Board
- Daily Special Panel
- Exterior Signage

Miscellaneous Equipment

- Telephone
- Filing Cabinet
- Safe
- Bulletin Board

- Mop & Broom Holder
- Tablet Computer, Printer and Software
- Cone Holders

Production Equipment

- Hand Wash Sink
- Dishwashing Sink
- Commercial Microwave
- Fudge Warmer
- Commercial Mixer
- Commercial Mixing Bowls
- Stainless Steel Prep Table
- Commercial Dishwasher
- Waffle Cone Iron

Seasonality

Anna's Homemade Ice Cream will be impacted by seasonal business patterns. Summertime clearly is the strongest season for ice cream producers and retailers. According to the National Ice Cream Retailers Association, industry production begins to intensify during the months of March and April, is busiest in June, and remains strong through August, after which production declines until the following spring.

LEGAL & REGULATORY

Anna's Homemade Ice Cream is in full compliance with all applicable legal and regulatory requirements enforced by the Wisconsin Department of Agriculture, Trade and Consumer Protection's Food Safety Division, which licenses, regulates, and inspects retail food stores (including ice cream shops) in conjunction with the Department of Health Services. In addition, the business has obtained an adequate level of business and liability insurance (policies available upon request).

PERSONNEL

The formation of Anna's Homemade Ice Cream represents the fulfillment of a long-time dream for the McNabbs. In addition, the business will provide them with a formal channel for sharing their family's own homemade ice cream recipes, several of which have been passed down for as many as three generations. In the past, the family has made several different kinds of ice cream for family and friends, and the response has always been overwhelmingly positive.

Anna McNabb will serve as the president of Anna's Homemade Ice Cream. Her son, Peter, a recent college graduate, will manage the business and work in partnership with Anna to develop its short- and long-term growth strategies, including opportunities to develop a potential franchising program. Long-term, Peter will assume total oversight of the business. Sarah, a third-year college student at a local university, will work as one of the business' part-time employees.

The following table provides an overview of Anna's Homemade Ice Cream's initial staff, with corresponding salaries, for the first year of operations:

Title	2016
Owner	$ 30,600
Manager	$ 35,000
1 Full-time associate	$ 22,725
2 Part-time associates	$ 20,000
	$108,325

Professional and Advisory Support

Anna McNabb has secured local accountant Bill Stewart to handle bookkeeping and provide tax advisory services. Additionally, commercial checking accounts have been established with Cedar Ridge Community Bank, which also will provide merchant accounts needed for accepting credit card and debit card payments.

GROWTH STRATEGY

Year One: Focus on establishing the business in the local/regional market and developing a reputation for quality and excellence. Achieve gross revenues of nearly $423,000.

Year Two: Add five new specialty flavors and introduce a range of specialty drinks (e.g., smoothies and floats). Add an additional five commercial customers in the primary market area. Generate gross revenues of approximately $440,000.

Year Three: Add an additional five specialty flavors and expand the specialty drinks menu to include mochas, flavored coffees, and lattes. Add an additional 10 commercial customers in the primary market area. Generate gross revenues of nearly $458,000.

MARKETING & SALES

A marketing plan has been developed for Anna's Homemade Ice Cream that includes the following main tactics:

1. *Social Media:* Guests will be able to follow the business on Facebook and Twitter, and take advantage of exclusive ice cream specials.

2. *Mobile Marketing:* Magnetic signage will be produced to display the Anna's Homemade Ice Cream name, Web site address, and phone number on the outside of the McNabbs' vehicles.

3. *Web Site:* A site will be developed, providing both retail and commercial customers with key information about Anna's Homemade Ice Cream, including available ice cream flavors, location, hours, and special discounts.

4. *Direct-Mail:* The McNabbs will send a postcard to area residents every spring (April), announcing the availability of new flavors and providing them with a coupon for one free scoop of ice cream.

5. *Advertising:* In order to generate buzz about the business, Anna's Homemade Ice Cream will run regular print ads in *The Cedar Ridge Gazette*, a free weekly newspaper serving the community. In addition, the monthly advertisement also will run in *Cedar Ridge Business*, a monthly business newspaper produced by the local Chamber of Commerce.

6. *Incentives:* To encourage prospective customers to visit the business, the McNabbs will hire local college students to personally distribute 1,000 coupons (good for one free scoop of ice cream) in the surrounding neighborhood.

7. *Community Outreach:* Because Anna's Homemade Ice Cream is committed to being a good neighbor, the McNabbs will participate in and support community events, including Cedar Ridge Days (an annual community festival), and the Memorial Day, Independence Day, and Labor Day parades.

FINANCIAL ANALYSIS

Anna McNabb is projecting that gross revenues for Anna's Homemade Ice Cream will grow at a compound annual rate of 4 percent during the first three years of operations, increasing from $423,000 in year one to $440,000 and $458,000 in years two and three, respectively:

Gross revenue

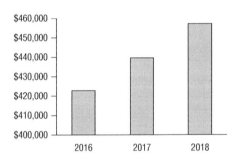

Funding

In addition to providing the real estate where Anna's Homemade Ice Cream will be located, Anna McNabb will invest $50,000 of her own money into the business, to be used for the purchase of initial inventory ($15,000) and ongoing operations. In addition, she is seeking a $100,000 business loan (five-year term, 6% interest). Anna McNabb will use the real estate, equipment, and opening inventory as collateral.

	Apr	May	Jun	Jul	Aug	Sep
	1	2	3	4	5	6
Income						
Total sales	$29,789	$31,306	$35,148	$40,973	$37,406	$37,808
Cost of goods sold	$ 9,533	$10,018	$11,247	$13,111	$12,787	$12,099
Labor cost	$ 5,444	$ 5,721	$ 6,423	$ 7,487	$ 7,302	$ 6,909
Total cost of goods sold	**$14,977**	**$15,739**	**$17,671**	**$20,598**	**$20,088**	**$19,008**
Gross profit	**$14,812**	**$15,568**	**$17,478**	**$20,375**	**$17,318**	**$18,800**
Expenses						
Advertising & marketing	$ 300	$ 300	$ 300	$ 300	$ 300	$ 300
Accounting & legal	$ 496	$ 496	$ 496	$ 496	$ 496	$ 496
Insurance	$ 691	$ 691	$ 691	$ 691	$ 691	$ 691
Interest expense (1)	$ 1,913	$ 1,913	$ 1,913	$ 1,913	$ 1,913	$ 1,913
Rent	$ 4,250	$ 4,250	$ 4,250	$ 4,250	$ 4,250	$ 4,250
Sales tax	$ 242	$ 242	$ 242	$ 242	$ 242	$ 242
Telephone	$ 128	$ 128	$ 128	$ 128	$ 128	$ 128
Utilities	$ 935	$ 935	$ 935	$ 935	$ 935	$ 935
Owner draw	$ 2,550	$ 2,550	$ 2,550	$ 2,550	$ 2,550	$ 2,550
Total expenses	**$11,505**	**$11,505**	**$11,505**	**$11,505**	**$11,505**	**$11,505**
Net income before taxes	**$ 3,307**	**$ 4,063**	**$ 5,973**	**$ 8,870**	**$ 5,813**	**$ 7,295**

	Oct	Nov	Dec	Jan	Feb	Mar	
	7	8	9	10	11	12	Total
Income							
Total sales	$30,719	$31,901	$51,986	$31,952	$30,719	$33,082	$422,790
Cost of goods sold	$ 9,830	$10,209	$16,635	$10,225	$10,185	$10,586	$136,464
Labor cost	$ 5,613	$ 5,829	$ 9,500	$ 5,839	$ 5,613	$ 6,045	$ 77,725
Total cost of goods sold	$15,444	$16,038	$26,135	$16,063	$15,798	$16,631	$214,189
Gross profit	$15,275	$15,863	$25,851	$15,889	$14,921	$16,451	$208,601
Expenses							
Advertising & marketing	$ 300	$ 300	$ 300	$ 300	$ 300	$ 300	$ 3,601
Accounting & legal	$ 496	$ 496	$ 496	$ 496	$ 496	$ 496	$ 5,957
Insurance	$ 691	$ 691	$ 691	$ 691	$ 691	$ 691	$ 8,293
Interest expense (1)	$ 1,913	$ 1,913	$ 1,913	$ 1,913	$ 1,913	$ 1,913	$ 22,950
Rent	$ 4,250	$ 4,250	$ 4,250	$ 4,250	$ 4,250	$ 4,250	$ 51,000
Sales tax	$ 242	$ 242	$ 242	$ 242	$ 242	$ 242	$ 2,907
Telephone	$ 128	$ 128	$ 128	$ 128	$ 128	$ 128	$ 1,530
Utilities	$ 935	$ 935	$ 935	$ 935	$ 935	$ 935	$ 11,220
Owner draw	$ 2,550	$ 2,550	$ 2,550	$ 2,550	$ 2,550	$ 2,550	$ 30,600
Total expenses	$11,505	$11,505	$11,505	$11,505	$11,505	$11,505	$138,057
Net income before taxes	$ 3,770	$ 4,358	$14,346	$ 4,384	$ 3,416	$ 4,946	$ 70,544

Land Clearing Business

New Ground Land Clearing Services, LLC

22567 Dothan Road
Headland, AL 36345

Fran Fletcher

New Ground Land Clearing Service, LLC is located in Headland, Alabama and is owned and operated by Terrell Hollis.

BUSINESS SUMMARY

New Ground Land Clearing Service, LLC is located in Headland, Alabama and is owned and operated by Terrell Hollis. Mr. Hollis got the idea for this business when his place of employment closed and he was forced to find another source of income. Mr. Hollis has 12 years of experience operating heavy equipment in the U.S. Air Force, so a land clearing business seems like the most logical choice.

Located in the Southeast Alabama, New Ground Land Clearing Service will serve customers within a 60-mile radius of Headland, Alabama. This area reaches into Barbour, Houston, and Dale counties. This area has an estimated population of 80,564 with 67,795 households present within a 2,000 square mile area. This should provide the business with a large customer base.

According to the Bureau of Labor Statistics, the job outlook for construction equipment operators is expected to increase by 19% over the next decade. According to the Alabama Forestry Commission, private landowners hold more than 19 million acres of timberland. As the population of Alabama grows and as residential areas continue to move out from the city, the need for land clearing will increase.

New Ground Land Clearing Service will offer the following services to residential and business clients:

- Bulldozer services
- Tree removal
- Stump removal
- Commercial or residential services
- Site clean-up
- Home site clearing
- Large and small acreage
- Pastureland reclamation

There are several businesses in the area offering similar services, but none more dedicated to success and to providing excellent customer service as Mr. Hollis.

111

The overall growth strategy of New Ground Land Clearing Service is to become the go-to business in the area for land clearing services. The owner understands the importance of referrals and the company will strive to provide excellent customer service. The owner also plans to bid on city and county contracts as opportunities arise.

The owner anticipates modest profits from the beginning. During the first year of operation, he expects a steady increase in income and profits as his advertising methods become established and as he starts receiving referrals from satisfied customers. If projections are correct, Mr. Hollis will need to hire additional workers and buy additional equipment during the second year.

Start-up costs will include purchasing used equipment that is in excellent working condition. The owner is currently seeking financing in the amount of $156,950 to cover start-up and operating expenses for the first month. Payments will be made monthly and 20 percent of the annual profits will be paid on the loan at the end of each year. If profits are obtained as anticipated, the loan should be repaid within five years.

COMPANY DESCRIPTION

Location
Mr. Hollis will operate New Ground Land Clearing Service from his home in Headland, Alabama.

Hours of Operation
New Ground Land Clearing Service will operate by appointment as follows:

Monday through Friday, 7 AM—6 PM

Personnel

Jason Hollis (owner)
Mr. Hollis will provide estimates, schedule jobs, provide services, and coordinate billing. Mr. Hollis served 12 years in the U.S. Air Force as a heavy equipment operator. During his service, he was trained in heavy equipment operation and OSHA safety regulations.

Kevin Hollis (foreman)
Mr. Hollis will serve as foreman of the land clearing crew. He has worked in the forestry industry for 7 years and has experience operating various types of heavy equipment.

Employees
One experienced full time employee will be hired when needed.

Products and Services

Services
New Ground Land Clearing Service will offer the following services:

- Bulldozer services
- Tree removal
- Stump removal
- Commercial or residential services
- Site clean-up
- Home site clearing
- Large and small acreage
- Pastureland reclamation

MARKET ANALYSIS

Industry Overview

According to the Bureau of Labor Statistics, the job outlook for construction equipment operators is expected to increase by 19% over the next decade. According to the Alabama Forestry Commission, private landowners hold more than 19 million acres of timberland. As the population of Alabama grows and as residential areas continue to move out from the city, the need for land clearing will increase. Additionally, reclamation of pastureland is also increasing as the demand for beef increases.

Target Market

New Ground Land Clearing Service will target customers within a 60-mile radius of Headland, Alabama. This area reaches into Barbour, Houston, and Dale counties. This area has an estimated population of 80,564 with 67,795 households present within a 2,000 square mile area. This should provide the business with a large customer base.

Competition

New Ground Land Clearing Service is not the only land clearing business in the Southeast Alabama area. The following businesses also offer similar services within parts of the same territory.

1. Allied Bulldozing Services, Dothan, Alabama. Offers land clearing services for both residential and commercial properties.

2. L & L Land Clearing, Eufaula, Alabama. Primarily offers tree removal and trimming services.

New Ground Land Clearing Service plans to set itself apart from the competition by offering land clearing services for all sizes of properties and providing services as quickly as possible.

GROWTH STRATEGY

The overall growth strategy of New Ground Land Clearing Service is to become well known in the area. The owner recognizes the importance of advertising and customer referrals. The company will make every effort to provide excellent customer service and to provide clearing services as quickly as possible.

The owner also plans to bid on city and county contracts as opportunities arise, and would be willing to extend the company's service area, purchase additional equipment, and hire more employees.

The owners expect the business to take off in the first year of operation and anticipate hiring additional workers and buying additional equipment later in the first year of operation.

Sales and Marketing

The company has identified key sales and marketing tactics to support the company's growth strategy.

Initial and ongoing advertising will include:

- Advertising in area newspapers
- Offering free estimates

FINANCIAL ANALYSIS

Start-up Costs

The owners will procure essential equipment to start the business. In order to cut costs, the company will purchase used equipment that is in good working condition. Equipment costs are expected to be the largest start-up expense.

Estimated start-up costs

Bulldozer	$ 70,000
Skid steer loader	$ 12,000
Stump grinder	$ 7,000
Chipper	$ 10,000
Dump truck	$ 17,000
Chain saws	$ 4,000
Trailer (2)	$ 8,000
Truck	$ 10,000
Business license	$ 1,000
Initial advertising	$ 500
Insurance	$ 4,000
Legal fees	$ 1,800
Total	**$145,300**

Estimated Monthly Expenses

Monthly expenses are expected to remain constant each month.

Monthly expenses

Loan payment	$ 1,000.00
Phone/Internet	$ 200.00
Advertising	$ 50.00
Insurance	$ 200.00
Wages owner	$ 4,000.00
Wages employees	$ 5,200.00
Equipment maintenance	$ 1,000.00
Total	**$11,650.00**

Estimated Monthly Income

The number of jobs will determine monthly income. Initially, the owner expects to provide land clearing services four days a week for an estimated monthly income of $19,200.

Prices for Services

Prices for services are dependent upon many factors:

- The size of the site

- The proximity to structures, streets, power lines

	Price per hour*		
Services	Hardwood	Brush	Pine
Tree removal with clean-up	$200	$100	$150
Tree removal with clean-up and stump grinding	$250	$150	$250
Home site clearing	$150	$100	$150
Bulldozer services	$ 75	$ 75	$ 75
Structure clearing	$100	$100	$100

*Four-hour minimum.

Profit/Loss

According to estimated expenses and income data, modest profits are expected from the beginning and are expected to steadily increase as referrals grow and advertising measures become established.

Demand for services should remain constant all year. Conservative estimates show that land clearing services will be provided four days per week at a rate of $150 per hour, for a monthly income of $19,200.

Income is expected to increase by 8% each year and expenses are expected to increase by 4% each year. Profits will be used to purchase additional equipment and hire employees as needed.

Monthly profit/loss

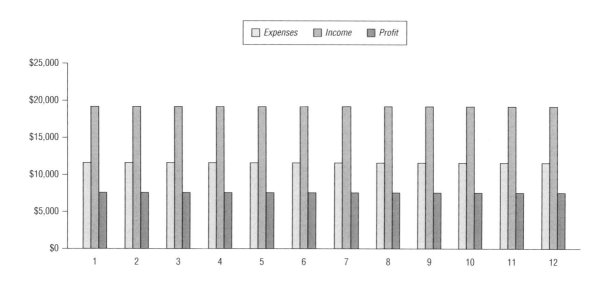

Yearly profit/loss

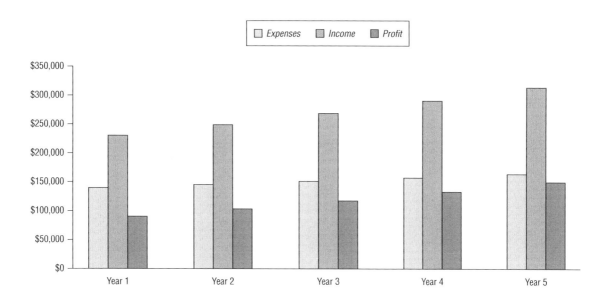

Financing

New Ground Land Clearing Service is currently seeking financing in the amount of $156,950. This would cover start-up and operating expenses for the first month of operation. The business will pay $1,000 per month toward repayment and will also pay 20% of the annual profit at the end of each year. The Repayment Plan chart shows that the loan will be paid within five years. The owner will replace or buy additional equipment with additional profits.

Repayment plan

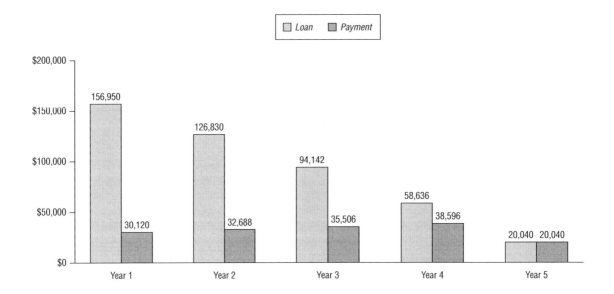

Mentally Disabled Care Facility

Welcome Home Organization

730 Grand River Avenue
Brighton, MI 48114

Andrew A. Westerfeld
Aaron L. Wappelhorst

Sunrise Care Organization plans to build and operate a Residential Care Facility for developmentally disabled adults. This facility will be available for individuals over the age of 18, who begin to reach the age of being too old to live at home, yet too young to live in a full-time nursing facility. This facility will serve the needs of those who are moderately mentally disabled, who require some habit training. By serving this particular group we can create an excellent living environment, including a social family–like atmosphere and active lifestyles for all of our residents.

Our services include full–time residential care, private rooms, direct–care staff and nursing staff for any necessary medical care, entertainment and recreational opportunities, and educational and job skills training. The facility will be equipped to care for 30 individuals, including 30 private rooms, a cafeteria, living and socializing areas, and entertainment facilities. Our goal is to meet the social, physical, mental, recreational, educational, and vocational needs of all of our residents.

EXECUTIVE SUMMARY

Welcome Home Organization will provide residential care for the mentally disabled. The organization will be certified as a 501 (c)(3) non–profit corporation. We are dedicated to helping those with developmental disabilities live their life to the fullest, while creating a family atmosphere that creates a better tomorrow and atmosphere that encourages the participation of residents' families in their day–to–day lives. We strive to offer a community that promotes self respect, independence, and improves the quality of life for all our residents.

We intend to offer the highest quality residential care and day program services in the Southwest Detroit area. Our facility will accommodate thirty residents, each of whom will have individual, fully–furnished bedrooms. Other amenities include several spacious living areas which provide a variety of atmospheres to meet individual needs. Residents will have available three full meals a day, which will accommodate their personal tastes and nutritional requirements. We will have employed a fully–trained staff who will assist the residents in day–to–day living. In addition, day programs will offer a variety of activities, and habit and work skills training to foster growth of the individual.

The facility's limited size will provide an opportunity for interaction between staff, volunteers and residents and will allow for personalized care. We will listen to the needs and desires of our residents to provide superior living conditions. We plan to construct a new $1.6 million facility, which will offer the amenities of a modern home. Our facility is large enough to operate efficiently, but small enough to feel like home. This type of atmosphere is the core objective of the organization. Residents should feel as though they are relaxed and in their living room, and not in an institution.

Welcome Home Organization will be operated by a five–person management team. The head of the facility will be our Chief Administrative Officer who will work with the management team and staff to operate the facility. A Chief Business Officer will oversee the day–to–day financial and fundraising activities of the organization. The Social Service Coordinator will be responsible for admissions and discharges, sales presentations, and general paperwork. In addition, the Residential Services Coordinator and the Day Program and Volunteer Coordinator will be responsible for their individual sectors.

The marketing plan of the organization is two–fold. First, the organization must market itself towards potential supporters and then to potential residents. Potential supporters will be recruited through personal relationships and an aggressive fundraising plan. Increasingly long waiting lists for residential care in the Detroit and Ann Arbor regions will provide the organization with a strong resident base. Currently the market for residential adult foster care facilities is underserved.

In order for the organization to be successful it must meet its fundraising goals. We plan to raise $1.6 million in initial fundraising, with $750,000 being contributed before the facility construction begins. The remaining $850,000 will be raised in the first year. Welcome Home Organization will fund the remaining portion of development costs through a long–term loan. Solid financial management will lead to an organization that will serve the community for years to come. The generosity of supporters is the key to the success of the organization.

Welcome Home Organization will be an asset to the developmentally disabled community, and the community as a whole. Our goal is to meet the social, physical, mental, recreational, educational, and vocational needs of all of our residents. At Welcome Home Organization we are committed to fostering compassion and improving tomorrow for those with mental disabilities.

Mission

At Welcome Home Organization we are committed to fostering compassion and improving tomorrow for those with mental disabilities. Welcome Home Organization is dedicated to helping those with developmental disabilities live their life to the fullest, while creating a family atmosphere that creates a better tomorrow. We strive to offer a community that promotes self respect, independence, and improves the quality of life for all of our residents.

Objectives

In order for Welcome Home Organization to attain its vision, the following objectives need to be achieved:

1. Secure initial financing by securing commitments from both corporate and individual donors.

2. Develop and construct a world-class residential facility that meets the needs of mentally handicapped persons in the Southwestern Detroit community.

3. Maintain full occupancy, thus serving the needs of as many individuals as possible.

4. Operate at only the highest standards, providing all residents with the ability to lead the best life possible.

5. Provide individualized programs to meet the residents' needs.

PRODUCTS & SERVICES

Residential Services

Welcome Home Organization seeks to offer the best living conditions possible for all of our residents. We plan to construct a 30–room facility so that each resident is able to enjoy a space all their own. Each person will have a comfortable room, matching a home environment as closely as possible. The rooms will be comfortably furnished and decorated. The residents will receive three prepared meals per day, and a snack will be offered in the evening. All food will be served family style, again matching as closely as possible a home environment. All meals will be prepared by a trained cooking staff, and therefore will be able to meet the individual nutritional requirements of all of our residents. Also, there will be a trained Dining Aide staff as well as many volunteers who will assist those individuals with special eating needs.

In addition to the private rooms, there will be numerous areas available for social activities and entertainment. These living spaces will offer residents an opportunity to socialize with one another as well as the facility's volunteers and staff. These areas will be equipped with furniture and decorations so as to again create an atmosphere of home.

Our staff will be on duty 24 hours a day, and will be able to meet all of the needs of our residents. This facility will surpass state–requirements in the number of direct–care staff on duty so that our residents will have the best living conditions possible. A full team of direct–care staff will be on duty 24–hours a day. In addition, a trained nursing staff will be on duty from 7:00 am to 11:00 pm to meet the medical needs of the residents. During the evening hours from 11:00 pm to 7:00 am, the direct–care staff on duty will be trained in emergency medical procedures as well as medication administration. The facility will also make arrangements with a physician and dentist to assume overall responsibility for medical and dental care. Each resident will have at least one physical examination per year by a licensed physician and dentist.

Day Program Services

Welcome Home Organization will offer a Day Program to provide our residents with opportunities to socialize, exercise, and learn. This program's intent is to improve the lives of our residents and to teach new skills through a variety of activities and programs. In doing this, we hope to give them the skills they need to live as independently as possible. Through these programs we hope to instill a variety of skills including communicating with others, making personal choices, eating independently, personal hygiene, domestic skills, developing hobbies and interests, and developing basic work skills. Each person's program will be individually designed to meet their personal needs and skills.

These skills will be emphasized through a variety of activities designed and coordinated by a trained Day Program staff. In addition, many entertainment and social activities will be incorporated. These include a variety of games and sports, exercise time, gardening activities, arts and crafts, table games, music and singing time, and many others. Another important aspect of the day program will be community service projects. This part of the program will teach our residents the importance of giving back to the community. All Day Program activities will primarily take place on campus, but field trips will be offered on occasion.

Within the facility there will be an area designated specifically for the Day Program. State law requires forty square feet of usable floor space for each resident. Our facility will house a maximum of 30 residents, and so our Day Program Activity Center will be 2,400 square feet in area. The Day Program will include a staff of four who will be responsible for developing individualized programs for each resident, planning activities, and working with volunteers. These volunteers will include family members of the residents. Both the residents' wants and needs will be taken into account in creating programs and planning activities. Overall, it is crucial that the program plan is person–centered, and is developed with active participation from the residents.

ORGANIZATION

Facility

One of the most important aspects of our organization will be our world–class residential care facility building. We plan to locate our 12,000 square foot facility in Brighton, Michigan on approximately three acres. Our building will have every convenience of home, so our residents are truly comfortable.

The building will consist of 30 bedrooms, each of which is approximately 140 square feet. The bedrooms will be fully furnished and contain a bed, pillows, blankets, a bedspread, other proper linens, a bedside stand, a chair, closet space, a dresser, and vanity and sink. The rooms will each have at least one window which will provide views of the outdoors.

In addition to the bedrooms, the facility will have several living room–type areas. In total, these areas will be approximately 2,400 square feet. These rooms will serve many needs from providing a relaxing place to watch television and socialize, to a place to play board games with fellow residents and volunteers. One room will be furnished with couches, chairs, and end tables and will supply a place for the residents to watch television. Another room will have couches, tables, chairs, and floor mats to provide a place for social activities and games. The room will be stocked with a variety of board games and cards for the residents' enjoyment. A third, smaller area will accommodate those seeking a quiet place. This area will also have couches, chairs, bookshelves, end tables, and lamps. We hope that by providing a variety of living areas, our residents will have ample opportunity to socialize and interact with those in our community as well as have individual time for peace and quiet.

Our facility will utilize communal bathrooms for the residents' use. These bathrooms will be conveniently located so that all residents have easy access. The bathrooms will have all the necessary equipment, including individual showering areas.

The Day Program will take place in our 2,400 square foot activity center. This center will be very flexible, allowing the spaced to be used for a variety of activities. The area will have collapsible tables and chairs, floor mats, and other appropriate equipment. This way, the facility can meet many different needs, from arts and crafts to exercise and dancing.

The kitchen will be approximately 750 square feet, and will be equipped with proper kitchen equipment. These items will include commercial-sized refrigerators and freezers, ovens, and dishwashing equipment. There will also be adequate preparation areas with necessary counter space and sinks. The dining area will be approximately 1,200 square feet and will have adequate number of tables and chairs so as to accommodate our residents. Finally, about 1,000 square feet will be devoted to offices, a nurses station, and general work space.

BUSINESS STRATEGY

Features and Benefits

At Welcome Home Organization, we believe that our benefits are quite simple. We want to create a quality home–like environment where our residents can live happily and successfully. We strive to create the best living environment possible, with modern and clean facilities. We believe that each person is important, and should be treated as such. We hope to have the best staff in the industry, whose only focus is the happiness and care of each individual living in our facility. We want to create the best activities, so that our residents can truly enjoy life and make the best out of it. We want our residents to learn, to socialize, and to be happy. At Welcome Home Organization we know all of these things will be accomplished.

Business Model

The Welcome Home Organization derives its revenues from three sources: government payments, residents' contributions, and donations. Government payments are broken into two categories: per diem reimbursements for residential care and monthly reimbursements for day programs. The per diem reimbursement rate is $150 per resident, and the day program rate is $850 per resident per month. These rates are set by the Michigan Department of Mental Health, and are indexed to the cost of living increases. Residents or their families pay a fee of $275 per month for residential care and day program services. Donations are put towards the construction and development of the facility, along with securing the organization's financial future. Government revenues and resident contributions alone are not enough to support the development and operation of the facility. Therefore, donations are essential to the organization's success. A portion of donations that do not go towards development and operations will be placed in an investment fund. This fund protects the organization against fluctuations in government revenues in the future.

Legal Business Description

Welcome Home Organization will receive certification as a non-profit corporation filed as a 501(c) (3) through the Internal Revenue Service and the Michigan Secretary of State's Office. In order to receive this status, the following steps must be taken:

1. Review IRS Publication 557, *Tax–Exempt Status for your Organization* as well as IRS Publication 578, *Tax Information for Private Foundations and Foundation Managers.*

2. File Michigan form *Articles of Incorporation of a Nonprofit Corporation* through the Michigan Secretary of State's Office.

3. File IRS Form SS–4, *Application for Employer Identification Number.*

4. File IRS Form SS–1028, *Application for Recognition of Exemption,* as well as IRS form 921–A, *Consent Fixing Period of Limitation Upon Assessment of Tax,* and IRS Form–8718, *User fee for Exempt Organization Letter Request,* in order to produce a Letter of Determination.

5. File Michigan Form 3372, *Michigan Sales/Use Tax Exemption Application,* through the Michigan Department of Revenue to receive a Michigan State Tax I.D. number.

6. Register as a Charitable Organization with the Michigan Attorney General's Office using form *Charitable Organization Initial Registration Statement.*

In addition to applying for non–profit status, because Welcome Home Organization is operating in the health care industry, we must be approved by the Michigan Certificate of Need Program, as well as receive state licensing through the Michigan Department of Licensing and Regulatory Affairs. The Certificate of Need program is designed to verify the need of services in the community the facility plans to locate. In order to receive this certificate, the following steps must be completed:

1. Letter of Intent

2. Proposed Expenditures

3. New or Additional Equipment Application

4. New or Additional Long-Term Care Bed Application

5. Proposed Project Budget

6. Applicant Identification and Certification

7. Representative Registration

8. Service–Specific Revenues and Expenses

9. Detailed Institutional Cash Flows

10. Periodic Progress Reports

The most important aspect of the Certificate of Need Program is the verification of need in the area for the services proposed. According to the Michigan Developmental Disabilities Council, as of December 31, 2013 there were 260 individuals in the Detroit Metropolitan area seeking adult foster care. This information was gathered through the Michigan Developmental Disabilities Council and is the most recent data available. According to the Council, this information is still current. Each of these individuals has been determined to be eligible to receive state funding.

To receive state licensing from the Michigan Department of Licensing and Regulatory Affairs, the following must be done:

1. Complete Michigan Department of Licensing and Regulatory Affairs form *Application for License to Operate an Adult Foster Care Group Home.*

2. Submit facility plans to the licensing office and the Michigan State Fire Marshal. These plans must also include a description of the utilization of each area.

In order to receive State Medicaid funding, we must apply for and receive a Provider Agreement through the Department of Social Services' Division of Medical Services. The DMS will issue this agreement if they have received a certificate of authorization or an acknowledgement of exemption from the Michigan Developmental Disabilities Council.

OPERATIONS

Location

Welcome Home Organization will be centrally located in Livingston County where we will be able to meet the needs of individuals from throughout the Southwest Detroit Metropolitan Area. The facility will serve people from Livingston County, Oakland County, Wayne County, Macomb County, and Washtenaw County. We chose this location because of our ability to raise money and public awareness in the community.

Organization

Our management team will consist of individuals with experience in the health care and nursing home industry. These individuals will be charged with maintaining the daily operations of the facility as well as supporting the long–term viability of the organization. The management team will include the following:

Chief Administrative Officer

1. This individual will be responsible for the overall operation and management of the facility.

2. He or she will oversee all activities in the organization, including marketing, services, staffing, and decision making.

3. He or she will work with the management team and the Board of Directors to promote the well–being of the residents as well as the long–term success of the organization.

Chief Business Officer

1. This individual is responsible for the business and finance operations of the facility.

2. He or she will manage all necessary financial information, and prepare financial forecasts and budgets.

3. He or she will also coordinate all fundraising efforts for the facility.

Residential Services Coordinator

1. This individual will work with the staff in order to maintain excellence in service and quality living conditions for all residents.

2. He or she will be in charge of operations including scheduling, disciplinary activities, and overall maintenance of the facility and its services.

Day Program and Volunteer Coordinator

1. This individual is responsible for the day-to-day activities and socializing of the residents through the Day Program.

2. He or she will also coordinate volunteers at the facility.

Social Service Coordinator

1. This individual will be responsible for residents' admissions and intakes. They will also give sales presentations to prospective residents, give tours of the facility, and be responsible for working with families to fill out paperwork for admissions.

2. He or she will also be responsible for the paperwork and duties associated with discharges.

3. He or she will be in charge of fulfilling the requirements of the state in terms of paperwork, including securing state funding.

Outside Management Support

Welcome Home Organization will also rely on a variety of outside sources for management support. These include both a Certified Public Accountant and an Attorney. These services will be donated by friends of the organization.

Accountant/CPA

1. This individual will work with the Chief Business Officer and the Chief Administrative Officer in order to create adequate financial statements.

Attorney

1. This individual will be responsible for representing Welcome Home Organization in any legal proceedings.

2. He or she will prepare and file any necessary legal documentation.

Board of Directors

An outside Board of Directors will be assembled, including highly qualified individuals from throughout the community. This board will consist of experts in the health care and nursing care field, as well as donors, family members of residents, and other respected members of the community. Working with the management team, they will aid in making appropriate and effective decisions that will benefit the lives of our residents as well as foster the long–term success of the organization.

Staffing

The state of Michigan gives specific guidelines for the staffing of residential adult foster care facilities. In order to achieve a higher level of personalized care, Welcome Home Organization will exceed these requirements. Welcome Home will be tailored to meet the needs of what the state classifies as mild to moderately disabled individuals. If the facility were to serve more severely disabled individuals, the staffing levels would have to be increased dramatically to meet state requirements. Our organization will consist of a direct care staff, a nursing staff, a day program staff, a dietary staff, an administrative staff, and a facility services staff. In total our staff will include approximately 28 full-time and 6 part-time employees.

Volunteers

Volunteers will be an integral component necessary for the success of Welcome Home Organization. They will be actively recruited from throughout the community, and will include all age levels and abilities. They will be utilized in nearly every aspect of the organization, from daily operations and care to fundraising. Volunteers will work closely with the Day Program and Volunteer Coordinator to help meet the needs of the residents and the facility as a whole. We hope to utilize an adequate number of volunteers to aid in areas such as general care, activities and entertainment, meal time assistance, and education and training. In addition to helping out, we hope that the volunteers will develop meaningful relationships with our residents, adding to the quality of their lives.

In addition to assisting with the daily operations, volunteers will also be needed to aid in all of our fundraising efforts. They will work with the Chief Business Officer and the Day Program and Volunteer Coordinator to organize and work at fundraising activities as discussed in the Fundraising Plan. Their efforts in this area are critical to the financial success of the organization.

BUSINESS STRATEGY

Strategic Alliances

Welcome Home Organization hopes to develop several strategic alliances, including the following:

1. Corporate Sponsorship—We hope to develop relationships with a variety of corporate sponsors willing to donate to our organization. We plan to put into place a variety of programs to support these activities. One of these programs is our Naming Rights Program. Through this program a company will be able to purchase naming rights for our facility. The facility will then be marked with a plaque to show our appreciation for their generous contribution. The facility will also then take on the corporate name permanently. We plan to work with the Founder's Committee to develop this relationship.

2. Physician and Dentist—Our facility will work with a local physician and dentist to take on responsibility for the overall care of our residents. These individuals will then have regularly scheduled times in which they will visit our facility and perform normal checkups and health evaluations. Also, they will be available in cases of emergency.

3. Hospital—According to state law, a formal written arrangement with a community hospital must be made for the treatment and hospitalization of our residents. We will work with a local hospital to make such arrangements.

MARKET ANALYSIS

Market Definition

Welcome Home Organization operates within the developmentally disabled community. More specifically, the organization works with individuals who range from mild to moderate developmental disability. These patients require habit training and some assistance with day-to-day living. This represents a significant percentage of the developmental disabled community.

Within the Detroit metro area there are approximately 260 individuals on the waiting list of residential adult foster care facilities. Each individual qualifies for state funding according the Michigan Developmental Disabilities Council.

The county breakdown is as follows:

1. Oakland County: 40 individuals

2. Livingston County 27 individuals

3. Washtenaw County: 37 individuals

4. Wayne County: 156 individuals

These people represent opportunity for the Welcome Home Organization. They will be the catalyst for a quick path to full occupancy of the facility.

Market Organization

Mild to moderately developmentally disabled people receive care from three primary sources: family, family in conjunction with day programs and residential adult foster care facilities. There are benefits and drawbacks to each type of care. Families are increasingly challenged to provide around-the-clock care to their developmentally disabled loved ones.

Family is almost always the first source of care received by the disabled individual. As the individual ages, providing full-time care can become increasingly challenging. The factors of dual careers and additional children make providing adequate care all the more difficult. During adolescence parents usually enroll their child in a day program for the disabled. These programs function like a daycare. The individuals are dropped off in the morning and picked up in the afternoon. Throughout the day the individuals interact with others, have recreational time and participate in habit training. Some patients will be involved with a work skills program. At some point parents must decide if they will be the primary care givers indefinitely, or if the now young adult will enter a residential care facility.

Residential adult foster care facilities cover a wide range of care needs. Individuals enrolled in these programs may require anything from habit training to full-time nursing care. Welcome Home Organization will specialize in the mild to moderately developmentally disabled community. By specializing in this sector the Welcome Home family can focus its abilities on making a significant impact upon its residents' lives. All the residents will take part in habit training, while some will also take part in an additional work skills training program. While the Welcome Home Organization believes that all individuals deserve care, we also believe that this niche market will provide us with the best opportunity to serve the community.

SWOT Analysis

S: Strengths

1. Welcome Home Organization will pride itself on having the newest and cleanest facilities in the market. Our dedication to continuing quality will only enhance this reputation over time.
2. The staff will have vast experience and training, and the staffing number will exceed state requirements.
3. The low number of beds allows for more personalized service and care.
4. Large-scale fundraising creates a moderate price structure.
5. Our central location will be convenient to the entire Detroit/Ann Arbor Region.

W: Weaknesses

1. Our strategy relies upon an excellent initial and ongoing fundraising campaign. By utilizing personal relationships and experienced supporters we will be able to reach our fundraising goals.
2. Any new organization faces the challenge of establishing itself in the community. We must establish ourselves in the hearts of our supporters and potential residents in order to gain trust.
3. The Welcome Home Organization must abide by the strict regulations associated with operating a facility of this nature. Through a thorough understanding of the regulations the Welcome Home Organization can accomplish this task.

O: Opportunities

1. With 260 people signed up on the waiting list of existing facilities, there should not be a problem reaching capacity.

2. Studies show that developmentally disabled adults are living longer, and often outliving their parents. This creates more demand as medical technologies continue to improve.

3. In the future the demand could warrant the construction and operation of a second facility. This facility would meet the same needs of the current operation and would not be developed for 7–10 years.

T: Threats

1. Decreased funding from the State of Michigan.

2. Established facilities have already gained trust and respect from the donor and developmentally disabled community.

3. New entries into the market pose a threat. We will overcome these competitors by always improving the total quality of the organization, and delivering personalized service to each resident.

4. Lack of fundraising jeopardizes the feasibility of the facility. But once again we believe that our fundraising plan is feasible, and will be executed successfully.

Customers

Due to the nature of our business, we have a very specific customer profile. Our residents fit within the following criteria:

1. Age: 18–40

2. Mild to Moderate Developmental Disability

3. Income: Varying

4. Family Status: Single

5. Location: Southwestern Detroit Metropolitan Region, including Wayne, Oakland, Washtenaw, Livingston and Macomb Counties.

6. Lifestyle: In need of habit and work skills training.

Our residents are looking for a personalized home-like atmosphere, which affords them the opportunity to socialize, learn and grow towards a better tomorrow. We plan to fulfill all of these needs.

Competition

The competition is from existing facilities operating in the Detroit/Ann Arbor Region. These facilities have established trust in the community, and have histories of reputable care. Only three facilities offer campus-style living similar to that of Welcome Home Organization.

Welcome Home Organization holds competitive advantages over these existing facilities. The facility itself will be new, and contain modern conveniences. The staff of the organization will be experienced and well trained, and also able to deliver personalized care. This is due to the low number of beds, which allows for more interaction between staff and residents. Overall the services we offer will be similar, but we pride ourselves on delivering them in a professional and personalized manner. Welcome Home is not just a facility, but truly a home for its residents.

MARKETING & SALES

Marketing Plan

Welcome Home Organization must market itself in two different spectrums, residents and benefactors. The initial thrust of the marketing campaign has two objectives–to demonstrate the demand for residential care, and to rally support for the organization. After the initial marketing campaign is complete, then the organization will transition its marketing efforts accordingly. Future marketing efforts will focus their attention towards producing a positive organizational image.

The organization's market differentiation is three–fold. First, the facility will be of the highest quality. Second, the staff will strive to deliver personalized care to the residents. Finally, the organization will adapt itself to meet the needs of its residents and their families. These three benefits will be the basis of the organization's competitive advantage.

Marketing Plan: Phase 1

Phase one carries out the immediate objectives of the organization. It begins ingratiating itself with the developmentally disabled community, and raises public awareness of the organization. In terms of the overall time line, this phase takes place during the initial fundraising and development, all the way up to the full occupancy of the facility. The marketing is directed to both potential residents and supporters.

Residents

The sales strategy of Welcome Home organization is multifaceted. Welcome Home will serve the needs of the underserved, provide quality care and offer assurance to the families of the developmentally disabled. In order to carry out these strategies the organization plans to have two essential marketing methods.

The Michigan Developmental Disabilities Council waiting list will provide an excellent source of potential residents. These residents are already seeking residential care and have been qualified by the State of Michigan to receive funding. Therefore, they are a target market that we will pursue.

In addition, during the development stage members of the organization will become involved in regional advocacy and support groups for the developmentally disabled and their families. The purpose of this involvement is to become acquainted with the influential people within the market, and to better understand the needs of the market. These types of networking events will also help to provide the original group of residents. When it comes to a loved one, families desire a personal connection to those providing the care of the individual.

This personal connection will be provided by the Social Services Director and Chief Administrative Officer, who will be the public face of the organization. Once the facility's construction is complete and in operation, they will give tours, help coordinate public relations events and act as a sounding board for the concerns of residents and their families. Welcome Home Organization will strive to be a learning organization; an organization that works to create a home-like atmosphere for its residents and peace of mind for their loved ones.

Providing quality care is a must, and it will be expressed throughout all the actions of the Welcome Home Organization. Marketing the quality of care will be accomplished through the development of positive public relations. Residents and their families will see an organization that prides itself on quality throughout. The most trusted form of advertising is an unsolicited endorsement, and that must be the foundation that supports Welcome Home Organization.

Two marketing methods have been adopted. The first is a personal sales method that focuses itself on becoming involved within the developmentally disabled community as well as personally contacting those on the waiting list. Welcome Home Organization believes that this personal bond is vital to success. Second, the organization will develop a positive public relations campaign to cast a wider net and raise the public awareness of the organization.

Supporters

Welcome Home Organization cannot exist without generous donations from its supporters. These donations are crucial for the initial startup including construction of the facility as well as funding a portion of ongoing operations. Marketing the organization to potential supporters means building a donor pool from a series of fundraising committees. The original or Founders Committee will be comprised of civic minded individuals who value the mission and vision of the organization. This committee will be responsible for the coordination of successive committees meant to broaden the scope of the fundraising. An altruistic sales strategy will be used to approach members of the Founders Committee.

Members of the Founders Committee will be solicited from personal connections and family members. Given the interpersonal relationships that already exist, this effort should meet with quick success. In order to meet the goal of fifteen members, Welcome Home plans to approach thirty potential donors. These donors will meet individually with the Welcome Home family to discuss their involvement in the organization. They will be asked to donate fifty thousand dollars, and support future fundraising efforts. Although a success rate of fifty percent for such a large commitment is ambitious, it is also achievable. The strength of personal connections and the nobleness of the Welcome Home mission will open the hearts of supporters.

The process of recruiting members of the Founder's Committee has already begun, and has been extraordinarily successful. Eight families have pledged to join Welcome Home Organization's Founder's Committee. A more detailed description of the fundraising activities can be found in the Fundraising Plan.

Marketing Plan: Phase 2

Phase two of the marketing effort begins after the facility has reached its full occupancy. This phase has two goals: to continue publicizing the tradition of quality care, and to become further involved in the developmentally disabled community. Much of this marketing effort will take place simultaneously with ongoing fundraising efforts. The effective planning and execution of fundraising events such as golf tournaments and dinner auctions will provide excellent public relations.

These events will be coordinated by the Chief Business Officer and Chief Administrative Officer. The Chief Business Officer's central fundraising role will be continuous contact and networking among present and potential supporters. Members of the Founders Committee will work in conjunction with the CBO to establish fundraising goals and strategies. The Founders Committee also coordinates with the CAO to aid in the planning and execution of the fundraising events.

Long-Term Competitive Plan

Welcome Home Organization envisions a bright future with continuous improvements in all facets of the organization. In order to maintain a long–term competitive advantage, Welcome Home must listen to the needs of its residents, expand and improve the facilities, and strive for extensive fundraising. These accomplishments advance the Welcome Home Organization vision of living life to the fullest, while working towards a better tomorrow.

The well–being of its residents is the mission of the organization. Accordingly, the organization is determined to adapt itself to the needs of its residents. One example of this personalized service we plan to implement is a customized activities schedule, which best reflects the interests of the resident. Each resident is a true individual, who deserves to be treated with dignity and respect. By fostering this atmosphere over the long–term Welcome Home establishes an advantage that cannot be matched by a newcomer to the market.

The facility will be updated and renovated to meet the stylistic and amenity demands of the time. Welcome Home is being constructed as a first–class operation, and will maintain that status as the facility ages. By staying current the Welcome Home Organization will maintain its advantage of truly being a home–like atmosphere.

While the initial plan calls for a single facility of thirty beds, future demands may require expansion. In this case, Welcome Home will consider the development of a second site to meet the demands of the market. A second facility would not be constructed until the initial operation has been running for seven to ten years. This period of time would allow the organization to establish itself as a leader in the developmentally disabled community.

If the heart of Welcome Home is its residents, then its lifeblood is fundraising. Welcome Home Organization will establish a competitive advantage through its extensive fundraising efforts. These efforts will establish funds for its operation, renovation and expansion. The fundraising effort will be well organized and well executed. The Chief Administrative Officer and Chief Business Officer are responsible for the success of the fundraising operations.

FUNDRAISING PLAN

Initial Fundraising Effort

Welcome Home Organization thrives upon the generosity of its friends and benefactors. In order to meet the initial start–up and operating costs Welcome Home has created an aggressive fundraising plan. The cornerstone of this plan is a Founders Committee consisting of 15 people, pledging to donate $50,000 each. These 15 people will not only donate money, but also their time to the initial fundraising effort. Once the Founder's Committee has been established, a broader group of supporters can be gathered. The Platinum Circle will include 20 people donating $25,000 apiece. The Gold Circle will seek out 25 donors pledging $10,000 per person. Finally, the Silver Circle includes 100 individuals each pledging $1,000. Given the importance of these initial supporters it is crucial to gather not just people, but the right people.

Our initial fundraising goal is $1.6 million. Construction on the project will begin once we have met half of the initial fundraising goal. This initial fundraising will be used to develop the facility, cover a portion of operating costs, and help to secure the financial future of the organization. We plan to have completed the initial fundraising effort in slightly over one year.

Founders Committee

The members of the Founders Committee represent the highest commitment to the Welcome Home Organization. They must donate as much through their time and energy as through their wallet. A member must have adequate financial resources, solid stature within the community, and a willingness to work with the organization into the future. Prospective members of this committee may very well have experience interacting with developmentally disabled individuals within their own lives. In addition to the traditional fundraising circles, Welcome Home Organization will utilize those for whom developmental disability is a special cause.

These members will be recruited through personal relationships of the Brumfeld and Wesley families. Currently, eight families have already pledged their support and agreed to join the Founders Committee. $400,000 has been pledged to date. This initial group will help to fill the rest of the Founders Committee as well as the Platinum, Gold, and Silver Circles.

A profile of each of the members follows:

1. Bart and Martha Brumfeld: Bart is currently the President of Operations for Transport USA. The couple is involved in many charity and community activities, and is very familiar with the donor community throughout the Detroit metropolitan area.

2. Don and Judith Booth: Don is currently the Vice-President and General Counsel of Railways Inc. He is also the owner and principal of Booth Law Group. In addition, he serves as a Grand Rapids Alderman. Judith is the Deputy Executive Director of the Michigan Democratic Party. Both are extremely active throughout the community.

3. Shelly Grabek: Shelly is an active member of her family's businesses. Pinnacle Newspapers Inc. is a media company based in Michigan. In addition, she is involved with UMAN, a manufacturing firm

based in San Diego, California. She donates much of her free time to worthy causes, including the St. Jude's Children's Hospital.

4. Rock and Cynthia Noetzol: Rock is a retired Ann Arbor physician, and currently donates his time as the Washtenaw County Health Commissioner, a position he has held for over thirty years. He is a third generation Washtenaw County practitioner, and has family roots going back over a century and a half. Cynthia is a retired registered nurse, and is involved in the National Multiple Sclerosis Society.

5. Rick Spivey: Rick is an anti–trust attorney with the firm of Holden–Nash LLP. He is also a Oakland County Councilman. Rick is active in the community, and has vast experience in fundraising.

6. Eric and Julie Gardner: Eric is a retired executive from Robotics LLC, and is actively involved with a variety of charities including Boy Scouts of America. Julie is a retired homemaker.

7. Robert and Janice Wesley: Robert is currently the President of Lumber Supplies, Inc. based in Brighton, MI. He and Janice are actively involved in the community and have done extensive fundraising for a variety of charitable causes.

8. Greer Frasier: Greer is a widowed homemaker. Her husband's businesses included Frasier Window Company, Inc. and a variety of real estate holdings. Currently, she is involved with a variety of local charities.

The members of the Founders Committee have graciously agreed to personally send out pledge letters to their contacts. From their resources we have gathered the names of nearly 1,000 potential donors. Each member will send out a personal letter to their own contacts. The members have graciously agreed to underwrite the cost of this mailing.

Platinum Circle
A platinum circle of donors shall be derived from these efforts of the Founders Committee. This platinum circle will be responsible for a $25,000 donation and assistance in future fundraising. Members of this committee will be drawn from the contacts and resources of the Founders Committee members. The platinum circle will then assist in securing the gold circle of donors.

Gold Circle
The gold circle comprises the next phase of the initial fundraising effort. $250,000 will be brought in by the gold circle of donors. Just as important, this effort will lay the groundwork for the silver circle.

Silver Circle
The silver circle offers the chance for smaller donors to join the Welcome Home Organization family. One hundred donors pledging one thousand dollars will raise a total of $100,000.

In total the initial fundraising effort will raise $1.6 million dollars.

Spring Gala Event
In order to get people excited about the organization, as well as seek donors, Eric and Julie Gardner have graciously offered to underwrite the cost of a spring gala event at the Detroit Zoo. Families will have the option to donate from $250 dollars a guest, all the way up to joining the Platinum Committee with a donation of $25,000. Julie Gardner has offered to plan and execute the entire event. This event will be mentioned in the initial appeal letter, along with an enclosed response card.

Ongoing Fundraising
Welcome Home Organization will support a portion of its operating costs through ongoing fundraising operations. These operations will include traditional and non–traditional fundraising. The non–traditional fundraising is to include corporate sponsorship and naming rights.

Traditional Fundraising

The traditional fundraising plan includes an annual campaign, dinner auction, collection day, golf tournament, a bequest program and, in the future, an annuity program. These fundraisers should offer opportunities for even the smallest donor to share in the Welcome Home Organization vision. Their success will be one of the main duties of the Chief Administrative Officer, Chief Business Officer and Day Program and Volunteer Coordinator. Each of these events is done by multiple organizations, and requires significant numbers of people. Our Volunteer list will include the families of residents, our donors and friends.

- **Annual Campaign:** An annual fundraising campaign shall be conducted to help meet fundraising goals. The initial contacts will come from the list of potential supporters provided by the Founders Committee. This campaign will be conducted primarily through a mail/call strategy. Potential donors will receive a letter outlining the mission of Welcome Home Organization, and asking for their support. Within a week, a volunteer from the organization will contact that person, asking if they have received the letter, and if they are interested in supporting the organization. If they are not interested in donating to the organization, then they will be eliminated from the annual campaign. However, if they would like to donate, then they will be given further information and supporting calls until the donation is received. Donors to the annual campaign will be submitted into the pool for other fundraising activities. The general strategy of the annual campaign will be the responsibility of the Chief Administrative Officer. Volunteers for the follow up calls will be organized by the Day Program and Volunteer Coordinator. The annual campaign will begin in the third year, after all initial fundraising has been completed.

- **Dinner Auction:** Welcome Home Organization will host an annual dinner auction. The event will have three streams of revenue: the dinner, auction and corporate sponsorship, and will be held in October. This annual event will begin in our first year of operation. Auction items will be primarily donated in order to minimize cost. Corporate sponsors will enjoy the public goodwill which accompanies having their name attached to a worthy cause.

- **Collection Day:** Each year the organization will conduct a collection day to be held in April. This day will be similar to those held by organizations such as Backstoppers, Old Newsboys and other charitable groups. The organization will utilize a large number of volunteers to blanket busy intersections and public places asking for small donations. This type of fundraiser has a high margin, and raises the public awareness of the organization. A higher public awareness means a greater annual campaign, and so we will begin our annual collection day in the third year. This way we will have developed a greater public awareness and built a volunteer base to utilize in these activities.

- **Golf Tournament:** Golf tournaments provide many revenue opportunities. The first is simply the tournament fee paid by the golfer. In addition golfers may have the chance to purchase mulligans, enter skins contest and participate in hole–in–one contests. All these enhance the dollars brought in by each individual. Once again corporate sponsors may be elicited for the entire event, and also for individual holes. Although golf tournaments do have a high overhead, they are an excellent method of getting new individuals into the donor pool. The event is scheduled in June.

- **Bequest Program:** Bequest programs offer supporters the chance to remember the Welcome Home Organization in their last will and testament. The organization will provide standardized forms to aid in the legal process of the will. Donors may find this a useful tool to not only support the organization, but also to lessen the effect of estate taxes.

- **Gift Annuity Program:** After the organization has been established and is financially sound, they will create a gift annuity program. This type of program accepts cash and publicly traded securities as a gift to the organization. In exchange for the gift, Welcome Home Organization will pay an annual annuity to the beneficiary for the remainder of his or her life. The rate is determined by the age of the youngest beneficiary, with the rate increasing accordingly with the age. Upon the death of the beneficiary the gift remains with the organization. Those who participate in this program enjoy lower taxes and secure income in addition to the altruistic benefit.

Non–Traditional Fundraising

Many organizations have turned to non–traditional methods of fundraising. Among the most popular is the use of naming rights and sponsorship. Welcome Home Organization plans to utilize these options during the development and maturing of the organization. We hope that the naming rights of our facility will raise $200,000. This amount will be pledged over a period of 10 years, with a $20,000 donation each January. Corporations reap a double benefit; their name becomes associated with a positive image, and their donations lessen their tax burden.

FINANCIAL ANALYSIS

Financial Explanation

Welcome Home Organization will be established on solid financial ground by the end of year five. Donations are used to develop the facility, cover a portion of operating expenses, and protect the organization against fluctuations in government revenues. The development of the facility includes construction, training, equipment, and staffing prior to full occupancy. Occupancy is scheduled to be ten individuals when the facility opens in January of year one, and is to raise by ten individuals each subsequent month, until the capacity of thirty is reached.

Year zero has no revenue from operations, because it is dedicated to fundraising and development. Employees receive payment for time worked during the development and training phase. Pre–construction activities such as architecture and engineering are to begin on January 1st. Construction is expected to begin in April and commence in November. A loan of $1.1 million dollars is received on April 1; it is figured as a thirty year loan at six percent interest. The loan goes towards the cost of land and construction. The collateral will include the cash on hand and the residual value of the land and building. If additional collateral is required, the Wesley family has agreed to pledge a parcel of land in Livingston County as collateral.

Operation of the facility begins in January of year one. Operating revenues climb steadily through the end of March, as the occupancy increases each month. Accounts Receivable is calculated as one month of government revenues. Accounts Payable is calculated as one month of supplies and miscellaneous expenses. Investments have been calculated as seventy–five percent of excess cash flow, beginning in February of year two. These investments are meant to secure the financial future of the organization.

APPENDIX

Job Descriptions

Direct Care Staff

- Responsible for the overall care of residents.

- Assist with daily activities and special needs.

- Assist with maintaining health standards and appropriate environmental conditions.

Registered Nurse

- Responsible for the overall health of the residents, and will be the dedicated nurse in charge.

- Responsible for development of drug control procedures, environmental health, safety, and dietary procedures.

- Responsible for drug distribution management.

- Maintains necessary medical and nursing records.

- Necessary medical care will include, but is not limited to injections, inhalation therapy, intravenous fluids, suctioning, ostomy irrigation, lesion dressing, aseptic dressing, catheter irrigation, care for pressure sores and physiotherapy.

Licensed Practical Nurse

- Responsible for the care of the residents.

- Responsible for medication distribution while on duty.

- Works with the dedicated nurse in charge to maintain adequate medical and nursing records.

Cooks

- Responsible for the development of meal plans, taking into consideration residents wants and needs.

- Responsible for planning and ordering necessary food and equipment.

- In charge of food preparation for the entire facility.

- Maintains adequate records on resident-specific needs so as to accommodate necessary dietary and nutritional requirements.

Dining Aides

- Work with the cooks in the preparation and serving of meals.

- Assists residents with special eating needs.

- Work with volunteers to meet the general dining needs of the residents.

Housekeeping Services

- These services will be outsourced through an outside firm.

- Responsible for cleaning and maintaining the facility, including all common areas, restrooms, the activity center and resident's individual rooms.

Linen Assistant

- Responsible for laundry services, including resident's clothing, bathroom linens, and bedroom linens.

Plant Maintenance Employee

- In charge of the overall maintenance of the facility and its property.

- Responsible for necessary indoor repairs and maintenance at the facility.

- Responsible for outdoor maintenance, including lawn mowing and landscaping.

Day Program Staff

- Work with the Day Program Coordinator to plan and administer day program activities.

- Responsible for the care of the residents throughout the day.

- Work with volunteers in the Activities Center and throughout the facility.

Administrative Assistant

- Assists the Chief Administrative Officer in day–to–day activities of management and operations of the facility.

Receptionist

- Responsible for answering phones, greeting guests and other administrative tasks.

Biographical Information

- **Chief Administrative Officer:** The CAO has already been chosen, but the name is being kept confidential. This individual has over three years of public accounting experience, and holds C.P.A. certification. In addition, for the past three years this individual has served as the Director of Finance for a similar facility in another state. This individual is an excellent candidate, and brings a great and wide variety of experience to the operation.

- **Jonathan Fisher:** Jonathan has over six years experience with his family business, and a lifetime of charitable activities. He has worked directly with the developmentally disabled in the past. In addition, he has experience organizing fundraisers, which has led to numerous political connections.

- **Robert Wesley:** Robert has also worked with the developmentally disabled in the past at the Riverside Home. His work experience involves a variety of roles in the political process. Both Jonathan and Robert have worked with numerous candidates on all levels, including local, state-wide and national. These connections will be beneficial to the fundraising and securing government support.

Supplies are estimated at $5,000 per resident annually, including medical, grooming, food, etc.

Occupancy is estimated at $5.50 per square foot annually, and includes utilities, trash services, etc.

Insurance is paid semi–annually and is estimated at $40,000 for professional liability insurance, $30,000 for property and casualty insurance, and $10,000 for general liability.

Miscellaneous Expenses include Office Supplies, Maintenance Supplies, Activity Center Supplies, etc.

Professional Fees will be donated.

Benefits are calculated as 13% of total salary.

FICA Taxes are calculated as 7.65% of total salary.

Income Statement

Cost of Living is calculated at 2% annually, and is used to calculate increases in government revenues, and all non–fixed expenses.

Ongoing Fundraising stays constant over years 3—5.

Statement of Cash Flows

Accounts Receivable is calculated as one month of government revenues.

Accounts Payable is calculated as one month's supplies and miscellaneous expenses.

Investments are calculated as 75% of excess cash flows.

Salaries

Management receives an annual cost of living increase of 2% and a raise of 3%.

Staff receives an annual cost of living increase of 2% and a raise of 2%.

Painting Contractor

Fowler Painting Inc.

4901 Fruitvale Rd.
Newcastle, CA 95648

Claire Moore

Fowler Painting will provide both interior and exterior painting services to owners of residences and commercial property in Placer County, CA.

EXECUTIVE SUMMARY

Fowler Painting will provide both interior and exterior painting services to owners of residences and commercial property in Placer County, CA. We have found through our research that the top concern of customers who engage painting services is the disruption that is caused during the painting process.

We aim to build our brand based on high quality customer service with an emphasis on making the entire experience as convenient as possible for the customer.

Fowler Painting is structured as a corporation and is registered in the State of California. The corporate officers include Dan Fowler and his wife Deanna who both will work full-time in the business. Dan is the president, business manager as well as painting foreman and Deanna serves as Secretary/Treasurer as well as Office Manager and bookkeeper. The corporate vice president is Jim Fowler, Dan's father. Jim operated his own painting business in the Sacramento area for thirty years and will provide his expertise in the operation of Fowler Painting, Inc.

The owners will be providing the startup capital for the company and do not seek outside funding at this time. The company has also obtained a $15,000 line of credit that will be used as needed to fund growth and expenses. As it has not been used, the line of credit does not appear on these financials.

The office for Fowler Painting is located in the home of Dan and Deanna Fowler on their ten-acre property at 4901 Fruitvale Rd. in Newcastle, CA. The office is in a separate building and a converted barn is used to house equipment, supplies and the company vans (which are being rented).

Services provided by the company include commercial and residential painting. Such services encompass any preparation that may be required such as pressure washing of exteriors, paint removal and plastering.

During our first three years of operation we will focus on customers within Placer County. Cities in the county include: Roseville, Lincoln and Rocklin. The Placer County Economic and Demographic Profile for 2014 listed these cities as having the top growth rates in the county.

Objectives

Our objectives for the first three year of operations include:

- To achieve gross sales of $360,000 by year three.
- To achieve a customer mix of 60 percent residential and 40 percent commercial.
- To expand our customer footprint into nearby counties including El Dorado and Nevada county.

Mission

Our mission is to provide the best quality painting services in a prompt and professional manner. We promise our customers the following:

- We will start and finish on time
- We will maintain a neat and clean project
- We ensure high quality
- We handle all the details
- We stand behind our work

Competitive Advantage

Painting services are standard so a company has to distinguish itself in other ways such as services provided or in customer service. We intend to ensure our place as the premier painting services company in Northern California through our people and our services.

Our staff will impress customers and build our brand because of the following:

- Our employees are reference checked including a criminal background check.
- All employees are paid as employees rather than as independent subcontractors.
- Our employees receive continuing education in painting, customer service and safety.

Our company is fully insured with $2 million in liability coverage and our employees are covered by workman's compensation insurance. We have an active license with the California State License Board (CLSB). Anyone without an active state contractor license could face felony charges and if convicted could serve time in state prison. Obtaining a license requires four years of experience and all licensed contractors must carry proper insurance. Prospects can check for our license on the CLSB web site.

We can also provide prospective customers with references that they can check as to the quality or our work.

We warrant our labor and materials for a period of ten years. We will supply labor and materials to correct the condition without cost if paint failure appears.

This warranty does not cover the following:

- Incidental damages by accident, abuse, normal wear and tear, temperature, moisture or settlement
- Cracks
- Walking surfaces
- Paint failure due to rotted wood, structural defects, moisture or insects

COMPANY SUMMARY

Fowler Painting, Inc. is a startup corporation registered in the state of California. The principal officers of the company include Dan Fowler, his wife Deanna and Dan's father, Jim Fowler. Together, Dan and Jim have almost fifty years of experience in the painting industry. Jim Fowler ran his own painting company, Pacifica Painting Services, for thirty years before retiring in 2013.

Jim will be Fowler Painting's estimator during its first years of operation. We believe that his experience will prove invaluable in helping to grow the business and increase profitability.

Dan grew up working in his father's painting business and will continue to benefit from Jim's advice and guidance in running Fowler Painting. The company officers will be contributing the startup capital for the company and have also obtained a line of credit in the amount of $15,000 to cover expenses and growth as needed.

Company Location and Facilities

Company offices and storage facilities are located in Newcastle, CA on the personal property of Dan Fowler. Facilities include a small office building and a storage building for supplies, inventory and the company vans which are rented.

The company plans to gain business from existing contacts and from a focused marketing campaign that develops a network of professionals who work with those who own property such as real estate agents and insurance providers.

Startup Summary

Startup costs for the company include the following.

List of equipment needed for startup

Item	Estimated cost
Computer/printer/copier/scanner/fax	$1,500
Brushes, rollers	$ 500
Storage/filing/shelving	$ 300
Adding machine	$ 50
Paper shredder	$ 50
Desk/table/chair/lamp	$ 350
Ladders	$1,250
Dropcloths, rags, scrapers	$ 325
Misc tools & safety equipment	$ 450
Uniforms & shoes	$ 650
Sprayers	$1,400
Cleaning solvents	$ 200
Misc. supplies	$ 350
	$7,375

Start-up expenses

Expense	Cost
Licenses	$ 150
Van rent deposit	$3,000
Advertising	$ 250
Web site development	$ 850
Legal fees incorporation	$1,500
Magnetic truck signs	$ 100
Insurance	$ 700
Total start-up expenses	**$6,550**

Startup costs of $13,925 plus $5,000 of working capital will be contributed by Dan and Deanna Fowler.

COMPETITIVE ANALYSIS

According to Entrepreneur.com it is possible to start a painting business with as little as $2,000. Because it is so easy, the competition is bound to be considerable. However, not all painting contractors are licensed and insured. Not all can afford to have a crew of workers. Not all are willing to provide a warranty of their work. Nor do they have a track record of references.

Buyers of painting services need a way to distinguish one company from another as first impressions usually do not offer the layperson any way to know a good company from a less reputable one.

When it is difficult for consumers to judge the reliability of a company, it is common for those companies to compete based on timeliness of delivery and on price for services.

Our research has shown that the following companies serve the Placer County area and provide service similar to our own for residential and commercial properties. All are licensed and insured, offer free estimates and a warranty on work performed.

Name	Years in business
Off the wall	24
Perryman painting	23
Calpro painting	18
Auburn painting	10

Because Dan worked with his father since he was fifteen years old, he can honestly say that he has 20 year of experience in the business and can produce references to back his claim.

Now that Jim, his father, has retired from running his own painting company in the Bay Area, he will be working with Dan as his estimator. We believe that because of Jim's extensive experience in the business, that Fowler Painting will be able to outstrip much of the competition in its ability to accurately cost and price a job. This ability is key to success.

MARKET ANALYSIS

Of all the counties in California, Placer County has experienced some of the highest rates in growth of jobs, income and population increase in the past ten years. Over the past five to ten years, the significant expansion in Placer County's housing supply prompted the development of many major retail centers in the area, mostly within the Valley Region and particularly along the Highway 65 Corridor in Roseville and Rocklin.

Many Californians migrate to Placer County for its quality of life, and in some cases, relatively less-expensive housing. Placer County's ten-year growth rate was about 26 percent, almost twice the Sacramento Region's growth rate of around 15 percent, nearly 4 times the Bay Area (7 percent), and close to three times California's rate of around 9 percent for total housing unit growth.

Lincoln had the highest housing unit growth of all incorporated cities in Placer County in the ten-year historical period with an increase of 120 percent from 2003 to 2013.

The need for painting services does not just come from sales of new homes and new construction, however. Those who wish to sell their home or rent out an apartment or commercial facility often paint the location in an effort to increase its marketability.

According to the Placer County Association of Realtors (PCAOR) August 2015 home sales set a new record. July 2015 set a new record with 613 closed escrows. As the economy continues to rebound from its 2008 collapse, we will continue to see an increase in home sales and commercial development as well as business growth. We believe that this trend is good news for painting contractors in the area who can play a pivotal role in helping homeowners and those who own and manage commercial property to increase the value of their holdings.

Fowler Painting will serve both the residential and commercial markets. These markets can be described as follows:

Residential: homes. Our marketing efforts will emphasize the value that can be derived from painting your home or condo every few years.

Commercial: rentals and office space as well as hospitals, nursing homes and retail establishments. These customers are most interested in minimizing the down-time from having a painting crew on premises. Therefore we have instituted procedures to ensure that there will be a minimum of disruption to normal business activity or loss of rental revenues.

SERVICES

Fowler Painting, Inc. offers both interior and exterior painting services for residential and commercial properties.

Commercial markets include apartments, condos, retirement homes, office buildings, and rentals.

Fowler Painting services include:

- Full prep of walls and surfaces
- Pressure washing of exterior walls
- Small repairs of walls and wood surfaces
- Acoustical ceilings
- Custom painting: textures, checkerboard, stripes, color washing, dry brush, sponging

We use many different maintenance and safety paints, including:

- Lead encapsulates
- Fungus/mildew resistant coatings
- Rot-resistant coatings
- Epoxy for a tile-like coating
- Fire resistant
- Rust preventative paint
- Water resistant coatings

Service Area

During our first three years of operation we will focus on customers within Placer County. Cities in the county include: Roseville, Lincoln and Rocklin. The Placer County Economic and Demographic Profile for 2014 listed these cities as having the top growth rates in the county.

Lincoln's population showed the greatest increase of Placer County cities almost 115 percent growth in the ten-year period from 2003 to 2013.

Both Roseville and Rocklin also experienced high ten-year increases with respective growth rates of approximately 31 percent and 27 percent. According to Department of Finance (DOF) rankings, the

City of Lincoln, with a population of around 44,000 had the second highest growth rate of all California cities from January 2003 to January 2013.

Overall, the County is projected to see growth of about 18 percent between 2013 and 2023, which is a higher rate than the Sacramento Region's, Bay Area's, and California's respective projected growth of 11 percent, 7 percent, and 10 percent.

The highest population growth from 2012 to 2022 in Placer County, the Sacramento Region, the Bay Area, and California is projected to be in the 60 to 69 and 70 to 79 age groups. Placer County's per capita personal income is projected to increase about 22 percent from 2012 to 2022 to just over $64,000.

In 2012, Placer County's median household income was around $70,000, the highest income among the counties within the Sacramento Region and much higher than California.

MARKETING PLAN

Market trends in the painting industry have followed that of real estate. After a steep decline in 2008 construction markets began to post gains starting in 2011. It is expected that in the coming years a strong recovery in the housing market along with increased spending due to job growth will drive steady industry growth.

According to IBISWorld.com the growth in the housing market has increased the demand for painting services over the past five years as the residential market accounts for half of industry revenue. Developers have broken ground on new projects and owners of existing properties have been more willing to pay for improvements.

According to FirstResearch.com, the U.S. painting and wall covering contractors industry includes about 31,000 companies with combined annual revenue of about $16 billion. Demand in this industry is driven by building construction, renovation and maintenance.

The profitability of individual companies depends on efficiency of operations with larger companies having the advantage in being able to work on multiple projects concurrently. Smaller companies must compete by specializing in either unusual or in difficult applications and by providing superior customer service.

The U.S. Bureau of Labor Statistics projects that the number of actively employed painting and wall-covering contractors will increase by 38.5 percent during the ten-year period from 2010 to 2020, or 3.85 percent annually. In contrast, the overall job market is projected to grow by 18.5 percent in the same ten-year period.

The Bureau of Labor Statistics (BLS) estimates that overall residential construction activity will increase by 34 percent from 2010 to 2010, compared to 20.4 percent for nonresidential construction. BLS projects concluded that the related sales of residential painting services are likely to similarly increase by an annual rate of 3 to 4 percent until 2020.

Market Analysis

Fowler Painting will focus on both the residential and commercial markets. Both types of customer are concerned with quick turnaround; however, commercial customers have an economic interest in experiencing as little disruption as possible. We will aim to grow our commercial segment to at least 30 percent of our overall revenues.

Our plan is to grow at a steady pace by first focusing our marketing efforts to cities in Placer County within 30 miles of Lincoln. This geographic area is one of the most active and growing areas in the state.

While the residential customer presents the most potential for sales, we have found that the public's ability to take classes and rent equipment from establishments such as Lowes and Home Depot presents a challenge to the marketplace.

Our research indicates that both residential and commercial customers are likely to contract for painting services in the spring and summer months. There is a decline in demand for services as we move from autumn into the winter months.

Marketing Strategy

In addition to searching the Yellow Pages, prospective customers tend to find contractors through referrals from friends and from the Internet.

Therefore our marketing efforts will concentrate on the following objectives:

*   Build a strong network of satisfied customers and professionals who refer us to others.
*   Employ the purchase of advertising in traditional media such as Yellow Pages directory and neighborhood newspapers.
*   Use of the Internet including: web site, Facebook page, YouTube Channel with videos, submission of our information to contractor directory web sites, submission of Local places citations to Bing, Yahoo and Google

To help us with our Internet marketing we have contracted the services of a media company that specializes in marketing services for contractors. Their services emphasize local search engine optimization and content which means that we will not be competing with their other clients.

The services in our contract include:

*   Custom direct mail pieces, door hangers, referral cards, and brochures
*   Web hosting and site design
*   Search engine optimization
*   Quarterly email newsletter

Other marketing strategies that we will use include:

*   Custom magnets on our company vans that list our name, phone number, web site address and a brief list of painting services.
*   Yard signs posted at our work locations containing contact information.
*   Direct mail of postcards to neighbors in the area of our job locations during our contract.
*   Periodic emails to past customers with a useful article about home maintenance and improvement.
*   Company uniforms of tees and hats that contain company logo and contact info.

In order to develop our network for referrals we will develop alliance partners. These are professionals in complementary industries who would benefit from a mutual relationship of referrals. This network includes professionals in the following areas:

*   Landscape contractors
*   Insurance agents
*   Interior designers
*   HVAC contractors
*   Real estate agents and brokers
*   Home stagers

- Architects

- General contractors

We have worked on developing a mailing list for professionals in these categories who serve our area and we have begun an email and LinkedIn campaign to contact them. So far we have sent our newsletter to them as well as Connect requests at LinkedIn. Our emails include a link to Unsubscribe so that we avoid alienating anyone.

We also make it a point to rent a booth at all home and garden shows in our area. These events give us the opportunity to meet potential customers face-to-face and demonstrate the benefits of our services. At these events we also take the time to visit the other booths and introduce ourselves to other vendors who may become alliance partners in our referral network.

Pricing and Sales Strategy

A key to our success is the skillset of Jim Fowler as our chief estimator. Because of Jim's extensive experience as a painter/contractor he will be able to most accurately price our jobs for profitability. When pricing jobs we make certain assumptions as follows:

- Labor and materials will comprise 50 percent of contract total price as direct costs

- Labor will comprise 75 percent of direct costs of the job

- We will strive to achieve an annual net profit of at least 15 percent and expect to meet this goal by year two of operations

MANAGEMENT SUMMARY

Management consists of three individuals as follows:

- Dan Fowler, president

- Deanna Fowler, secretary/treasurer

- Jim Fowler, vice president

Jim Fowler operated his own painting company in the Bay Area for thirty years before retiring in 2013. For the last 20 of those years Dan worked for the company first as an assistant and eventually became a project foreman. Both Dan and Jim have extensive training and experience in providing excellent customer service, estimates and quality painting services.

Jim will be Fowler Painting's chief estimator and we believe that his years of experience will us to accurately price our jobs for profitability. As Jim is essentially retired and will be working part-time, he has agreed to take a reduced salary for the first two years of operation in order to help with cash flow.

Deanna has an associate's degree in business and 15 years' experience as a bookkeeper. Her experience in handling paperwork and her people skills will keep our office running smoothly.

Personnel Plan

In addition to Dan Fowler, we currently employ three part-time painters and we plan to add more employees as the work load increases. We also intend to move our painters into full-time status as soon as we can.

Personnel	Year 1	Year 2	Year 3
Foreman	$35,000	$ 35,000	$ 40,000
Foreman		$ 25,000	$ 25,000
Painters	$30,625	$ 43,125	$ 92,500
Estimator	$12,000	$ 12,000	$ 24,000
Office Mgr/Bookkeeper	$12,000	$ 12,000	$ 12,000
Totals	**$89,625**	**$127,125**	**$193,500**

FINANCIAL PLAN

Fowler Painting has formulated the following projections.

Pro forma profit and loss

	Year 1	Year 2	Year 3
Sales	**$175,000**	**$288,000**	**$420,000**
Direct costs			
Labor, material, supplies	$ 87,500	$144,000	$210,000
Gross profit	$ 87,500	$144,000	$210,000
Expenses			
Admin. payroll	$ 24,000	$ 24,000	$ 36,000
Employee insurance & benefits	$ 13,444	$ 19,800	$ 29,025
Depreciation	$ 230	$ 230	$ 230
Phone/Internet	$ 3,600	$ 3,600	$ 3,600
Insurance: liability, property, auto, errors omissions	$ 7,500	$ 8,000	$ 8,500
Payroll taxes	$ 8,963	$ 13,200	$ 19,350
Professional dues/memberships	$ 700	$ 850	$ 1,000
Advertising: print	$ 1,500	$ 1,800	$ 2,200
Advertising: web site and Internet marketing	$ 2,000	$ 2,000	$ 2,600
Office supplies	$ 420	$ 420	$ 420
Auto: gas & maintenance	$ 4,000	$ 5,500	$ 6,500
Software: estimating	$ 420	$ 420	$ 420
Software: Zoho	$ 360	$ 360	$ 360
Van rental	$ 9,600	$ 9,600	$ 9,600
Repairs & maintenance	$ 1,500	$ 1,500	$ 1,800
Accounting & legal	$ 1,800	$ 1,800	$ 2,000
Other expenses	$ 1,200	$ 1,200	$ 1,500
Total operating expenses	**$ 81,236**	**$ 94,280**	**$125,105**
Profit before interest and taxes	$ 6,264	$ 49,720	$ 84,895
Taxes incurred	$ 940	$ 7,458	$ 12,734
Net profit	**$ 5,324**	**$ 42,262**	**$ 72,161**
Net profit/sales	**3%**	**15%**	**17%**
Break-even revenue	$164,352	$203,476	$275,679
Monthly break-even revenue	$ 13,696	$ 16,956	$ 22,973
Estimated monthly fixed cost	$ 5,098	$ 5,630	$ 7,297

Break-even projection based on year two figures

Break-even hours	Painters	Hours	
Monthly budget			$24,000
Painters average budget hours	4	120	480
Projected sales price per hour including materials			$ 50
If BE revenue is			$16,956
Break-even hours for month			339

Projected balance sheet

	Year 1	Year 2	Year 3
Assets			
Cash in bank	$ 2,400	$43,317	$115,113
Accounts receivable	$ 1,500	$ 2,700	$ 3,200
Inventory	$ 1,000	$ 1,600	$ 1,800
Other current assets			
Total current assets	**$ 4,900**	**$47,617**	**$120,113**
Fixed assets			
Office furniture & equipment	$ 2,300	$ 2,300	$ 2,300
Less: depreciation	($ 230)	($ 460)	($ 690)
Total assets	**$ 6,970**	**$49,457**	**$121,723**
Liabilities			
Current liabilities			
Accounts payable	$ 350	$ 575	$ 680
Current maturities loan			
Total current liabilities	**$ 350**	**$ 575**	**$ 680**
Long term liabilities loan	0	0	0
Total liabilities	**$ 350**	**$ 575**	**$ 680**
Paid-in capital	$ 1,296	$ 1,296	$ 1,296
Retained earnings	$ 5,324	$47,586	$119,747
Total capital	**$ 5,324**	**$47,586**	**$119,747**
Total liabilities & capital	**$ 6,970**	**$49,457**	**$121,723**

Scrap Metal Salvage Business

LMI Salvage Inc.

23776 Cedar St.
Mason Ridge, Ohio 56609

Paul Greenland

LMI Salvage Inc. is a part-time scrap peddling business owned by Larry Irving and his son, Mark Irving.

EXECUTIVE SUMMARY

As owner of Irving Appliance Repair, Larry Irving frequently encounters customers with appliances that cannot be repaired, and which must be disposed of. This situation served as the inspiration to form LMI Salvage Inc. Initially a part-time scrap peddling business, Larry will own LMI Salvage in partnership with his son, Mark, who is interested in owning and operating his own business. In addition to a small start-up investment, Larry will contribute 15 years of small business management knowledge to LMI, providing Mark (who will be responsible for day-to-day operations) with valuable guidance.

LMI Salvage will immediately benefit from a steady supply of used appliances provided by customers of Irving Appliance Repair. Building on this foundation, Mark Irving will obtain metal items in need of disposal from other residential customers, and will began pursuing a strategy to develop a network of commercial customers that will supply him with a regular stream of both ferrous and non-ferrous scrap metal, positioning him for success in a lucrative industry with strong growth potential.

INDUSTRY ANALYSIS

According to a 2013 Huffington Post article by Ilana Greene, economic contributions associated with the scrap metal industry exceed $90 billion annually. Although the scrap metal industry is a major economic force, it is highly fragmented, with thousands of participants. Some analysts estimate that the leading 50 players generate approximately half of industry revenues.

Participants in the recycling industry are represented by the Washington, D.C.-based National Waste & Recycling Association, whose mission is to be "The leading organization providing leadership, advocacy, research, education and safety expertise to promote the North American waste and recycling industries, serve as their voice and create a climate where members prosper and provide safe, economically sustainable and environmentally sound services." With roots dating back to 1962 the organization has members from all 50 states. Additionally, the association serves its members through numerous regional offices and state chapters.

MARKET ANALYSIS

The cost to recycle metal is much lower than mining and refining new metal sources. Limited resources and a growing emphasis on recycling are factors that are driving steady demand for scrap metal nationwide, and in LMI Salvage's home market of Mason Ridge, Ohio.

Consumer Market

In 2015 the population of Mason Ridge included approximately 197,000 people. At that time, 62 percent of the community's housing units were single-family homes, 32 percent were structures with two or more rental units, and 6 percent were mobile homes or trailers. Because all property owners, including landlords, are in need of haul-away services, the opportunity within this market segment is both strong and consistent.

Commercial Market

Although the commercial segment initially will represent a small portion of LMI Salvage's business, commercial customers will become an increasingly important revenue source as the business pursues its growth strategy. From machine shops and automotive repair businesses to plumbers and retail stores, commercial operations produce a wide variety of scrap metal waste. In 2015 Mason Ridge included 5,313 businesses. Of particular interest are operations in the following categories:

- Apparel and Accessory Stores (60)
- Automotive Dealers and Gasoline Service Stations (118)
- Automotive Repair, Services and Parking (174)
- Building Construction—General Contractors & Operative Builders (81)
- Building Materials, Hardware, Garden Supply & Mobile Home Dealers (23)
- Communications (41)
- Construction—Special Trade Contractors (151)
- Electric, Gas and Sanitary Services (16)
- Fabricated Metal Products, Except Machinery & Transport Equipment (59)
- Furniture and Fixtures (6)
- General Merchandise Stores (30)
- Heavy Construction, Except Building Construction—Contractors (16)
- Home Furniture, Furnishings and Equipment Stores (80)
- Industrial and Commercial Machinery and Computer Equipment (140)
- Miscellaneous Manufacturing Industries (22)
- Miscellaneous Repair Services (86)
- Miscellaneous Retail (238)
- Primary Metal Industries (11)
- Printing, Publishing and Allied Industries (37)
- Transportation Equipment (11)

Competition

Scrap metal hauling is a highly fragmented industry. Significant competition exists due to the low cost of entry. Many businesses enter and exit the market every day. LMI Salvage has analyzed local conditions and determined that the following businesses, all of which have been in operation for five years or more, will present the greatest competition:

- Hassle-Free Haul Away

- Johnson Enterprises Inc.

- Junk King

- Larry's Hauling Service

- Simpson Salvage LLC

SERVICES

LMI Salvage will pick up both ferrous and non-ferrous metals from residential and commercial customers in need of disposal services. The business will then bring metals to area scrap yards for sale.

For commercial customers with large amounts of metal, LMI Salvage will negotiate a disposal fee, based on weight and volume (every job is different), providing additional revenue beyond what is received from the scrap yard. For large sources of scrap metal, LMI Salvage will concentrate its efforts on:

- Automotive Repair Shops

- Demolition Sites

- Manufacturing Companies (e.g., Operational Waste)

- Manufacturing Plant Closures

- Office Building Closures

- Plumbing Businesses

- Residential/Commercial Contractors/Remodelers

- Retail Store Closures

Ferrous Metal

Ferrous metal contains iron and offers the lowest reimbursement per pound. However, it also is the most common (widely available), and market prices tend to be stable. Common types of ferrous metal include:

- Carbon Steel

- Cast Iron

- Mild Steel

- Stainless Steel

- Wrought Iron

Common sources of recyclable ferrous items (and approximate weights) include:

- Barbecue Grills (150-180 Pounds)

- Cast Iron Bathtubs (250-300 Pounds)

- Dryers (100-125 Pounds)

- Engine Blocks (250-500 Pounds)

- Ornamental Gates/Fencing (Variable Weight)

- Ovens & Ranges (100-150 Pounds)

- Refrigerators (175-250 Pounds)

- Washing Machines (175-225 Pounds)

Non-ferrous Metals

Non-ferrous metals do not contain iron and offer the highest reimbursement per pound. However, they are more difficult to find and obtain, and prices may fluctuate considerably. Common types of non-ferrous metals include:

- Aluminum

- Brass

- Copper

- Gold

- Lead

- Nickel

- Silver

- Tin

- Titanium

- Zinc

Common sources of recyclable non-ferrous items include:

- Aluminum Cans

- Aluminum Radiators

- Aluminum Transmissions

- Aluminum Turnings

- Aluminum Wheels

- Aluminum Wire

- Auto Radiators (Brass)

- Batteries (Lead)

- Cast Aluminum

- Copper Piping

- Heater Cores

- Insulated Copper Wire

- Painted Aluminum

- Red Brass

- Sheet Copper

- Yellow Brass

PERSONNEL

Larry & Mark Irving (Owners)

Larry Irving has been the owner of Irving Appliance Repair for 15 years. In his work, Larry frequently encounters customers with appliances that cannot be repaired, and which must be disposed of. This situation served as the inspiration to form LMI Salvage Inc. Larry will own LMI Salvage in partnership with his son, Mark, who is interested in owning and operating his own business. A part-time community college student, Mark has a strong work ethic. He is responsible, dependable, and physically strong. In addition to a small start-up investment, Larry will contribute 15 years of knowledge as a small business owner/operator to LMI, providing Mark (who will be responsible for day-to-day operations) with valuable guidance.

Professional and Advisory Support

LMI Salvage will use a local accounting firm for assistance with tax preparation and bookkeeping. The business also has established a commercial checking account with a local bank.

GROWTH STRATEGY

The owners will gradually increase capacity by buying the largest truck the business can afford, thus lowering operational costs by consolidating loads and minimizing trips to local scrapyards. As capacity increases, LMI Salvage will attempt to secure more competitive volume-based reimbursement rates from area scrapyards (some offer tiers based on volume). LMI Salvage will differentiate itself from the competition by offering exception customer service and picking up pre-scheduled items from customers the same day they call.

The following targets have been established for the business for its first four years of operations:

Year One: Begin operations with one full-sized, used pick-up truck (class 2/capacity of less than 6,000 pounds). Develop an initial base of five commercial customers. Achieve gross revenues of $31,500 as a part-time operation, with commercial clients accounting for 25 percent of sales.

Year Two: Transition LMI Salvage to a full-time business. Expand hauling capacity via the purchase of a flat-bed trailer. Grow the business' commercial client base by adding five additional customers. Achieve gross revenues of $46,000, with commercial clients accounting for 35 percent of sales.

Year Three: Continue to expand hauling capacity by purchasing a used, heavy-duty pick-up truck (class 3). Expand the business' commercial client base by adding five additional customers. Achieve gross revenues of $60,500, with commercial clients accounting for 45 percent of sales.

Year Four: Expand the business' commercial client base by adding five additional customers. Achieve gross revenues of $75,000, with commercial clients accounting for 55 percent of sales.

The following graph and table show LMI Salvage's projected financial growth targets:

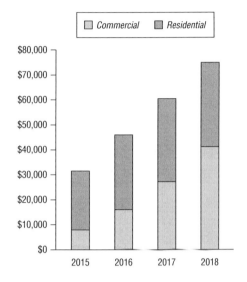

Category	2015	2016	2017	2018
Commercial	$ 7,875	$16,100	$27,225	$41,250
Residential	$23,625	$29,900	$33,275	$33,750
Total	**$31,500**	**$46,000**	**$60,500**	**$75,000**

OPERATIONS

Several pieces of equipment are critical for LMI Salvage to begin operations:

1. Full-Sized, Used Pickup Truck ($3,500)

2. Portable Floor Scale ($400)

3. Small Jib Crane/Winch ($350)

In addition, the owner will purchase the following items from a local used tool shop for approximately $400:

- Magnet (for ferrous/non-ferrous metal determination)

- Grinding Wheel

- Tin Snips

- Aviation Snips

- Hammers

- Prybars

- Drills

- Wire Cutters

- Safety Goggles

- First Aid Kit

Finally, Mark Irving has obtained a smartphone equipped with GPS navigation technology (for locating pickup sites), which will be used for all customer communications. An annual contract has been established with a leading wireless communications company.

The owners realize they will need to devote a portion of time pursuing leads, marketing the business, and doing administrative tasks.

MARKETING & SALES

LMI Salvage has developed a marketing plan with the following tactics:

1. Look for free items on CraigsList.

2. Post a free ad on CraigsList to promote the business.

3. Conduct research to learn about garbage pickup days in various residential neighborhoods and gain an advantage over competitors by arriving early to reclaim metal items that are being disposed of.

4. Relationship building with banks and landlords, who often need haul-away services in foreclosure/ eviction situations.

5. Development of a four-color promotional flyer, which can be left behind at various locations.

6. Magnetic business cards, which can be given to prospective customers.

7. Signage for LMI Salvage's truck (mobile advertising).

8. A simple Web site with details about the business and how to arrange pickups.

9. Development of a Facebook page.

FINANCIAL ANALYSIS

Following are four-year financial projections for LMI Salvage:

	2015	2016	2017	2018
Revenue				
Ferrous metal	$26,775	$36,800	$45,375	$52,500
Non-ferrous metal	$ 4,725	$ 9,200	$15,125	$22,500
Total	**$31,500**	**$46,000**	**$60,500**	**$75,000**
Expenses				
Salaries	$20,000	$30,000	$40,000	$50,000
Payroll taxes	$ 1,000	$ 1,500	$ 2,000	$ 2,500
Fuel	$ 1,050	$ 1,575	$ 2,100	$ 2,625
Auto insurance	$ 1,200	$ 1,300	$ 1,400	$ 1,500
Vehicle purchases	$ 3,500	$ 0	$ 7,500	$ 0
Office supplies	$ 200	$ 200	$ 200	$ 200
Equipment	$ 1,150	$ 500	$ 500	$ 500
Marketing & advertising	$ 450	$ 450	$ 450	$ 450
Telecommunications	$ 1,200	$ 1,200	$ 1,200	$ 1,200
Fees/certifications	$ 200	$ 200	$ 200	$ 200
Total expenses	**$29,950**	**$36,925**	**$55,550**	**$59,175**
Net income/loss	**$ 1,550**	**$ 9,075**	**$ 4,950**	**$15,825**

SWOT ANALYSIS

Strengths: Low-start-up costs; dump fees and fuel costs are proportionate to income; steady supply of used appliances provided by customers of Irving Appliance Repair; no expenses needed for a physical office.

Weaknesses: One-man/one-truck operation (injury, illness and mechanical failure may jeopardize sales).

Opportunities: Strong potential to differentiate with exceptional customer service, especially with regular commercial customers.

Threats: Reimbursement rates for non-ferrous metals may be volatile; significant competition due to low-entry cost.

Self-Published Author

Mark Sutton Inc.

29 Main St.
Abbington, AZ 85333

Paul Greenland

Mark Sutton is a former sportswriter who is leveraging the latest self-publishing and e-book technology to introduce and market a series of sports books.

EXECUTIVE SUMMARY

Before becoming the executive editor of a leading manufacturing trade magazine, author Mark Sutton spent 10 years as a sports reporter for the *Trenton Globe*. At that time he wrote a book about the history of the Trenton Tigers, one of the nation's oldest professional football teams. After winning the national championship in 2013, the Tigers have a new generation of fans, many of whom know little or nothing about the team's proud heritage. For this reason, Sutton has decided to produce and market a series of new sports books about the Tigers, utilizing a self-publishing model that capitalizes on the burgeoning popularity of e-books and print-on-demand technology.

INDUSTRY ANALYSIS

Several factors (the Internet, digital printing/print-on-demand distribution, and the adoption of e-books) have significantly changed the book publishing industry. In the May/June 2012 issue of *Writer's Digest,* literary agent April Eberhardt wrote: "Whereas just a few years ago the 'Big Six' publishers (Random House, HarperCollins, Penguin Group, Macmillan, Simon & Schuster and Hachette Book Group) were the gatekeepers to a book's success, and self-publishing was considered by many to be the option of last resort, perceptions—and the realities driving them—have shifted dramatically in recent months."

Indeed, emerging models have led a number of mainstream publishers to establish self-publishing and e-publishing divisions, and literary agencies are now beginning to offer self-publishing consulting services for authors. As a result, the lines between publishing models are blurring rapidly. At the same time, traditional book publishers (large publishing houses and smaller presses alike) have become extremely selective about the titles they decide to publish. Oftentimes, the odds are stacked against titles that are specialized or have a limited market.

Additionally, e-books have resulted in new opportunities for authors. Because they are distributed electronically, e-books are available immediately to a global audience, providing authors with the broadest distribution possible. Also, since they require a smaller commitment compared to traditional models, which involve large print runs, e-books allow authors and publishers to test the popularity of content with readers.

According to an article by Jeremy Greenfield in the February 2014 issue of *Writer's Digest,* data from the Association of American Publishers found that almost 29 percent of U.S. trade publishing revenues were attributed to e-books by the early part of 2014. Additionally, data from the Pew Internet & American Life Project found that about 25 percent of Americans read an e-book in 2012. The future of the format's popularity seems certain, considering that nearly 55 percent of children between the ages of two and 13 read e-books, based on a survey conducted by PlayCollective and *Digital Book World.*

MARKET ANALYSIS

Target Audiences

Trenton Tigers fans represent the primary market for Sutton's sports books. The team is fortunate to have one of the strongest followings in the Professional League. Even during the Great Recession, when many team struggled with lower attendance figures, the Tigers consistently enjoyed near-sellout crowds. Additionally, the team has benefited from exceptionally strong merchandise sales, thanks to its popular logo and strong fan base. Because team-related merchandise, including books, sells so strongly, Sutton is confident in the marketability of his titles.

Unlike other non-fiction titles (e.g., cookbooks, do-it-yourself, self-improvement, health, spirituality, etc.), which are many in number, the universe of books about the Trenton Tigers is very small. Sutton knows that fans of the team will find his titles easily when doing keyword searches for print books and e-books via leading channels such as Amazon, Barnes and Noble, etc.

SERVICES

Sutton will develop and market the following two titles (in both print and e-book form) in 2015:

- *Great Moments in Trenton Tigers History* ($14.95 print/$9.99 e-book/200 pages)
- *Trenton Tigers Trivia* ($9.99 print/$7.99 e-book/100 pages)

Based on the success of these titles in 2015, Sutton will develop future books in both print and digital format, including:

- *The Little Book of Trenton Tigers Facts* (2016)
- *Trenton Tigers: The Greatest Players* (2017)

PERSONNEL

Author/Owner

Before becoming the executive editor of a leading manufacturing trade magazine, author Mark Sutton spent 10 years as a sports reporter for the Trenton Globe. In that role, he covered a number of sports and teams, including the Trenton Tigers, one of the nation's oldest professional football teams.

A major highlight of Sutton's sports writing career occurred in 2001 when he authored a book called *Tiger Tales—The History of the Trenton Tigers: 1900-2000.* Although the book was successful, it eventually became out-of-print. Sutton retained the rights to his history book and still has all of the original research and interviews used in its development. After winning the national championship in

2013, the Tigers have a new generation of fans, many of whom know little or nothing about the team's proud heritage. For this reason, Sutton has decided to produce and market a series of new sports books, utilizing a self-publishing model that capitalizes on the burgeoning popularity of e-books and print-on-demand technology.

Professional and Advisory Support

To gain personal liability protection, Sutton will incorporate his author business, forming Mark Sutton Inc., using affordable documents available from a popular online legal document service. In addition, he will use the local firm, A-1 Accounting, for assistance with tax preparation and bookkeeping. In addition, he has identified an attorney who specializes in the publishing field, in the event that related legal services are needed, and has established a business banking account with his local bank. Finally, Sutton has hired a freelance developmental editor, graphic designer, and proofreader to assist him with the development of his sports books. These professionals were identified from listings in *Literary Market Place,* a leading directory for the publishing industry.

GROWTH STRATEGY

Year One: Release *Great Moments in Trenton Tigers History* and *Trenton Tigers Trivia.* Generate royalties of $51,850 on sales of both books.

Year Two: Release *The Little Book of Trenton Tigers Facts.* Generate royalties of $74,974 from the sale of three books.

Year Three: Release *Trenton Tigers: The Greatest Players.* Generate royalties of $106,835 from the sale of four books.

OPERATIONS

Mark Sutton will manage the marketing and sale of his sports book from a home office. Although he is a professional writer, Sutton will hire a developmental editor and a proofreader to ensure the quality of his manuscript. In addition, he will hire a professional designer to create dynamic covers for his titles.

The author has identified print-on-demand (POD) publishing as the best solution for his sports books. POD publishing is ideal for highly specialized books that primarily will be marketed and distributed online, as opposed to large concentrations of copies sold through traditional brick-and-mortar stores. Unlike traditional self-publishing, in which authors invest their own money to produce and print large quantities of books, which they must then distribute and sell, the POD model is similar to that of traditional publishers, in that authors are paid on a royalty basis. The difference is that books are printed and bound on-demand, thanks to the advent of digital technology.

A POD publisher named BookLocker has been identified as the best publishing solution. BookLocker considers a title once the complete manuscript is available for review, so that it can be evaluated for marketability/salability. Once accepted, authors pay a nominal setup fee that covers manuscript formatting, galley proofs, barcode, the assignment of an ISBN, etc. Authors retain all rights, and are not required to engage in a long-term contract, allowing the title to be quickly picked up by a traditional publisher if desired.

Upon publication, BookLocker distributes printed books through Ingram (the world's largest book distributor), Amazon.com, BarnesandNoble.com, and many other online stores. In addition, e-books are produced and made available through leading e-book stores, including Apple's iBookstore and Barnes & Noble. In addition to online orders, it is possible for customers to order books via their local brick-and-mortar store if desired.

MARKETING & SALES

Regardless of the publishing model, marketing is a critical factor that determines the success or failure of any book. There is no standard/one-size-fits-all approach to book marketing. Tactics that are successful for promoting one type of book may be unsuccessful for others. Unlike years past, when books existed mainly in printed form, the advent of e-books (and the burgeoning number of available titles) has made discoverability a primary marketing concern. Additionally, there is a greater need to sustain marketing efforts over a longer period of time. With this in mind, Mark Sutton has developed the following marketing strategy for his titles:

1. Develop a professionally-produced book video trailer that includes brief comments from both the author and former players. Distribution will occur via YouTube to potential customers, bloggers, and book reviewers.

2. Provide readers with an opportunity to view advanced review copies through the service, NetGalley, with a goal of generating positive early reviews on channels such as Amazon.com and Goodreads.

3. Identify and send review copies to leading sports bloggers.

4. Drive e-book sales by utilizing the e-mail book promotion service, BookBub, which notifies subscribers about new e-books for Nook, Kindle, iBook, Kobo, and other channels via daily alerts.

5. Develop and distribute a press kit that includes: review copy, press release, and author bio.

6. Send press kits and review copies to the following major book review magazine editors and reviewers:

- *Booklist,* American Library Association (www.booklistonline.com)

- *BookPage* (www.bookpage.com): Monthly tabloid review distributed in hundreds of bookstores.

- *ForeWord* (www.forewordmagazine.com): Focuses solely on independently published books.

- *Kirkus Reviews* (www.kirkusreviews.com): Reviews more than 500 pre-publication books monthly.

- *Library Journal* (www.libraryjournal.com): Monthly book review journal for librarians.

- *New York Review of Books* (www.nybooks.com)

- *Publishers Weekly* (www.publishersweekly.com): Weekly trade magazine for the book publishing industry in the United States.

7. Use the free service, MailChimp, to develop and maintain mailing lists for (1) bloggers/reviewers and (2) readers.

8. Use the free service, Rafflecopter, to build a proprietary database via giveaway campaigns (prizes to include free book copies, Amazon.com gift certificates, etc.).

9. Personally contact managers of leading bookstores in the target market and encourage them to host book signings, especially at key times (e.g., beginning of the football season; holiday shopping season; during the playoffs, etc.).

10. Use Twitter and Instagram to generate buzz about books among Tigers fans and among also drive attendance at book signings.

FINANCIAL ANALYSIS

The following table provides a snapshot of the books that Sutton will release in 2015, along with terms and volume projections:

Book title	Book type	Terms	Unit list price	Unit net price
Greatest moments	Print (Booklocker)	35%/list	$14.95	N/A
Greatest moments	print (other)	15%/list	$14.95	N/A
Greatest moments	e-book (Booklocker)	70%/list	$ 9.99	N/A
Greatest moments	e-book (other)	55%/net	$ 9.99	$6.99
Trivia	print (Booklocker)	35%/list	$ 9.99	N/A
Trivia	print (other)	15%/list	$ 9.99	N/A
Trivia	e-book (Booklocker)	70%/list	$ 7.99	N/A
Trivia	e-book (other)	55%/net	$ 7.99	$4.99

Additionally, this table provides projected royalties for each title in 2015:

Book title	Book type	Volume	Unit royalty	Total
Greatest moments	Print (Booklocker)	3,500	$5.23	$18,305
Greatest moments	print (other)	1,500	$2.24	$ 3,360
Greatest moments	e-book (Booklocker)	500	$4.89	$ 2,445
Greatest moments	e-book (other)	1,000	$3.84	$ 3,840
				$27,950
Trivia	Print (Booklocker)	4,500	$3.50	$15,750
Trivia	print (other)	1,500	$1.50	$ 2,250
Trivia	e-book (Booklocker)	750	$5.59	$ 4,193
Trivia	e-book (other)	1,500	$2.75	$ 4,125
				$26,318

A complete set of pro forma financial statements has been prepared for the business and is available upon request. Following are key projections for the first three years:

	2015	2016	2017
Sales			
Greatest moments	$27,950	$30,745	$ 33,820
Trivia	$26,318	$28,950	$ 31,845
Little book of facts	$ 0	$26,318	$ 28,950
Greatest players	$ 0	$ 0	$ 27,950
	$54,268	**$86,013**	**$122,564**
Expenses			
Salary	$35,000	$55,000	$ 80,000
Payroll taxes	$ 5,250	$ 8,250	$ 12,000
Accounting & legal	$ 2,000	$ 1,000	$ 1,000
Travel	$ 1,500	$ 2,000	$ 2,500
Marketing	$ 3,500	$ 5,000	$ 7,500
Software	$ 500	$ 500	$ 500
Equipment	$ 1,500	$ 500	$ 500
Internet	$ 750	$ 788	$ 827
Dues	$ 350	$ 386	$ 406
Telecommunications	$ 1,000	$ 1,050	$ 1,103
Miscellaneous	$ 500	$ 500	$ 500
Total expenses	**$51,850**	**$74,974**	**$106,835**
Net profit/loss	**$ 2,418**	**$11,039**	**$ 15,729**

Seminar Retreat Business Plan

Work Spirit Events

4075 Westerly Road
Santa Rosa, CA 95482

Claire Moore

Work Spirit Events is dedicated to helping new and established entrepreneurs to find the individual spirit that drives their work. Founded in 2014 by Kerri Stahl, the company aims to become a valuable source of information and inspiration that will infuse a new sense of spirituality in American enterprise.

EXECUTIVE SUMMARY

Work Spirit Events is dedicated to helping new and established entrepreneurs to find the individual spirit that drives their work. Founded in 2014 by Kerri Stahl, the company aims to become a valuable source of information and inspiration that will infuse a new sense of spirituality in American enterprise.

Kerri began the business after spending years climbing the corporate ladder of success only to find that the room at the top is empty without true purpose. She invested countless hours in searching for inner purpose and meaning. Finally Kerri felt that she was ready to move on to the next chapter in her life.

She left her high-paying corporate career and spent the next four years working with a well-known speaker and spiritual leader. Eventually Kerri took on the role of manager for that speaker and became proficient in booking his appearances and retreats.

At the end of the four years Kerri went on her own to found Work Spirit Events where she can truly express her life's calling and share her knowledge with others.

The business began with personal consulting and group workshops held at meeting rooms in banks and corporate offices. Kerri held her first retreat in the fall of 2014 at a resort on the Northern California coast. Through her workshops, consulting, retreats and web site, Kerri has assembled a membership list of 500 names. She intends to build on this foundation to grow the company.

Mission
The mission of Work Spirit Events is to provide our clients with an immersive retreat experience that will inspire their life's purpose long after the retreat ends.

Keys to Success
Our keys to success include:

- A focus on female success without guilt

- Helping our clients to infuse spirituality in all areas of their lives

- Personal attention to the needs and goals of our clients

- Cultivation of a membership list through marketing efforts

Objectives

- Complete business plan.

- Sales of $85K by year three.

- Sales of $150K by year five.

COMPANY SUMMARY

Located on the Northern California Coast of Sonoma County, Work Spirit Events offers seminars and retreats in one of the most beautiful settings on earth. We offer women the opportunity to explore the place of spirituality in their lives as it expresses itself in their work.

We offer retreats with different themes during the year. Retreats take place at Sonoma area resorts that offer guests access to many scenic and cultural experiences. During our retreats, which last from three to five days, participants can spend their free time either exploring or relaxing.

Future plans include offering retreats at locations such as the Caribbean, East Coast and Europe.

Company History

Kerri Stahl created Work Spirit Events in 2014. After reaching a position of success and influence in her field, Kerri found herself lonely and unfulfilled as a person. She finally took a much needed vacation at a meditation retreat in Colorado. The experience was the beginning of a life changing process.

Kerri continued to explore her life's purpose and the place of spirituality in her life. After years of study and introspections she decided to start Work Spirit Events where she can share what she has learned with other women entrepreneurs.

START-UP SUMMARY

We anticipate total start-up costs to eventually reach the following amounts based on our experience thus far and projections of near future expenditures.

List of equipment needed for startup

Item	Estimated cost
Computer/printer/copier/scanner/fax	$1,700
Telephone/cell phone	$ 200
Storage/filing/shelving	$ 150
Adding machine	$ 25
Paper shredder	$ 50
Desk/table/chair/lamp	$ 375
	$2,500

Requirements

Start-up expenses

Licenses	$ 350
Supplies	$ 150
Advertising	$ 650
Web site development	$2,000
Legal/accounting	$2,200
Total start-up expenses	**$5,350**

COMPANY LOCATION/FACILITIES

Work Spirit Events offices are located in the home of Kerri Stahl in Santa Rosa, CA. The seminars take place in Santa Rosa which is directly accessible by air from Los Angeles, Portland, San Diego and Seattle by way of Alaska Airlines.

Currently retreats are set to be held three times a year at the Sea Ranch Lodge in The Sea Ranch, California. Sea Ranch is located 61 miles west of Santa Rosa on the California coast. Attendees can fly into the Charles M. Schulz - Sonoma County Airport and then drive an hour and 45 minutes to Sea Ranch.

In the future we plan to offer retreats at other Northern California locations including: Calistoga and Lake Tahoe. Eventually we plan on offering retreats at locations such as the Caribbean, East Coast and Europe.

Work Spirit also holds workshops and seminars in Santa Rosa. Workshops are three hours in length and serve to provide an introduction to Kerri. We also hold two day seminars in Santa Rosa.

Work Spirit currently rents facilities to hold its seminars and intends to continue doing so for at least the next few years. Although renting gives us less flexibility in scheduling, we are able to contain costs by not having to maintain a physical location. As seminars are only given a few times a year, there is no need at this time to take on the expense of a physical facility year-round.

COMPANY OWNERSHIP

At this time Work Spirit is a sole proprietorship owned by Kerri Stahl, founder and president. It has been registered with the city and county of Santa Rosa. The formation of a corporation will be considered in the future as our business and our needs grow.

SERVICES

Seminars

Two-day seminars are held in Santa Rosa several times per year.

Seminar topics include:

- Finding and preserving meaning in your job and career

- Awareness meditation and the search for your authenticity

- *Write for life:* Your Journey of Self-Discover Through Writing

Retreats

Retreats taking place over three to five days are currently held at the Sea Ranch Lodge in The Sea Ranch, CA on the coast.

Topics of workshops will include:

- *Passion, Purpose, Profit:* Creating A Business That Reflects Your Truth
- *From Darkness to Light:* Reinventing Your Life After Crisis or Loss
- *Meaningful Leadership:* From Self-Empowerment to Stewardship

We plan to expand the number of locations where we offer retreats to include venues on the East Coast, Caribbean and Europe.

Personal Coaching

Kerri offers personal coaching sessions ranging from 20 minutes to an hour. Clients can schedule and pay for their sessions through our web site. The registration process includes an application form that allows for the collection of background information on what the client needs to accomplish in the coaching session.

Group Coaching program

Coaching programs offered run either for three months, six months or a year. The coaching programs include group calls for discussion and accountability to help participants determine their path and meet their goals. Longer programs include scheduled gatherings at luxurious locations. We are currently working on plans to offer our first gathering at a Lake Tahoe resort in the fall of 2016.

Prices

- Prices for two-day retreats range from $400 to $700 depending on the topic.
- Prices for three-day retreats range from $1,200 to $1,900 depending on the topic.
- Prices for five-day retreats range from $2,400 to $3,500 depending on the topic.
- Prices for group coaching range from $2,000 to $4,000
- Prices for personal coaching average $125 per hour

Topics

Some retreats have special guest speakers or activities that entail an additional charge to cover costs. When this is the case, retreat fee is adjusted to ensure that all costs are covered.

Course materials and activities included in the fees typically include the following:

- Daily breakfast and lunch
- Daily movement and meditation classes
- Course workbook

A non-refundable deposit of 20 percent of the total retreat fee is required for retreats payable at time of registration. The balance of the fee can be paid in two installments within 60 and 45 days of registration deadline. Cancellations result in a loss of 50 percent of the retreat price if made up 60 days prior to the retreat. Cancellations within six weeks of the retreat date will result in the total loss of funds. All cancellations must be made in writing. We strongly recommend that our clients use travel guard travel insurance.

We reserve the right to cancel the trip if it is not booked to the trip minimum and if we do so we will refund all deposits in full.

COMPETITION

There are many business seminars available to the public and there are also a wide variety of spiritually themed seminars and retreats. Our service meets at the intersection of these services. Moreover, we target our services to women who are now or who wish to be involved in expressing their spiritually at work or in business. Therefore, our target audience is more tightly defined as is our competition.

Through our research we have located other retreat centers in Northern California. Each of the retreats listed below maintains a physical facility and its programs are held on site. It is also possible to rent these facilities for seminars, retreats and events.

- *Total Woman Retreats and Seminars in Carmichael, CA:* specializes in religion and spirituality.

- *Santa Sabina Center in San Rafael, CA:* founded by the Dominican Sisters of San Rafael; open to spiritual seekers of all traditions; a place of study, prayer and community in support of contemplative spiritual exploration.

- *Angela Center in Santa Rosa, CA:* Sponsored by the Ursuline Sisters and grounded in the Catholic tradition. Open to people of diverse faiths and cultural backgrounds; offers a place for groups and non-profits for their own conferences or retreats.

- *Esalen in Big Sur, CA:* A retreat center and educational institute is comprised of a world-wide network of seekers. Holds workshops on site year-round ranging from one day to seven days.

Other possible competition includes any organization that offers the public similar programs to our own especially if they present their programs in the Northern California area. Because retreat and event planners often choose a variety of locations rather than one stable location, this competition could include anyone from religious groups to universities, many of which offer free or low-cost seminars.

The ranks of professional seminar and retreat providers are large and varied. The public has little to go on to judge the value of any particular seminar/retreat provider as the industry has little oversight.

A few possible competitors include:

- *Connie Clark:* Has held "Spa for the Spirit" retreats for women at Northern California locations.

- *Sheri Rosenthal:* Offers "The Art of Audacious Living" retreat and individual programs.

- *Margaret Wheatley:* Holds her program "A Path for Warriors of the Human Spirit" several times a year in Provo, UT and other locations.

INDUSTRY PROFILE

According to a report from Marketdata Enterprises, Inc., the self-improvement (SI) industry was worth an estimated $9.9 billion in the U.S. alone in 2005. The industry includes various market segments: infomercials, books, audio books, motivational speakers, seminars, personal coaching, weight loss, stress management and online education programs. Growth rate for the industry is projected at 6.1 percent average per year from 2012 to 2016.

Trends associated with the self-help industry include:

- Rising popularity of webinars due to lower cost.

- The development of women as a target market.

- Infomercials provide the largest sales volume.

- Self-improvement customers are most likely to be female, middle-aged, affluent and live on the two U.S. coasts.

The value of SI market segments in 2005 illustrates the most profitable segments. Of seminar attendees and SI book buyers, 70 percent are female.

The top market segments in descending order were:

- Weight loss programs

- Personal coaching

- Infomercials

- Holistic Institutes and training

- Books

- Audiotapes

- Public Seminars

Personal coaching is a largely unregulated industry segment. Coaches charge a monthly fee that ranges between $200 and $500 for weekly phone calls. Marketdata estimates that Personal Coaching is growing at a rate of 6 percent per year.

MARKET ANALYSIS

There are several markets that would be interested in our seminars:

- People who are transitioning in their lives and are seeking to make major changes and move in a new direction yet to be determined

- People who are working to develop a mindset of expansion and abundance

- Those who are considering starting their own business or moving their business to the next level

- Owners of small businesses

Target Market

Our target market exhibits the following characteristics:

- Women over age 30 that have income of at least $50,000 per year

- Those seeking to make a transition in their lives

- Those interested in finding meaning through their work or business

- Women interested in starting a business that brings a sense of fulfillment

Our marketing efforts will include levering off organizations, publications and web sites that cater to this demographic.

Strategy and Implementation

According to Marketdata, the self-improvement industry is experiencing the following challenges:

- No regulation or certification of the industry

- Passing of the old guard and few, if any, new names emerging on the scene

- Big name speakers are giving away more content as incentives to buy

- Higher priced retreats are not selling well

- Consumers are choosing books, CDs, free webinars, and podcasts over monthly coaching

Every successful self-help "guru" or expert has built their business on a book. We live in an information age where people expect to get information at the touch of a button. More than that, people are seeking solutions.

According to LiteraryMarketing.com, expertise in any field can be established by writing articles and books.

> "The ability to send your clients, and prospective clients, a book you have authored, or co-authored, for them to keep on their shelves and refer to on a regular basis provides an almost unparalleled tool for establishing yourself in your specialty area and making consistent contact with your target market."

Examples of self-help experts who have established their credibility with a book include:

- Tim Ferris —"The Four-Hour Work Week"

- Louise Hay—"You Can Heal Your Life"

- Deepak Chopra—"The Seven Spiritual Laws of Success"

Kerri Stahl has written her own book to express her beliefs and to tell her story. The book is called, "The Work Spirit: Finding Your Life's Purpose at Home and the Workplace."

Thanks to new digital technologies it is possible to publish and sell a book without investing thousands of dollars. Kerri self-published through Lightning Source, Inc. (LSI) and sells her book as a "print on demand" item. Because Lightning Source is part of the Ingram Content Group, books that they publish on demand are made available through Amazon, Barnes and Noble and other online book sales sites.

For print runs of at least 2,000 copies, LSI will print and send you the books for about $7 per copy.

Kerri has listed her book on her web site with a clickable link that takes customers to Amazon.com where they can buy the book. Every quarter LSI sends Kerri a sales report and a check for her share of the sale after costs. Kerri makes about $2 on each book sale.

While the book is not a significant profit center for her business, it does give her credibility and a platform to launch speaking engagements, coaching, retreats and seminars.

Marketing Programs

Our marketing efforts will be conducted largely online. Our web site and Facebook page will be most important. Our web site will house a blog with video posts of Kerri discussing topics of interest to our target demographic and will include links to buy her book, sign up for a personal coaching session and a link to sign up for our events. It will also include contact information and a contact form as well as a link so that visitors can join our mailing list to be informed of our events and updates.

To summarize, our marketing efforts will focus on the following:

- The website and video blog

- Email newsletter list

- Guest blogging on sites that cater to our target market

- Kerri's book

- Social media: Facebook, Pinterest, Instagram, LinkedIn, Google

Pricing Strategy

It's most important to price our seminars and retreats in such a way that all costs are covered and that we realize a gross profit of at least 40 percent. To that end we have set in place certain stipulations such as:

- A non-refundable deposit: this ensures that required non-refundable deposits we pay for facilities are covered

- Return policy: our return policy ensures that costs are covered even if an attendee cancels

- Discount for early registration: by offering a deep discount for early registration we increase the odds of completing the event and making a profit

- We aim for an average of $400 per participant, per day

Costs that must be covered in the pricing include:

- Transportation costs including cost of day tours for attendees

- Advertising

- Food and lodging for Kerri

- Meals for attendees

- Supplies

- Fee for assistant

- Fee for yoga/movement teachers

- Cost of group tours, entrance fees, tips

- Meeting rooms

The seminar and retreat prices must also include an appropriate profit.

Sales Strategy

Our sales strategy makes maximum use of web-based technologies such as:

- Email to our list

- Webinar with follow-up

- Blog articles with videos of Kerri

- Book

- Link to free webinar

- Link to schedule individual coaching session

- Testimonials from past attendees with links to their sites

- Links on our web site to our social media sites

The web site houses a calendar of upcoming events and links that enable customers to either contact us or sign up for seminars and retreats. Once they sign up, they will receive regular updates by email. These updates will include "homework" that they can do to prepare for the event.

Longer retreats have built-in time for attendees to relax and do whatever they want. We will use this down time to schedule a limited number of personal coaching sessions that attendees can book for an additional fee. Pre-registration is not required for these sessions as many attendees will not decide that they need one-on-one assistance until they start working through the main program materials.

Another source of revenue that leverages the retreat is the Intensive session. We offer a one-day Intensive prior to the event for an additional fee. We also offer a two-day Intensive following the event where clients will meet with Kerri for three hours each day. This gives attendees a mix of free time and personal coaching that will add value to their experience.

The day before the end of the retreat we present attendees with the opportunity to sign up for a Post-Retreat Course that consists of a series of webinars over the next three months.

Finally, we offer our retreat attendees the opportunity to join a long-term Post-Retreat Coaching Program lasting for six months. At a price of about $4,000 each, this strategy alone has the potential to add thousands to our bottom line.

Milestones

We plan to accomplish the following milestones over the next year.

Milestone	Start	End	Budget	Manager
Web site	October 2014	Feb 2015	1,200	Kerri
Social media sites	October 2014	Dec 2014	800	Kerri
Recruit social media admin	October 2014	Oct 2014	1,000	Kerri
First seminar	November 2014	Nov 2014	1,000	Kerri
Second seminar	February 2015	April 2015	1,000	Kerri
First retreat	September 2015	March 2016	3,000	Kerri
Totals			**8,000**	

MANAGEMENT SUMMARY

This is a small company with one key person at the helm, Kerri Stahl. So far we have added a freelance web site designer and a freelance social media consultant to our team. We hope to be able to employ a part-time administrative assistant in 2016 and move this person to full-time status as soon as possible.

For the present, we are using the services of a freelance virtual assistant to help us in our marketing activities, scheduling, emails and registration for events.

In an effort to automate as many processes as possible, we are utilizing a number of web-based tools including:

• *Acuity Scheduling:* handles bookings, cancellation, reminders and payments

• *GoogleDocs:* houses forms such as the application for Intensives

• *InfusionSoft:* email marketing and CRM (customer relationship management)

• *QuickBooks Online:* accounting in the cloud from any Internet-connected computer or device and the ability to take payments

Management Team

Kerri Stahl is the owner of Work Spirit Events. She earned her MBA at UC Berkeley and then began her rise up the corporate ladder. After 20 years Kerri realized that money and success do not automatically translate into personal fulfillment.

Two marriages and multiple relocations failed to bring the inner satisfaction that Kerri longer for. So she decided to leave the corporate race in search of the next step. Thanks to a successful IPO from one of her employers along with her savings, Kerri invested four years in study and personal reflection under the guidance of a well-known spiritual leader.

Kerri eventually took on the role of personal assistant to her teacher and helped him to manage and design his retreats.

Eventually Kerri wrote her own book based on her experiences and personal journey, "The Work Spirit: Finding Your Life's Purpose at Home and the Workplace."

PERSONNEL PLAN

We anticipate the following personnel implementations.

	Year 1	Year 2	Year 3
Owner	$25,000	$30,000	$40,000
Virtual assist	$12,000	$12,000	$12,000
Other contractors	$ 7,600	$ 6,300	$ 5,800
Total people	**5**	**5**	**5**
Total payroll	**$44,600**	**$48,300**	**$57,800**

FINANCIAL PLAN

Currently the company has received all funding from the owner Kerri Stahl who has invested $15,000 to cover the costs of equipment and initial services for startup.

In year one, we experienced a severe loss but this was expected because it takes several months to build up interest and registration in seminar and retreat events. The owner is committed to infusing the business with additional funding as needed but we fully expect to show profitability starting in year two.

Because we are able to contain costs by operating out of Kerri's home and by using online services and a virtual assistant, we do not anticipate the need to seek outside funding at this time.

Pro forma profit and loss

	Year 1	Year 2	Year 3
Sales	**$25,000**	**$65,000**	**$85,000**
Direct costs of sales	$ 6,250	$16,250	$21,250
Gross margin	$18,750	$48,750	$63,750
Gross margin %	75%	75%	75%
Expenses			
Virtual assistant	$12,000	$12,000	$12,000
Depreciation	$ 100	$ 100	$ 100
Rent	$ 0	$ 0	$ 0
Phone/Internet	$ 640	$ 960	$ 960
Insurance: liability life/disability	$ 1,350	$ 1,350	$ 1,350
Professional dues/memberships	$ 300	$ 300	$ 350
Advertising	$ 1,800	$ 1,800	$ 1,800
Office supplies	$ 200	$ 250	$ 300
Travel	$ 3,000	$ 3,400	$ 4,000
Web site services	$ 3,000	$ 2,500	$ 2,000
Other expenses	$ 400	$ 600	$ 800
Quickbooks	$ 350	$ 400	$ 500
Legal/accounting	$ 2,800	$ 2,000	$ 2,000
Social media services	$ 1,800	$ 1,800	$ 1,800
Total operating expenses	**$27,740**	**$27,460**	**$27,960**
Profit before interest and taxes	($ 8,990)	($21,290)	$35,790
Taxes incurred	($ 1,798)	($ 4,258)	$ 7,158
Net profit	**($ 7,192)**	**($17,032)**	**$28,632**
Net profit/sales	**−29%**	**−26%**	**34%**

Projected balance sheet

	Year 1	Year 2	Year 3
Assets			
Cash in bank	$5,000	$22,282	$51,164
Other current assets			
Total current assets	**$5,000**	**$22,282**	**$51,164**
Fixed assets			
Office furniture & equipment	$2,500	$ 2,500	$ 2,500
Less: depreciation	($ 250)	($ 500)	($ 750)
Total assets	**$7,250**	**$24,282**	**$52,914**
Liabilities			
Current liabilities			
Accounts payable	—	—	
Current maturities loan			
Total current liabilities	—	—	
Long term liabilities loan	$ 0		
Total liabilities	—	—	
Kerri Stahl, capital	$7,250	$24,282	$52,914
Total owner's equity	**$7,250**	**$24,282**	**$52,914**
Total liabilities & equity	**$7,250**	**$24,282**	**$52,914**

Senior Citizen Yoga Instructor Business

Youngberg Yoga LLC

5819 Centerville Ln.
Johnstown, NC 28500

Paul Greenland

Youngberg Yoga LLC is a yoga instruction business focusing on the senior citizen population.

EXECUTIVE SUMMARY

Youngberg Yoga LLC is a yoga instruction business focusing on the senior citizen population. The business' operations will consist mainly of two group classes (Yoga Foundations and Yoga Progressions) that are gentle in nature and emphasize stretching, strengthening, breathing and relaxation, awareness, range of movement, and alignment. In addition to physical health, these classes also provide participants with potential psychological benefits such as stress reduction, improved confidence, and lower rates of depression.

Youngberg Yoga is owned by Patricia Youngberg, whose professional background includes working as a full-time activities director for Johnstown Nursing Home. In addition, Youngberg has taught local yoga classes at several studios on a part-time basis for the past 11 years and has earned the Registered Yoga Teacher (RYT) designation after meeting the appropriate teaching experience requirements of the non-profit Yoga Alliance. The business will begin as a part-time operation and transition to a full-time enterprise, laying the foundation for the eventual establishment of a physical yoga studio specifically for the senior population.

INDUSTRY ANALYSIS

According to the Yoga Alliance (the largest non-profit association serving the yoga industry), there were more than 3,700 Registered Yoga Schools and approximately 60,000 Registered Yoga Teachers in 2015. The organization's mission is "to promote and support the integrity and diversity of the teaching of yoga." The Yoga Alliance recognizes many different yoga styles and is committed to industry advocacy. Its member teachers and schools benefit from guidance related to effective business practices. In addition, the organization supports scholarship programs and is involved in developing strategic alliances that benefit the yoga industry. More information is available at www.yogaalliance.org.

MARKET ANALYSIS

National & State Outlook

According to *The State of Aging and Health in America 2013*, a report developed by the Centers for Disease Control and Prevention, U.S. Department of Health and Human Services, the population of older adults in the United States is experiencing unprecedented growth. Key drivers for this growth include the aging baby boomer population, as well as longer life spans in general.

Based on data from the U.S. Census Bureau, the number of individuals over the age of 65 totaled 40.2 million in 2010 (13% of the population). This figure is projected to reach 54.8 million (16.1%) by 2020 and 72.1 million (19.3%) by 2030. In North Carolina, specifically, adults over age 65 accounted for 12.4 percent of the population in 2010. Consistent with national trends, this figure is projected to increase, reaching 13.7 percent by 2015, 15.1 percent by 2020, 16.6 percent by 2025, and 17.8 percent by 2030.

Local Outlook

The population of Johnstown, North Carolina, included 102,599 people in 2014. Individuals over the age of 55 accounted for 34.3 percent of the population (much higher than the national average of 25.4 percent). By 2019 the population is projected to reach 132,712, at which time individuals over 55 will account for 34.5 percent of the population (compared to 27.3 percent nationally).

Key Prospects

Specifically, Youngberg Yoga will concentrate its marketing efforts on area retirement communities, senior centers, senior apartment facilities, and nursing homes. Key prospects include Wind Pointe Center, Sharingham Estates, Highfield Towers, Greenview Terrace, Timberline Center, and Parkview Plaza. These retirement communities and apartment complexes are home to nearly 1,000 senior citizen residents.

Beyond Johnstown, significant senior populations also exist in the nearby communities of Fenton, Streeter, Wentworth, Lexington Ridge, and Cantwell, offering opportunities for growth beyond the business' initial primary market. Key prospects in these communities include, but are not limited to, The Village, Vista Cove, Terraces at Langford, and Regency Park.

SERVICES

Encompassing the heart, spirit, body, and mind, yoga essentially is a wellness program dating back more than 2,000 years to ancient India. There are many different styles of yoga. Youngberg Yoga's classes are based on Hatha yoga, which includes meditation skills, postures (asana), and breathing practice (pranayama). Youngberg Yoga will begin by offering two levels of fitness-based group classes:

1. *Yoga Foundations:* Participants in Yoga Foundations do all exercises standing or seated in a chair. This course is ideal for older seniors (ages 70+) and those with physical limitations.

2. *Yoga Progressions:* This course follows the same approach as Yoga Foundations, but is designed for younger seniors (ages 55-69), or those with greater flexibility, strength, and mobility.

Both Yoga Foundations and Yoga Progressions are gentle classes emphasizing stretching, strengthening, breathing and relaxation, awareness, range of movement, and alignment. The courses build participants' confidence by progressing from basic versions of yoga poses to more complicated ones. The environment is non-competitive, and each individual's unique capabilities and circumstances are honored at all times.

Youngberg Yoga will charge participants a fee of $12.50 per week ($50/month) for each class. Sessions will last 1 hour and will be offered twice per week.

Benefits

Seniors who attend Yoga Foundations or Yoga Progressions may reap a number of potential benefits, including, but not limited to:

- Blood Sugar Control

- Chronic Pain Management

- Decreased Fall Risks

- Depression Reduction

- Enhanced Sleep Quality

- Higher Energy Levels

- Improved Balance

- Improved Body Awareness

- Improved Bone Density

- Improved Respiratory Function

- Increased Confidence

- Stress Reduction

PERSONNEL

Youngberg Yoga is owned by Patricia Youngberg, whose professional background includes working as a full-time activities director for Johnstown Nursing Home. In addition, Youngberg has taught local yoga classes at several studios on a part-time basis for the past 11 years. After teaching a course specifically for seniors at Johnstown Nursing Home, Youngberg was inspired to bring the program to more seniors, realizing that this growing population is in need of exercise, but often faces limited options when physical conditions prevent participation in classes such as spinning, weightlifting, or walking. In addition to physical health, yoga also provides elderly participants with potential psychological benefits such as stress reduction, improved confidence, and lower rates of depression. Youngberg's passion for and experience working with the senior population, as well as her yoga instruction experience, position her for success in this new venture.

Youngberg has earned the Registered Yoga Teacher (RYT) designation after meeting the appropriate teaching experience requirements at a Registered Yoga School (RYS) recognized by the non-profit Yoga Alliance. Specifically, she presently holds a RYT 500 designation, and will soon meet the qualifications for Experienced Registered Yoga Teacher (E-RYT 200). Additionally, because she will be teaching yoga on her own and not for a local studio, Youngberg has completed a small business certificate program at a local community college, providing with foundational business management skills.

Professional and Advisory Support

Youngberg Yoga has established her LLC using documents from a popular online legal document service. In addition, she will utilize accounting and tax preparation software programs to handle her own bookkeeping and tax preparation. A commercial checking account has been established with a local community bank. Although most class registrations will be paid for via check, Youngberg also will use a popular mobile point-of-sale service to accept credit card and debit card payments from customers.

GROWTH STRATEGY

Year One: Begin offering Yoga Foundations and Yoga Progressions sessions at local retirement communities, senior centers, senior apartment facilities, and nursing homes on a part-time basis. Achieve gross revenues of $24,000.

Year Two: Transition Youngberg Yoga to a full-time operation. Introduce private (one-on-one) lessons for seniors with mild dementia and Alzheimer's, as well as a class designed specifically for joint attendance by both seniors and their caregivers. Achieve gross revenues of $48,000.

Year Three: Begin exploring options to establish a dedicated local studio. Achieve gross revenues of $72,000.

OPERATIONS

Location

Youngberg Yoga will begin operations as a part-time business. Patricia Youngberg will handle administrative tasks from a dedicated home office and provide courses directly at local facilities (retirement communities, senior centers, senior apartment facilities, and nursing homes). She will contract directly with program directors and administrators to provide group classes 48 weeks per year.

Equipment

Patricia Youngberg will invest in a set of yoga mats and yoga blocks for use during her courses. Facilities will be responsible for providing chairs that participants can use.

Legal

Youngberg Yoga has secured an appropriate level of liability insurance. However, participants will be required to obtain a physician's release and sign a liability waiver prior to taking any class.

MARKETING & SALES

Youngberg Yoga has developed a marketing strategy that includes the following tactics:

1. Publication of an online profile in the Yoga Alliance Registry, providing others with verification that Patricia Youngberg has met the organization's minimum teaching experience requirements.

2. Relationship building with area retirement communities, senior centers, senior apartment facilities, and nursing homes.

3. Four-color flyers showing photographs of seniors participating in yoga and describing the Yoga Foundations and Yoga Progression courses.

4. A regular schedule of presentations to local retirement groups, churches, and service clubs.

5. Word-of-mouth marketing to drive referrals and increase attendance.

6. A Web site with complete details about Youngberg Yoga. Specifically, the site will feature video clips of seniors participating in the Yoga Foundations or Yoga Progressions classes, in order to make prospective attendees receptive to the idea of participating. The site also will feature information about Patricia Youngberg, as well as general information about the benefits of yoga.

7. A media relations strategy that involves guest appearances/columns focused on the benefits of yoga for seniors. This will entail participation on noon and morning shows of local network affiliates

(e.g., ABC, NBC, CBS, and FOX), as well as interviews on a popular local AM radio station that has a strong senior citizen following. Youngberg also will submit occasional articles to local newspapers that reach older readers in the market.

This marketing plan will be reviewed semi-annually.

FINANCIAL ANALYSIS

Youngberg Yoga has prepared a complete set of pro forma financial statements, which are available upon request. The following table provides an overview of key projections for years one through three:

	2015	2016	2017
Revenue	**$24,000**	**$48,000**	**$72,000**
Expenses			
Salary	$14,500	$30,000	$50,000
Payroll taxes	$ 2,175	$ 4,500	$ 7,500
Insurance	$ 2,500	$ 2,625	$ 2,756
Office supplies	$ 350	$ 350	$ 350
Equipment	$ 750	$ 500	$ 500
Marketing & advertising	$ 2,000	$ 3,000	$ 4,000
Telecommunications & Internet	$ 1,200	$ 1,200	$ 1,200
Professional development	$ 350	$ 350	$ 350
Subscriptions & dues	$ 75	$ 75	$ 75
Total expenses	**$23,900**	**$42,600**	**$66,731**
Net income	**$ 100**	**$ 5,400**	**$ 5,269**

Tree Removal and Stump Grinding Service

Sapp's Tree Removal and Stump Grinding, LLC

2256 Denton-Hazlehurst Rd.
Denton, Georgia 31532

Fran Fletcher

Sapp's Tree Removal and Stump Grinding, LLC is located in Denton, Georgia and is owned a
Terrell Sapp.

BUSINESS SUMMARY

Sapp's Tree Removal and Stump Grinding, LLC is located in Denton, Georgia and is own
operated by Terrell Sapp. Mr. Sapp got the idea for this business when his place of employment
and he was forced to find another source of income.

Located in the heart of South Georgia, Sapp's Tree Removal and Stump Grinding will serve custor
within a 60-mile radius of Denton. According to census data, there are more than 41,000 househo
located within the service area, and many businesses as well.

According to the Bureau of Labor Statistics, the jobs in the grounds maintenance category are expected
to increase by 13% over the next decade. South Georgia is plagued with storms, especially during the
summer and fall, which leads to downed trees that need to be removed.

Sapp's Tree Removal and Stump Grinding will offer the following services to residential and business
clients:

- Tree removal

- Stump grinding

- Fallen tree removal

- Limb removal

- Clean-up services

- Emergency removal

There are several businesses in the area offering similar services, but none more dedicated to success and
to providing excellent customer service as Sapp's.

The overall growth strategy of Sapp's Tree Removal and Stump Grinding is to become the go-to
business in the area for tree removal and stump grinding services. The owner understands the
importance of referrals and the company will strive to provide excellent customer service. The owner
also plans to bid on city and county contracts as opportunities arise.

The owner anticipates modest profits from the beginning. During the first year of operation, he expects a steady increase in income and profits as his advertising methods become established and as he starts receiving referrals from satisfied customers. If projections are correct, Mr. Sapp will need to hire additional workers and buy additional equipment during the second year.

Start-up costs will include purchasing used tools and machinery that are in excellent working condition. Associated costs for start-up are estimated at $81,300. The owner is currently seeking financing in the form of a business line of credit in the amount of $118,800 to cover start-up and operating expenses for the first three months. Payments to the line of credit will be paid monthly and a percentage of the profits will be paid on the principal each year. If profits are obtained as anticipated, the loan should be repaid within five years.

COMPANY DESCRIPTION

Location

Mr. Sapp will operate Sapp's Tree Removal and Stump Grinding from his home office in Denton, Georgia.

Hours of Operation

Sapp's Tree Removal and Stump Grinding will operate by appointment as follows:

Monday—Thursday, 7 AM—6 PM

Friday—Sunday (Emergencies Only)

Personnel

Terrell Sapp (owner)

Mr. Sapp will provide estimates, schedule jobs, provide services, and coordinate billing. Mr. Sapp has 20 years experience working in industrial maintenance. During his tenure, he was trained in heavy equipment operation and OSHA safety regulations.

Trevor Sapp

Mr. Sapp will serve as foreman and provide tree removal and stump grinding services. Mr. Sapp worked at a commercial landscaping business for two years, where he learned to prune limbs from different types of trees, eliminate unsightly stumps, and provide clean-up after rendering services.

Employees

Two experienced full-time employees will be hired to assist with tree removal and stump grinding services.

Products and Services

Services

Sapp's Tree Removal and Stump Grinding will offer the following services:

- Tree removal
- Stump grinding
- Fallen tree removal
- Limb removal
- Clean-up services
- Emergency removal

MARKET ANALYSIS

Industry Overview

According to the Bureau of Labor Statistics, the job outlook for grounds maintenance workers is expected to increase by 13% over the next decade. South Georgia is plagued with storms, especially during the summer and fall, which leads to downed trees that need to be removed.

Target Market

Sapp's Tree Removal and Stump Grinding will target customers within a 60-mile radius of Denton, Georgia.

According to census data, there are more than 41,000 households within a 60-mile radius of Denton, which is located in Jeff Davis County, Georgia. Those households and businesses in the area will serve as a large customer base for Mr. Sapp.

Competition

Sapp's Tree Removal and Stump Grinding is not the only business of this type in the area. The following businesses also offer similar services within parts of the same territory.

1. Bill's Stump Grinding, Douglas, Georgia. Offers stump grinding services on both residential and commercial properties.

2. Osplunge, Savannah, Georgia. Primarily offers tree removal and trimming services to electric companies. The Savannah office also offers residential services in south central Georgia.

3. Ocilla Tree Trimming, Ocilla, Georgia. Trims trees for residential and commercial properties.

Sapp's Tree Removal and Stump Grinding plans to set itself apart from the competition by specializing in tree removal and stump grinding. The business will also strive to perform emergency services within two hours and to schedule normal services within one week.

GROWTH STRATEGY

The overall growth strategy of Sapp's Tree Removal and Stump Grinding is to become the go-to business in the area for tree removal and stump grinding services. The owner understands the importance of referrals and the company will strive to provide excellent customer service and timely maintenance services.

The owner also plans to bid on city and county contracts as opportunities arise.

The owners expect the business to take off in the first year of operation and anticipate hiring additional workers and buying additional equipment during the second year of operation.

Sales and Marketing

The company has identified key sales and marketing tactics to support the company's growth strategy.

Initial advertising will include:

*   Advertising in area newspapers

Ongoing marketing strategies include:

*   Advertising in area newspapers

*   Free estimates

*   A referral rewards program—20% discount for a single tree removal

FINANCIAL ANALYSIS

Start-up Costs

The owners will have to purchase some essential equipment to start the business. In order to cut costs, used equipment that is in good working condition will be purchased. Equipment costs will be the largest start-up expense.

Estimated start-up costs

Bucket truck	$20,000
Stump grinder	$ 7,000
Chipper	$10,000
Dump truck	$17,000
Chain saws	$ 4,000
Trailer	$ 5,000
Truck	$10,000
Climbing equipment	$ 1,000
Business license	$ 1,000
Initial advertising	$ 500
Insurance	$ 4,000
Legal fees	$ 1,800
Total	**$81,300**

Estimated Monthly Expenses

Monthly expenses are expected to remain constant each month.

Monthly expenses

Loan payment	$ 1,000.00
Phone/Internet	$ 150.00
Advertising	$ 100.00
Insurance	$ 250.00
Wages owner	$ 4,000.00
Wages employees	$ 6,000.00
Equipment maintenance	$ 1,000.00
Total	**$12,500.00**

Estimated Monthly Income

The number of jobs will determine monthly income. The owner expects to at least provide one tree removal and one stump grinding service each day (Monday through Thursday) for an estimated monthly income of $16,000.

Prices for Services

Prices for services are dependent upon many factors:

- The size of the tree (height, diameter, number of limbs)

- The proximity to structures, streets, power lines

- The type of tree

- The condition of the tree (healthy, dead, or dying)

Services	Price	
	Hardwood	Pine
Tree removal	$ 500–$2,000	$ 500–$1,000
Tree removal with clean-up	$1,000–$5,000	$1,000–$3,000
Tree removal with stump grinding	$1,000–$3,500	$1,000–$2,800
Tree removal with clean-up and stump grinding	$1,000–$5,000	$1,000–$3,000
Stump grinding	$ 75–$ 350	$ 35–$ 75
Fallen tree removal	$ 300–$1,000	$ 300–$1,000
Limb removal	$ 150 per hour	$ 150 per hour
Emergency removal	$ 500 + cost	$ 500 + cost

Profit/Loss

According to conservative estimated expenses and income data, modest profits are expected from the beginning and are expected to steadily increase as referrals grow and advertising measures become established.

The summer and fall months should see an increase in demand for services since the service area is prone to summer storms and hurricanes in the fall. Conservative estimates show that one tree removal and stump grinding service will be provided four days per week for a monthly income of $16,000. For the months of June to November, conservative estimates show that in addition to the monthly income, an additional $2,000 per month will be earned for emergency calls.

Income is expected to increase by 10% each year and expenses are expected to increase by 6% each year. Profits will be used to purchase additional equipment and hire employees as needed.

Monthly profit/loss

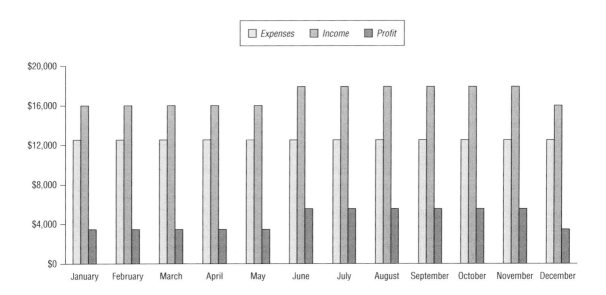

Yearly profit/loss

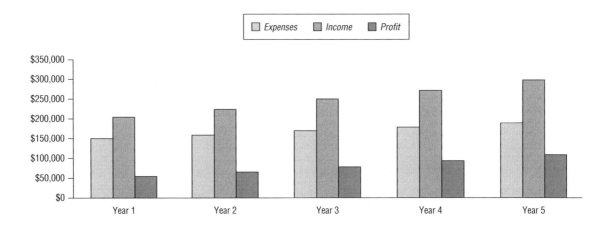

Financing

Sapp's Tree Removal and Stump Grinding is currently seeking financing in the form of a business line of credit in the amount of $118,800. This would cover start-up and operating expenses for the first three months. The business will pay $1,000 per month toward repayment and will also pay 20% of the annual profit at the end of each year. The Repayment Plan chart shows that the loan will be paid within five years. The owner will reinvest remaining profits into the company by buying additional equipment.

Repayment plan

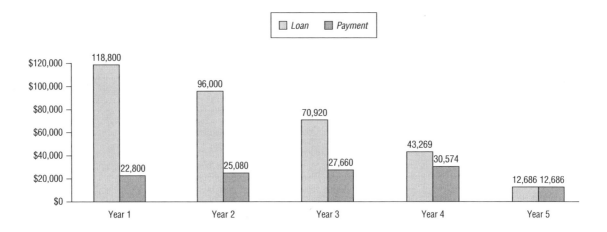

BUSINESS PLAN TEMPLATE

USING THIS TEMPLATE

A business plan carefully spells out a company's projected course of action over a period of time, usually the first two to three years after the start-up. In addition, banks, lenders, and other investors examine the information and financial documentation before deciding whether or not to finance a new business venture. Therefore, a business plan is an essential tool in obtaining financing and should describe the business itself in detail as well as all important factors influencing the company, including the market, industry, competition, operations and management policies, problem solving strategies, financial resources and needs, and other vital information. The plan enables the business owner to anticipate costs, plan for difficulties, and take advantage of opportunities, as well as design and implement strategies that keep the company running as smoothly as possible.

This template has been provided as a model to help you construct your own business plan. Please keep in mind that there is no single acceptable format for a business plan, and that this template is in no way comprehensive, but serves as an example.

The business plans provided in this section are fictional and have been used by small business agencies as models for clients to use in compiling their own business plans.

GENERIC BUSINESS PLAN

Main headings included below are topics that should be covered in a comprehensive business plan. They include:

Business Summary

Purpose
Provides a brief overview of your business, succinctly highlighting the main ideas of your plan.

Includes

- Name and Type of Business
- Description of Product/Service
- Business History and Development
- Location
- Market

- Competition
- Management
- Financial Information
- Business Strengths and Weaknesses
- Business Growth

Table of Contents

Purpose
Organized in an Outline Format, the Table of Contents illustrates the selection and arrangement of information contained in your plan.

Includes

- Topic Headings and Subheadings
- Page Number References

Business History and Industry Outlook

Purpose
Examines the conception and subsequent development of your business within an industry specific context.

Includes

- Start-up Information
- Owner/Key Personnel Experience
- Location
- Development Problems and Solutions
- Investment/Funding Information
- Future Plans and Goals
- Market Trends and Statistics
- Major Competitors
- Product/Service Advantages
- National, Regional, and Local Economic Impact

Product/Service

Purpose
Introduces, defines, and details the product and/or service that inspired the information of your business.

Includes

- Unique Features
- Niche Served
- Market Comparison
- Stage of Product/Service Development
- Production
- Facilities, Equipment, and Labor
- Financial Requirements
- Product/Service Life Cycle
- Future Growth

Market Examination

Purpose
Assessment of product/service applications in relation to consumer buying cycles.

Includes

- Target Market
- Consumer Buying Habits
- Product/Service Applications
- Consumer Reactions
- Market Factors and Trends
- Penetration of the Market
- Market Share
- Research and Studies
- Cost
- Sales Volume and Goals

Competition

Purpose
Analysis of Competitors in the Marketplace.

Includes

- Competitor Information
- Product/Service Comparison
- Market Niche
- Product/Service Strengths and Weaknesses
- Future Product/Service Development

Marketing

Purpose

Identifies promotion and sales strategies for your product/service.

Includes

- Product/Service Sales Appeal
- Special and Unique Features
- Identification of Customers
- Sales and Marketing Staff
- Sales Cycles
- Type of Advertising/ Promotion
- Pricing
- Competition
- Customer Services

Operations

Purpose

Traces product/service development from production/inception to the market environment.

Includes

- Cost Effective Production Methods
- Facility
- Location
- Equipment
- Labor
- Future Expansion

Administration and Management

Purpose

Offers a statement of your management philosophy with an in-depth focus on processes and procedures.

Includes

- Management Philosophy
- Structure of Organization
- Reporting System
- Methods of Communication
- Employee Skills and Training
- Employee Needs and Compensation
- Work Environment
- Management Policies and Procedures
- Roles and Responsibilities

Key Personnel

Purpose

Describes the unique backgrounds of principle employees involved in business.

Includes

- Owner(s)/Employee Education and Experience
- Positions and Roles
- Benefits and Salary
- Duties and Responsibilities
- Objectives and Goals

Potential Problems and Solutions

Purpose

Discussion of problem solving strategies that change issues into opportunities.

Includes

- Risks
- Litigation
- Future Competition
- Economic Impact
- Problem Solving Skills

Financial Information

Purpose

Secures needed funding and assistance through worksheets and projections detailing financial plans, methods of repayment, and future growth opportunities.

Includes

- Financial Statements
- Bank Loans
- Methods of Repayment
- Tax Returns

- Start-up Costs
- Projected Income (3 years)
- Projected Cash Flow (3 Years)
- Projected Balance Statements (3 years)

Appendices

Purpose

Supporting documents used to enhance your business proposal.

Includes

- Photographs of product, equipment, facilities, etc.
- Copyright/Trademark Documents
- Legal Agreements
- Marketing Materials
- Research and or Studies

- Operation Schedules
- Organizational Charts
- Job Descriptions
- Resumes
- Additional Financial Documentation

New program starting January 4th, 2024

Nuevo programa a partir del 4 de Enero de 2024

Open Play/Juego Abierto

**Thursdays/Jueves 2 - 3pm
Ages 0-5 & Cargivers/
Edades 0-5 y Adultos**

 **EAGLE VALLEY LIBRARY DISTRICT**

Gypsum Public Library
47 Lundgren Blvd. | P.O. Box 979
Gypsum, Colorado 81637
970-524-5080
www.evld.org

Fictional Food Distributor

Commercial Foods, Inc.

3003 Avondale Ave.
Knoxville, TN 37920

This plan demonstrates how a partnership can have a positive impact on a new business. It demonstrates how two individuals can carve a niche in the specialty foods market by offering gourmet foods to upscale restaurants and fine hotels. This plan is fictional and has not been used to gain funding from a bank or other lending institution.

STATEMENT OF PURPOSE

Commercial Foods, Inc. seeks a loan of $75,000 to establish a new business. This sum, together with $5,000 equity investment by the principals, will be used as follows:

- Merchandise inventory $25,000
- Office fixture/equipment $12,000
- Warehouse equipment $14,000
- One delivery truck $10,000
- Working capital $39,000
- Total $100,000

DESCRIPTION OF THE BUSINESS

Commercial Foods, Inc. will be a distributor of specialty food service products to hotels and upscale restaurants in the geographical area of a 50 mile radius of Knoxville. Richard Roberts will direct the sales effort and John Williams will manage the warehouse operation and the office. One delivery truck will be used initially with a second truck added in the third year. We expect to begin operation of the business within 30 days after securing the requested financing.

MANAGEMENT

A. Richard Roberts is a native of Memphis, Tennessee. He is a graduate of Memphis State University with a Bachelor's degree from the School of Business. After graduation, he worked for a major manufacturer of specialty food service products as a detail sales person for five years, and, for the past three years, he has served as a product sales manager for this firm.

B. John Williams is a native of Nashville, Tennessee. He holds a B.S. Degree in Food Technology from the University of Tennessee. His career includes five years as a product development chemist in gourmet food products and five years as operations manager for a food service distributor.

Both men are healthy and energetic. Their backgrounds complement each other, which will ensure the success of Commercial Foods, Inc. They will set policies together and personnel decisions will be made jointly. Initial salaries for the owners will be $1,000 per month for the first few years. The spouses of both principals are successful in the business world and earn enough to support the families.

They have engaged the services of Foster Jones, CPA, and William Hale, Attorney, to assist them in an advisory capacity.

PERSONNEL

The firm will employ one delivery truck driver at a wage of $8.00 per hour. One office worker will be employed at $7.50 per hour. One part-time employee will be used in the office at $5.00 per hour. The driver will load and unload his own trucks. Mr. Williams will assist in the warehouse operation as needed to assist one stock person at $7.00 per hour. An additional delivery truck and driver will be added the third year.

LOCATION

The firm will lease a 20,000 square foot building at 3003 Avondale Ave., in Knoxville, which contains warehouse and office areas equipped with two-door truck docks. The annual rental is $9,000. The building was previously used as a food service warehouse and very little modification to the building will be required.

PRODUCTS AND SERVICES

The firm will offer specialty food service products such as soup bases, dessert mixes, sauce bases, pastry mixes, spices, and flavors, normally used by upscale restaurants and nice hotels. We are going after a niche in the market with high quality gourmet products. There is much less competition in this market than in standard run of the mill food service products. Through their work experiences, the principals have contacts with supply sources and with local chefs.

THE MARKET

We know from our market survey that there are over 200 hotels and upscale restaurants in the area we plan to serve. Customers will be attracted by a direct sales approach. We will offer samples of our products and product application data on use of our products in the finished prepared foods. We will cultivate the chefs in these establishments. The technical background of John Williams will be especially useful here.

COMPETITION

We find that we will be only distributor in the area offering a full line of gourmet food service products. Other foodservice distributors offer only a few such items in conjunction with their standard product line. Our survey shows that many of the chefs are ordering products from Atlanta and Memphis because of a lack of adequate local supply.

SUMMARY

Commercial Foods, Inc. will be established as a foodservice distributor of specialty food in Knoxville. The principals, with excellent experience in the industry, are seeking a $75,000 loan to establish the business. The principals are investing $25,000 as equity capital.

The business will be set up as an S Corporation with each principal owning 50% of the common stock in the corporation.

FICTIONAL HARDWARE STORE

OSHKOSH HARDWARE, INC.

123 Main St.
Oshkosh, WI 54901

The following plan outlines how a small hardware store can survive competition from large discount chains by offering products and providing expert advice in the use of any product it sells. This plan is fictional and has not been used to gain funding from a bank or other lending institution.

EXECUTIVE SUMMARY

Oshkosh Hardware, Inc. is a new corporation that is going to establish a retail hardware store in a strip mall in Oshkosh, Wisconsin. The store will sell hardware of all kinds, quality tools, paint, and housewares. The business will make revenue and a profit by servicing its customers not only with needed hardware but also with expert advice in the use of any product it sells.

Oshkosh Hardware, Inc. will be operated by its sole shareholder, James Smith. The company will have a total of four employees. It will sell its products in the local market. Customers will buy our products because we will provide free advice on the use of all of our products and will also furnish a full refund warranty.

Oshkosh Hardware, Inc. will sell its products in the Oshkosh store staffed by three sales representatives. No additional employees will be needed to achieve its short and long range goals. The primary short range goal is to open the store by October 1, 1994. In order to achieve this goal a lease must be signed by July 1, 1994 and the complete inventory ordered by August 1, 1994.

Mr. James Smith will invest $30,000 in the business. In addition, the company will have to borrow $150,000 during the first year to cover the investment in inventory, accounts receivable, and furniture and equipment. The company will be profitable after six months of operation and should be able to start repayment of the loan in the second year.

THE BUSINESS

The business will sell hardware of all kinds, quality tools, paint, and housewares. We will purchase our products from three large wholesale buying groups.

In general our customers are homeowners who do their own repair and maintenance, hobbyists, and housewives. Our business is unique in that we will have a complete line of all hardware items and will be able to get special orders by overnight delivery. The business makes revenue and profits by servicing our customers not only with needed hardware but also with expert advice in the use of any product we sell. Our major costs for bringing our products to market are cost of merchandise of 36%, salaries of $45,000, and occupancy costs of $60,000.

191

Oshkosh Hardware, Inc.'s retail outlet will be located at 1524 Frontage Road, which is in a newly developed retail center of Oshkosh. Our location helps facilitate accessibility from all parts of town and reduces our delivery costs. The store will occupy 7500 square feet of space. The major equipment involved in our business is counters and shelving, a computer, a paint mixing machine, and a truck.

THE MARKET

Oshkosh Hardware, Inc. will operate in the local market. There are 15,000 potential customers in this market area. We have three competitors who control approximately 98% of the market at present. We feel we can capture 25% of the market within the next four years. Our major reason for believing this is that our staff is technically competent to advise our customers in the correct use of all products we sell.

After a careful market analysis, we have determined that approximately 60% of our customers are men and 40% are women. The percentage of customers that fall into the following age categories are:

Under 16: 0%
17-21: 5%
22-30: 30%
31-40: 30%
41-50: 20%
51-60: 10%
61-70: 5%
Over 70: 0%

The reasons our customers prefer our products is our complete knowledge of their use and our full refund warranty.

We get our information about what products our customers want by talking to existing customers. There seems to be an increasing demand for our product. The demand for our product is increasing in size based on the change in population characteristics.

SALES

At Oshkosh Hardware, Inc. we will employ three sales people and will not need any additional personnel to achieve our sales goals. These salespeople will need several years experience in home repair and power tool usage. We expect to attract 30% of our customers from newspaper ads, 5% of our customers from local directories, 5% of our customers from the yellow pages, 10% of our customers from family and friends, and 50% of our customers from current customers. The most cost effect source will be current customers. In general our industry is growing.

MANAGEMENT

We would evaluate the quality of our management staff as being excellent. Our manager is experienced and very motivated to achieve the various sales and quality assurance objectives we have set. We will use a management information system that produces key inventory, quality assurance, and sales data on a weekly basis. All data is compared to previously established goals for that week, and deviations are the primary focus of the management staff.

GOALS IMPLEMENTATION

The short term goals of our business are:

1. Open the store by October 1, 1994
2. Reach our breakeven point in two months
3. Have sales of $100,000 in the first six months

In order to achieve our first short term goal we must:

1. Sign the lease by July 1, 1994
2. Order a complete inventory by August 1, 1994

In order to achieve our second short term goal we must:

1. Advertise extensively in Sept. and Oct.
2. Keep expenses to a minimum

In order to achieve our third short term goal we must:

1. Promote power tool sales for the Christmas season
2. Keep good customer traffic in Jan. and Feb.

The long term goals for our business are:

1. Obtain sales volume of $600,000 in three years
2. Become the largest hardware dealer in the city
3. Open a second store in Fond du Lac

The most important thing we must do in order to achieve the long term goals for our business is to develop a highly profitable business with excellent cash flow.

FINANCE

Oshkosh Hardware, Inc. Faces some potential threats or risks to our business. They are discount house competition. We believe we can avoid or compensate for this by providing quality products complimented by quality advice on the use of every product we sell. The financial projections we have prepared are located at the end of this document.

JOB DESCRIPTION-GENERAL MANAGER

The General Manager of the business of the corporation will be the president of the corporation. He will be responsible for the complete operation of the retail hardware store which is owned by the corporation. A detailed description of his duties and responsibilities is as follows.

Sales

Train and supervise the three sales people. Develop programs to motivate and compensate these employees. Coordinate advertising and sales promotion effects to achieve sales totals as outlined in budget. Oversee purchasing function and inventory control procedures to insure adequate merchandise at all times at a reasonable cost.

Finance

Prepare monthly and annual budgets. Secure adequate line of credit from local banks. Supervise office personnel to insure timely preparation of records, statements, all government reports, control of receivables and payables, and monthly financial statements.

Administration

Perform duties as required in the areas of personnel, building leasing and maintenance, licenses and permits, and public relations.

Organizations, Agencies, & Consultants

A listing of Associations and Consultants of interest to entrepreneurs, followed by the Small Business Administration Regional Offices, Small Business Development Centers, Service Corps of Retired Executives offices, and Venture Capital and Finance Companies.

Associations

This section contains a listing of associations and other agencies of interest to the small business owner. Entries are listed alphabetically by organization name.

American Business Women's Association
9100 Ward Pkwy.
PO Box 8728
Kansas City, MO 64114-0728
(800)228-0007
E-mail: abwa@abwa.org
Website: http://www.abwa.org
Jeanne Banks, National President

American Franchisee Association
53 W Jackson Blvd., Ste. 1157
Chicago, IL 60604
(312)431-0545
E-mail: info@franchisee.org
Website: http://www.franchisee.org
Susan P. Kezios, President

American Independent Business Alliance
222 S Black Ave.
Bozeman, MT 59715
(406)582-1255
E-mail: info@amiba.net
Website: http://www.amiba.net
Jennifer Rockne, Director

American Small Businesses Association
206 E College St., Ste. 201
Grapevine, TX 76051
800-942-2722
E-mail: info@asbaonline.org
Website: http://www.asbaonline.org/

American Women's Economic Development Corporation
216 East 45th St., 10th Floor
New York, NY 10017
(917)368-6100
Fax: (212)986-7114
E-mail: info@awed.org
Website: http://www.awed.org
Roseanne Antonucci, Exec. Dir.

Association for Enterprise Opportunity
1601 N Kent St., Ste. 1101
Arlington, VA 22209
(703)841-7760
Fax: (703)841-7748
E-mail: aeo@assoceo.org
Website: http://www.microenterprise works.org
Bill Edwards, Exec.Dir.

Association of Small Business Development Centers
c/o Don Wilson
8990 Burke Lake Rd.
Burke, VA 22015
(703)764-9850
Fax: (703)764-1234
E-mail: info@asbdc-us.org
Website: http://www.asbdc-us.org
Don Wilson, Pres./CEO

BEST Employers Association
2505 McCabe Way
Irvine, CA 92614
(949)253-4080
800-433-0088
Fax: (714)553-0883
E-mail: info@bestlife.com
Website: http://www.bestlife.com
Donald R. Lawrenz, CEO

Center for Family Business
PO Box 24219
Cleveland, OH 44124
(440)460-5409
E-mail: grummi@aol.com
Dr. Leon A. Danco, Chm.

Coalition for Government Procurement
1990 M St. NW, Ste. 400
Washington, DC 20036
(202)331-0975
E-mail: info@thecgp.org
Website: http://www.coalgovpro.org
Paul Caggiano, Pres.

Employers of America
PO Box 1874
Mason City, IA 50402-1874
(641)424-3187
800-728-3187
Fax: (641)424-1673
E-mail: employer@employerhelp.org
Website: http://www.employerhelp.org
Jim Collison, Pres.

Family Firm Institute
200 Lincoln St., Ste. 201
Boston, MA 02111
(617)482-3045
Fax: (617)482-3049
E-mail: ffi@ffi.org
Website: http://www.ffi.org
Judy L. Green, Ph.D., Exec.Dir.

Independent Visually Impaired Enterprisers
500 S 3rd St., Apt. H
Burbank, CA 91502
(818)238-9321
E-mail: abazyn@bazyncommunications.com
Website: http://www.acb.org/affiliates
Adris Bazyn, Pres.

International Association for Business Organizations
3 Woodthorn Ct., Ste. 12
Owings Mills, MD 21117
(410)581-1373
E-mail: nahbb@msn.com
Rudolph Lewis, Exec. Officer

International Council for Small Business
The George Washington University School of Business and Public Management
2115 G St. NW, Ste. 403
Washington, DC 20052
(202)994-0704
Fax: (202)994-4930
E-mail: icsb@gwu.edu
Website: http://www.icsb.org
Susan G. Duffy. Admin.

International Small Business Consortium
3309 Windjammer St.
Norman, OK 73072
E-mail: sb@isbc.com
Website: http://www.isbc.com

Kauffman Center for Entrepreneurial Leadership
4801 Rockhill Rd.
Kansas City, MO 64110-2046
(816)932-1000
E-mail: info@kauffman.org
Website: http://www.entreworld.org

National Alliance for Fair Competition
3 Bethesda Metro Center, Ste. 1100
Bethesda, MD 20814
(410)235-7116
Fax: (410)235-7116
E-mail: ampesq@aol.com
Tony Ponticelli, Exec.Dir.

National Association for the Self-Employed
PO Box 612067
DFW Airport
Dallas, TX 75261-2067
(800)232-6273
E-mail: mpetron@nase.org
Website: http://www.nase.org
Robert Hughes, Pres.

National Association of Business Leaders
4132 Shoreline Dr., Ste. J & H
Earth City, MO 63045
Fax: (314)298-9110
E-mail: nabl@nabl.com
Website: http://www.nabl.com/
Gene Blumenthal, Contact

National Association of Private Enterprise
PO Box 15550
Long Beach, CA 90815
888-224-0953
Fax: (714)844-4942

Website: http://www.napeonline.net
Laura Squiers, Exec.Dir.

National Association of Small Business Investment Companies
666 11th St. NW, Ste. 750
Washington, DC 20001
(202)628-5055
Fax: (202)628-5080
E-mail: nasbic@nasbic.org
Website: http://www.nasbic.org
Lee W. Mercer, Pres.

National Business Association
PO Box 700728
5151 Beltline Rd., Ste. 1150
Dallas, TX 75370
(972)458-0900
800-456-0440
Fax: (972)960-9149
E-mail: info@nationalbusiness.org
Website: http://www.nationalbusiness.org
Raj Nisankarao, Pres.

National Business Owners Association
PO Box 111
Stuart, VA 24171
(276)251-7500
(866)251-7505
Fax: (276)251-2217
E-mail: membershipservices@nboa.org
Website: http://www.rvmdb.com.nboa
Paul LaBarr, Pres.

National Center for Fair Competition
PO Box 220
Annandale, VA 22003
(703)280-4622
Fax: (703)280-0942
E-mail: kentonp1@aol.com
Kenton Pattie, Pres.

National Family Business Council
1640 W. Kennedy Rd.
Lake Forest, IL 60045
(847)295-1040
Fax: (847)295-1898
E-mail: lmsnfbc@email.msn.com
Jogn E. Messervey, Pres.

National Federation of Independent Business
53 Century Blvd., Ste. 250
Nashville, TN 37214
(615)872-5800
800-NFIBNOW
Fax: (615)872-5353
Website: http://www.nfib.org
Jack Faris, Pres. and CEO

National Small Business Association
1156 15th St. NW, Ste. 1100
Washington, DC 20005
(202)293-8830
800-345-6728
Fax: (202)872-8543
E-mail: press@nsba.biz
Website: http://www.nsba.biz
Rob Yunich, Dir. of Communications

PUSH Commercial Division
930 E 50th St.
Chicago, IL 60615-2702
(773)373-3366
Fax: (773)373-3571
E-mail: info@rainbowpush.org
Website: http://www.rainbowpush.org
Rev. Willie T. Barrow, Co-Chm.

Research Institute for Small and Emerging Business
722 12th St. NW
Washington, DC 20005
(202)628-8382
Fax: (202)628-8392
E-mail: info@riseb.org
Website: http://www.riseb.org
Allan Neece, Jr., Chm.

Sales Professionals USA
PO Box 149
Arvada, CO 80001
(303)534-4937
888-736-7767
E-mail: salespro@salesprofessionals-usa.com
Website: http://www.salesprofessionals-usa.com
Sharon Herbert, Natl. Pres.

Score Association - Service Corps of Retired Executives
409 3rd St. SW, 6th Fl.
Washington, DC 20024
(202)205-6762
800-634-0245
Fax: (202)205-7636
E-mail: media@score.org
Website: http://www.score.org
W. Kenneth Yancey, Jr., CEO

Small Business and Entrepreneurship Council
1920 L St. NW, Ste. 200
Washington, DC 20036
(202)785-0238
Fax: (202)822-8118
E-mail: membership@sbec.org
Website: http://www.sbecouncil.org
Karen Kerrigan, Pres./CEO

Small Business in Telecommunications
1331 H St. NW, Ste. 500
Washington, DC 20005
(202)347-4511
Fax: (202)347-8607
E-mail: sbt@sbthome.org
Website: http://www.sbthome.org
Lonnie Danchik, Chm.

Small Business Legislative Council
1010 Massachusetts Ave. NW, Ste. 540
Washington, DC 20005
(202)639-8500
Fax: (202)296-5333
E-mail: email@sblc.org
Website: http://www.sblc.org
John Satagaj, Pres.

Small Business Service Bureau
554 Main St.
PO Box 15014
Worcester, MA 01615-0014
(508)756-3513
800-343-0939
Fax: (508)770-0528
E-mail: membership@sbsb.com
Website: http://www.sbsb.com
Francis R. Carroll, Pres.

Small Publishers Association of North America
1618 W Colorado Ave.
Colorado Springs, CO 80904
(719)475-1726
Fax: (719)471-2182
E-mail: span@spannet.org
Website: http://www.spannet.org
Scott Flora, Exec. Dir.

SOHO America
PO Box 941
Hurst, TX 76053-0941
800-495-SOHO
E-mail: soho@1sas.com
Website: http://www.soho.org

Structured Employment Economic Development Corporation
915 Broadway, 17th Fl.
New York, NY 10010
(212)473-0255
Fax: (212)473-0357
E-mail: info@seedco.org
Website: http://www.seedco.org
William Grinker, CEO

Support Services Alliance
107 Prospect St.
Schoharie, NY 12157
800-836-4772
E-mail: info@ssamembers.com

Website: http://www.ssainfo.com
Steve COle, Pres.

United States Association for Small Business and Entrepreneurship
975 University Ave., No. 3260
Madison, WI 53706
(608)262-9982
Fax: (608)263-0818
E-mail: jgillman@wisc.edu
Website: http://www.ususbe.org
Joan Gillman, Exec. Dir.

Consultants

This section contains a listing of consultants specializing in small business development. It is arranged alphabetically by country, then by state or province, then by city, then by firm name.

Canada

Alberta

Tenato
1229A 9th Ave. SE
Calgary, AB, Canada T2G 0S9
(403)242-1127
Fax: (403)261-5693
E-mail: jdrew@tenato.com
Website: http://www.tenato.com

Varsity Consulting Group
School of Business
University of Alberta
Edmonton, AB, Canada T6G 2R6
(780)492-2994
Fax: (780)492-5400

British Columbia

Andrew R. De Boda Consulting
1523 Milford Ave.
Coquitlam, BC, Canada V3J 2V9
(604)936-4527
Fax: (604)936-4527
E-mail: deboda@intergate.bc.ca

Reality Marketing Associates
3049 Sienna Ct.
Coquitlam, BC, Canada V3E 3N7
(604)944-8603
Fax: (604)944-4708
E-mail: info@realityassociates.com
Website: http://www.realityassociates.com

Pinpoint Tactics Business Consulting
5525 West Blvd., Ste. 330
Vancouver, BC, Canada V6M 3W6
(604)263-4698

E-mail: info@pinpointtactics.com
Website: http://www.pinpointtactics.com

Ketch Consulting Inc.
6890 Winnifred Pl.
Victoria, BC, Canada V8M 1N1
(250)661-1208
E-mail: info@ketch.ca
Website: http://www.ketch.ca

Mahigan Consulting Services
334 Skawshen Rd.
West Vancouver, BC, Canada V7P 3T1
(604)210-3833
Fax: (778)285-2736
E-mail: info@mahiganconsulting.com
Website: http://www.mahiganconsulting.com

Nova Scotia

The Marketing Clinic
1384 Bedford Hwy.
Bedford, NS, Canada B4A 1E2
(902)835-4122
Fax: (902)832-9389
E-mail: office@themarketingclinic.ca
Website: http://www.themarketingclinic.ca

Ontario

The Cynton Co.
17 Massey St.
Brampton, ON, Canada L6S 2V6
(905)792-7769
Fax: (905)792-8116
E-mail: cynton@home.com
Website: http://www.cynton.com

CRO Engineering Ltd.
1895 William Hodgins Ln.
Carp, ON, Canada K0A 1L0
(613)839-1108
Fax: (613)839-1406
E-mail: J.Grefford@ieee.ca

Business Plan World
PO Box 1322, Sta. B
Mississauga, ON, Canada L4Y 4B6
(709)643-8544
E-mail: theboss@businessplanworld.com
Website: http://www.businessplanworld.com

JPL Consulting
236 Millard Ave.
Newmarket, ON, Canada L3Y 1Z2
(416)606-9124
E-mail: sales@jplbiz.ca
Website: http://www.jplbiz.ca

Black Eagle Consulting 2000 Inc.
451 Barclay Cres.
Oakville, ON , Canada L6J 6H8
(905)842-3010
Fax: (905)842-9586
E-mail: info@blackeagle.ca
Website: http://www.blackeagle.ca

Care Concepts & Communications
21 Spruce Hill Rd.
Toronto, ON, Canada M4E 3G2
(416)420-8840
E-mail: info@cccbizconsultants.com
Website: http://www.cccbizconsultants
.com

FHG International Inc.
14 Glengrove Ave. W
Toronto, ON, Canada M4R 1N4
(416)402-8000
E-mail: info@fhgi.com
Website: http://www.fhgi.com

Harrison Pricing Strategy Group Inc.
1235 Bay St., Ste. 400
Toronto, ON, Canada M5R 3K4
(416)218-1103
Fax: (416) 827-8595

Ken Wyman & Associates Inc.
64 Lamb Ave.
Toronto, ON, Canada V
(416)362-2926
Fax: (416)362-3039
E-mail: kenwyman@compuserve.com

Quebec

PGP Consulting
17 Linton
Dollard-des-Ormeaux, QC, Canada H9B
1P2
(514)796-7613
Fax: (866)750-0947
E-mail: pierre@pgpconsulting.com
Website: http://www.pgpconsulting.com

Komand Consulting
1250 Rene Levesque Blvd.,W
22nd Fl., Ste. 2200
Montreal, QC, Canada H3B 4W8
(514)934-9281
Fax: (514)934-0770
E-mail: info@komand.ca
Website: http://www.komand.ca

Saskatchewan

Banda Marketing Group
410 - 22nd St. E, Ste. 810
Saskatoon, SK, Canada S7K 5T6
(306) 343-6100

Fax: (306) 652-1340
E-mail: admin@bandagroup.com
Website: http://www.bandagroup.com

Oracle Planning
106 28th St. W
Saskatoon, SK, Canada, S7L 0K2
(306) 717-5001
Fax: (650)618-2742

United states

Alabama

Business Planning Inc.
2090 Columbiana Rd., Ste. 2950
Vestavia Hills, AL 35216
(205)824-8969
Fax: (205)824-8939
E-mail: kmiller@businessplanninginc.
com
Website: http://www.business
planninginc.com

Tradebank of Eastern Alabama
400 S St. E
Talladega, AL 35160
(256)761-9051
Fax: (256)761-9227

Alaska

Alaska Business Development Center
840 K St., Ste. 202
Anchorage, AK 99501
(907)562-0335
Free: 800-478-3474
Fax: (907)562-6988
E-mail: info@abdc.org
Website: http://www.abdc.org

Arizona

Carefree Direct Marketing Corp.
8001 E Serene St.
PO Box 3737
Carefree, AZ 85377-3737
(480)488-4227
Fax: (480)488-2841

Management 2000
39342 S Winding Trl.
Oro Valley, AZ 85737
(520)818-9988
Fax: (520)818-3277
E-mail: m2000@mgmt2000.com
Website: http://www.mgmt2000.com

CMAS
5125 N 16th St.
Phoenix, AZ 85016

(602)395-1001
Fax: (602)604-8180

Moneysoft Inc.
1 E Camelback Rd. #550
Phoenix, AZ 85012
Free: 800-966-7797
E-mail: mbray@moneysoft.com
Website: http://www.moneysoft.com

Harvey C. Skoog
7151 E Addis Ave.
Prescott Valley, AZ 86314
(928)772-1448

The De Angelis Group Inc.
9815 E Bell Rd., Ste. 120
Scottsdale, AZ 85260
(480)609-4868
Fax: (480)452-0401
E-mail: info@thedeangelisgroup.com
Website: http://www.thedeangelisgroup.com

Incendo Marketing L.L.C.
7687 E Thunderhawk Rd., Ste. 100
Scottsdale, AZ 85255
(480)513-4208
Fax: (509)561-9011

Sauerbrun Technology Group Ltd.
7979 E Princess Dr., Ste. 5
Scottsdale, AZ 85255-5878
(602)502-4950
Fax: (602)502-4292
E-mail: info@sauerbrun.com
Website: http://www.sauerbrun.com

Van Cleve Associates
6932 E 2nd St.
Tucson, AZ 85710
(520)296-2587
Fax: (520)296-3358

Variantia
6161 N Canon del Pajaro
Tucson, AZ 85750
(520)577-7680

Louws Management Corp.
PO Box 130
Vail, AZ 85641
(520)664-1881
Fax: (928)222-0086
E-mail: info@louwstraining.com
Website: http://www.louwsmanagement
.com

California

Thomas E. Church & Associates Inc.
PO Box 2439
Aptos, CA 95001
(831) 662-7950

Fax:(831) 684-0173
E-mail: thomase2@trueyellow.net
Website: http://www.thomas_church
.ypgs.net

AB Manley Partners Worldwide L.L.C.
1428 S Marengo Ave.
Alhambra, CA 91803-3096
(626) 457-8841

Lindquist Consultants-Venture Planning
225 Arlington Ave.
Berkeley, CA 94707
(510)524-6685
Fax: (510)527-6604

One Page Business Plan Co.
1798 Fifth St.
Berkeley, CA 94710
(510)705-8400
Fax: (510)705-8403
E-mail: info@onepagebusinessplan.com
Website: http://www.onepagebusiness
plan.com

WordCraft Creative Services
2687 Shasta Rd.
Berkeley, CA 94708
(510) 848-5177
Fax:(510) 868-1006
E-mail: info@wordcraftcreative.com
Website: http://www.wordcraft
creative.com

Growth Partners
1566 La Pradera Dr., Ste. 5
Campbell, CA 95008
(408) 871-7925
Fax: (408) 871-7924
E-mail: mark@growth-partners.com
Website: http://www.growth-partners
.com

The Success Resource
25773 Flanders Pl.
Carmel, CA 93923
(831) 236-0732

W and J PARTNERSHIP
PO Box 2499
18876 Edwin Markham Dr.
Castro Valley, CA 94546
(510)583-7751
Fax: (510)583-7645
E-mail: wamorgan@wjpartnership.com
Website: http://www.wjpartnership.com

JB Associates
21118 Gardena Dr.
Cupertino, CA 95014
(408)257-0214

Fax: (408)257-0216
E-mail: semarang@sirius.com

House Agricultural Consultants
1105 Kennedy Pl., Ste. 1
Davis, CA 95616
(916)753-3361
Fax: (916)753-0464
E-mail: infoag@houseag.com
Website: http://www.houseag.com/

3C Systems Co.
16161 Ventura Blvd., Ste. 815
Encino, CA 91436
(818)907-1302
Fax: (818)907-1357
E-mail: mark@3CSysCo.com
Website: http://www.3CSysCo.com

Technical Management Consultants
3624 Westfall Dr.
Encino, CA 91436-4154
(818)784-0626
Fax: (818)501-5575
E-mail: tmcrs@aol.com

Rainwater-Gish & Associates
317 3rd St., Ste. 3
Eureka, CA 95501
(707)443-0030
Fax: (707)443-5683

MedMarket Diligence L.L.C.
51 Fairfield
Foothill Ranch, CA 92610-1856
(949) 859-3401
Fax: (949) 837-4558
E-mail: info@mediligence.com
Website: http://www.mediligence.com

Global Tradelinks
451 Pebble Beach Pl.
Fullerton, CA 92835
(714)441-2280
Fax: (714)441-2281
E-mail: info@globaltradelinks.com
Website: http://www.globaltradelinks.com

Larson Associates
1440 Harbor Blvd., Ste. 800
Fullerton, CA 92835
(714)529-4121
Fax: (714)572-3606
E-mail: ray@consultlarson.com
Website: http://www.consultlarson.com

Strategic Business Group
800 Cienaga Dr.
Fullerton, CA 92835-1248
(714)449-1040
Fax: (714)525-1631

Burnes Consulting
20537 Wolf Creek Rd.
Grass Valley, CA 95949
(530)346-8188
Free: 800-949-9021
Fax: (530)346-7704
E-mail: kent@burnesconsulting.com
Website: http://www.burnesconsulting
.com

International Health Resources
PO Box 2738
Grass Valley, CA 95945
Website: http://www.futureofhealthcare
.com

Pioneer Business Consultants
9042 Garfield Ave., Ste. 211
Huntington Beach, CA 92646
(714)964-7600

Fluor Daniel Inc.
3353 Michelson Dr.
Irvine, CA 92612-0650
(949)975-2000
Fax: (949)975-5271
E-mail: sales.consulting@fluordaniel.com
Website: http://www.fluor.com

MCS Associates
18881 Von Karman, Ste. 1175
Irvine, CA 92612
(949)263-8700
Fax: (949)263-0770
E-mail: info@mcsassociates.com
Website: http://www.mcsassociates.com

Savvy Communications
9730 Soda Bay Rd., Ste. 5035
Kelseyville, CA 95451-9576
(707) 277-8078
Fax:(707) 277-8079

Sky Blue Consulting Inc.
4165 Executive Dr.
Lafayette, CA 94549
(925) 283-8272

Comprehensive Business Services
3201 Lucas Cir.
Lafayette, CA 94549
(925)283-8272
Fax: (925)283-8272

The Ribble Group
27601 Forbes Rd., Ste. 52
Laguna Niguel, CA 92677
(714)582-1085
Fax: (714)582-6420
E-mail: ribble@deltanet.com

Norris Bernstein, CMC
9309 Marina Pacifica Dr. N
Long Beach, CA 90803

(562)493-5458
Fax: (562)493-5459
E-mail: norris@ctecomputer.com
Website: http://foodconsultants.com/
bernstein/

Horizon Consulting Services
1315 Garthwick Dr.
Los Altos, CA 94024
(415)967-0906
Fax: (650)967-0906

Blue Garnet Associates L.L.C.
8055 W Manchester Ave., Ste. 430
Los Angeles, CA 90293
(310) 439-1930
Fax: (310) 388-1657
E-mail: hello@bluegarnet.net
Website: http://www.bluegarnet.net

CAST Management Consultants Inc.
700 S Flower St., Ste. 1900
Los Angeles, CA 90017
(213) 614-8066
Fax: (213) 614-0760
E-mail: info@castconsultants.com
Website: http://www.castconsultants.com

Rubenstein/Justman Management Consultants
11620 Wilshire Blvd., Ste. 750
Los Angeles, CA 90025
(310)445-5300
Fax: (310)496-1450
E-mail: info@rjmc.net
Website: http://www.rjmc.net

F.J. Schroeder & Associates
1926 Westholme Ave.
Los Angeles, CA 90025
(310)470-2655
Fax: (310)470-6378
E-mail: fjsacons@aol.com
Website: http://www.mcninet.com/
GlobalLook/Fjschroe.html

Western Management Associates
5777 W Century Blvd., Ste. 1220
Los Angeles, CA 90045
(310)645-1091
Free: (888)788-6534
Fax: (310)645-1092
E-mail: gene@cfoforrent.com
Website: http://www.cfoforrent.com

Inspiration Quest Inc.
PO Box 90
Mendocino, CA 95460
(415) 235-6002
E-mail: info@inspirationquest.com
Website: http://www.inspirationquest
.com

Heron Advisory Group
9 Heron Dr.
Mill Valley, CA 94941
(415) 380-8611
Fax: (415) 381-9044
E-mail: janetmca@pacbell.net
Website: http://www.hagroup.biz

Emacula Consulting Group
131 Draeger Dr., Ste. A
Moraga, CA 94556
(925) 388-6083
Fax: (267) 589-3151
E-mail: drochlin@emacula.com
Website: http://www.emacula.com

BizplanSource
1048 Irvine Ave., Ste. 621
Newport Beach, CA 92660
Free: 888-253-0974
Fax: 800-859-8254
E-mail: info@bizplansource.com
Website: http://www.bizplansource.com
Adam Greengrass, President

The Market Connection
20051 SW Birch St., Ste 310
Newport Beach, CA 92660
(949)851-6313
Fax: (949)833-0283

Intelequest Corp.
722 Gailen Ave.
Palo Alto, CA 94303
(415)968-3443
Fax: (415)493-6954
E-mail: frits@iqix.com

Beblie, Brandt & Jacobs Inc.
19 Brista del Lago
Rancho Santa Margarita, CA 92618
(949)589-5120
Fax: (949)203-6225
E-mail: darcy@bbjinc.com

California Business Incubation Network
225 Broadway, Ste. 2250
San Diego, CA 92101
(619)237-0559
Fax: (619)237-0521

The Drake Group
824 Santa Clara Pl.
San Diego, CA 92109-7224
(858) 488-3911
Fax: (810) 454-4593
E-mail: cdrake@drakegroup.com
Website: http://www.drakegroup.com

G.R. Gordetsky Consultants Inc.
11414 Windy Summit Pl.
San Diego, CA 92127

(858)487-4939
E-mail: gordet@pacbell.net

Noorany Marketing Resources
3830 Valley Centre Dr., Ste. 705
San Diego, CA 92130
(858) 792-9559
Fax: (858) 259-2320
E-mail: heidi@noorany.com
Website: http://www.noorany.com

Freeman, Sullivan & Co.
1101 Montgomery St., 15th Fl.
San Francisco, CA 94104
Website: http://www.fscgroup.com

PKF Consulting Corp.
50 California St., 19th Fl.
San Francisco, CA 94111
(415)788-3102
Fax: (415)433-7844
E-mail: callahan@pkfc.com
Website: http://www.pkfc.com

Welling & Woodard Inc.
1067 Broadway
San Francisco, CA 94133
(415)776-4500
Fax: (415)776-5067

Highland Associates
16174 Highland Dr.
San Jose, CA 95127
(408)272-7008
Fax: (408)272-4040

Leckrone Law Corp.
4010 Moorpark Ave., Ste. 215
San Jose, CA 95117-1843
(408) 243-9898
Fax: (408) 296-6637

ORDIS Inc.
6815 Trinidad Dr.
San Jose, CA 95120-2056
(408)268-3321
Free: 800-446-7347
Fax: (408)268-3582
E-mail: ordis@ordis.com
Website: http://www.ordis.com

Bay Area Tax Consultants and Bayhill Financial Consultants
1840 Gateway Dr.
San Mateo, CA 94404
(650)378-1373
Fax: (650)585-5444
E-mail: admin@baytax.com
Website: http://www.baytax.com/

Helfert Associates
111 St. Matthews, Ste. 307
San Mateo, CA 94401

(650)377-0540
Fax: (650)377-0472

Mykytyn Consulting Group Inc.
185 N Redwood Dr., Ste. 200
San Rafael, CA 94903
(415)491-1770
Fax: (415)491-1251
E-mail: info@mcgi.com

Omega Management Systems Inc.
3 Mount Darwin Ct.
San Rafael, CA 94903-1109
(415)499-1300
Fax: (415)492-9490
E-mail: information@omegamgt.com

Manex Consulting
2010 Crow Canyon Pl., Ste. 320
San Ramon, CA 94583
(925) 807-5100
Website: http://www.manexconsulting
.com

Brincko Associates Inc.
530 Wilshire Blvd., Ste. 201
Santa Monica, CA 90401
(310)553-4523
Fax: (310)553-6782

hE Myth
131B Stony Cir., Ste. 2000
Santa Rosa, CA 95401
(541)552-4600
Free: 800-300-3531
E-mail: info@emyth.com
Website: http://www.emyth.com

Figueroa Farms L.L.C.
PO Box 206
Santa Ynez, CA 93460
(805) 686-4890
Fax: (805) 686-2887
E-mail: info@figueroafarms.com
Website: http://www.FigueroaFarms.com

Reilly, Connors & Ray
1743 Canyon Rd.
Spring Valley, CA 91977
(619)698-4808
Fax: (619)460-3892
E-mail: davidray@adnc.com

RJR Associates
1639 Lewiston Dr.
Sunnyvale, CA 94087
(408)737-7720
E-mail: bobroy@rjrassoc.com
Website: http://www.rjrassoc.com

Schwafel Associates
333 Cobalt Way, Ste. 107
Sunnyvale, CA 94085

(408)720-0649
Fax: (408)720-1796
E-mail: schwafel@ricochet.net
Website: http://www.patca.org

The International Coverting Institute
5200 Badger Rd
Terrebonne, CA 97760
(503) 548-1447
Fax: (503) 548-1618

GlobalReady
1521 Kirk Ave.
Thousand Oaks, CA 91360
(805) 427-4131
E-mail: info@globalready.com
Website: http://www.globalready.com

Staubs Business Services
23320 S Vermont Ave.
Torrance, CA 90502-2940
(310)830-9128
Fax: (310)830-9128
E-mail: Harry_L_Staubs@Lamg.com

Enterprise Management Corp.
17461 Irvine Blvd., Ste. M
Tustin, CA 92780
(714) 505-1925
Fax: (714) 505-9691
E-mail: cfotogo@companycfo.com
Website: http://www.companycfo.com

Out of Your Mind...and Into the Marketplace
13381 White Sands Dr.
Tustin, CA 92780-4565
(714)544-0248
Free: 800-419-1513
Fax: (714)730-1414
Website: http://www.business-plan.com

Ingman Company Inc.
7949 Woodley Ave., Ste. 120
Van Nuys, CA 91406-1232
(805)650-9353
Fax: (805)984-2979

Innovative Technology Associates
3639 E Harbor Blvd., Ste. 203E
Ventura, CA 93001
(805)650-9353

Grid Technology Associates
20404 Tufts Cir.
Walnut, CA 91789
(909)444-0922
Fax: (909)444-0922

Bell Springs Publishing
PO Box 1240
Willits, CA 95490
(707)459-6372

E-mail: bellsprings@sabernet
Website: http://www.bellsprings.com

Hutchinson Consulting and Appraisal
23245 Sylvan St., Ste. 103
Woodland Hills, CA 91367
(818)888-8175
Free: 800-977-7548
Fax: (818)888-8220
E-mail: r.f.hutchinson-cpa@worldnet
.att.net

Colorado

Sam Boyer & Associates
4255 S Buckley Rd., No. 136
Aurora, CO 80013
(303)766-1557
Free: 800-785-0485
Fax: (303)766-8740
E-mail: samboyer@samboyer.com
Website: http://www.samboyer.com/

Associated Enterprises Ltd.
183 Pauls Ln.
Bailey, CO 80421

Comer & Associates LLC
5255 Holmes Pl.
Boulder, CO 80303
(303) 786-7986
Fax: (303)895-2347
E-mail: jerry@comerassociates.com
Website: http://www.comerassociates
.com

Ameriwest Business Consultants Inc.
3725 E. Wade Ln.
Colorado Springs, CO 80917
(719)380-7096
Fax: (719)380-7096
E-mail: email@abchelp.com
Website: http://www.abchelp.com

GVNW Consulting Inc.
2270 La Montana Way
Colorado Springs, CO 80936
(719)594-5800
Fax: (719)594-5803
Website: http://www.gvnw.com

M-Squared Inc.
755 San Gabriel Pl.
Colorado Springs, CO 80906
(719)576-2554
Fax: (719)576-2554

Foxhall Consulting Services
2532 Dahlia St.
Denver, CO 80207
(303)355-7995
Fax: (303)377-0716

E-mail: michael@foxhallconsulting.com
Website: http://www.foxhallconsulting
.com

KLA Associates
2352 Humboldt St.
Denver, CO 80205-5332
(303)830-8042

Wilson Hughes Consulting LLC
2100 Humboldt St., Ste. 302
Denver, CO 80205
Website: http://www.wilsonhughes
consultingllc.com

Co-Active Communications Corp.
400 Inverness Pkwy., Ste. 200
Englewood, CO 80112-6415
(303)771-6181
Fax: (303)771-0080

Thornton Financial FNIC
1024 Centre Ave., Bldg. E
Fort Collins, CO 80526-1849
(970)221-2089
Fax: (970)484-5206

Extelligent Inc.
8400 E Crescent Pky., Ste. 600
Greenwood Village, CO 80111
(720)201-5672
E-mail: info@extelligent.com
Website: http://www.extelligent.com

**Western Capital Holdings Inc.10050 E
Applwood Dr.**
Parker, CO 80138
(303)841-1022
Fax: (303)770-1945

Connecticut

Christiansen Consulting
56 Scarborough St.
Hartford, CT 06105
(860)586-8265
Fax: (860)233-3420
Website: http://www.Christiansen
Consulting.com

Follow-up News
185 Pine St., Ste. 818
Manchester, CT 06040
(860)647-7542
Free: 800-708-0696
Fax: (860)646-6544
E-mail: Followupnews@aol.com

Musevue360
555 Millbrook Rd.
Middletown, CT 06457
(860)463-7722
Fax: (860)346-3013

E-mail: jennifer.eifrig@musevue360.com
Website: http://www.musevue360.com

Alltis Corp.
747 Farmington Ave., Ste. 6
New Britain, CT 06053
(860)224-1300
Fax: (860)224-1700
E-mail: info@alltis.com
Website: http://www.alltis.com

Kalba International Inc.
116 McKinley Ave.
New Haven, CT 06515
(203)397-2199
Fax: (781)240-2657
E-mail: kalba@comcast.net
Website: http://www.kalbainternational
.com

Lovins & Associates Consulting
357 Whitney Ave.
New Haven, CT 06511
(203)787-3367
Fax: (203)624-7599
E-mail: Alovinsphd@aol.com
Website: http://www.lovinsgroup.com

JC Ventures Inc.
4 Arnold St.
Old Greenwich, CT 06870-1203
(203)698-1990
Free: 800-698-1997
Fax: (203)698-2638

**Charles L. Hornung
Associates**
52 Ned's Mountain Rd.
Ridgefield, CT 06877
(203)431-0297

Greenwich Associates
6 High Ridge Park
Stamford, CT 06905
(203)629-1200
Fax: (203)629-1229
E-mail: lisa@greenwich.com
Website: http://www.greenwich.com

Management Practice Inc.
216 W Hill Rd.
Stamford, CT 06902
(203)973-0535
Fax: (203)978-9034
E-mail: mpayne@mpiweb.com
Website: http://www.mpiweb.com

RealBusinessPlans.com
156 Westport Rd.
Wilton, CT 06897
(914)837-2886

E-mail: ct@realbusinessplans.com
Website: http://www.RealBusinessPlans
.com

Wellspring Consulting LLC
198 Amity Rd., 2nd Fl.
Woodbridge, CT 06525
(203)387-7192
Fax: (203)387-1345
E-mail: info@wellspringconsulting.net
Website: http://www.wellspring
consulting.net

Delaware

Focus Marketing
61-7 Habor Dr.
Claymont, DE 19703
(302)793-3064

Daedalus Ventures Ltd.
PO Box 1474
Hockessin, DE 19707
(302)239-6758
Fax: (302)239-9991
E-mail: daedalus@mail.del.net

The Formula Group
PO Box 866
Hockessin, DE 19707
(302)456-0952
Fax: (302)456-1354
E-mail: formula@netaxs.com

Selden Enterprises Inc.
2502 Silverside Rd., Ste. 1
Wilmington, DE 19810-3740
(302)529-7113
Fax: (302)529-7442
E-mail: selden2@bellatlantic.net
Website: http://www.seldenenterprises
.com

District of Columbia

The Breen Consulting Group LLC
1101 Pennsylvania Ave, NW, 7th Fl.
Washington, DC 20004
(877)881-4688
E-mail: sales@joebreen.com
Website: http://www.joebreen.com

Catalysr IpF
1514Upshur St. NW
Washington, DC 20011
(202)230-2662
E-mail: contact@catalystipf.com
Website: http://www.catalystipf.com

Smith, Dawson & Andrews Inc.
1150 Connecticut Ave., Ste. 1025
Washington, DC 20036
(202)835-0740

Fax: (202)775-8526
E-mail: webmaster@sda-inc.com
Website: http://www.sda-inc.com

1000 Cranes LLC
1425 K St. NW, Ste. 350
Washington, DC 20005
(202)587-2737
E-mail: info@1000cranes.com
Website: http://www.1000cranes.com

Florida

BackBone, Inc.
20404 Hacienda Court
Boca Raton, FL 33498
(561)470-0965
Fax: 516-908-4038
E-mail: BPlans@backboneinc.com
Website: http://www.backboneinc.com

Dr. Eric H Shaw and Associates
500 South Ocean Blvd., Ste. 2105
Boca Raton, FL 33432
(561)338-5151
E-mail: ericshaw@bellsouth.net
Website: http://www.ericshaw.com

E.N. Rysso & Associates
180 Bermuda Petrel Ct.
Daytona Beach, FL 32119
(386)760-3028
E-mail: erysso@aol.com

Eric Sands Consulting Services
6750 N. Andrews Ave., Ste. 200
Fort Lauderdale, FL 33309
(954)721-4767
Fax: (954)720-2815
E-mail: easands@aol.com
Website: http://www.ericsandsconsultig
.com

F.A. McGee Inc.
800 Claughton Island Dr., Ste. 401
Miami, FL 33131
(305)377-9123

Strategic Business Planning Co.
12000 Biscayne Blvd., Ste. 203
Miami, FL 33181
(954)704-9100
E-mail: info@bizplan.com
Website: http://www.bizplan.com

Professional Planning Associates, Inc.
1440 NE 35th St.
Oakland Park, FL 33334
(954)829-2523
Fax:(954)537-7945
E-mail: Mgoldstein@proplana.com
Website: http://proplana.com
Michael Goldstein, President

Hunter G. Jackson Jr.
3409 Canoga Dr.
Orlando, FL 32861-8272
(407)245-7682
E-mail: hunterjackson@juno.com

F. Newton Parks
210 El Brillo Way
Palm Beach, FL 33480
(561)833-1727
Fax: (561)833-4541

Hughes Consulting Services LLC
522 Alternate 19
Palm Harbor, FL 34683
(727)631-2536
Fax: (727)474-9818
Website: http://consultinghughes.com

Avery Business Development Services
2506 St. Michel Ct.
Ponte Vedra Beach, FL 32082
(904)280-8840
Fax: (904)285-6033

Dufresne Consulting Group Inc.
10014 N Dale Mabry, Ste. 101
Tampa, FL 33618-4426
(813)264-4775
Fax: (813)264-9300
Website: http://www.dcgconsult.com

Tunstall Consulting LLC
13153 N. Dale Mabry Hwy., Ste. 200
Tampa, FL 33618
(813)968-4461
Fax: (813)961-2315
Website: http://www.tunstallconsulting
.com

The Business Planning Institute, LLC.
580 Village Blvd., Ste. 150
West Palm Beach, FL 33409
(561)236-5533
Fax: (561)689-5546
Website: http://www.bpiplans.com

Georgia

Fountainhead Consulting Group, Inc.
3970 Old Milton Pkwy, Ste. 210
Atlanta, GA 30005
(770)642-4220
Website: http://www.fountainhead
consultinggroup.com/

CHScottEnterprises
227 Sandy Springs P., NE, Ste. 720702
Atlanta, GA 30358
(770)356-4808
E-mail: info@chscottenterprises.com
Website: http://www.chscottenter
prises.com

US Business Plan Inc.
1200 Barrett Pky., Ste. 4-400
Kennesaw, GA 30144
(770)794-8000
Website: http://www.usbusinessplan.com

Business Ventures Corp.
1650 Oakbrook Dr., Ste. 405
Norcross, GA 30093
(770)729-8000
Fax: (770)729-8028

Tom C. Davis CPA LLC
1808-A Plum St.
Valdosta, GA 31601
(229)247-9801
Fax:(229) 244-7704
E-mail: mail@tcdcpa.com
Website: http://www.tcdcpa.com/

Illinois

TWD and Associates
431 S Patton
Arlington Heights, IL 60005
(847)398-6410
Fax: (847)255-5095
E-mail: tdoo@aol.com

Management Planning Associates Inc.
2275 Half Day Rd., Ste. 350
Bannockburn, IL 60015-1277
(847)945-2421
Fax: (847)945-2425

Phil Faris Associates
86 Old Mill Ct.
Barrington, IL 60010
(847)382-4888
Fax: (847)382-4890
E-mail: pfaris@meginsnet.net

Seven Continents Technology
787 Stonebridge
Buffalo Grove, IL 60089
(708)577-9653
Fax: (708)870-1220

Grubb & Blue Inc.
2404 Windsor Pl.
Champaign, IL 61820
(217)366-0052
Fax: (217)356-0117

ACE Accounting Service Inc.
3128 N Bernard St.
Chicago, IL 60618
(773)463-7854
Fax: (773)463-7854

AON Consulting Worldwide
200 E Randolph St., 10th Fl.
Chicago, IL 60601

(312)381-4800
Free: 800-438-6487
Fax: (312)381-0240
Website: http://www.aon.com

FMS Consultants
5801 N Sheridan Rd., Ste. 3D
Chicago, IL 60660
(773)561-7362
Fax: (773)561-6274

Grant Thornton
800 1 Prudential Plz.
130 E Randolph St.
Chicago, IL 60601
(312)856-0001
Fax: (312)861-1340
E-mail: gtinfo@gt.com
Website: http://www.grantthornton.com

Kingsbury International Ltd.
5341 N Glenwood Ave.
Chicago, IL 60640
(773)271-3030
Fax: (773)728-7080
E-mail: jetlag@mcs.com
Website: http://www.kingbiz.com

MacDougall & Blake Inc.
1414 N Wells St., Ste. 311
Chicago, IL 60610-1306
(312)587-3330
Fax: (312)587-3699
E-mail: jblake@compuserve.com

James C. Osburn Ltd.
6445 N. Western Ave., Ste. 304
Chicago, IL 60645
(773)262-4428
Fax: (773)262-6755
E-mail: osburnltd@aol.com

Tarifero & Tazewell Inc.
211 S Clark
Chicago, IL 60690
(312)665-9714
Fax: (312)665-9716

Human Energy Design Systems
620 Roosevelt Dr.
Edwardsville, IL 62025
(618)692-0258
Fax: (618)692-0819

China Business Consultants Group
931 Dakota Cir.
Naperville, IL 60563
(630)778-7992
Fax: (630)778-7915
E-mail: cbcq@aol.com

Center for Workforce Effectiveness
500 Skokie Blvd., Ste. 222
Northbrook, IL 60062
(847)559-8777

Fax: (847)559-8778
E-mail: office@cwelink.com
Website: http://www.cwelink.com

Smith Associates
1320 White Mountain Dr.
Northbrook, IL 60062
(847)480-7200
Fax: (847)480-9828

Francorp Inc.
20200 Governors Dr.
Olympia Fields, IL 60461
(708)481-2900
Free: 800-372-6244
Fax: (708)481-5885
E-mail: francorp@aol.com
Website: http://www.francorpinc.com

Camber Business Strategy Consultants
1010 S Plum Tree Ct
Palatine, IL 60078-0986
(847)202-0101
Fax: (847)705-7510
E-mail: camber@ameritech.net

Partec Enterprise Group
5202 Keith Dr.
Richton Park, IL 60471
(708)503-4047
Fax: (708)503-9468

Rockford Consulting Group Ltd.
Century Plz., Ste. 206
7210 E State St.
Rockford, IL 61108
(815)229-2900
Free: 800-667-7495
Fax: (815)229-2612
E-mail: rligus@RockfordConsulting.com
Website: http://www.Rockford
Consulting.com

RSM McGladrey Inc.
1699 E Woodfield Rd., Ste. 300
Schaumburg, IL 60173-4969
(847)413-6900
Fax: (847)517-7067
Website: http://www.rsmmcgladrey.com

A.D. Star Consulting
320 Euclid
Winnetka, IL 60093
(847)446-7827
Fax: (847)446-7827
E-mail: startwo@worldnet.att.net

Indiana

Bingham Economic Development Advisors
8900 Keystone Xing
Indianapolis, IN 46240
(317)968-5576

Ketchum Consulting Group
7575 Copperfield Way
Indianapolis, IN 46256
(317)845-5411
Fax: (317)842-9941

Cox and Company
3930 Mezzanine Dr. Ste A
Lafayette, IN, 47905
(765)449-4495
Fax: (765)449-1218
E-mail: stan@coxpa.com

Iowa

McCord Consulting Group Inc.
3425 Sycamore Ct. NE
Cedar Rapids, IA 52402
(319)378-0077
Fax: (319)378-1577
E-mail: sam@mccordgroup.com

Management Solutions L.L.C.
3815 Lincoln Pl. Dr.
Des Moines, IA 50312
(515)277-6408
Fax: (515)277-3506

Kansas

Aspire Business Development
10955 Lowell Ave., Ste. 400
Overland Park, KS 66210
(913)660-9400
Free: (888)548-1504
Website: http://www.aspirekc.com

Maine

Pan Atlantic SMS Group Inc.
6 City Ctr., Ste. 200
Portland, ME 04101
(207)871-8622
Fax: (207)772-4842
E-mail: pmurphy@panatlanticsmsgroup.com
Website: http://www.panatlanticsms
group.com

Maryland

Clemons & Associates Inc.
5024-R Campbell Blvd.
Baltimore, MD 21236
(410)931-8100
Fax: (410)931-8111
E-mail: info@clemonsmgmt.com
Website: http://www.clemonsmgmt.com

Employee Benefits Group Inc.
4405 E West Hwy., Ste. 202
Bethesda, MD 20814
(301) 718-4637

Fax: (301) 907-0176
E-mail: info@ebg.com
Website: http://www.ebg.com

Burdeshaw Associates Ltd.
4701 Sangamore Rd.
Bethesda, MD 20816-2508
(301)229-5800
Fax: (301)229-5045
E-mail: jstacy@burdeshaw.com
Website: http://www.burdeshaw.com

Michael E. Cohen
5225 Pooks Hill Rd., Ste. 1119 S
Bethesda, MD 20814
(301)530-5738
Fax: (301)530-2988
E-mail: mecohen@crosslink.net

World Development Group Inc.
5800 Madaket Rd., Ste. 100
Bethesda, MD 20816
(301) 320-0971
Fax: (301) 320-0978
E-mail: wdg@worlddg.com
Website: http://www.worlddg.com

Creative Edge Consulting
6047 Wild Ginger Ct.
Columbia, MD 21044
(443) 545-5863
Website: http://www.creativeedge
consulting.org

Paul Yelder Consulting
9581 Standon Pl.
Columbia, MD 21045
(410) 740-8417
E-mail: consulting@yelder.com
Website: http://www.yelder.com

Hammer Marketing Resources
19118 Silver Maple Ct.
Hagerstown, MD 21742
(301) 733-8891
Fax: (305) 675-3277

Strategies
8 Park Center Ct., Ste. 200
Owings Mills, MD 21117
(410)363-6669
Fax: (410)363-1231
E-mail: info@strategiescorp.net
Website: http://www.strategiescorp.net

Managance Consulting and Coaching
1708 Chester Mill Rd.
Silver Spring, MD 20906
(301) 260-9503
E-mail: info@managance.com
Website: http://www.managance.com

Andrew Sussman & Associates
13731 Kretsinger
Smithsburg, MD 21783
(301)824-2943
Fax: (301)824-2943

Massachusetts

Geibel Marketing and Public Relations
PO Box 611
Belmont, MA 02478-0005
(617)484-8285
Fax: (617)489-3567
E-mail: jgeibel@geibelpr.com
Website: http://www.geibelpr.com

Bain & Co.
131 Dartmouth St.
Boston, MA 02116
(617)572-2000
Fax: (617)572-2427
E-mail: corporate.inquiries@bain.com
Website: http://www.bain.com

Fairmont Consulting Group
470 Atlantic Ave., 4th Fl.
Boston, MA 02210
(617)217-2401
Fax: (617)939-0262
E-mail: info@fairmontcg.com
Website: http://www.fairmontcg.com

Information & Research Associates
PO Box 3121
Framingham, MA 01701
(508)788-0784

Walden Consultants Ltd.
252 Pond St.
Hopkinton, MA 01748
(508)435-4882
Fax: (508)435-3971
Website: http://www.waldenconsultants
.com

Consulting Resources Corp.
6 Northbrook Park
Lexington, MA 02420
(781)863-1222
Fax: (781)863-1441
E-mail: res@consultingresources.net
Website: http://www.consultingre
sources.net

Mehr & Co.
31 Woodcliffe Rd.
Lexington, MA 02421
(781)372-1055

Real Resources
27 Indian Hill Rd.
Medfield, MA 02052
(508)359-6780

VMB Associates Inc.
115 Ashland St.
Melrose, MA 02176
(781)665-0623
Fax: (425)732-7142
E-mail: vmbinc@aol.com

The Company Doctor
14 Pudding Stone Ln.
Mendon, MA 01756
(508)478-1747
Fax: (508)478-0520

Data and Strategies Group Inc.
190 N Main St.
Natick, MA 01760
(508)653-9990
Fax: (508)653-7799
E-mail: dsginc@dsggroup.com
Website: http://www.dsggroup.com

The Enterprise Group
73 Parker Rd.
Needham, MA 02494
(617)444-6631
Fax: (617)433-9991
E-mail: lsacco@world.std.com
Website: http://www.enterprise-group
.com

PSMJ Resources Inc.
10 Midland Ave.
Newton, MA 02458
(617)965-0055
Free: 800-537-7765
Fax: (617)965-5152
E-mail: psmj@tiac.net
Website: http://www.psmj.com

Non Profit Capital Management
41 Main St.
Sterling, MA 01564
(781)933-6726
Fax: (781)933-6734

Michigan

BBC Entrepreneurial Training & Consulting LLC
803 N Main St.
Ann Arbor, MI 48104
(734)930-9741
Fax: (734)930-6629
E-mail: info@bioconsultants.com
Website: http://www.bioconsultants.com

Center for Simplified Strategic Planning Inc.
2219 Packard Rd., Ste. 13
Ann Arbor, MI 48104
(734)995-3465
E-mail: tidd@cssp.com
Website: http://www.cssp.com

Walter Frederick Consulting
1719 South Blvd.
Ann Arbor, MI 48104
(313)662-4336
Fax: (313)769-7505

Aimattech Consulting LLC
568 Woodway Ct., Ste. 1
Bloomfield Hills, MI 48302
(248) 540-3758
Fax: (248) 540-3011
E-mail: dpwconsult@aol.com
Website: http://www.aimattech.com

QualSAT International Inc.
30777 NW Highway., Ste. 101
Farmington Hills, MI 48334
866-899-0020
Fax: (248)932-3801
E-mail: info@qualsat.com
Website: http://www.qualsat.com

Fox Enterprises
6220 W Freeland Rd.
Freeland, MI 48623
(989)695-9170
Fax: (989)695-9174

T. L. Cramer Associates LLC
1788 Broadstone Rd.
Grosse Pointe Woods, MI 48236
(313)332-0182
E-mail: info@tlcramerassociates.com
Website: http://www.tlcramerassociates
.com

G.G.W. and Associates
1213 Hampton
Jackson, MI 49203
(517)782-2255
Fax: (517)782-2255

BHM Associates Inc.
2817 Canterbury Dr.
Midland, MI 48642
(989) 631-7109
E-mail: smiller@bhmassociates.net
Website: http://www.bhmassociates.net

MarketingHelp Inc.
6647 Riverwoods Ct. NE
Rockford, MI 49341
(616) 866-1198
Website: http://www.mktghelp.com

Rehmann, Robson PC
5800 Gratiot
Saginaw, MI 48605
(989)799-9580
Fax: (989)799-0227
E-mail: info@rehmann.com
Website: http://www.rehmann.com

Private Ventures Inc.
16000 W 9 Mile Rd., Ste. 504
Southfield, MI 48075
(248)569-1977
Free: 800-448-7614
Fax: (248)569-1838
E-mail: pventuresi@aol.com

JGK Associates
14464 Kerner Dr.
Sterling Heights, MI 48313
(810)247-9055
Fax: (248)822-4977
E-mail: kozlowski@home.com

Cool & Associates Inc.
921 Village Green Ln., Ste. 1068
Waterford, MI 48328
(248)683-1130
E-mail: jcool@cool-associates.com
Website: http://www.cool-associates.com

Griffioen Consulting Group Inc.
6689 Orchard Lake Rd., Ste. 295
West Bloomfield, MI 48322
(888)262-5850
Fax: (248)855-4084
Website: http://www.griffioenconsulting
.com

Minnesota

Health Fitness Corp.
31700 W 82nd St., Ste. 200
Minneapolis, MN 55431
(952)831-6830
E-mail: info@hfit.com
Website: http://www.hfit.com

Consatech Inc.
PO Box 1047
Burnsville, MN 55337
(612)953-1088
Fax: (612)435-2966

Kaes Analytics Inc.
14960 Ironwood Ct.
Eden Prairie, MN 55346
(952)942-2912

DRI Consulting
2 Otter Ln.
Saint Paul, MN 55127
(651)415-1400
Fax: (651)415-9968
E-mail: dric@dric.com
Website: http://www.dric.com

Markin Consulting
12072 87th Pl. N
Maple Grove, MN 55369
(763)493-3568
Fax: (763)322-5013

E-mail: markin@markinconsulting.com
Website: http://www.markinconsulting
.com

**Minnesota Cooperation Office for
Small Business & Job Creation Inc.**
5001 W 80th St., Ste. 825
Minneapolis, MN 55437
(612)830-1230
Fax: (612)830-1232
E-mail: mncoop@msn.com
Website: http://www.mnco.org

Power Systems Research
1365 Corporate Center Curve, 2nd Fl.
St. Paul, MN 55121
(612)905-8400
Free: (888)625-8612
Fax: (612)454-0760
E-mail: Barb@Powersys.com
Website: http://www.powersys.com

Missouri

**Business Planning and Development
Corp.**
4030 Charlotte St.
Kansas City, MO 64110
(816)753-0495
E-mail: humph@bpdev.demon.co.uk
Website: http://www.bpdev.demon.co.uk

CFO Service
10336 Donoho
St. Louis, MO 63131
(314)750-2940
E-mail: jskae@cfoservice.com
Website: http://www.cfoservice.com

Nebraska

**International Management Consulting
Group Inc.**
1309 Harlan Dr., Ste. 205
Bellevue, NE 68005
(402)291-4545
Free: 800-665-IMCG
Fax: (402)291-4343
E-mail: imcg@neonramp.com
Website: http://www.mgtconsulting.com

**Heartland Management Consulting
Group**
1904 Barrington Pky.
Papillion, NE 68046
(402)952-5339
Fax: (402)339-1319

Nevada

The DuBois Group
865 Tahoe Blvd., Ste. 108
Incline Village, NV 89451

(775)832-0550
Free: 800-375-2935
Fax: (775)832-0556
E-mail: DuBoisGrp@aol.com

New Hampshire

Wolff Consultants
10 Buck Rd.
Hanover, NH 03755
(603)643-6015

BPT Consulting Associates Ltd.
12 Parmenter Rd., Ste. B-6
Londonderry, NH 03053
(603)437-8484
Free: (888)278-0030
Fax: (603)434-5388
E-mail: bptcons@tiac.net
Website: http://www.bptconsulting.com

New Jersey

Delta Planning Inc.
138 Hillcrest Dr.
Denville, NJ 07834
(913)625-1742
Free: 800-672-0762
Fax: (973)625-3531
E-mail: DeltaP@worldnet.att.net
Website: http://deltaplanning.com

Kumar Associates Inc.
1004 Cumbermeade Rd.
Fort Lee, NJ 07024
(201)224-9480
Fax: (201)585-2343
E-mail: mail@kumarassociates.com
Website: http://kumarassociates.com

John Hall & Company Inc.
14 Houston Rd.
Little Falls, NJ 07424
(973)680-4449
Fax: (973)680-4581
E-mail: jhcompany@aol.com

Market Focus
12 Maryland Rd.
Maplewood, NJ 07040
(973)378-2470
Fax: (973)378-2470
E-mail: mcss66@marketfocus.com

Distinctive Marketing Inc.
516 Bloomfield Ave., Ste. 7
Montclair, NJ 07042
(973)746-9114
Fax: (973)783-5555
Website: http://www.distinctive
mktg.com

Vanguard Communications Corp.
45 S Park Pl., Ste. 210
Morristown, NJ 07960
(973)605-8000
Fax: (973)605-8329
Website: http://www.vanguard.net/

Bedminster Group Inc.
16 Arrowhead Dr.
Neshanic Station, NJ 08853
(908)347-0006
Fax: (908)369-4767
E-mail: info@bedminstergroup.com
Website: http://www.bedminstergroup
.com

ConMar International Ltd.
1405 Rte. 18, Ste. 200
Old Bridge, NJ 08857
(732)607-6415
Fax: (732)607-6480
Website: http://www.conmar-intl.com

PA Consulting Group
600 Alexander Pk., Ste. 209A
Princeton, NJ 08540
(609)806-0800
Fax: (609)936-8811
E-mail: info@paconsulting.com
Website: http://www.pa-consulting.com

Aurora Marketing Management Inc.
66 Witherspoon St., Ste. 600
Princeton, NJ 08542
(908)904-1125
Fax: (908)359-1108
E-mail: aurora2@voicenet.com
Website: http://www.auroramarketing
.net

Schkeeper Inc.
130-6 Bodman Pl.
Red Bank, NJ 07701
(732)219-1965
Fax: (732)530-3703
Website: http://www.schkeeper.com

Henry Branch Associates
2502 Harmon Cove Twr.
Secaucus, NJ 07094
(201)866-2008
Fax: (201)601-0101
E-mail: hbranch161@home.com

Robert Gibbons & Company Inc.
46 Knoll Rd.
Tenafly, NJ 07670-1050
(201)871-3933
Fax: (201)871-2173

PMC Management Consultants Inc.
6 Thistle Ln.
Three Bridges, NJ 08887-0332

(908)788-1014
Free: 800-PMC-0250
Fax: (908)806-7287
E-mail: inguiry@pmc-management.com
Website: http://www.pmc-management
.com

R.W. Bankart & Associates
20 Valley Ave., Ste. D-2
Westwood, NJ 07675-3607
(201)664-7672

New Mexico

Vondle & Associates Inc.
4926 Calle de Tierra, NE
Albuquerque, NM 87111
(505)292-8961
Fax: (505)296-2790
E-mail: vondle@aol.com

InfoNewMexico
2207 Black Hills Rd., NE
Rio Rancho, NM 87124
(505)891-2462
Fax: (505)896-8971

New York

Powers Research and Training Institute
PO Box 78
Bayville, NY 11709
(516)628-2250
Fax: (516)628-2252
E-mail: powercocch@compuserve.com
Website: http://www.nancypowers.com

Consortium House
296 Wittenberg Rd.
Bearsville, NY 12409
(845)679-8867
Fax: (845)679-9248
E-mail: eugenegs@aol.com
Website: http://www.chpub.com

Progressive Finance Corp.
3549 Tiemann Ave.
Bronx, NY 10469
(718)405-9029
Free: 800-225-8381
Fax: (718)405-1170

Wave Hill Associates Inc.
2621 Palisade Ave., Ste. 15-C
Bronx, NY 10463
(718)549-7368
Fax: (718)601-9670
E-mail: pepper@compuserve.com

Management Insight
96 Arlington Rd.
Buffalo, NY 14221
(716)631-3319

Fax: (716)631-0203
E-mail: michalski@foodservice
insight.com
Website: http://www.foodserviceinsight
.com

**Samani International Enterprises,
Marions Panyaught Consultancy**
2028 Parsons
Flushing, NY 11357-3436
(917)287-8087
Fax: 800-873-8939
E-mail: vjp2@biostrategist.com
Website: http://www.biostrategist.com

Marketing Resources Group
71-58 Austin St.
Forest Hills, NY 11375
(718)261-8882

**Mangabay Business Plans &
Development**

Subsidiary of Innis Asset Allocation
125-10 Queens Blvd., Ste. 2202
Kew Gardens, NY 11415
(905)527-1947
Fax: 509-472-1935
E-mail: mangabay@mangabay.com
Website: http://www.mangabay.com
Lee Toh, Managing Partner

ComputerEase Co.
1301 Monmouth Ave.
Lakewood, NY 08701
(212)406-9464
Fax: (914)277-5317
E-mail: crawfordc@juno.com

Boice Dunham Group
30 W 13th St.
New York, NY 10011
(212)924-2200
Fax: (212)924-1108

Elizabeth Capen
27 E 95th St.
New York, NY 10128
(212)427-7654
Fax: (212)876-3190

Haver Analytics
60 E 42nd St., Ste. 2424
New York, NY 10017
(212)986-9300
Fax: (212)986-5857
E-mail: data@haver.com
Website: http://www.haver.com

The Jordan, Edmiston Group Inc.
150 E 52nd Ave., 18th Fl.
New York, NY 10022
(212)754-0710
Fax: (212)754-0337

KPMG International
345 Park Ave.
New York, NY 10154-0102
(212)758-9700
Fax: (212)758-9819
Website: http://www.kpmg.com

Mahoney Cohen Consulting Corp.
111 W 40th St., 12th Fl.
New York, NY 10018
(212)490-8000
Fax: (212)790-5913

Management Practice Inc.
342 Madison Ave.
New York, NY 10173-1230
(212)867-7948
Fax: (212)972-5188
Website: http://www.mpiweb.com

Moseley Associates Inc.
342 Madison Ave., Ste. 1414
New York, NY 10016
(212)213-6673
Fax: (212)687-1520

Practice Development Counsel
60 Sutton Pl. S
New York, NY 10022
(212)593-1549
Fax: (212)980-7940
E-mail: pwhaserot@pdcounsel.com
Website: http://www.pdcounsel.com

Unique Value International Inc.
575 Madison Ave., 10th Fl.
New York, NY 10022-1304
(212)605-0590
Fax: (212)605-0589

The Van Tulleken Co.
126 E 56th St.
New York, NY 10022
(212)355-1390
Fax: (212)755-3061
E-mail: newyork@vantulleken.com

Vencon Management Inc.
301 W 53rd St.
New York, NY 10019
(212)581-8787
Fax: (212)397-4126
Website: http://www.venconinc.com

Werner International Inc.
55 E 52nd, 29th Fl.
New York, NY 10055
(212)909-1260
Fax: (212)909-1273
E-mail: richard.downing@rgh.com
Website: http://www.wernertex.com

Zimmerman Business Consulting Inc.
44 E 92nd St., Ste. 5-B
New York, NY 10128
(212)860-3107
Fax: (212)860-7730
E-mail: ljzzbci@aol.com
Website: http://www.zbcinc.com

Overton Financial
7 Allen Rd.
Peekskill, NY 10566
(914)737-4649
Fax: (914)737-4696

Stromberg Consulting
2500 Westchester Ave.
Purchase, NY 10577
(914)251-1515
Fax: (914)251-1562
E-mail: strategy@stromberg_
consulting.com
Website: http://www.stromberg_
consulting.com

**Innovation Management
Consulting Inc.**
209 Dewitt Rd.
Syracuse, NY 13214-2006
(315)425-5144
Fax: (315)445-8989
E-mail: missonneb@axess.net

M. Clifford Agress
891 Fulton St.
Valley Stream, NY 11580
(516)825-8955
Fax: (516)825-8955

Destiny Kinal Marketing Consultancy
105 Chemung St.
Waverly, NY 14892
(607)565-8317
Fax: (607)565-4083

Valutis Consulting Inc.
5350 Main St., Ste. 7
Williamsville, NY 14221-5338
(716)634-2553
Fax: (716)634-2554
E-mail: valutis@localnet.com
Website: http://www.valutisconsulting
.com

North Carolina

Best Practices L.L.C.
6320 Quadrangle Dr., Ste. 200
Chapel Hill, NC 27514
(919)403-0251
Fax: (919)403-0144
E-mail: best@best:in/class
Website: http://www.best-in-class.com

Norelli & Co.
1340 Harding Pl.
Charlotte, NC 28204
(704)376-5484
Fax: (704)376-5485
E-mail: consult@norelli.com
Website: http://www.norelli.com

North Dakota

Center for Innovation
Ina Mae Rude Entrepreneur Ctr.
4200 James Ray Dr.
Grand Forks, ND 58203
(701)777-3132
Fax: (701)777-2339
E-mail: info@innovators.net
Website: http://www.innovators.net

Ohio

Transportation Technology Services
208 Harmon Rd.
Aurora, OH 44202
(330)562-3596

Empro Systems Inc.
4777 Red Bank Expy., Ste. 1
Cincinnati, OH 45227-1542
(513)271-2042
Fax: (513)271-2042

Alliance Management International Ltd.
1440 Windrow Ln.
Cleveland, OH 44147-3200
(440)838-1922
Fax: (440)838-0979
E-mail: bgruss@amiltd.com
Website: http://www.amiltd.com

Bozell Kamstra Public Relations
1301 E 9th St., Ste. 3400
Cleveland, OH 44114
(216)623-1511
Fax: (216)623-1501
E-mail: jfeniger@cleveland.bozell
kamstra.com
Website: http://www.bozellkamstra.com

Cory Dillon Associates
111 Schreyer Pl. E
Columbus, OH 43214
(614)262-8211
Fax: (614)262-3806

Holcomb Gallagher Adams
300 Marconi, Ste. 303
Columbus, OH 43215
(614)221-3343
Fax: (614)221-3367
E-mail: riadams@acme.freenet.oh.us

Young & Associates
PO Box 711
Kent, OH 44240
(330)678-0524
Free: 800-525-9775
Fax: (330)678-6219
E-mail: online@younginc.com
Website: http://www.younginc.com

Robert A. Westman & Associates
8981 Inversary Dr. SE
Warren, OH 44484-2551
(330)856-4149
Fax: (330)856-2564

Oklahoma

Innovative Partners L.L.C.
4900 Richmond Sq., Ste. 100
Oklahoma City, OK 73118
(405)840-0033
Fax: (405)843-8359
E-mail: ipartners@juno.com

Oregon

INTERCON - The International Converting Institute
5200 Badger Rd.
Crooked River Ranch, OR 97760
(541)548-1447
Fax: (541)548-1618
E-mail: johnbowler@crookedriverranch.com

Talbott ARM
HC 60, Box 5620
Lakeview, OR 97630
(541)635-8587
Fax: (503)947-3482

Management Technology Associates Ltd.
2768 SW Sherwood Dr, Ste. 105
Portland, OR 97201-2251
(503)224-5220
Fax: (503)224-5334
E-mail: lcuster@mta-ltd.com
Website: http://www.mgmt-tech.com

Pennsylvania

Healthscope Inc.
400 Lancaster Ave.
Devon, PA 19333
(610)687-6199
Fax: (610)687-6376
E-mail: health@voicenet.com
Website: http://www.healthscope.net/

Elayne Howard & Associates Inc.
3501 Masons Mill Rd., Ste. 501
Huntingdon Valley, PA 19006-3509
(215)657-9550

GRA Inc.
115 West Ave., Ste. 201
Jenkintown, PA 19046
(215)884-7500
Fax: (215)884-1385
E-mail: gramail@gra-inc.com
Website: http://www.gra-inc.com

Mifflin County Industrial Development Corp.
Mifflin County Industrial Plz.
6395 SR 103 N
Bldg. 50
Lewistown, PA 17044
(717)242-0393
Fax: (717)242-1842
E-mail: mcide@acsworld.net

Autech Products
1289 Revere Rd.
Morrisville, PA 19067
(215)493-3759
Fax: (215)493-9791
E-mail: autech4@yahoo.com

Advantage Associates
434 Avon Dr.
Pittsburgh, PA 15228
(412)343-1558
Fax: (412)362-1684
E-mail: ecocba1@aol.com

Regis J. Sheehan & Associates
Pittsburgh, PA 15220
(412)279-1207

James W. Davidson Company Inc.
23 Forest View Rd.
Wallingford, PA 19086
(610)566-1462

Puerto Rico

Diego Chevere & Co.
Metro Parque 7, Ste. 204
Metro Office
Caparra Heights, PR 00920
(787)774-9595
Fax: (787)774-9566
E-mail: dcco@coqui.net

Manuel L. Porrata and Associates
898 Munoz Rivera Ave., Ste. 201
San Juan, PR 00927
(787)765-2140
Fax: (787)754-3285
E-mail: m_porrata@manuelporrata.com
Website: http://manualporrata.com

South Carolina

Aquafood Business Associates
PO Box 13267
Charleston, SC 29422

(843)795-9506
Fax: (843)795-9477
E-mail: rraba@aol.com

Profit Associates Inc.
PO Box 38026
Charleston, SC 29414
(803)763-5718
Fax: (803)763-5719
E-mail: bobrog@awod.com
Website: http://www.awod.com/gallery/
business/proasc

Strategic Innovations International
12 Executive Ct.
Lake Wylie, SC 29710
(803)831-1225
Fax: (803)831-1177
E-mail: stratinnov@aol.com
Website: http://www.strategic
innovations.com

Minus Stage
Box 4436
Rock Hill, SC 29731
(803)328-0705
Fax: (803)329-9948

Tennessee

Daniel Petchers & Associates
8820 Fernwood CV
Germantown, TN 38138
(901)755-9896

Business Choices
1114 Forest Harbor, Ste. 300
Hendersonville, TN 37075-9646
(615)822-8692
Free: 800-737-8382
Fax: (615)822-8692
E-mail: bz-ch@juno.com

**RCFA Healthcare Management
Services L.L.C.**
9648 Kingston Pke., Ste. 8
Knoxville, TN 37922
(865)531-0176
Free: 800-635-4040
Fax: (865)531-0722
E-mail: info@rcfa.com
Website: http://www.rcfa.com

Growth Consultants of America
3917 Trimble Rd.
Nashville, TN 37215
(615)383-0550
Fax: (615)269-8940
E-mail: 70244.451@compuserve.com

Texas

**Integrated Cost Management
Systems Inc.**
6001 W I-20, Ste. 209
Arlington, TX 76094-0206
(817)475-2945
E-mail: abm@icms.net
Website: http://www.icms.net

Business Resource Software Inc.
1779 Wells Branch Pky.
Austin, TX 78728
Free: 800-423-1228
Fax: (512)251-4401
E-mail: info@brs-inc.com
Website: http://www.brs-inc.com

Erisa Adminstrative Services Inc.
12325 Hymeadow Dr., Bldg. 4
Austin, TX 78750-1847
(512)250-9020
Fax: (512)250-9487
Website: http://www.cserisa.com

R. Miller Hicks & Co.
1011 W 11th St.
Austin, TX 78703
(512)477-7000
Fax: (512)477-9697
E-mail: millerhicks@rmhicks.com
Website: http://www.rmhicks.com

Pragmatic Tactics Inc.
3303 Westchester Ave.
College Station, TX 77845
(409)696-5294
Free: 800-570-5294
Fax: (409)696-4994
E-mail: ptactics@aol.com
Website: http://www.ptatics.com

Zaetric Business Solutions LLC
27350 Blueberry Hill, Ste. 14
Conroe, TX 77385
(713)621-4885
Fax: (713)824-1654
E-mail: inquiries@zaetric.com
Website: http://www.zaetric.com

Perot Systems
12404 Park Central Dr.
Dallas, TX 75251
(972)340-5000
Free: 800-688-4333
Fax: (972)455-4100
E-mail: corp.comm@ps.net
Website: http://www.perotsystems.com

ReGENERATION Partners
3811 Turtle Creek Blvd., Ste. 300
Dallas, TX 75219

(214)559-3999
Free: 800-406-1112
E-mail: info@regeneration-partner.com
Website: http://www.regeneration-
partners.com

High Technology Associates
5739 Longmont Ln.
Houston, TX 77057
(713)963-9300
Fax: (713)963-8341
E-mail: baker@hta-usa.com
Website: http://www.high-technology-
associates.com

SynerImages LLC
1 Riverway, Ste. 1700
Houston, TX 77056
(713)840-6442
Fax: (713)963-8341
Website: http://www.synerimages.com

PROTEC
4607 Linden Pl.
Pearland, TX 77584
(281)997-9872
Fax: (281)997-9895
E-mail: p.oman@ix.netcom.com

Bastian Public Relations
614 San Dizier
San Antonio, TX 78232
(210)404-1839
E-mail: lisa@bastianpr.com
Website: http://www.bastianpr.com
Lisa Bastian CBC

**Business Strategy Development
Consultants**
PO Box 690365
San Antonio, TX 78269
(210)696-8000
Free: 800-927-BSDC
Fax: (210)696-8000

Utah

Vector Resources
7651 S Main St., Ste. 106
Midvale, UT 84047-7158
(801) 352-8500
Fax: (801) 352-8506
E-mail: info@vectorresources.com
Website: http://www.vectorresources
.com

StreetMaker Inc.
524 West 440 South
Orem, UT 84058-6115
(801)607-2246
Fax: (800)561-4928
E-mail: contact@streetmaker.com
Website: http://www.streetmaker.com

Biomedical Management Resources
PO Box 521125
Salt Lake City, UT 84152-1125
(801)272-4668
Fax: (801)277-3290
E-mail: SeniorManagement@Biomedical
Management.com
Website: http://www.biomedical
management.com

Marriott Consulting Inc.
6945 S Knudsen Ridge Cir.
Salt Lake City, UT 84121
(801)944-5000
Fax: (801)947-9022
E-mail: info@marriottconsulting.com
Website: http://www.marriott
consulting.com

Virginia

Crown Consulting Inc.
1400 Key Blvd., Ste. 1100
Arlington, VA 22209
(703)650-0663
Fax: (703)243-1280
E-mail: info@crownci.com
Website: http://www.crownci.com

Dare Mighty Things
901 N Glebe Rd., Ste. 1005
Arlington, VA 22203
(703)752-4331
Fax: (703)752-4332
E-mail: info@daremightythings.com
Website: http://www.daremightythings
.com

Elliott B. Jaffa
2530-B S Walter Reed Dr.
Arlington, VA 22206
(703)931-0040

Koach Enterprises - USA
5529 N 18th St.
Arlington, VA 22205
(703)241-8361
Fax: (703)241-8623

AMX International Inc.
9016 Triple Ridge Rd.
Fairfax Station, VA 22039-3003
(703)864-7046
Fax: (703)690-9994
E-mail: info@amxi.com
Website: http://www.amxi.com

Joel Greenstein & Associates
6212 Nethercombe Ct.
McLean, VA 22101
(703) 893-1888

John C. Randall and Associates Inc.
10197 Georgetown Rd.
Mechanicsville, VA 23116
(804)746-4450

Charles Scott Pugh (Investor)
4101 Pittaway Dr.
Richmond, VA 23235-1022
(804)560-0979
Fax: (804)560-4670

Robert Martens & Co.
2226 Floyd Ave.
Richmond, VA 23220
(804) 342-8850
Fax: (804)342-8860
E-mail: rm@robertmartens.com
Website: http://www.robertmartens.com

William W. Garry Inc.
PO Box 61662
Virginia Beach, VA 23466
(757) 467-7874
E-mail: drbillgarry@freeyellow.com

Regis J. Sheehan & Associates
500 Belmont Bay Dr.
Woodbridge, VA 22191-5445
(703)491-7377

Washington

Burlington Consultants
10900 NE 8th St., Ste. 900
Bellevue, WA 98004
(425)688-3060
Fax: (425)454-4383
E-mail: partners@burlington
consultants.com
Website: http://www.burlington
consultants.com

Perry L. Smith Consulting
800 Bellevue Way NE, Ste. 400
Bellevue, WA 98004-4208
(425)462-2072
Fax: (425)462-5638

St. Charles Consulting Group
1420 NW Gilman Blvd.
Issaquah, WA 98027
(425)557-8708
Fax: (425)557-8731
E-mail: info@stcharlesconsulting.com
Website: http://www.stcharlesconsulting
.com

**Independent Automotive Training
Services**
PO Box 334
Kirkland, WA 98083
(425)822-5715
E-mail: ltunney@autosvccon.com
Website: http://www.autosvccon.com

Kahle Associate Inc.
6203 204th Dr. NE
Redmond, WA 98053
(425)836-8763
Fax: (425)868-3770
E-mail: randykahle@kahleassociates.com
Website: http://www.kahleassociates.com

Dan Collin
3419 Wallingord Ave N, No. 2
Seattle, WA 98103
(206)634-9469
E-mail: dc@dancollin.com
Website: http://members.home.net/
dcollin/

ECG Management Consultants Inc.
1111 3rd Ave., Ste. 2700
Seattle, WA 98101-3201
(206)689-2200
Fax: (206)689-2209
E-mail: ecg@ecgmc.com
Website: http://www.ecgmc.com

**Northwest Trade Adjustment
Assistance Center**
900 4th Ave., Ste. 2430
Seattle, WA 98164-1001
(206)622-2730
Free: 800-667-8087
Fax: (206)622-1105
E-mail: matchingfunds@nwtaac.org
Website: http://www.taacenters.org

Business Planning Consultants
S 3510 Ridgeview Dr.
Spokane, WA 99206
(509)928-0332
Fax: (509)921-0842
E-mail: bpci@nextdim.com

West Virginia

**Stanley & Associates Inc./
BusinessandMarketingPlans.com**
1687 Robert C. Byrd Dr.
Beckley, WV 25801
(304)252-0324
Free: 888-752-6720
Fax: (304)252-0470
E-mail: cclay@charterinternet.com
Website: http://www.Businessand
MarketingPlans.com
Christopher Clay

Wisconsin

White & Associates Inc.
5349 Somerset Ln. S
Greenfield, WI 53221
(414)281-7373
Fax: (414)281-7006
E-mail: wnaconsult@aol.com

Small business administration regional offices

This section contains a listing of Small Business Administration offices arranged numerically by region. Service areas are provided. Contact the appropriate office for a referral to the nearest field office, or visit the Small Business Administration online at www.sba.gov.

Region 1

U.S. Small Business Administration
Region I Office
10 Causeway St., Ste. 812
Boston, MA 02222-1093
Phone: (617)565-8415
Fax: (617)565-8420
Serves Connecticut, Maine, Massachusetts, New Hampshire, Rhode Island, and Vermont.

Region 2

U.S. Small Business Administration
Region II Office
26 Federal Plaza, Ste. 3108
New York, NY 10278
Phone: (212)264-1450
Fax: (212)264-0038
Serves New Jersey, New York, Puerto Rico, and the Virgin Islands.

Region 3

U.S. Small Business Administration
Region III Office
1150 First Avenue Suite 1001
King of Prussia, PA 19406
(610)382-3092
Serves Delaware, the District of Columbia, Maryland, Pennsylvania, Virginia, and West Virginia.

Region 4

U.S. Small Business Administration
Region IV Office
233 Peachtree St. NE
Harris Tower 1800
Atlanta, GA 30303
Phone: (404)331-4999
Fax: (404)331-2354
Serves Alabama, Florida, Georgia, Kentucky, Mississippi, North Carolina, South Carolina, and Tennessee.

Region 5

U.S. Small Business Administration
Region V Office

500 W. Madison St.
Citicorp Center, Ste. 1150
Chicago, IL 60661
Phone: (312)353-0357
Fax: (312)353-3426
Serves Illinois, Indiana, Michigan, Minnesota, Ohio, and Wisconsin.

Region 6

U.S. Small Business Administration
Region VI Office
4300 Amon Carter Blvd., Ste. 108
Fort Worth, TX 76155
Phone: (817)684-5581
Fax: (817)684-5588
Serves Arkansas, Louisiana, New Mexico, Oklahoma, and Texas.

Region 7

U.S. Small Business Administration
Region VII Office
1000 Walnut Suite 530
Kansas City, MO 64106
Phone: (816)426-4840
Fax: (816)426-4848
Serves Iowa, Kansas, Missouri, and Nebraska.

Region 8

U.S. Small Business Administration
Region VIII Office
721 19th St., Ste. 400
Denver, CO 80202
Phone: (303)844-0500
Fax: (303)844-0506
Serves Colorado, Montana, North Dakota, South Dakota, Utah, and Wyoming.

Region 9

U.S. Small Business Administration
Region IX Office
330 N Brand Blvd., Ste. 1200
Glendale, CA 91203
Phone: (818)552-3437
Fax: (818)552-0344
Serves American Samoa, Arizona, California, Guam, Hawaii, Nevada, and the Trust Territory of the Pacific Islands.

Region 10

U.S. Small Business Administration
Region X Office
2401 Fourth Ave., Ste. 400
Seattle, WA 98121
Phone: (206)553-5676
Fax: (206)553-4155

Serves Alaska, Idaho, Oregon, and Washington.

Small business development centers

This section contains a listing of all Small Business Development Centers, organized alphabetically by state/U.S. territory, then by city, then by agency name.

Alabama

Alabama SBDC

UNIVERSITY OF ALABAMA
2800 Milan Court Suite 124
Birmingham, AL 35211-6908
Phone: 205-943-6750
Fax: 205-943-6752
E-Mail: wcampbell@provost.uab.edu
Website: http://www.asbdc.org
Mr. William Campbell Jr, State Director

Alaska

Alaska SBDC

UNIVERSITY OF ALASKA - ANCHORAGE
430 West Seventh Avenue, Suite 110
Anchorage, AK 99501
Phone: 907-274 -7232
Fax: 907-272-0565
E-Mail: Isaac.Vanderburg@aksbdc.org
Website: http://www.aksbdc.org
Isaac Vanderburg, State Director

American Samoa

American Samoa SBDC

AMERICAN SAMOA COMMUNITY COLLEGE
P.O. Box 2609
Pago Pago, American Samoa 96799
Phone: 011-684-699-4830
Fax: 011-684-699-6132
E-Mail: hthweatt.sbdc@hotmail.com
Website: www.as-sbdc.org
Mr. Herbert Thweatt, Director

Arizona

Arizona SBDC

MARICOPA COUNTY COMMUNITY COLLEGE
2411 West 14th Street, Suite 114
Tempe, AZ 85281
Phone: 480-731-8720
Fax: 480-731-8729

E-Mail: janice.washington@domail
.maricopa.edu
Website: http://www.azsbdc.net
Janice Washington, State Director

Arkansas

Arkansas SBDC

UNIVERSITY OF ARKANSAS

2801 South University Avenue
Little Rock, AR 72204
Phone: 501-683-7700
Fax: 501-683-7720
E-Mail: jmroderick@ualr.edu
Website: http://asbtdc.org
Ms. Janet M. Roderick, State Director

California

California - Northern California Regional SBDC

Northern California SBDC

HUMBOLDT STATE UNIVERSITY

1 Harpst Street 2006A, 209 Siemens Hall
Arcata, CA, 95521
Phone: 707-826-3920
Fax: 707-826-3912
E-Mail: Kristin.Johnson@humboldt.edu
Website: https://www.norcalsbdc.org
Kristin Johnson, Regional Director

California - Northern California SBDC

CALIFORNIA STATE UNIVERSITY - CHICO

35 Main St., Rm 203rr
Chico, CA 95929-0765
Phone: 530-898-5443
Fax: 530-898-4734
E-Mail: dripke@csuchico.edu
Website: https://www.necsbdc.org
Mr. Dan Ripke, Interim Regional Director

California - San Diego and Imperial SBDC

SOUTHWESTERN COMMUNITY COLLEGE

880 National City Boulevard, Suite 103
National City, CA 91950
Phone: 619-216-6721
Fax: 619-216-6692
E-Mail: awilson@swccd.edu
Website: http://www.SBDCRegional
Network.org
Aleta Wilson, Regional Director

California - UC Merced SBDC

UC Merced Lead Center

UNIVERSITY OF CALIFORNIA - MERCED

550 East Shaw, Suite 105A
Fresno, CA 93710
Phone: 559-241-6590
Fax: 559-241-7422
E-Mail: dhowerton@ucmerced.edu
Website: http://sbdc.ucmerced.edu
Diane Howerton, State Director

California - Orange County/Inland Empire SBDC

Tri-County Lead SBDC

CALIFORNIA STATE UNIVERSITY - FULLERTON

800 North State College Boulevard, SGMH 5313
Fullerton, CA 92834
Phone: 714-278-5168
Fax: 714-278-7101
E-Mail: kmpayne@fullerton.edu
Website: http://www.leadsbdc.org
Katrina Payne Smith, Lead Center Director

California - Los Angeles Region SBDC

LONG BEACH CITY COLLEGE

4900 E. Conant Street, Building 2
Long Beach, CA 90808
Phone: 562-938-5006
Fax: 562-938-5030
E-Mail: jtorres@lbcc.edu
Website: http://www.smallbizla.org
Jesse Torres, Lead Center Director

Colorado

Colorado SBDC

COLORADO SBDC

1625 Broadway, Suite 2700
Denver, CO 80202
Phone: 303-892-3864
Fax: 303-892-3848
E-Mail: Kelly.Manning@state.co.us
Website: http://www.www.coloradosbdc
.org
Ms. Kelly Manning, State Director

Connecticut

Connecticut SBDC

UNIVERSITY OF CONNECTICUT

2100 Hillside Road, Unit 1044
Storrs, CT 06269
Phone: 855-428-7232

E-Mail: ecarter@uconn.edu
Website: www.ctsbdc.com
Emily Carter, State Director

Delaware

Delaware SBDC

DELAWARE TECHNOLOGY PARK

1 Innovation Way, Suite 301
Newark, DE 19711
Phone: 302-831-4283
Fax: 302-831-1423
E-Mail: jmbowman@udel.edu
Website: http://www.delawaresbdc.org
Mike Bowman, State Director

District of Columbia

District of Columbia SBDC

HOWARD UNIVERSITY

2600 6th Street, NW Room 128
Washington, DC 20059
Phone: 202-806-1550
Fax: 202-806-1777
E-Mail: darrell.brown@howard.edu
Website: http://www.dcsbdc.com/
Darrell Brown, Executive Director

Florida

Florida SBDC

UNIVERSITY OF WEST FLORIDA

11000 University Parkway, Building 38
Pensacola, FL 32514
Phone: 850-473-7800
Fax: 850-473-7813
E-Mail: mmyhre@uwf.edu
Website: http://www.floridasbdc.com
Michael Myhre, State Director

Georgia

Georgia SBDC

UNIVERSITY OF GEORGIA

1180 East Broad Street
Athens, GA 30602
Phone: 706-542-6762
Fax: 706-542-7935
E-mail: aadams@georgiasbdc.org
Website: http://www.georgiasbdc.org
Mr. Allan Adams, State Director

Guam

Guam Small Business Development Center

UNIVERSITY OF GUAM

Pacific Islands SBDC
P.O. Box 5014 - U.O.G. Station

Mangilao, GU 96923
Phone: 671-735-2590
Fax: 671-734-2002
E-mail: casey@pacificsbdc.com
Website: http://www.uog.edu/sbdc
Mr. Casey Jeszenka, Director

Hawaii

Hawaii SBDC

UNIVERSITY OF HAWAII - HILO
200 W. Kawili Street, Suite 107
Hilo, HI 96720
Phone: 808-974-7515
Fax: 808-974-7683
E-Mail: cathy.wiltse@hisbdc.org
Website: http://www.hisbdc.org
Cathy Wiltse, State Director

Idaho

Idaho SBDC

BOISE STATE UNIVERSITY
1910 University Drive
Boise, ID 83725
Phone: 208-426-3838
Fax: 208-426-3877
E-mail: ksewell@boisestate.edu
Website: http://www.idahosbdc.org
Katie Sewell, State Director

Illinois

Illinois SBDC

DEPARTMENT OF COMMERCE AND ECONOMIC OPPORTUNITY
500 E. Monroe
Springfield, IL 62701
Phone: 217-524-5700
Fax: 217-524-0171
E-mail: mark.petrilli@illinois.gov
Website: http://www.ilsbdc.biz
Mr. Mark Petrilli, State Director

Indiana

Indiana SBDC

INDIANA ECONOMIC DEVELOPMENT CORPORATION
One North Capitol, Suite 700
Indianapolis, IN 46204
Phone: 317-232-8805
Fax: 317-232-8872
E-mail: JSchpok@iedc.in.gov
Website: http://www.isbdc.org
Jacob Schpok, State Director

Iowa

Iowa SBDC

IOWA STATE UNIVERSITY
2321 North Loop Drive, Suite 202
Ames, IA 50010
Phone: 515-294-2030
Fax: 515-294-6522
E-mail: lshimkat@iastate.edu
Website: http://www.iowasbdc.org
Lisa Shimkat, State Director

Kansas

Kansas SBDC

FORT HAYS STATE UNIVERSITY
214 SW Sixth Street, Suite 301
Topeka, KS 66603
Phone: 785-296-6514
Fax: 785-291-3261
E-mail: panichello@ksbdc.net
Website: http://www.fhsu.edu/ksbdc
Greg Panichello, State Director

Kentucky

Kentucky SBDC

UNIVERSITY OF KENTUCKY
One Quality Street
Lexington, KY 40507
Phone: 859-257-7668
Fax: 859-323-1907
E-mail: lrnaug0@uky.edu
Website: http://www.ksbdc.org
Becky Naugle, State Director

Louisiana

Louisiana SBDC

UNIVERSITY OF LOUISIANA - MONROE

College of Business Administration
700 University Avenue
Monroe, LA 71209
Phone: 318-342-5507
Fax: 318-342-5510
E-mail: rkessler@lsbdc.org
Website: http://www.lsbdc.org
Rande Kessler, State Director

Maine

Maine SBDC

UNIVERSITY OF SOUTHERN MAINE
96 Falmouth Street P.O. Box 9300
Portland, ME 04104
Phone: 207-780-4420
Fax: 207-780-4810

E-mail: mark.delisle@maine.edu
Website: http://www.mainesbdc.org
Mark Delisle, State Director

Maryland

Maryland SBDC

UNIVERSITY OF MARYLAND
7100 Baltimore Avenue, Suite 401
College Park, MD 20742
Phone: 301-403-8300
Fax: 301-403-8303
E-mail: rsprow@mdsbdc.umd.edu
Website: http://www.mdsbdc.umd.edu
Renee Sprow, State Director

Massachusetts

Massachusetts SBDC

UNIVERSITY OF MASSACHUSETTS
23 Tillson Farm Road
Amherst, MA 01003
Phone: 413-545-6301
Fax: 413-545-1273
E-mail: gparkin@msbdc.umass.edu
Website: http://www.www.msbdc.org
Georgianna Parkin, State Director

Michigan

Michigan SBTDC

GRAND VALLEY STATE UNIVERSITY
510 West Fulton Avenue
Grand Rapids, MI 49504
Phone: 616-331-7480
Fax: 616-331-7485
E-mail: boesen@gvsu.edu
Website: http://www.misbtdc.org
Nancy Boese, State Director

Minnesota

Minnesota SBDC

MINNESOTA SMALL BUSINESS DEVELOPMENT CENTER
1st National Bank Building
332 Minnesota Street, Suite E200
St. Paul, MN 55101-1349
Phone: 651-259-7420
Fax: 651-296-5287
E-mail: Bruce.Strong@state.mn.us
Website: http://www.mnsbdc.com
Bruce H. Strong, State Director

Mississippi

Mississippi SBDC

UNIVERSITY OF MISSISSIPPI
122 Jeanette Phillips Drive
P.O. Box 1848

University, MS 38677
Phone: 662-915-5001
Fax: 662-915-5650
E-mail: wgurley@olemiss.edu
Website: http://www.mssbdc.org
Doug Gurley, Jr., State Director

Missouri

Missouri SBDC

UNIVERSITY OF MISSOURI

410 South 6th Street, ?200
Engineering North
Columbia, MO 65211
Phone: 573-882-9206
Fax: 573-884-4297
E-mail: bouchardc@missouri.edu
Website: http://www.missouribusiness.net
Chris Bouchard, State Director

Montana

Montana SBDC

DEPARTMENT OF COMMERCE

301 S. Park Avenue, Room 114
Helena, MT 59601
Phone: 406-841-2746
Fax: 406-841-2728
E-mail: adesch@mt.gov
Website: http://www.sbdc.mt.gov
Ms. Ann Desch, State Director

Nebraska

Nebraska SBDC

UNIVERSITY OF NEBRASKA - OMAHA

200 Mammel Hall, 67th & Pine Streets
Omaha, NE 68182
Phone: 402-554-2521
Fax: 402-554-3473
E-mail: rbernier@unomaha.edu
Website: http://nbdc.unomaha.edu
Robert Bernier, State Director

Nevada

Nevada SBDC

UNIVERSITY OF NEVADA - RENO

Reno College of Business, Room 411
Reno, NV 89557-0100
Phone: 775-784-1717
Fax: 775-784-4337
E-mail: males@unr.edu
Website: http://www.nsbdc.org
Sam Males, State Director

New Hampshire

New Hampshire SBDC

UNIVERSITY OF NEW HAMPSHIRE

10 Garrison Avenue
Durham, NH 03824-3593
Phone: 603-862-2200
Fax: 603-862-4876
E-mail: Mary.Collins@unh.edu
Website: http://www.nhsbdc.org
Mary Collins, State Director

New Jersey

New Jersey SBDC

RUTGERS UNIVERSITY

1 Washington Park, 3rd Floor
Newark, NJ 07102
Phone: 973-353-1927
Fax: 973-353-1110
E-mail: bhopper@njsbdc.com
Website: http://www.njsbdc.com
Brenda Hopper, State Director

New Mexico

New Mexico SBDC

SANTA FE COMMUNITY COLLEGE

6401 Richards Avenue
Santa Fe, NM 87508
Phone: 505-428-1362
Fax: 505-428-1469
E-mail: russell.wyrick@sfcc.edu
Website: http://www.nmsbdc.org
Russell Wyrick, State Director

New York

New York SBDC

STATE UNIVERSITY OF NEW YORK

22 Corporate Woods, 3rd Floor
Albany, NY 12246
Phone: 518-443-5398
Fax: 518-443-5275
E-mail: j.king@nyssbdc.org
Website: http://www.nyssbdc.org
Jim King, State Director

North Carolina

North Carolina SBDTC

UNIVERSITY OF NORTH CAROLINA

5 West Hargett Street, Suite 600
Raleigh, NC 27601
Phone: 919-715-7272
Fax: 919-715-7777
E-mail: sdaugherty@sbtdc.org
Website: http://www.sbtdc.org
Scott Daugherty, State Director

North Dakota

North Dakota SBDC

UNIVERSITY OF NORTH DAKOTA

1200 Memorial Highway, PO Box 5509
Bismarck, ND 58506
Phone: 701-328-5375
Fax: 701-250-4304
E-mail: dkmartin@ndsbdc.org
Website: http://www.ndsbdc.org
David Martin, State Director

Ohio

Ohio SBDC

OHIO DEPARTMENT OF DEVELOPMENT

77 South High Street, 28th Floor
Columbus, OH 43216
Phone: 614-466-2711
Fax: 614-466-1789
E-mail: ezra.escudero@development.ohio.gov
Website: http://www.ohiosbdc.org
Ezra Escudero, State Director

Oklahoma

Oklahoma SBDC

SOUTHEAST OKLAHOMA STATE UNIVERSITY

1405 N. 4th Avenue, PMB 2584
Durant, OK 74701
Phone: 580-745-2955
Fax: 580-745-7471
E-mail: wcarter@se.edu
Website: http://www.osbdc.org
Grady Pennington, State Director

Oregon

Oregon SBDC

LANE COMMUNITY COLLEGE

1445 Willamette Street, Suite 5
Eugene, OR 97401
Phone: 541-463-5250
Fax: 541-345-6006
E-mail: gregorym@lanecc.edu
Website: http://www.bizcenter.org
Mark Gregory, State Director

Pennsylvania

Pennsylvania SBDC

UNIVERSITY OF PENNSYLVANIA

The Wharton School

3819-33 Chestnut Street, Suite 325
Philadelphia, PA 19104

Phone: 215-898-1219
Fax: 215-573-2135
E-mail: cconroy@wharton.upenn.edu
Website: http://pasbdc.org
Christian Conroy, State Director

Puerto Rico

Puerto Rico SBDC

INTER-AMERICAN UNIVERSITY OF PUERTO RICO
416 Ponce de Leon Avenue, Union Plaza, Tenth Floor
Hato Rey, PR 00918
Phone: 787-763-6811
Fax: 787-763-6875
E-mail: cmarti@prsbdc.org
Website: http://www.prsbdc.org
Carmen Marti, Executive Director

Rhode Island

Rhode Island SBDC

UNIVERSITY OF RHODE ISLAND
75 Lower College Road, 2nd Floor
Kingston, RI 02881
Phone: 401-874-4576
E-mail: gsonnenfeld@uri.edu
Website: http://www.risbdc.org
Gerald Sonnenfeld, State Director

South Carolina

South Carolina SBDC

UNIVERSITY OF SOUTH CAROLINA

Moore School of Business
1014 Greene Street
Columbia, SC 29208
Phone: 803-777-0749
Fax: 803-777-6876
E-mail: michele.abraham@moore.sc.edu
Website: http://www.scsbdc.com
Michele Abraham, State Director

South Dakota

South Dakota SBDC

UNIVERSITY OF SOUTH DAKOTA
414 East Clark Street, Patterson Hall
Vermillion, SD 57069
Phone: 605-677-5103
Fax: 605-677-5427
E-mail: jeff.eckhoff@usd.edu
Website: http://www.usd.edu/sbdc
Jeff Eckhoff, State Director

Tennessee

Tennessee SBDC

MIDDLE TENNESSEE STATE UNIVERSITY
3050 Medical Center Parkway, Ste. 200
Nashville, TN 37129
Phone: 615-849-9999
Fax: 615-893-7089
E-mail: pgeho@tsbdc.org
Website: http://www.tsbdc.org
Patrick Geho, State Director

Texas

Texas-North SBDC

DALLAS COUNTY COMMUNITY COLLEGE
1402 Corinth Street
Dallas, TX 75215
Phone: 214-860-5832
Fax: 214-860-5813
E-mail: m.langford@dcccd.edu
Website: http://www.ntsbdc.org
Mark Langford, Region Director

Texas Gulf Coast SBDC

UNIVERSITY OF HOUSTON
2302 Fannin, Suite 200
Houston, TX 77002
Phone: 713-752-8444
Fax: 713-756-1500
E-mail: fyoung@uh.edu
Website: http://sbdcnetwork.uh.edu
Mike Young, Executive Director

Texas-NW SBDC

TEXAS TECH UNIVERSITY
2579 South Loop 289, Suite 114
Lubbock, TX 79423
Phone: 806-745-3973
Fax: 806-745-6207
E-mail: c.bean@nwtsbdc.org
Website: http://www.nwtsbdc.org
Craig Bean, Executive Director

Texas-South-West Texas Border Region SBDC

UNIVERSITY OF TEXAS - SAN ANTONIO
501 West Durango Boulevard
San Antonio, TX 78207-4415
Phone: 210-458-2480
Fax: 210-458-2425
E-mail: albert.salgado@utsa.edu
Website: https://www.txsbdc.org
Alberto Salgado, Region Director

Utah

Utah SBDC

SALT LAKE COMMUNITY COLLEGE
9750 South 300 West
Salt Lake City, UT 84070
Phone: 801-957-5384
Fax: 801-985-5300
E-mail: Sherm.Wilkinson@slcc.edu
Website: http://www.utahsbdc.org
Sherm Wilkinson, State Director

Vermont

Vermont SBDC

VERMONT TECHNICAL COLLEGE
PO Box 188, 1 Main Street
Randolph Center, VT 05061-0188
Phone: 802-728-9101
Fax: 802-728-3026
E-mail: lrossi@vtsbdc.org
Website: http://www.vtsbdc.org
Linda Rossi, State Director

Virgin Islands

Virgin Islands SBDC

UNIVERSITY OF THE VIRGIN ISLANDS
8000 Nisky Center, Suite 720
St. Thomas, VI 00802
Phone: 340-776-3206
Fax: 340-775-3756
E-mail: ldottin@uvi.edu
Website: http://www.sbdcvi.org
Leonor Dottin, State Director

Virginia

Virginia SBDC

GEORGE MASON UNIVERSITY
4031 University Drive, Suite100
Fairfax, VA 22030
Phone: 703-277-7727
Fax: 703-352-8518
E-mail: jkeenan@gmu.edu
Website: http://www.virginiasbdc.org
Jody Keenan, Director

Washington

Washington SBDC

WASHINGTON STATE UNIVERSITY
1235 N. Post Street, Suite 201
Spokane, WA 99201
Phone: 509-358-7765
Fax: 509-358-7764
E-mail: duane.fladland@wsbdc.org
Website: http://www.wsbdc.org
Duane Fladland, State Director

West Virginia

West Virginia SBDC

**WEST VIRGINIA DEVELOPMENT
OFFICE**
Capital Complex, Building 6, Room 652
1900 Kanawha Boulevard
Charleston, WV 25305
Phone: 304-957-2087
Fax: 304-558-0127
E-mail: Kristina.J.Oliver@wv.gov
Website: http://www.wvsbdc.org
Mr. Conley Salyor, State Director

Wisconsin

Wisconsin SBDC

UNIVERSITY OF WISCONSIN
432 North Lake Street, Room 423
Madison, WI 53706
Phone: 608-263-7794
Fax: 608-263-7830
E-mail: bon.wikenheiser@uwex.edu
Website: http://www.uwex.edu/sbdc
Bon Wikenheiser, State Director

Wyoming

Wyoming SBDC

UNIVERSITY OF WYOMING
1000 E. University Ave., Dept. 3922
Laramie, WY 82071-3922
Phone: 307-766-3405
Fax: 307-766-3406
E-mail: jkline@uwyo.edu
Website: http://www.wyomingentre
preneur.biz
Jill Kline, Acting State Director

Service corps of retired executives (score) offices

*This section contains a listing of all
SCORE offices organized alphabetically by
state/U.S. territory, then by city, then by
agency name.*

Alabama

SCORE Office (Northeast Alabama)
1400 Commerce Blvd., Northeast
Anniston, AL 36207
(256)241-6111

SCORE Office (North Alabama)
1731 1st Ave. North, Ste. 200
Birmingham, AL 35203
(205)264-8425
Fax: (205)934-0538

SCORE Office (Baldwin County)
327 Fairhope Avenue
Fairhope, AL 36532
(251)928-6387

SCORE Office (Mobile)
451 Government Street
Mobile, AL 36652
(251)431-8614
Fax: (251)431-8646

SCORE Office (Alabama Capitol City)
600 S. Court St.
Montgomery, AL 36104
(334)240-6868
Fax: (334)240-6869

SCORE Office (Tuscaloosa)
2200 University Blvd.
Tuscaloosa, AL 35402
(205)758-7588

Alaska

SCORE Office (Anchorage)
420 L St., Ste. 300
Anchorage, AK 99501
(907)271-4022
Fax: (907)271-4545

Arizona

SCORE Office (Greater Phoenix)
2828 N. Central Ave., Ste. 800
Phoenix, AZ 85004
(602)745-7250
Fax: (602)745-7210
E-mail: e-mail@SCORE-phoenix.org
Website: http://www.greaterphoenix
.score.org/

SCORE Office (Northern Arizona)
1228 Willow Creek Rd., Ste. 2
Prescott, AZ 86301
(928)778-7438
Fax: (928)778-0812
Website: http://www.northernarizona
.score.org/

SCORE Office (Southern Arizona)
1400 W Speedway Blvd.
Tucson, AZ 85745
(520)505-3636
Fax: (520)670-5011
Website: http://www.southernarizona
.score.org/

Arkansas

SCORE Office (South Central)
201 N. Jackson Ave.
El Dorado, AR 71730-5803
(870)863-6113
Fax: (870)863-6115

SCORE Office (Northwest Arkansas)
614 E. Emma St., Room M412
Springdale, AR 72764
(479)725-1809
Website: http://www.northwestarkansas
.score.org

SCORE Office (Little Rock)
2120 Riverfront Dr., Ste. 250
Little Rock, AR 72202-1747
(501)324-7379
Fax: (501)324-5199
Website: http://www.littlerock.score.org

SCORE Office (Southeast Arkansas)
P.O. Box 5069
Pine Bluff, AR 71611-5069
(870)535-0110
Fax: (870)535-1643

California

SCORE Office (Bakersfield)
P.O. Box 2426
Bakersfield, CA 93303
(661)861-9249
Fax: (661)395-4134
Website: http://www.bakersfield.score.org

SCORE Office (Santa Cruz County)
716 G Capitola Ave.
Capitola, CA 95010
(831)621-3735
Fax: (831)475-6530
Website: http://santacruzcounty.score.org

SCORE Office (Greater Chico Area)
1324 Mangrove St., Ste. 114
Chico, CA 95926
(530)342-8932
Fax: (530)342-8932
Website: http://www.greaterchicoarea
.score.org

SCORE Office (El Centro)
1850 W. Main St, Ste. C
El Centro, CA 92243
(760)337-2692
Website: http://www.sandiego.score.org/

SCORE Office (Central Valley)
801 R St., Ste. 201
Fresno, CA 93721
(559)487-5605
Fax: (559)487-5636
Website: http://www.centralvalley.score
.org

SCORE Office (Los Angeles)
330 N. Brand Blvd., Ste. 190
Glendale, CA 91203-2304
(818)552-3206

Fax: (818)552-3323
Website: http://www.greaterlosangeles.
score.org

SCORE Office (Modesto Merced)
1880 W. Wardrobe Ave.
Merced, CA 95340
(209)725-2033
Fax: (209)577-2673
Website: http://www.modestomerced.
score.org

SCORE Office (Monterey Bay)
Monterey Chamber of Commerce
30 Ragsdale Dr.
Monterey, CA 93940
(831)648-5360
Website: http://www.montereybay.score
.org

SCORE Office (East Bay)
492 9th St., Ste. 350
Oakland, CA 94607
(510)273-6611
Fax: (510)273-6015
E-mail: webmaster@eastbayscore.org
Website: http://www.eastbay.score.org/

SCORE Office (Ventura County)
400 E. Esplanade Dr., Ste. 301
Oxnard, CA 93036
(805)204-6022
Fax: (805)650-1414
Website: http://www.ventura.score.org

SCORE Office (Coachella)
43100 Cook St., Ste. 104
Palm Desert, CA 92211
(760)773-6507
Fax: (760)773-6514
Website: http://www.coachellavalley
.score.org

SCORE Office (Antelope Valley)
1212 E. Avenue, S Ste. A3
Palmdale, CA 93550
(661)947-7679
Website: http://www.antelopevalley
.score.org/

SCORE Office (Inland Empire)
11801 Pierce St., 2nd Fl.
Riverside, CA 92505
(951)-652-4390
Fax: (951)929-8543
Website: http://www.inlandempire
.score.org/

SCORE Office (Sacramento)
4990 Stockton Blvd.
Sacramento, CA 95820
(916)635-9085

Fax: (916)635-9089
Website: http://www.sacramento
.score.org

SCORE Office (San Diego)
550 West C. St., Ste. 550
San Diego, CA 92101-3540
(619)557-7272
Website: http://www.sandiego.score.org/

SCORE Office (San Francisco)
455 Market St., 6th Fl.
San Francisco, CA 94105
(415)744-6827
Fax: (415)744-6750
E-mail: sfscore@sfscore.
Website: http://www.sanfrancisco
.score.org/

SCORE Office (Silicon Valley)
234 E. Gish Rd., Ste. 100
San Jose, CA 95112
(408)453-6237
Fax: (408)494-0214
E-mail: info@svscore.org
Website: http://www.siliconvalley
.score.org/

SCORE Office (San Luis Obispo)
711 Tank Farm Rd., Ste. 210
San Luis Obispo, CA 93401
(805)547-0779
Website: http://www.sanluisobispo
.score.org

SCORE Office (Orange County)
200 W. Santa Anna Blvd., Ste. 700
Santa Ana, CA 92701
(714)550-7369
Fax: (714)550-0191
Website: http://www.orangecounty.
score.org

SCORE Office (Santa Barbara)
924 Anacapa St.
Santa Barbara, CA 93101
(805)563-0084
Website: http://www.santabarbara
.score.org/

SCORE Office (North Coast)
777 Sonoma Ave., Rm. 115E
Santa Rosa, CA 95404
(707)571-8342
Fax: (707)541-0331
Website: http://www.northcoast.score
.org

SCORE Office (Tuolumne County)
222 S. Shepherd St.
Sonora, CA 95370
(209)532-4316

Fax: (209)588-0673
Website: http://www.tuolumnecounty
.score.org/

Colorado

SCORE Office (Colorado Springs)
3595 E. Fountain Blvd., Ste. E-1
Colorado Springs, CO 80910
(719)636-3074
Fax: (719)635-1571
Website: http://www.coloradosprings
.score.org/

SCORE Office (Denver)
US Custom's House, 4th Fl.
721 19th St.
Denver, CO 80202
(303)844-3985
Fax: (303)844-6490
Website: http://www.denver.score.org/

SCORE Office (Tri-River)
1102 Grand Ave.
Glenwood Springs, CO 81601
(970)945-6589

SCORE Office (Grand Junction)
2591 B & 3/4 Rd.
Grand Junction, CO 81503
(970)243-5242

SCORE Office (Gunnison)
608 N. 11th
Gunnison, CO 81230
(303)641-4422

SCORE Office (Montrose)
1214 Peppertree Dr.
Montrose, CO 81401
(970)249-6080

SCORE Office (Pagosa Springs)
PO Box 4381
Pagosa Springs, CO 81157
(970)731-4890

SCORE Office (Rifle)
0854 W. Battlement Pky., Apt. C106
Parachute, CO 81635
(970)285-9390

SCORE Office (Pueblo)
302 N. Santa Fe
Pueblo, CO 81003
(719)542-1704
Fax: (719)542-1624
Website: http://www.pueblo.score.org

SCORE Office (Ridgway)
143 Poplar Pl.
Ridgway, CO 81432

SCORE Office (Silverton)
PO Box 480
Silverton, CO 81433
(303)387-5430

SCORE Office (Minturn)
PO Box 2066
Vail, CO 81658
(970)476-1224

Connecticut

SCORE Office (Greater Bridgeport)
230 Park Ave.
Bridgeport, CT 06604
(203)450-9484
Fax: (203)576-4388

SCORE Office (Western Connecticut)
155 Deer Hill Ave.
Danbury, CT 06010
(203)794-1404
Website: http://www.westernconnecticut
.score.org

SCORE Office (Greater Hartford County)
330 Main St., 2nd Fl.
Hartford, CT 06106
(860)240-4700
Fax: (860)240-4659
Website: http://www.greaterhartford
.score.org

SCORE Office (Manchester)
20 Hartford Rd.
Manchester, CT 06040
(203)646-2223
Fax: (203)646-5871

SCORE Office (New Britain)
185 Main St., Ste. 431
New Britain, CT 06051
(203)827-4492
Fax: (203)827-4480

SCORE Office (New Haven)
60 Sargent Dr.
New Haven, CT 06511
(203)865-7645
Website: http://www.newhaven.score.org

SCORE Office (Fairfield County)
111 East Ave.
Norwalk, CT 06851
(203)847-7348
Fax: (203)849-9308
Website: http://www.fairfieldcounty
.score.org

SCORE Office (Southeastern Connecticut)
665 Boston Post Rd.
Old Saybrook, CT 06475

(860)388-9508
Website: http://www.southeastern
connecticut.score.org

SCORE Office (Northwest Connecticut)
 333 Kennedy Dr.
Torrington, CT 06790
(560)482-6586
Website: http://www.northwest
connecticut.score.org

Delaware

SCORE Office (Dover)
Treadway Towers
PO Box 576
Dover, DE 19903
(302)678-0892
Fax: (302)678-0189

SCORE Office (Lewes)
PO Box 1
Lewes, DE 19958
(302)645-8073
Fax: (302)645-8412

SCORE Office (Milford)
204 NE Front St.
Milford, DE 19963
(302)422-3301

SCORE Office (Wilmington)
824 Market St., Ste. 610
Wilmington, DE 19801
(302)573-6652
Fax: (302)573-6092
Website: http://www.scoredelaware.com

District of Columbia

SCORE Office (George Mason University)
409 3rd St. SW, 4th Fl.
Washington, DC 20024
800-634-0245

SCORE Office (Washington DC)
1110 Vermont Ave. NW, 9th Fl.
Washington, DC 20043
(202)606-4000
Fax: (202)606-4225
E-mail: dcscore@hotmail.com
Website: http://www.scoredc.org/

Florida

SCORE Office (Desota County Chamber of Commerce)
16 South Velucia Ave.
Arcadia, FL 34266
(941)494-4033

SCORE Office (Suncoast/Pinellas)
Airport Business Ctr.
4707 - 140th Ave. N, No. 311
Clearwater, FL 33755
(813)532-6800
Fax: (813)532-6800

SCORE Office (DeLand)
336 N. Woodland Blvd.
DeLand, FL 32720
(904)734-4331
Fax: (904)734-4333

SCORE Office (South Palm Beach)
1050 S. Federal Hwy., Ste. 132
Delray Beach, FL 33483
(561)278-7752
Fax: (561)278-0288

SCORE Office (Ft. Lauderdale)
Federal Bldg., Ste. 123
299 E. Broward Blvd.
Ft. Lauderdale, FL 33301
(954)356-7263
Fax: (954)356-7145

SCORE Office (Southwest Florida)
The Renaissance
8695 College Pky., Ste. 345 & 346
Ft. Myers, FL 33919
(941)489-2935
Fax: (941)489-1170

SCORE Office (Treasure Coast)
Professional Center, Ste. 2
3220 S. US, No. 1
Ft. Pierce, FL 34982
(561)489-0548

SCORE Office (Gainesville)
101 SE 2nd Pl., Ste. 104
Gainesville, FL 32601
(904)375-8278

SCORE Office (Hialeah Dade Chamber)
59 W. 5th St.
Hialeah, FL 33010
(305)887-1515
Fax: (305)887-2453

SCORE Office (Daytona Beach)
921 Nova Rd., Ste. A
Holly Hills, FL 32117
(904)255-6889
Fax: (904)255-0229
E-mail: score87@dbeach.com

SCORE Office (South Broward)
3475 Sheridian St., Ste. 203
Hollywood, FL 33021
(305)966-8415

SCORE Office (Citrus County)
5 Poplar Ct.
Homosassa, FL 34446
(352)382-1037

SCORE Office (Jacksonville)
7825 Baymeadows Way, Ste. 100-B
Jacksonville, FL 32256
(904)443-1911
Fax: (904)443-1980
E-mail: scorejax@juno.com
Website: http://www.scorejax.org/

SCORE Office (Jacksonville Satellite)
3 Independent Dr.
Jacksonville, FL 32256
(904)366-6600
Fax: (904)632-0617

SCORE Office (Central Florida)
5410 S. Florida Ave., No. 3
Lakeland, FL 33801
(941)687-5783
Fax: (941)687-6225

SCORE Office (Lakeland)
100 Lake Morton Dr.
Lakeland, FL 33801
(941)686-2168

SCORE Office (St. Petersburg)
800 W. Bay Dr., Ste. 505
Largo, FL 33712
(813)585-4571

SCORE Office (Leesburg)
9501 US Hwy. 441
Leesburg, FL 34788-8751
(352)365-3556
Fax: (352)365-3501

SCORE Office (Cocoa)
1600 Farno Rd., Unit 205
Melbourne, FL 32935
(407)254-2288

SCORE Office (Melbourne)
Melbourne Professional Complex
1600 Sarno, Ste. 205
Melbourne, FL 32935
(407)254-2288
Fax: (407)245-2288

SCORE Office (Merritt Island)
1600 Sarno Rd., Ste. 205
Melbourne, FL 32935
(407)254-2288
Fax: (407)254-2288

SCORE Office (Space Coast)
Melbourn Professional Complex
1600 Sarno, Ste. 205
Melbourne, FL 32935
(407)254-2288
Fax: (407)254-2288

SCORE Office (Dade)
49 NW 5th St.
Miami, FL 33128
(305)371-6889
Fax: (305)374-1882
E-mail: score@netrox.net
Website: http://www.netrox.net/~score/

SCORE Office (Naples of Collier)
International College
2654 Tamiami Trl. E
Naples, FL 34112
(941)417-1280
Fax: (941)417-1281
E-mail: score@naples.net
Website: http://www.naples.net/clubs/
score/index.htm

SCORE Office (Pasco County)
6014 US Hwy. 19, Ste. 302
New Port Richey, FL 34652
(813)842-4638

SCORE Office (Southeast Volusia)
115 Canal St.
New Smyrna Beach, FL 32168
(904)428-2449
Fax: (904)423-3512

SCORE Office (Ocala)
110 E. Silver Springs Blvd.
Ocala, FL 34470
(352)629-5959

Clay County SCORE Office
Clay County Chamber of Commerce
1734 Kingsdey Ave.
PO Box 1441
Orange Park, FL 32073
(904)264-2651
Fax: (904)269-0363

SCORE Office (Orlando)
80 N. Hughey Ave.
Rm. 445 Federal Bldg.
Orlando, FL 32801
(407)648-6476
Fax: (407)648-6425

SCORE Office (Emerald Coast)
19 W. Garden St., No. 325
Pensacola, FL 32501
(904)444-2060
Fax: (904)444-2070

SCORE Office (Charlotte County)
201 W. Marion Ave., Ste. 211
Punta Gorda, FL 33950
(941)575-1818
E-mail: score@gls3c.com
Website: http://www.charlotte-florida
.com/business/scorepg01.htm

SCORE Office (St. Augustine)
1 Riberia St.
St. Augustine, FL 32084
(904)829-5681
Fax: (904)829-6477

SCORE Office (Bradenton)
2801 Fruitville, Ste. 280
Sarasota, FL 34237
(813)955-1029

SCORE Office (Manasota)
2801 Fruitville Rd., Ste. 280
Sarasota, FL 34237
(941)955-1029
Fax: (941)955-5581
E-mail: score116@gte.net
Website: http://www.score-suncoast.org/

SCORE Office (Tallahassee)
200 W. Park Ave.
Tallahassee, FL 32302
(850)487-2665

SCORE Office (Hillsborough)
4732 Dale Mabry Hwy. N, Ste. 400
Tampa, FL 33614-6509
(813)870-0125

SCORE Office (Lake Sumter)
122 E. Main St.
Tavares, FL 32778-3810
(352)365-3556

SCORE Office (Titusville)
2000 S. Washington Ave.
Titusville, FL 32780
(407)267-3036
Fax: (407)264-0127

SCORE Office (Venice)
257 N. Tamiami Trl.
Venice, FL 34285
(941)488-2236
Fax: (941)484-5903

SCORE Office (Palm Beach)
500 Australian Ave. S, Ste. 100
West Palm Beach, FL 33401
(561)833-1672
Fax: (561)833-1712

SCORE Office (Wildwood)
103 N. Webster St.
Wildwood, FL 34785

Georgia

SCORE Office (Atlanta)
Harris Tower, Suite 1900
233 Peachtree Rd., NE
Atlanta, GA 30309
(404)347-2442
Fax: (404)347-1227

SCORE Office (Augusta)
3126 Oxford Rd.
Augusta, GA 30909
(706)869-9100

SCORE Office (Columbus)
School Bldg.
PO Box 40
Columbus, GA 31901
(706)327-3654

SCORE Office (Dalton-Whitfield)
305 S. Thorton Ave.
Dalton, GA 30720
(706)279-3383

SCORE Office (Gainesville)
PO Box 374
Gainesville, GA 30503
(770)532-6206
Fax: (770)535-8419

SCORE Office (Macon)
711 Grand Bldg.
Macon, GA 31201
(912)751-6160

SCORE Office (Brunswick)
4 Glen Ave.
St. Simons Island, GA 31520
(912)265-0620
Fax: (912)265-0629

SCORE Office (Savannah)
111 E. Liberty St., Ste. 103
Savannah, GA 31401
(912)652-4335
Fax: (912)652-4184
E-mail: info@scoresav.org
Website: http://www.coastalempire.com/
score/index.htm

Guam

SCORE Office (Guam)
Pacific News Bldg., Rm. 103
238 Archbishop Flores St.
Agana, GU 96910-5100
(671)472-7308

Hawaii

SCORE Office (Hawaii, Inc.)
1111 Bishop St., Ste. 204
PO Box 50207
Honolulu, HI 96813
(808)522-8132
Fax: (808)522-8135
E-mail: hnlscore@juno.com

SCORE Office (Kahului)
250 Alamaha, Unit N16A
Kahului, HI 96732
(808)871-7711

SCORE Office (Maui, Inc.)
590 E. Lipoa Pkwy., Ste. 227
Kihei, HI 96753
(808)875-2380

Idaho

SCORE Office (Treasure Valley)
1020 Main St., No. 290
Boise, ID 83702
(208)334-1696
Fax: (208)334-9353

SCORE Office (Eastern Idaho)
2300 N. Yellowstone, Ste. 119
Idaho Falls, ID 83401
(208)523-1022
Fax: (208)528-7127

Illinois

SCORE Office (Fox Valley)
40 W. Downer Pl.
PO Box 277
Aurora, IL 60506
(630)897-9214
Fax: (630)897-7002

SCORE Office (Greater Belvidere)
419 S. State St.
Belvidere, IL 61008
(815)544-4357
Fax: (815)547-7654

SCORE Office (Bensenville)
1050 Busse Hwy. Suite 100
Bensenville, IL 60106
(708)350-2944
Fax: (708)350-2979

SCORE Office (Central Illinois)
402 N. Hershey Rd.
Bloomington, IL 61704
(309)644-0549
Fax: (309)663-8270
E-mail: webmaster@central-illinois-score
.org
Website: http://www.central-illinois-score
.org/

SCORE Office (Southern Illinois)
150 E. Pleasant Hill Rd.
Box 1
Carbondale, IL 62901
(618)453-6654
Fax: (618)453-5040

SCORE Office (Chicago)
Northwest Atrium Ctr.
500 W. Madison St., No. 1250
Chicago, IL 60661
(312)353-7724
Fax: (312)886-5688
Website: http://www.mcs.net/~bic/

SCORE Office (Chicago–Oliver Harvey College)
Pullman Bldg.
1000 E. 11th St., 7th Fl.
Chicago, IL 60628
Fax: (312)468-8086

SCORE Office (Danville)
28 W. N. Street
Danville, IL 61832
(217)442-7232
Fax: (217)442-6228

SCORE Office (Decatur)
Milliken University
1184 W. Main St.
Decatur, IL 62522
(217)424-6297
Fax: (217)424-3993
E-mail: charding@mail.millikin.edu
Website: http://www.millikin.edu/
academics/Tabor/score.html

SCORE Office (Downers Grove)
925 Curtis
Downers Grove, IL 60515
(708)968-4050
Fax: (708)968-8368

SCORE Office (Elgin)
24 E. Chicago, 3rd Fl.
PO Box 648
Elgin, IL 60120
(847)741-5660
Fax: (847)741-5677

SCORE Office (Freeport Area)
26 S. Galena Ave.
Freeport, IL 61032
(815)233-1350
Fax: (815)235-4038

SCORE Office (Galesburg)
292 E. Simmons St.
PO Box 749
Galesburg, IL 61401
(309)343-1194
Fax: (309)343-1195

SCORE Office (Glen Ellyn)
500 Pennsylvania
Glen Ellyn, IL 60137
(708)469-0907
Fax: (708)469-0426

SCORE Office (Greater Alton)
Alden Hall
5800 Godfrey Rd.
Godfrey, IL 62035-2466
(618)467-2280

Fax: (618)466-8289
Website: http://www.altonweb.com/score/

SCORE Office (Grayslake)
19351 W. Washington St.
Grayslake, IL 60030
(708)223-3633
Fax: (708)223-9371

SCORE Office (Harrisburg)
303 S. Commercial
Harrisburg, IL 62946-1528
(618)252-8528
Fax: (618)252-0210

SCORE Office (Joliet)
100 N. Chicago
Joliet, IL 60432
(815)727-5371
Fax: (815)727-5374

SCORE Office (Kankakee)
101 S. Schuyler Ave.
Kankakee, IL 60901
(815)933-0376
Fax: (815)933-0380

SCORE Office (Macomb)
216 Seal Hall, Rm. 214
Macomb, IL 61455
(309)298-1128
Fax: (309)298-2520

SCORE Office (Matteson)
210 Lincoln Mall
Matteson, IL 60443
(708)709-3750
Fax: (708)503-9322

SCORE Office (Mattoon)
1701 Wabash Ave.
Mattoon, IL 61938
(217)235-5661
Fax: (217)234-6544

SCORE Office (Quad Cities)
622 19th St.
Moline, IL 61265
(309)797-0082
Fax: (309)757-5435
E-mail: score@qconline.com
Website: http://www.qconline.com/
business/score/

SCORE Office (Naperville)
131 W. Jefferson Ave.
Naperville, IL 60540
(708)355-4141
Fax: (708)355-8355

SCORE Office (Northbrook)
2002 Walters Ave.
Northbrook, IL 60062

(847)498-5555
Fax: (847)498-5510

SCORE Office (Palos Hills)
10900 S. 88th Ave.
Palos Hills, IL 60465
(847)974-5468
Fax: (847)974-0078

SCORE Office (Peoria)
124 SW Adams, Ste. 300
Peoria, IL 61602
(309)676-0755
Fax: (309)676-7534

SCORE Office (Prospect Heights)
1375 Wolf Rd.
Prospect Heights, IL 60070
(847)537-8660
Fax: (847)537-7138

SCORE Office (Quincy Tri-State)
300 Civic Center Plz., Ste. 245
Quincy, IL 62301
(217)222-8093
Fax: (217)222-3033

SCORE Office (River Grove)
2000 5th Ave.
River Grove, IL 60171
(708)456-0300
Fax: (708)583-3121

SCORE Office (Northern Illinois)
515 N. Court St.
Rockford, IL 61103
(815)962-0122
Fax: (815)962-0122

SCORE Office (St. Charles)
103 N. 1st Ave.
St. Charles, IL 60174-1982
(847)584-8384
Fax: (847)584-6065

SCORE Office (Springfield)
511 W. Capitol Ave., Ste. 302
Springfield, IL 62704
(217)492-4416
Fax: (217)492-4867

SCORE Office (Sycamore)
112 Somunak St.
Sycamore, IL 60178
(815)895-3456
Fax: (815)895-0125

SCORE Office (University)
Hwy. 50 & Stuenkel Rd. Ste. C3305
University Park, IL 60466
(708)534-5000
Fax: (708)534-8457

Indiana

SCORE Office (Anderson)
205 W. 11th St.
Anderson, IN 46015
(317)642-0264

SCORE Office (Bloomington)
Star Center
216 W. Allen
Bloomington, IN 47403
(812)335-7334
E-mail: wtfische@indiana.edu
Website: http://www.brainfreezemedia
.com/score527/

SCORE Office (South East Indiana)
500 Franklin St.
Box 29
Columbus, IN 47201
(812)379-4457

SCORE Office (Corydon)
310 N. Elm St.
Corydon, IN 47112
(812)738-2137
Fax: (812)738-6438

SCORE Office (Crown Point)
Old Courthouse Sq. Ste. 206
PO Box 43
Crown Point, IN 46307
(219)663-1800

SCORE Office (Elkhart)
418 S. Main St.
Elkhart, IN 46515
(219)293-1531
Fax: (219)294-1859

SCORE Office (Evansville)
1100 W. Lloyd Expy., Ste. 105
Evansville, IN 47708
(812)426-6144

SCORE Office (Fort Wayne)
1300 S. Harrison St.
Ft. Wayne, IN 46802
(219)422-2601
Fax: (219)422-2601

SCORE Office (Gary)
973 W. 6th Ave., Rm. 326
Gary, IN 46402
(219)882-3918

SCORE Office (Hammond)
7034 Indianapolis Blvd.
Hammond, IN 46324
(219)931-1000
Fax: (219)845-9548

SCORE Office (Indianapolis)
429 N. Pennsylvania St., Ste. 100
Indianapolis, IN 46204-1873

(317)226-7264
Fax: (317)226-7259
E-mail: inscore@indy.net
Website: http://www.score-indianapolis
.org/

SCORE Office (Jasper)
PO Box 307
Jasper, IN 47547-0307
(812)482-6866

SCORE Office (Kokomo/Howard Counties)
106 N. Washington St.
Kokomo, IN 46901
(765)457-5301
Fax: (765)452-4564

SCORE Office (Logansport)
300 E. Broadway, Ste. 103
Logansport, IN 46947
(219)753-6388

SCORE Office (Madison)
301 E. Main St.
Madison, IN 47250
(812)265-3135
Fax: (812)265-2923

SCORE Office (Marengo)
Rt. 1 Box 224D
Marengo, IN 47140
Fax: (812)365-2793

SCORE Office (Marion/Grant Counties)
215 S. Adams
Marion, IN 46952
(765)664-5107

SCORE Office (Merrillville)
255 W. 80th Pl.
Merrillville, IN 46410
(219)769-8180
Fax: (219)736-6223

SCORE Office (Michigan City)
200 E. Michigan Blvd.
Michigan City, IN 46360
(219)874-6221
Fax: (219)873-1204

SCORE Office (South Central Indiana)
4100 Charleston Rd.
New Albany, IN 47150-9538
(812)945-0066

SCORE Office (Rensselaer)
104 W. Washington
Rensselaer, IN 47978

SCORE Office (Salem)
210 N. Main St.
Salem, IN 47167

(812)883-4303
Fax: (812)883-1467

SCORE Office (South Bend)
300 N. Michigan St.
South Bend, IN 46601
(219)282-4350
E-mail: chair@southbend-score.org
Website: http://www.southbend-score.org/

SCORE Office (Valparaiso)
150 Lincolnway
Valparaiso, IN 46383
(219)462-1105
Fax: (219)469-5710

SCORE Office (Vincennes)
27 N. 3rd
PO Box 553
Vincennes, IN 47591
(812)882-6440
Fax: (812)882-6441

SCORE Office (Wabash)
PO Box 371
Wabash, IN 46992
(219)563-1168
Fax: (219)563-6920

Iowa

SCORE Office (Burlington)
Federal Bldg.
300 N. Main St.
Burlington, IA 52601
(319)752-2967

SCORE Office (Cedar Rapids)
2750 1st Ave. NE, Ste 350
Cedar Rapids, IA 52401-1806
(319)362-6405
Fax: (319)362-7861
E:mail: score@scorecr.org
Website: http://www.scorecr.org

SCORE Office (Illowa)
333 4th Ave. S
Clinton, IA 52732
(319)242-5702

SCORE Office (Council Bluffs)
7 N. 6th St.
Council Bluffs, IA 51502
(712)325-1000

SCORE Office (Northeast Iowa)
3404 285th St.
Cresco, IA 52136
(319)547-3377

SCORE Office (Des Moines)
Federal Bldg., Rm. 749
210 Walnut St.

Des Moines, IA 50309-2186
(515)284-4760

SCORE Office (Ft. Dodge)
Federal Bldg., Rm. 436
205 S. 8th St.
Ft. Dodge, IA 50501
(515)955-2622

SCORE Office (Independence)
110 1st. St. east
Independence, IA 50644
(319)334-7178
Fax: (319)334-7179

SCORE Office (Iowa City)
210 Federal Bldg.
PO Box 1853
Iowa City, IA 52240-1853
(319)338-1662

SCORE Office (Keokuk)
401 Main St.
Pierce Bldg., No. 1
Keokuk, IA 52632
(319)524-5055

SCORE Office (Central Iowa)
Fisher Community College
709 S. Center
Marshalltown, IA 50158
(515)753-6645

SCORE Office (River City)
15 West State St.
Mason City, IA 50401
(515)423-5724

SCORE Office (South Central)
SBDC, Indian Hills Community College
525 Grandview Ave.
Ottumwa, IA 52501
(515)683-5127
Fax: (515)683-5263

SCORE Office (Dubuque)
10250 Sundown Rd.
Peosta, IA 52068
(319)556-5110

SCORE Office (Southwest Iowa)
614 W. Sheridan
Shenandoah, IA 51601
(712)246-3260

SCORE Office (Sioux City)
Federal Bldg.
320 6th St.
Sioux City, IA 51101
(712)277-2324
Fax: (712)277-2325

SCORE Office (Iowa Lakes)
122 W. 5th St.
Spencer, IA 51301
(712)262-3059

SCORE Office (Vista)
119 W. 6th St.
Storm Lake, IA 50588
(712)732-3780

SCORE Office (Waterloo)
215 E. 4th
Waterloo, IA 50703
(319)233-8431

Kansas

SCORE Office (Southwest Kansas)
501 W. Spruce
Dodge City, KS 67801
(316)227-3119

SCORE Office (Emporia)
811 Homewood
Emporia, KS 66801
(316)342-1600

SCORE Office (Golden Belt)
1307 Williams
Great Bend, KS 67530
(316)792-2401

SCORE Office (Hays)
PO Box 400
Hays, KS 67601
(913)625-6595

SCORE Office (Hutchinson)
1 E. 9th St.
Hutchinson, KS 67501
(316)665-8468
Fax: (316)665-7619

SCORE Office (Southeast Kansas)
404 Westminster Pl.
PO Box 886
Independence, KS 67301
(316)331-4741

SCORE Office (McPherson)
306 N. Main
PO Box 616
McPherson, KS 67460
(316)241-3303

SCORE Office (Salina)
120 Ash St.
Salina, KS 67401
(785)243-4290
Fax: (785)243-1833

SCORE Office (Topeka)
1700 College
Topeka, KS 66621
(785)231-1010

SCORE Office (Wichita)
100 E. English, Ste. 510
Wichita, KS 67202

(316)269-6273
Fax: (316)269-6499

SCORE Office (Ark Valley)
205 E. 9th St.
Winfield, KS 67156
(316)221-1617

Kentucky

SCORE Office (Ashland)
PO Box 830
Ashland, KY 41105
(606)329-8011
Fax: (606)325-4607

SCORE Office (Bowling Green)
812 State St.
PO Box 51
Bowling Green, KY 42101
(502)781-3200
Fax: (502)843-0458

SCORE Office (Tri-Lakes)
508 Barbee Way
Danville, KY 40422-1548
(606)231-9902

SCORE Office (Glasgow)
301 W. Main St.
Glasgow, KY 42141
(502)651-3161
Fax: (502)651-3122

SCORE Office (Hazard)
B & I Technical Center
100 Airport Gardens Rd.
Hazard, KY 41701
(606)439-5856
Fax: (606)439-1808

SCORE Office (Lexington)
410 W. Vine St., Ste. 290, Civic C
Lexington, KY 40507
(606)231-9902
Fax: (606)253-3190
E-mail: scorelex@uky.campus.mci.net

SCORE Office (Louisville)
188 Federal Office Bldg.
600 Dr. Martin L. King Jr. Pl.
Louisville, KY 40202
(502)582-5976

SCORE Office (Madisonville)
257 N. Main
Madisonville, KY 42431
(502)825-1399
Fax: (502)825-1396

SCORE Office (Paducah)
Federal Office Bldg.
501 Broadway, Rm. B-36

Paducah, KY 42001
(502)442-5685

Louisiana

SCORE Office (Central Louisiana)
802 3rd St.
Alexandria, LA 71309
(318)442-6671

SCORE Office (Baton Rouge)
564 Laurel St.
PO Box 3217
Baton Rouge, LA 70801
(504)381-7130
Fax: (504)336-4306

SCORE Office (North Shore)
2 W. Thomas
Hammond, LA 70401
(504)345-4457
Fax: (504)345-4749

SCORE Office (Lafayette)
804 St. Mary Blvd.
Lafayette, LA 70505-1307
(318)233-2705
Fax: (318)234-8671
E-mail: score302@aol.com

SCORE Office (Lake Charles)
120 W. Pujo St.
Lake Charles, LA 70601
(318)433-3632

SCORE Office (New Orleans)
365 Canal St., Ste. 3100
New Orleans, LA 70130
(504)589-2356
Fax: (504)589-2339

SCORE Office (Shreveport)
400 Edwards St.
Shreveport, LA 71101
(318)677-2536
Fax: (318)677-2541

Maine

SCORE Office (Augusta)
40 Western Ave.
Augusta, ME 04330
(207)622-8509

SCORE Office (Bangor)
Peabody Hall, Rm. 229
One College Cir.
Bangor, ME 04401
(207)941-9707

SCORE Office (Central & Northern Arroostock)
111 High St.
Caribou, ME 04736

(207)492-8010
Fax: (207)492-8010

SCORE Office (Penquis)
South St.
Dover Foxcroft, ME 04426
(207)564-7021

SCORE Office (Maine Coastal)
Mill Mall
Box 1105
Ellsworth, ME 04605-1105
(207)667-5800
E-mail: score@arcadia.net

SCORE Office (Lewiston-Auburn)
BIC of Maine-Bates Mill Complex
35 Canal St.
Lewiston, ME 04240-7764
(207)782-3708
Fax: (207)783-7745

SCORE Office (Portland)
66 Pearl St., Rm. 210
Portland, ME 04101
(207)772-1147
Fax: (207)772-5581
E-mail: Score53@score.maine.org
Website: http://www.score.maine.org/
chapter53/

SCORE Office (Western Mountains)
255 River St.
PO Box 252
Rumford, ME 04257-0252
(207)369-9976

SCORE Office (Oxford Hills)
166 Main St.
South Paris, ME 04281
(207)743-0499

Maryland

SCORE Office (Southern Maryland)
2525 Riva Rd., Ste. 110
Annapolis, MD 21401
(410)266-9553
Fax: (410)573-0981
E-mail: score390@aol.com
Website: http://members.aol.com/
score390/index.htm

SCORE Office (Baltimore)
The City Crescent Bldg., 6th Fl.
10 S. Howard St.
Baltimore, MD 21201
(410)962-2233
Fax: (410)962-1805

SCORE Office (Bel Air)
108 S. Bond St.
Bel Air, MD 21014

(410)838-2020
Fax: (410)893-4715

SCORE Office (Bethesda)
7910 Woodmont Ave., Ste. 1204
Bethesda, MD 20814
(301)652-4900
Fax: (301)657-1973

SCORE Office (Bowie)
6670 Race Track Rd.
Bowie, MD 20715
(301)262-0920
Fax: (301)262-0921

SCORE Office (Dorchester County)
203 Sunburst Hwy.
Cambridge, MD 21613
(410)228-3575

SCORE Office (Upper Shore)
210 Marlboro Ave.
Easton, MD 21601
(410)822-4606
Fax: (410)822-7922

SCORE Office (Frederick County)
43A S. Market St.
Frederick, MD 21701
(301)662-8723
Fax: (301)846-4427

SCORE Office (Gaithersburg)
9 Park Ave.
Gaithersburg, MD 20877
(301)840-1400
Fax: (301)963-3918

SCORE Office (Glen Burnie)
103 Crain Hwy. SE
Glen Burnie, MD 21061
(410)766-8282
Fax: (410)766-9722

SCORE Office (Hagerstown)
111 W. Washington St.
Hagerstown, MD 21740
(301)739-2015
Fax: (301)739-1278

SCORE Office (Laurel)
7901 Sandy Spring Rd. Ste. 501
Laurel, MD 20707
(301)725-4000
Fax: (301)725-0776

SCORE Office (Salisbury)
300 E. Main St.
Salisbury, MD 21801
(410)749-0185
Fax: (410)860-9925

Massachusetts

SCORE Office (NE Massachusetts)
100 Cummings Ctr., Ste. 101 K
Beverly, MA 01923
(978)922-9441
Website: http://www1.shore.net/~score/

SCORE Office (Boston)
10 Causeway St., Rm. 265
Boston, MA 02222-1093
(617)565-5591
Fax: (617)565-5598
E-mail: boston-score-20@worldnet
.att.net
Website: http://www.scoreboston.org/

**SCORE office (Bristol/Plymouth
County)**
53 N. 6th St., Federal Bldg.
Bristol, MA 02740
(508)994-5093

SCORE Office (SE Massachusetts)
60 School St.
Brockton, MA 02401
(508)587-2673
Fax: (508)587-1340
Website: http://www.metrosouth
chamber.com/score.html

SCORE Office (North Adams)
820 N. State Rd.
Cheshire, MA 01225
(413)743-5100

SCORE Office (Clinton Satellite)
1 Green St.
Clinton, MA 01510
Fax: (508)368-7689

SCORE Office (Greenfield)
PO Box 898
Greenfield, MA 01302
(413)773-5463
Fax: (413)773-7008

SCORE Office (Haverhill)
87 Winter St.
Haverhill, MA 01830
(508)373-5663
Fax: (508)373-8060

SCORE Office (Hudson Satellite)
PO Box 578
Hudson, MA 01749
(508)568-0360
Fax: (508)568-0360

SCORE Office (Cape Cod)
Independence Pk., Ste. 5B
270 Communications Way
Hyannis, MA 02601

(508)775-4884
Fax: (508)790-2540

SCORE Office (Lawrence)
264 Essex St.
Lawrence, MA 01840
(508)686-0900
Fax: (508)794-9953

SCORE Office (Leominster Satellite)
110 Erdman Way
Leominster, MA 01453
(508)840-4300
Fax: (508)840-4896

SCORE Office (Bristol/Plymouth Counties)
53 N. 6th St., Federal Bldg.
New Bedford, MA 02740
(508)994-5093

SCORE Office (Newburyport)
29 State St.
Newburyport, MA 01950
(617)462-6680

SCORE Office (Pittsfield)
66 West St.
Pittsfield, MA 01201
(413)499-2485

SCORE Office (Haverhill-Salem)
32 Derby Sq.
Salem, MA 01970
(508)745-0330
Fax: (508)745-3855

SCORE Office (Springfield)
1350 Main St.
Federal Bldg.
Springfield, MA 01103
(413)785-0314

SCORE Office (Carver)
12 Taunton Green, Ste. 201
Taunton, MA 02780
(508)824-4068
Fax: (508)824-4069

SCORE Office (Worcester)
33 Waldo St.
Worcester, MA 01608
(508)753-2929
Fax: (508)754-8560

Michigan

SCORE Office (Allegan)
PO Box 338
Allegan, MI 49010
(616)673-2479

SCORE Office (Ann Arbor)
425 S. Main St., Ste. 103
Ann Arbor, MI 48104
(313)665-4433

SCORE Office (Battle Creek)
34 W. Jackson Ste. 4A
Battle Creek, MI 49017-3505
(616)962-4076
Fax: (616)962-6309

SCORE Office (Cadillac)
222 Lake St.
Cadillac, MI 49601
(616)775-9776
Fax: (616)768-4255

SCORE Office (Detroit)
477 Michigan Ave., Rm. 515
Detroit, MI 48226
(313)226-7947
Fax: (313)226-3448

SCORE Office (Flint)
708 Root Rd., Rm. 308
Flint, MI 48503
(810)233-6846

SCORE Office (Grand Rapids)
111 Pearl St. NW
Grand Rapids, MI 49503-2831
(616)771-0305
Fax: (616)771-0328
E-mail: scoreone@iserv.net
Website: http://www.iserv.net/
~scoreone/

SCORE Office (Holland)
480 State St.
Holland, MI 49423
(616)396-9472

SCORE Office (Jackson)
209 East Washington
PO Box 80
Jackson, MI 49204
(517)782-8221
Fax: (517)782-0061

SCORE Office (Kalamazoo)
345 W. Michigan Ave.
Kalamazoo, MI 49007
(616)381-5382
Fax: (616)384-0096
E-mail: score@nucleus.net

SCORE Office (Lansing)
117 E. Allegan
PO Box 14030
Lansing, MI 48901
(517)487-6340
Fax: (517)484-6910

SCORE Office (Livonia)
15401 Farmington Rd.
Livonia, MI 48154
(313)427-2122
Fax: (313)427-6055

SCORE Office (Madison Heights)
26345 John R
Madison Heights, MI 48071
(810)542-5010
Fax: (810)542-6821

SCORE Office (Monroe)
111 E. 1st
Monroe, MI 48161
(313)242-3366
Fax: (313)242-7253

SCORE Office (Mt. Clemens)
58 S/B Gratiot
Mt. Clemens, MI 48043
(810)463-1528
Fax: (810)463-6541

SCORE Office (Muskegon)
PO Box 1087
230 Terrace Plz.
Muskegon, MI 49443
(616)722-3751
Fax: (616)728-7251

SCORE Office (Petoskey)
401 E. Mitchell St.
Petoskey, MI 49770
(616)347-4150

SCORE Office (Pontiac)
Executive Office Bldg.
1200 N. Telegraph Rd.
Pontiac, MI 48341
(810)975-9555

SCORE Office (Pontiac)
PO Box 430025
Pontiac, MI 48343
(810)335-9600

SCORE Office (Port Huron)
920 Pinegrove Ave.
Port Huron, MI 48060
(810)985-7101

SCORE Office (Rochester)
71 Walnut Ste. 110
Rochester, MI 48307
(810)651-6700
Fax: (810)651-5270

SCORE Office (Saginaw)
901 S. Washington Ave.
Saginaw, MI 48601
(517)752-7161
Fax: (517)752-9055

SCORE Office (Upper Peninsula)
2581 I-75 Business Spur
Sault Ste. Marie, MI 49783
(906)632-3301

SCORE Office (Southfield)
21000 W. 10 Mile Rd.
Southfield, MI 48075
(810)204-3050
Fax: (810)204-3099

SCORE Office (Traverse City)
202 E. Grandview Pkwy.
PO Box 387
Traverse City, MI 49685
(616)947-5075
Fax: (616)946-2565

SCORE Office (Warren)
30500 Van Dyke, Ste. 118
Warren, MI 48093
(810)751-3939

Minnesota

SCORE Office (Aitkin)
Aitkin, MN 56431
(218)741-3906

SCORE Office (Albert Lea)
202 N. Broadway Ave.
Albert Lea, MN 56007
(507)373-7487

SCORE Office (Austin)
PO Box 864
Austin, MN 55912
(507)437-4561
Fax: (507)437-4869

SCORE Office (South Metro)
Ames Business Ctr.
2500 W. County Rd., No. 42
Burnsville, MN 55337
(612)898-5645
Fax: (612)435-6972
E-mail: southmetro@scoreminn.org
Website: http://www.scoreminn.org/
southmetro/

SCORE Office (Duluth)
1717 Minnesota Ave.
Duluth, MN 55802
(218)727-8286
Fax: (218)727-3113
E-mail: duluth@scoreminn.org
Website: http://www.scoreminn.org

SCORE Office (Fairmont)
PO Box 826
Fairmont, MN 56031
(507)235-5547
Fax: (507)235-8411

SCORE Office (Southwest Minnesota)
112 Riverfront St.
Box 999
Mankato, MN 56001

(507)345-4519
Fax: (507)345-4451
Website: http://www.scoreminn.org/

SCORE Office (Minneapolis)
North Plaza Bldg., Ste. 51
5217 Wayzata Blvd.
Minneapolis, MN 55416
(612)591-0539
Fax: (612)544-0436
Website: http://www.scoreminn.org/

SCORE Office (Owatonna)
PO Box 331
Owatonna, MN 55060
(507)451-7970
Fax: (507)451-7972

SCORE Office (Red Wing)
2000 W. Main St., Ste. 324
Red Wing, MN 55066
(612)388-4079

SCORE Office (Southeastern Minnesota)
220 S. Broadway, Ste. 100
Rochester, MN 55901
(507)288-1122
Fax: (507)282-8960
Website: http://www.scoreminn.org/

SCORE Office (Brainerd)
St. Cloud, MN 56301

SCORE Office (Central Area)
1527 Northway Dr.
St. Cloud, MN 56301
(320)240-1332
Fax: (320)255-9050
Website: http://www.scoreminn.org/

SCORE Office (St. Paul)
350 St. Peter St., No. 295
Lowry Professional Bldg.
St. Paul, MN 55102
(651)223-5010
Fax: (651)223-5048
Website: http://www.scoreminn.org/

SCORE Office (Winona)
Box 870
Winona, MN 55987
(507)452-2272
Fax: (507)454-8814

SCORE Office (Worthington)
1121 3rd Ave.
Worthington, MN 56187
(507)372-2919
Fax: (507)372-2827

Mississippi

SCORE Office (Delta)
915 Washington Ave.
PO Box 933
Greenville, MS 38701
(601)378-3141

SCORE Office (Gulfcoast)
1 Government Plaza
2909 13th St., Ste. 203
Gulfport, MS 39501
(228)863-0054

SCORE Office (Jackson)
1st Jackson Center, Ste. 400
101 W. Capitol St.
Jackson, MS 39201
(601)965-5533

SCORE Office (Meridian)
5220 16th Ave.
Meridian, MS 39305
(601)482-4412

Missouri

SCORE Office (Lake of the Ozark)
University Extension
113 Kansas St.
PO Box 1405
Camdenton, MO 65020
(573)346-2644
Fax: (573)346-2694
E-mail: score@cdoc.net
Website: http://sites.cdoc.net/score/

Chamber of Commerce (Cape Girardeau)
PO Box 98
Cape Girardeau, MO 63702-0098
(314)335-3312

SCORE Office (Mid-Missouri)
1705 Halstead Ct.
Columbia, MO 65203
(573)874-1132

SCORE Office (Ozark-Gateway)
1486 Glassy Rd.
Cuba, MO 65453-1640
(573)885-4954

SCORE Office (Kansas City)
323 W. 8th St., Ste. 104
Kansas City, MO 64105
(816)374-6675
Fax: (816)374-6692
E-mail: SCOREBIC@AOL.COM
Website: http://www.crn.org/score/

SCORE Office (Sedalia)
Lucas Place
323 W. 8th St., Ste.104

Kansas City, MO 64105
(816)374-6675

SCORE office (Tri-Lakes)
PO Box 1148
Kimberling, MO 65686
(417)739-3041

SCORE Office (Tri-Lakes)
HCRI Box 85
Lampe, MO 65681
(417)858-6798

SCORE Office (Mexico)
111 N. Washington St.
Mexico, MO 65265
(314)581-2765

SCORE Office (Southeast Missouri)
Rte. 1, Box 280
Neelyville, MO 63954
(573)989-3577

SCORE office (Poplar Bluff Area)
806 Emma St.
Poplar Bluff, MO 63901
(573)686-8892

SCORE Office (St. Joseph)
3003 Frederick Ave.
St. Joseph, MO 64506
(816)232-4461

SCORE Office (St. Louis)
815 Olive St., Rm. 242
St. Louis, MO 63101-1569
(314)539-6970
Fax: (314)539-3785
E-mail: info@stlscore.org
Website: http://www.stlscore.org/

SCORE Office (Lewis & Clark)
425 Spencer Rd.
St. Peters, MO 63376
(314)928-2900
Fax: (314)928-2900
E-mail: score01@mail.win.org

SCORE Office (Springfield)
620 S. Glenstone, Ste. 110
Springfield, MO 65802-3200
(417)864-7670
Fax: (417)864-4108

SCORE office (Southeast Kansas)
1206 W. First St.
Webb City, MO 64870
(417)673-3984

Montana

SCORE Office (Billings)
815 S. 27th St.
Billings, MT 59101
(406)245-4111

SCORE Office (Bozeman)
1205 E. Main St.
Bozeman, MT 59715
(406)586-5421

SCORE Office (Butte)
1000 George St.
Butte, MT 59701
(406)723-3177

SCORE Office (Great Falls)
710 First Ave. N
Great Falls, MT 59401
(406)761-4434
E-mail: scoregtf@in.tch.com

SCORE Office (Havre, Montana)
518 First St.
Havre, MT 59501
(406)265-4383

SCORE Office (Helena)
Federal Bldg.
301 S. Park
Helena, MT 59626-0054
(406)441-1081

SCORE Office (Kalispell)
2 Main St.
Kalispell, MT 59901
(406)756-5271
Fax: (406)752-6665

SCORE Office (Missoula)
723 Ronan
Missoula, MT 59806
(406)327-8806
E-mail: score@safeshop.com
Website: http://missoula.bigsky.net/
score/

Nebraska

SCORE Office (Columbus)
Columbus, NE 68601
(402)564-2769

SCORE Office (Fremont)
92 W. 5th St.
Fremont, NE 68025
(402)721-2641

SCORE Office (Hastings)
Hastings, NE 68901
(402)463-3447

SCORE Office (Lincoln)
8800 O St.
Lincoln, NE 68520
(402)437-2409

SCORE Office (Panhandle)
150549 CR 30
Minatare, NE 69356

(308)632-2133
Website: http://www.tandt.com/SCORE

SCORE Office (Norfolk)
3209 S. 48th Ave.
Norfolk, NE 68106
(402)564-2769

SCORE Office (North Platte)
3301 W. 2nd St.
North Platte, NE 69101
(308)532-4466

SCORE Office (Omaha)
11145 Mill Valley Rd.
Omaha, NE 68154
(402)221-3606
Fax: (402)221-3680
E-mail: infoctr@ne.uswest.net
Website: http://www.tandt.com/score/

Nevada

SCORE Office (Incline Village)
969 Tahoe Blvd.
Incline Village, NV 89451
(702)831-7327
Fax: (702)832-1605

SCORE Office (Carson City)
301 E. Stewart
PO Box 7527
Las Vegas, NV 89125
(702)388-6104

SCORE Office (Las Vegas)
300 Las Vegas Blvd. S, Ste. 1100
Las Vegas, NV 89101
(702)388-6104

SCORE Office (Northern Nevada)
SBDC, College of Business
Administration
Univ. of Nevada
Reno, NV 89557-0100
(702)784-4436
Fax: (702)784-4337

New Hampshire

SCORE Office (North Country)
PO Box 34
Berlin, NH 03570
(603)752-1090

SCORE Office (Concord)
143 N. Main St., Rm. 202A
PO Box 1258
Concord, NH 03301
(603)225-1400
Fax: (603)225-1409

SCORE Office (Dover)
299 Central Ave.
Dover, NH 03820

(603)742-2218
Fax: (603)749-6317

SCORE Office (Monadnock)
34 Mechanic St.
Keene, NH 03431-3421
(603)352-0320

SCORE Office (Lakes Region)
67 Water St., Ste. 105
Laconia, NH 03246
(603)524-9168

SCORE Office (Upper Valley)
Citizens Bank Bldg., Rm. 310
20 W. Park St.
Lebanon, NH 03766
(603)448-3491
Fax: (603)448-1908
E-mail: billt@valley.net
Website: http://www.valley.net/~score/

SCORE Office (Merrimack Valley)
275 Chestnut St., Rm. 618
Manchester, NH 03103
(603)666-7561
Fax: (603)666-7925

SCORE Office (Mt. Washington Valley)
PO Box 1066
North Conway, NH 03818
(603)383-0800

SCORE Office (Seacoast)
195 Commerce Way, Unit-A
Portsmouth, NH 03801-3251
(603)433-0575

New Jersey

SCORE Office (Somerset)
Paritan Valley Community College,
Rte. 28
Branchburg, NJ 08807
(908)218-8874
E-mail: nj-score@grizbiz.com.
Website: http://www.nj-score.org/

SCORE Office (Chester)
5 Old Mill Rd.
Chester, NJ 07930
(908)879-7080

SCORE Office (Greater Princeton)
4 A George Washington Dr.
Cranbury, NJ 08512
(609)520-1776

SCORE Office (Freehold)
36 W. Main St.
Freehold, NJ 07728
(908)462-3030
Fax: (908)462-2123

SCORE Office (North West)
Picantinny Innovation Ctr.
3159 Schrader Rd.
Hamburg, NJ 07419
(973)209-8525
Fax: (973)209-7252
E-mail: nj-score@grizbiz.com
Website: http://www.nj-score.org/

SCORE Office (Monmouth)
765 Newman Springs Rd.
Lincroft, NJ 07738
(908)224-2573
E-mail: nj-score@grizbiz.com
Website: http://www.nj-score.org/

SCORE Office (Manalapan)
125 Symmes Dr.
Manalapan, NJ 07726
(908)431-7220

SCORE Office (Jersey City)
2 Gateway Ctr., 4th Fl.
Newark, NJ 07102
(973)645-3982
Fax: (973)645-2375

SCORE Office (Newark)
2 Gateway Center, 15th Fl.
Newark, NJ 07102-5553
(973)645-3982
Fax: (973)645-2375
E-mail: nj-score@grizbiz.com
Website: http://www.nj-score.org

SCORE Office (Bergen County)
327 E. Ridgewood Ave.
Paramus, NJ 07652
(201)599-6090
E-mail: nj-score@grizbiz.com
Website: http://www.nj-score.org/

SCORE Office (Pennsauken)
4900 Rte. 70
Pennsauken, NJ 08109
(609)486-3421

SCORE Office (Southern New Jersey)
4900 Rte. 70
Pennsauken, NJ 08109
(609)486-3421
E-mail: nj-score@grizbiz.com
Website: http://www.nj-score.org/

SCORE Office (Greater Princeton)
216 Rockingham Row
Princeton Forrestal Village
Princeton, NJ 08540
(609)520-1776
Fax: (609)520-9107
E-mail: nj-score@grizbiz.com
Website: http://www.nj-score.org/

SCORE Office (Shrewsbury)
Hwy. 35
Shrewsbury, NJ 07702
(908)842-5995
Fax: (908)219-6140

SCORE Office (Ocean County)
33 Washington St.
Toms River, NJ 08754
(732)505-6033
E-mail: nj-score@grizbiz.com
Website: http://www.nj-score.org/

SCORE Office (Wall)
2700 Allaire Rd.
Wall, NJ 07719
(908)449-8877

SCORE Office (Wayne)
2055 Hamburg Tpke.
Wayne, NJ 07470
(201)831-7788
Fax: (201)831-9112

New Mexico

SCORE Office (Albuquerque)
525 Buena Vista, SE
Albuquerque, NM 87106
(505)272-7999
Fax: (505)272-7963

SCORE Office (Las Cruces)
Loretto Towne Center
505 S. Main St., Ste. 125
Las Cruces, NM 88001
(505)523-5627
Fax: (505)524-2101
E-mail: score.397@zianet.com

SCORE Office (Roswell)
Federal Bldg., Rm. 237
Roswell, NM 88201
(505)625-2112
Fax: (505)623-2545

SCORE Office (Santa Fe)
Montoya Federal Bldg.
120 Federal Place, Rm. 307
Santa Fe, NM 87501
(505)988-6302
Fax: (505)988-6300

New York

SCORE Office (Northeast)
1 Computer Dr. S
Albany, NY 12205
(518)446-1118
Fax: (518)446-1228

SCORE Office (Auburn)
30 South St.
PO Box 675

Auburn, NY 13021
(315)252-7291

SCORE Office (South Tier Binghamton)
Metro Center, 2nd Fl.
49 Court St.
PO Box 995
Binghamton, NY 13902
(607)772-8860

SCORE Office (Queens County City)
12055 Queens Blvd., Rm. 333
Borough Hall, NY 11424
(718)263-8961

SCORE Office (Buffalo)
Federal Bldg., Rm. 1311
111 W. Huron St.
Buffalo, NY 14202
(716)551-4301
Website: http://www2.pcom.net/score/
buf45.html

SCORE Office (Canandaigua)
Chamber of Commerce Bldg.
113 S. Main St.
Canandaigua, NY 14424
(716)394-4400
Fax: (716)394-4546

SCORE Office (Chemung)
333 E. Water St., 4th Fl.
Elmira, NY 14901
(607)734-3358

SCORE Office (Geneva)
Chamber of Commerce Bldg.
PO Box 587
Geneva, NY 14456
(315)789-1776
Fax: (315)789-3993

SCORE Office (Glens Falls)
84 Broad St.
Glens Falls, NY 12801
(518)798-8463
Fax: (518)745-1433

SCORE Office (Orange County)
40 Matthews St.
Goshen, NY 10924
(914)294-8080
Fax: (914)294-6121

SCORE Office (Huntington Area)
151 W. Carver St.
Huntington, NY 11743
(516)423-6100

SCORE Office (Tompkins County)
904 E. Shore Dr.
Ithaca, NY 14850
(607)273-7080

SCORE Office (Long Island City)
120-55 Queens Blvd.
Jamaica, NY 11424
(718)263-8961
Fax: (718)263-9032

SCORE Office (Chatauqua)
101 W. 5th St.
Jamestown, NY 14701
(716)484-1103

SCORE Office (Westchester)
2 Caradon Ln.
Katonah, NY 10536
(914)948-3907
Fax: (914)948-4645
E-mail: score@w-w-w.com
Website: http://w-w-w.com/score/

SCORE Office (Queens County)
Queens Borough Hall
120-55 Queens Blvd. Rm. 333
Kew Gardens, NY 11424
(718)263-8961
Fax: (718)263-9032

SCORE Office (Brookhaven)
3233 Rte. 112
Medford, NY 11763
(516)451-6563
Fax: (516)451-6925

SCORE Office (Melville)
35 Pinelawn Rd., Rm. 207-W
Melville, NY 11747
(516)454-0771

SCORE Office (Nassau County)
400 County Seat Dr., No. 140
Mineola, NY 11501
(516)571-3303
E-mail: Counse1998@aol.com
Website: http://members.aol.com/
Counse1998/Default.htm

SCORE Office (Mt. Vernon)
4 N. 7th Ave.
Mt. Vernon, NY 10550
(914)667-7500

SCORE Office (New York)
26 Federal Plz., Rm. 3100
New York, NY 10278
(212)264-4507
Fax: (212)264-4963
E-mail: score1000@erols.com
Website: http://users.erols.com/
score-nyc/

SCORE Office (Newburgh)
47 Grand St.
Newburgh, NY 12550
(914)562-5100

SCORE Office (Owego)
188 Front St.
Owego, NY 13827
(607)687-2020

SCORE Office (Peekskill)
1 S. Division St.
Peekskill, NY 10566
(914)737-3600
Fax: (914)737-0541

SCORE Office (Penn Yan)
2375 Rte. 14A
Penn Yan, NY 14527
(315)536-3111

SCORE Office (Dutchess)
110 Main St.
Poughkeepsie, NY 12601
(914)454-1700

SCORE Office (Rochester)
601 Keating Federal Bldg., Rm. 410
100 State St.
Rochester, NY 14614
(716)263-6473
Fax: (716)263-3146
Website: http://www.ggw.org/score/

SCORE Office (Saranac Lake)
30 Main St.
Saranac Lake, NY 12983
(315)448-0415

SCORE Office (Suffolk)
286 Main St.
Setauket, NY 11733
(516)751-3886

SCORE Office (Staten Island)
130 Bay St.
Staten Island, NY 10301
(718)727-1221

SCORE Office (Ulster)
Clinton Bldg., Rm. 107
Stone Ridge, NY 12484
(914)687-5035
Fax: (914)687-5015
Website: http://www.scoreulster.org/

SCORE Office (Syracuse)
401 S. Salina, 5th Fl.
Syracuse, NY 13202
(315)471-9393

SCORE Office (Utica)
SUNY Institute of Technology, Route 12
Utica, NY 13504-3050
(315)792-7553

SCORE Office (Watertown)
518 Davidson St.
Watertown, NY 13601

(315)788-1200
Fax: (315)788-8251

North Carolina

SCORE office (Asheboro)
317 E. Dixie Dr.
Asheboro, NC 27203
(336)626-2626
Fax: (336)626-7077

SCORE Office (Asheville)
Federal Bldg., Rm. 259
151 Patton
Asheville, NC 28801-5770
(828)271-4786
Fax: (828)271-4009

SCORE Office (Chapel Hill)
104 S. Estes Dr.
PO Box 2897
Chapel Hill, NC 27514
(919)967-7075

SCORE Office (Coastal Plains)
PO Box 2897
Chapel Hill, NC 27515
(919)967-7075
Fax: (919)968-6874

SCORE Office (Charlotte)
200 N. College St., Ste. A-2015
Charlotte, NC 28202
(704)344-6576
Fax: (704)344-6769
E-mail: CharlotteSCORE47@AOL.com
Website: http://www.charweb.org/
business/score/

SCORE Office (Durham)
411 W. Chapel Hill St.
Durham, NC 27707
(919)541-2171

SCORE Office (Gastonia)
PO Box 2168
Gastonia, NC 28053
(704)864-2621
Fax: (704)854-8723

SCORE Office (Greensboro)
400 W. Market St., Ste. 103
Greensboro, NC 27401-2241
(910)333-5399

SCORE Office (Henderson)
PO Box 917
Henderson, NC 27536
(919)492-2061
Fax: (919)430-0460

SCORE Office (Hendersonville)
Federal Bldg., Rm. 108
W. 4th Ave. & Church St.
Hendersonville, NC 28792
(828)693-8702
E-mail: score@circle.net
Website: http://www.wncguide.com/
score/Welcome.html

SCORE Office (Unifour)
PO Box 1828
Hickory, NC 28603
(704)328-6111

SCORE Office (High Point)
1101 N. Main St.
High Point, NC 27262
(336)882-8625
Fax: (336)889-9499

SCORE Office (Outer Banks)
Collington Rd. and Mustain
Kill Devil Hills, NC 27948
(252)441-8144

SCORE Office (Down East)
312 S. Front St., Ste. 6
New Bern, NC 28560
(252)633-6688
Fax: (252)633-9608

SCORE Office (Kinston)
PO Box 95
New Bern, NC 28561
(919)633-6688

SCORE Office (Raleigh)
Century Post Office Bldg., Ste. 306
300 Federal St. Mall
Raleigh, NC 27601
(919)856-4739
E-mail: jendres@ibm.net
Website: http://www.intrex.net/score96/
score96.htm

SCORE Office (Sanford)
1801 Nash St.
Sanford, NC 27330
(919)774-6442
Fax: (919)776-8739

SCORE Office (Sandhills Area)
1480 Hwy. 15-501
PO Box 458
Southern Pines, NC 28387
(910)692-3926

SCORE Office (Wilmington)
Corps of Engineers Bldg.
96 Darlington Ave., Ste. 207
Wilmington, NC 28403
(910)815-4576
Fax: (910)815-4658

North Dakota

SCORE Office (Bismarck-Mandan)
700 E. Main Ave., 2nd Fl.
PO Box 5509
Bismarck, ND 58506-5509
(701)250-4303

SCORE Office (Fargo)
657 2nd Ave., Rm. 225
Fargo, ND 58108-3083
(701)239-5677

SCORE Office (Upper Red River)
4275 Technology Dr., Rm. 156
Grand Forks, ND 58202-8372
(701)777-3051

SCORE Office (Minot)
100 1st St. SW
Minot, ND 58701-3846
(701)852-6883
Fax: (701)852-6905

Ohio

SCORE Office (Akron)
1 Cascade Plz., 7th Fl.
Akron, OH 44308
(330)379-3163
Fax: (330)379-3164

SCORE Office (Ashland)
Gill Center
47 W. Main St.
Ashland, OH 44805
(419)281-4584

SCORE Office (Canton)
116 Cleveland Ave. NW, Ste. 601
Canton, OH 44702-1720
(330)453-6047

SCORE Office (Chillicothe)
165 S. Paint St.
Chillicothe, OH 45601
(614)772-4530

SCORE Office (Cincinnati)
Ameritrust Bldg., Rm. 850
525 Vine St.
Cincinnati, OH 45202
(513)684-2812
Fax: (513)684-3251
Website: http://
www.score.chapter34.org/

SCORE Office (Cleveland)
Eaton Center, Ste. 620
1100 Superior Ave.
Cleveland, OH 44114-2507
(216)522-4194
Fax: (216)522-4844

ORGANIZATIONS, AGENCIES, & CONSULTANTS

SCORE Office (Columbus)
2 Nationwide Plz., Ste. 1400
Columbus, OH 43215-2542
(614)469-2357
Fax: (614)469-2391
E-mail: info@scorecolumbus.org
Website: http://www.scorecolumbus.org/

SCORE Office (Dayton)
Dayton Federal Bldg., Rm. 505
200 W. Second St.
Dayton, OH 45402-1430
(513)225-2887
Fax: (513)225-7667

SCORE Office (Defiance)
615 W. 3rd St.
PO Box 130
Defiance, OH 43512
(419)782-7946

SCORE Office (Findlay)
123 E. Main Cross St.
PO Box 923
Findlay, OH 45840
(419)422-3314

SCORE Office (Lima)
147 N. Main St.
Lima, OH 45801
(419)222-6045
Fax: (419)229-0266

SCORE Office (Mansfield)
55 N. Mulberry St.
Mansfield, OH 44902
(419)522-3211

SCORE Office (Marietta)
Thomas Hall
Marietta, OH 45750
(614)373-0268

SCORE Office (Medina)
County Administrative Bldg.
144 N. Broadway
Medina, OH 44256
(216)764-8650

SCORE Office (Licking County)
50 W. Locust St.
Newark, OH 43055
(614)345-7458

SCORE Office (Salem)
2491 State Rte. 45 S
Salem, OH 44460
(216)332-0361

SCORE Office (Tiffin)
62 S. Washington St.
Tiffin, OH 44883
(419)447-4141
Fax: (419)447-5141

SCORE Office (Toledo)
608 Madison Ave, Ste. 910
Toledo, OH 43624
(419)259-7598
Fax: (419)259-6460

SCORE Office (Heart of Ohio)
377 W. Liberty St.
Wooster, OH 44691
(330)262-5735
Fax: (330)262-5745

SCORE Office (Youngstown)
306 Williamson Hall
Youngstown, OH 44555
(330)746-2687

Oklahoma

SCORE Office (Anadarko)
PO Box 366
Anadarko, OK 73005
(405)247-6651

SCORE Office (Ardmore)
410 W. Main
Ardmore, OK 73401
(580)226-2620

SCORE Office (Northeast Oklahoma)
210 S. Main
Grove, OK 74344
(918)787-2796
Fax: (918)787-2796
E-mail: Score595@greencis.net

SCORE Office (Lawton)
4500 W. Lee Blvd., Bldg. 100, Ste. 107
Lawton, OK 73505
(580)353-8727
Fax: (580)250-5677

SCORE Office (Oklahoma City)
210 Park Ave., No. 1300
Oklahoma City, OK 73102
(405)231-5163
Fax: (405)231-4876
E-mail: score212@usa.net

SCORE Office (Stillwater)
439 S. Main
Stillwater, OK 74074
(405)372-5573
Fax: (405)372-4316

SCORE Office (Tulsa)
616 S. Boston, Ste. 406
Tulsa, OK 74119
(918)581-7462
Fax: (918)581-6908
Website: http://www.ionet.net/~tulscore/

Oregon

SCORE Office (Bend)
63085 N. Hwy. 97
Bend, OR 97701
(541)923-2849
Fax: (541)330-6900

SCORE Office (Willamette)
1401 Willamette St.
PO Box 1107
Eugene, OR 97401-4003
(541)465-6600
Fax: (541)484-4942

SCORE Office (Florence)
3149 Oak St.
Florence, OR 97439
(503)997-8444
Fax: (503)997-8448

SCORE Office (Southern Oregon)
33 N. Central Ave., Ste. 216
Medford, OR 97501
(541)776-4220
E-mail: pgr134f@prodigy.com

SCORE Office (Portland)
1515 SW 5th Ave., Ste. 1050
Portland, OR 97201
(503)326-3441
Fax: (503)326-2808
E-mail: gr134@prodigy.com

SCORE Office (Salem)
416 State St. (corner of Liberty)
Salem, OR 97301
(503)370-2896

Pennsylvania

SCORE Office (Altoona-Blair)
1212 12th Ave.
Altoona, PA 16601-3493
(814)943-8151

SCORE Office (Lehigh Valley)
Rauch Bldg. 37
Lehigh University
621 Taylor St.
Bethlehem, PA 18015
(610)758-4496
Fax: (610)758-5205

SCORE Office (Butler County)
100 N. Main St.
PO Box 1082
Butler, PA 16003
(412)283-2222
Fax: (412)283-0224

SCORE Office (Harrisburg)
4211 Trindle Rd.
Camp Hill, PA 17011

(717)761-4304
Fax: (717)761-4315

SCORE Office (Cumberland Valley)
75 S. 2nd St.
Chambersburg, PA 17201
(717)264-2935

SCORE Office (Monroe County-Stroudsburg)
556 Main St.
East Stroudsburg, PA 18301
(717)421-4433

SCORE Office (Erie)
120 W. 9th St.
Erie, PA 16501
(814)871-5650
Fax: (814)871-7530

SCORE Office (Bucks County)
409 Hood Blvd.
Fairless Hills, PA 19030
(215)943-8850
Fax: (215)943-7404

SCORE Office (Hanover)
146 Broadway
Hanover, PA 17331
(717)637-6130
Fax: (717)637-9127

SCORE Office (Harrisburg)
100 Chestnut, Ste. 309
Harrisburg, PA 17101
(717)782-3874

SCORE Office (East Montgomery County)
Baederwood Shopping Center
1653 The Fairways, Ste. 204
Jenkintown, PA 19046
(215)885-3027

SCORE Office (Kittanning)
2 Butler Rd.
Kittanning, PA 16201
(412)543-1305
Fax: (412)543-6206

SCORE Office (Lancaster)
118 W. Chestnut St.
Lancaster, PA 17603
(717)397-3092

SCORE Office (Westmoreland County)
300 Fraser Purchase Rd.
Latrobe, PA 15650-2690
(412)539-7505
Fax: (412)539-1850

SCORE Office (Lebanon)
252 N. 8th St.
PO Box 899

Lebanon, PA 17042-0899
(717)273-3727
Fax: (717)273-7940

SCORE Office (Lewistown)
3 W. Monument Sq., Ste. 204
Lewistown, PA 17044
(717)248-6713
Fax: (717)248-6714

SCORE Office (Delaware County)
602 E. Baltimore Pike
Media, PA 19063
(610)565-3677
Fax: (610)565-1606

SCORE Office (Milton Area)
112 S. Front St.
Milton, PA 17847
(717)742-7341
Fax: (717)792-2008

SCORE Office (Mon-Valley)
435 Donner Ave.
Monessen, PA 15062
(412)684-4277
Fax: (412)684-7688

SCORE Office (Monroeville)
William Penn Plaza
2790 Mosside Blvd., Ste. 295
Monroeville, PA 15146
(412)856-0622
Fax: (412)856-1030

SCORE Office (Airport Area)
986 Brodhead Rd.
Moon Township, PA 15108-2398
(412)264-6270
Fax: (412)264-1575

SCORE Office (Northeast)
8601 E. Roosevelt Blvd.
Philadelphia, PA 19152
(215)332-3400
Fax: (215)332-6050

SCORE Office (Philadelphia)
1315 Walnut St., Ste. 500
Philadelphia, PA 19107
(215)790-5050
Fax: (215)790-5057
E-mail: score46@bellatlantic.net
Website: http://www.pgweb.net/score46/

SCORE Office (Pittsburgh)
1000 Liberty Ave., Rm. 1122
Pittsburgh, PA 15222
(412)395-6560
Fax: (412)395-6562

SCORE Office (Tri-County)
801 N. Charlotte St.
Pottstown, PA 19464
(610)327-2673

SCORE Office (Reading)
601 Penn St.
Reading, PA 19601
(610)376-3497

SCORE Office (Scranton)
Oppenheim Bldg.
116 N. Washington Ave., Ste. 650
Scranton, PA 18503
(717)347-4611
Fax: (717)347-4611

SCORE Office (Central Pennsylvania)
200 Innovation Blvd., Ste. 242-B
State College, PA 16803
(814)234-9415
Fax: (814)238-9686
Website: http://countrystore.org/
business/score.htm

SCORE Office (Monroe-Stroudsburg)
556 Main St.
Stroudsburg, PA 18360
(717)421-4433

SCORE Office (Uniontown)
Federal Bldg.
Pittsburg St.
PO Box 2065 DTS
Uniontown, PA 15401
(412)437-4222
E-mail: uniontownscore@lcsys.net

SCORE Office (Warren County)
315 2nd Ave.
Warren, PA 16365
(814)723-9017

SCORE Office (Waynesboro)
323 E. Main St.
Waynesboro, PA 17268
(717)762-7123
Fax: (717)962-7124

SCORE Office (Chester County)
Government Service Center, Ste. 281
601 Westtown Rd.
West Chester, PA 19382-4538
(610)344-6910
Fax: (610)344-6919
E-mail: score@locke.ccil.org

SCORE Office (Wilkes-Barre)
7 N. Wilkes-Barre Blvd.
Wilkes Barre, PA 18702-5241
(717)826-6502
Fax: (717)826-6287

SCORE Office (North Central Pennsylvania)
240 W. 3rd St., Rm. 227
PO Box 725
Williamsport, PA 17703

(717)322-3720
Fax: (717)322-1607
E-mail: score234@mail.csrlink.net
Website: http://www.lycoming.org/score/

SCORE Office (York)
Cyber Center
2101 Pennsylvania Ave.
York, PA 17404
(717)845-8830
Fax: (717)854-9333

Puerto Rico

SCORE Office (Puerto Rico & Virgin Islands)
PO Box 12383-96
San Juan, PR 00914 0383
(787)726-8040
Fax: (787)726-8135

Rhode Island

SCORE Office (Barrington)
281 County Rd.
Barrington, RI 02806
(401)247-1920
Fax: (401)247-3763

SCORE Office (Woonsocket)
640 Washington Hwy.
Lincoln, RI 02865
(401)334-1000
Fax: (401)334-1009

SCORE Office (Wickford)
8045 Post Rd.
North Kingstown, RI 02852
(401)295-5566
Fax: (401)295-8987

SCORE Office (J.G.E. Knight)
380 Westminster St.
Providence, RI 02903
(401)528-4571
Fax: (401)528-4539
Website: http://www.riscore.org

SCORE Office (Warwick)
3288 Post Rd.
Warwick, RI 02886
(401)732-1100
Fax: (401)732-1101

SCORE Office (Westerly)
74 Post Rd.
Westerly, RI 02891
(401)596-7761
800-732-7636
Fax: (401)596-2190

South Carolina

SCORE Office (Aiken)
PO Box 892
Aiken, SC 29802
(803)641-1111
800-542-4536
Fax: (803)641-4174

SCORE Office (Anderson)
Anderson Mall
3130 N. Main St.
Anderson, SC 29621
(864)224-0453

SCORE Office (Coastal)
284 King St.
Charleston, SC 29401
(803)727-4778
Fax: (803)853-2529

SCORE Office (Midlands)
Strom Thurmond Bldg., Rm. 358
1835 Assembly St., Rm 358
Columbia, SC 29201
(803)765-5131
Fax: (803)765-5962
Website: http://www.scoremidlands.org/

SCORE Office (Piedmont)
Federal Bldg., Rm. B-02
300 E. Washington St.
Greenville, SC 29601
(864)271-3638

SCORE Office (Greenwood)
PO Drawer 1467
Greenwood, SC 29648
(864)223-8357

SCORE Office (Hilton Head Island)
52 Savannah Trail
Hilton Head, SC 29926
(803)785-7107
Fax: (803)785-7110

SCORE Office (Grand Strand)
937 Broadway
Myrtle Beach, SC 29577
(803)918-1079
Fax: (803)918-1083
E-mail: score381@aol.com

SCORE Office (Spartanburg)
PO Box 1636
Spartanburg, SC 29304
(864)594-5000
Fax: (864)594-5055

South Dakota

SCORE Office (West River)
Rushmore Plz. Civic Ctr.
444 Mount Rushmore Rd., No. 209
Rapid City, SD 57701
(605)394-5311
E-mail: score@gwtc.net

SCORE Office (Sioux Falls)
First Financial Center
110 S. Phillips Ave., Ste. 200
Sioux Falls, SD 57104-6727
(605)330-4231
Fax: (605)330-4231

Tennessee

SCORE Office (Chattanooga)
Federal Bldg., Rm. 26
900 Georgia Ave.
Chattanooga, TN 37402
(423)752-5190
Fax: (423)752-5335

SCORE Office (Cleveland)
PO Box 2275
Cleveland, TN 37320
(423)472-6587
Fax: (423)472-2019

SCORE Office (Upper Cumberland Center)
1225 S. Willow Ave.
Cookeville, TN 38501
(615)432-4111
Fax: (615)432-6010

SCORE Office (Unicoi County)
PO Box 713
Erwin, TN 37650
(423)743-3000
Fax: (423)743-0942

SCORE Office (Greeneville)
115 Academy St.
Greeneville, TN 37743
(423)638-4111
Fax: (423)638-5345

SCORE Office (Jackson)
194 Auditorium St.
Jackson, TN 38301
(901)423-2200

SCORE Office (Northeast Tennessee)
1st Tennessee Bank Bldg.
2710 S. Roan St., Ste. 584
Johnson City, TN 37601
(423)929-7686
Fax: (423)461-8052

SCORE Office (Kingsport)
151 E. Main St.
Kingsport, TN 37662
(423)392-8805

SCORE Office (Greater Knoxville)
Farragot Bldg., Ste. 224
530 S. Gay St.
Knoxville, TN 37902
(423)545-4203
E-mail: scoreknox@ntown.com
Website: http://www.scoreknox.org/

SCORE Office (Maryville)
201 S. Washington St.
Maryville, TN 37804-5728
(423)983-2241
800-525-6834
Fax: (423)984-1386

SCORE Office (Memphis)
Federal Bldg., Ste. 390
167 N. Main St.
Memphis, TN 38103
(901)544-3588

SCORE Office (Nashville)
50 Vantage Way, Ste. 201
Nashville, TN 37228-1500
(615)736-7621

Texas

SCORE Office (Abilene)
2106 Federal Post Office and Court Bldg.
Abilene, TX 79601
(915)677-1857

SCORE Office (Austin)
2501 S. Congress
Austin, TX 78701
(512)442-7235
Fax: (512)442-7528

SCORE Office (Golden Triangle)
450 Boyd St.
Beaumont, TX 77704
(409)838-6581
Fax: (409)833-6718

SCORE Office (Brownsville)
3505 Boca Chica Blvd., Ste. 305
Brownsville, TX 78521
(210)541-4508

SCORE Office (Brazos Valley)
3000 Briarcrest, Ste. 302
Bryan, TX 77802
(409)776-8876
E-mail: 102633.2612@compuserve.com

SCORE Office (Cleburne)
Watergarden Pl., 9th Fl., Ste. 400
Cleburne, TX 76031
(817)871-6002

SCORE Office (Corpus Christi)
651 Upper North Broadway, Ste. 654
Corpus Christi, TX 78477

(512)888-4322
Fax: (512)888-3418

SCORE Office (Dallas)
6260 E. Mockingbird
Dallas, TX 75214-2619
(214)828-2471
Fax: (214)821-8033

SCORE Office (El Paso)
10 Civic Center Plaza
El Paso, TX 79901
(915)534-0541
Fax: (915)534-0513

SCORE Office (Bedford)
100 E. 15th St., Ste. 400
Ft. Worth, TX 76102
(817)871-6002

SCORE Office (Ft. Worth)
100 E. 15th St., No. 24
Ft. Worth, TX 76102
(817)871-6002
Fax: (817)871-6031
E-mail: fwbac@onramp.net

SCORE Office (Garland)
2734 W. Kingsley Rd.
Garland, TX 75041
(214)271-9224

SCORE Office (Granbury Chamber of Commerce)
416 S. Morgan
Granbury, TX 76048
(817)573-1622
Fax: (817)573-0805

SCORE Office (Lower Rio Grande Valley)
222 E. Van Buren, Ste. 500
Harlingen, TX 78550
(956)427-8533
Fax: (956)427-8537

SCORE Office (Houston)
9301 Southwest Fwy., Ste. 550
Houston, TX 77074
(713)773-6565
Fax: (713)773-6550

SCORE Office (Irving)
3333 N. MacArthur Blvd., Ste. 100
Irving, TX 75062
(214)252-8484
Fax: (214)252-6710

SCORE Office (Lubbock)
1205 Texas Ave., Rm. 411D
Lubbock, TX 79401
(806)472-7462
Fax: (806)472-7487

SCORE Office (Midland)
Post Office Annex
200 E. Wall St., Rm. P121
Midland, TX 79701
(915)687-2649

SCORE Office (Orange)
1012 Green Ave.
Orange, TX 77630-5620
(409)883-3536
800-528-4906
Fax: (409)886-3247

SCORE Office (Plano)
1200 E. 15th St.
PO Drawer 940287
Plano, TX 75094-0287
(214)424-7547
Fax: (214)422-5182

SCORE Office (Port Arthur)
4749 Twin City Hwy., Ste. 300
Port Arthur, TX 77642
(409)963-1107
Fax: (409)963-3322

SCORE Office (Richardson)
411 Belle Grove
Richardson, TX 75080
(214)234-4141
800-777-8001
Fax: (214)680-9103

SCORE Office (San Antonio)
Federal Bldg., Rm. A527
727 E. Durango
San Antonio, TX 78206
(210)472-5931
Fax: (210)472-5935

SCORE Office (Texarkana State College)
819 State Line Ave.
Texarkana, TX 75501
(903)792-7191
Fax: (903)793-4304

SCORE Office (East Texas)
RTDC
1530 SSW Loop 323, Ste. 100
Tyler, TX 75701
(903)510-2975
Fax: (903)510-2978

SCORE Office (Waco)
401 Franklin Ave.
Waco, TX 76701
(817)754-8898
Fax: (817)756-0776
Website: http://www.brc-waco.com/

SCORE Office (Wichita Falls)
Hamilton Bldg.
900 8th St.

Organizations, Agencies, & Consultants

Wichita Falls, TX 76307
(940)723-2741
Fax: (940)723-8773

Utah

SCORE Office (Northern Utah)
160 N. Main
Logan, UT 84321
(435)746-2269

SCORE Office (Ogden)
1701 E. Windsor Dr.
Ogden, UT 84604
(801)629-8613
E-mail: score158@netscape.net

SCORE Office (Central Utah)
1071 F. Windsor Dr.
Provo, UT 84604
(801)373-8660

SCORE Office (Southern Utah)
225 South 700 East
St. George, UT 84770
(435)652-7751

SCORE Office (Salt Lake)
310 S Main St.
Salt Lake City, UT 84101
(801)746-2269
Fax: (801)746-2273

Vermont

SCORE Office (Champlain Valley)
Winston Prouty Federal Bldg.
11 Lincoln St., Rm. 106
Essex Junction, VT 05452
(802)951-6762

SCORE Office (Montpelier)
87 State St., Rm. 205
PO Box 605
Montpelier, VT 05601
(802)828-4422
Fax: (802)828-4485

SCORE Office (Marble Valley)
256 N. Main St.
Rutland, VT 05701-2413
(802)773-9147

SCORE Office (Northeast Kingdom)
20 Main St.
PO Box 904
St. Johnsbury, VT 05819
(802)748-5101

Virgin Islands

SCORE Office (St. Croix)
United Plaza Shopping Center
PO Box 4010, Christiansted

St. Croix, VI 00822
(809)778-5380

SCORE Office (St. Thomas-St. John)
Federal Bldg., Rm. 21
Veterans Dr.
St. Thomas, VI 00801
(809)774-8530

Virginia

SCORE Office (Arlington)
2009 N. 14th St., Ste. 111
Arlington, VA 22201
(703)525-2400

SCORE Office (Blacksburg)
141 Jackson St.
Blacksburg, VA 24060
(540)552-4061

SCORE Office (Bristol)
20 Volunteer Pkwy.
Bristol, VA 24203
(540)989-4850

SCORE Office (Central Virginia)
1001 E. Market St., Ste. 101
Charlottesville, VA 22902
(804)295-6712
Fax: (804)295-7066

SCORE Office (Alleghany Satellite)
241 W. Main St.
Covington, VA 24426
(540)962-2178
Fax: (540)962-2179

SCORE Office (Central Fairfax)
3975 University Dr., Ste. 350
Fairfax, VA 22030
(703)591-2450

SCORE Office (Falls Church)
PO Box 491
Falls Church, VA 22040
(703)532-1050
Fax: (703)237-7904

SCORE Office (Glenns)
Glenns Campus
Box 287
Glenns, VA 23149
(804)693-9650

SCORE Office (Peninsula)
6 Manhattan Sq.
PO Box 7269
Hampton, VA 23666
(757)766-2000
Fax: (757)865-0339
E-mail: score100@seva.net

SCORE Office (Tri-Cities)
108 N. Main St.
Hopewell, VA 23860
(804)458-5536

SCORE Office (Lynchburg)
Federal Bldg.
1100 Main St.
Lynchburg, VA 24504-1714
(804)846-3235

SCORE Office (Greater Prince William)
8963 Center St
Manassas, VA 20110
(703)368-4813
Fax: (703)368-4733

SCORE Office (Martinsvile)
115 Broad St.
Martinsville, VA 24112-0709
(540)632-6401
Fax: (540)632-5059

SCORE Office (Hampton Roads)
Federal Bldg., Rm. 737
200 Grandby St.
Norfolk, VA 23510
(757)441-3733
Fax: (757)441-3733
E-mail: scorehr60@juno.com

SCORE Office (Norfolk)
Federal Bldg., Rm. 737
200 Granby St.
Norfolk, VA 23510
(757)441-3733
Fax: (757)441-3733

SCORE Office (Virginia Beach)
Chamber of Commerce
200 Grandby St., Rm 737
Norfolk, VA 23510
(804)441-3733

SCORE Office (Radford)
1126 Norwood St.
Radford, VA 24141
(540)639-2202

SCORE Office (Richmond)
Federal Bldg.
400 N. 8th St., Ste. 1150
PO Box 10126
Richmond, VA 23240-0126
(804)771-2400
Fax: (804)771-8018
E-mail: scorechapter12@yahoo.com
Website: http://www.cvco.org/score/

SCORE Office (Roanoke)
Federal Bldg., Rm. 716
250 Franklin Rd.
Roanoke, VA 24011

(540)857-2834
Fax: (540)857-2043
E-mail: scorerva@juno.com
Website: http://hometown.aol.com/
scorerv/Index.html

SCORE Office (Fairfax)
8391 Old Courthouse Rd., Ste. 300
Vienna, VA 22182
(703)749-0400

SCORE Office (Greater Vienna)
513 Maple Ave. West
Vienna, VA 22180
(703)281-1333
Fax: (703)242-1482

SCORE Office (Shenandoah Valley)
301 W. Main St.
Waynesboro, VA 22980
(540)949-8203
Fax: (540)949-7740
E-mail: score427@intelos.net

SCORE Office (Williamsburg)
201 Penniman Rd.
Williamsburg, VA 23185
(757)229-6511
E-mail: wacc@williamsburgcc.com

SCORE Office (Northern Virginia)
1360 S. Pleasant Valley Rd.
Winchester, VA 22601
(540)662-4118

Washington

SCORE Office (Gray's Harbor)
506 Duffy St.
Aberdeen, WA 98520
(360)532-1924
Fax: (360)533-7945

SCORE Office (Bellingham)
101 E. Holly St.
Bellingham, WA 98225
(360)676-3307

SCORE Office (Everett)
2702 Hoyt Ave.
Everett, WA 98201-3556
(206)259-8000

SCORE Office (Gig Harbor)
3125 Judson St.
Gig Harbor, WA 98335
(206)851-6865

SCORE Office (Kennewick)
PO Box 6986
Kennewick, WA 99336
(509)736-0510

SCORE Office (Puyallup)
322 2nd St. SW
PO Box 1298
Puyallup, WA 98371
(206)845-6755
Fax: (206)848-6164

SCORE Office (Seattle)
1200 6th Ave., Ste. 1700
Seattle, WA 98101
(206)553-7320
Fax: (206)553-7044
E-mail: score55@aol.com
Website: http://www.scn.org/civic/
score-online/index55.html

SCORE Office (Spokane)
801 W. Riverside Ave., No. 240
Spokane, WA 99201
(509)353-2820
Fax: (509)353-2600
E-mail: score@dmi.net
Website: http://www.dmi.net/score/

SCORE Office (Clover Park)
PO Box 1933
Tacoma, WA 98401-1933
(206)627-2175

SCORE Office (Tacoma)
1101 Pacific Ave.
Tacoma, WA 98402
(253)274-1288
Fax: (253)274-1289

SCORE Office (Fort Vancouver)
1701 Broadway, S-1
Vancouver, WA 98663
(360)699-1079

SCORE Office (Walla Walla)
500 Tausick Way
Walla Walla, WA 99362
(509)527-4681

SCORE Office (Mid-Columbia)
1113 S. 14th Ave.
Yakima, WA 98907
(509)574-4944
Fax: (509)574-2943
Website: http://www.ellensburg.com/
~score/

West Virginia

SCORE Office (Charleston)
1116 Smith St.
Charleston, WV 25301
(304)347-5463
E-mail: score256@juno.com

SCORE Office (Virginia Street)
1116 Smith St., Ste. 302
Charleston, WV 25301
(304)347-5463

SCORE Office (Marion County)
PO Box 208
Fairmont, WV 26555-0208
(304)363-0486

SCORE Office (Upper Monongahela Valley)
1000 Technology Dr., Ste. 1111
Fairmont, WV 26555
(304)363-0486
E-mail: score537@hotmail.com

SCORE Office (Huntington)
1101 6th Ave., Ste. 220
Huntington, WV 25701-2309
(304)523-4092

SCORE Office (Wheeling)
1310 Market St.
Wheeling, WV 26003
(304)233-2575
Fax: (304)233-1320

Wisconsin

SCORE Office (Fox Cities)
227 S. Walnut St.
Appleton, WI 54913
(920)734-7101
Fax: (920)734-7161

SCORE Office (Beloit)
136 W. Grand Ave., Ste. 100
PO Box 717
Beloit, WI 53511
(608)365-8835
Fax: (608)365-9170

SCORE Office (Eau Claire)
Federal Bldg., Rm. B11
510 S. Barstow St.
Eau Claire, WI 54701
(715)834-1573
E-mail: score@ecol.net
Website: http://www.ecol.net/~score/

SCORE Office (Fond du Lac)
207 N. Main St.
Fond du Lac, WI 54935
(414)921-9500
Fax: (414)921-9559

SCORE Office (Green Bay)
835 Potts Ave.
Green Bay, WI 54304
(414)496-8930
Fax: (414)496-6009

SCORE Office (Janesville)
20 S. Main St., Ste. 11
PO Box 8008
Janesville, WI 53547
(608)757-3160
Fax: (608)757-3170

SCORE Office (La Crosse)
712 Main St.
La Crosse, WI 54602-0219
(608)784-4880

SCORE Office (Madison)
505 S. Rosa Rd.
Madison, WI 53719
(608)441-2820

SCORE Office (Manitowoc)
1515 Memorial Dr.
PO Box 903
Manitowoc, WI 54221-0903
(414)684-5575
Fax: (414)684-1915

**SCORE Office
(Milwaukee)**
310 W. Wisconsin Ave., Ste. 425
Milwaukee, WI 53203
(414)297-3942
Fax: (414)297-1377

**SCORE Office
(Central Wisconsin)**
1224 Lindbergh Ave.
Stevens Point, WI 54481
(715)344-7729

SCORE Office (Superior)
Superior Business Center Inc.
1423 N. 8th St.
Superior, WI 54880
(715)394-7388
Fax: (715)393-7414

SCORE Office (Waukesha)
223 Wisconsin Ave.
Waukesha, WI 53186-4926
(414)542-4249

SCORE Office (Wausau)
300 3rd St., Ste. 200
Wausau, WI 54402-6190
(715)845-6231

**SCORE Office
(Wisconsin Rapids)**
2240 Kingston Rd.
Wisconsin Rapids, WI 54494
(715)423-1830

Wyoming

SCORE Office (Casper)
Federal Bldg., No. 2215
100 East B St.
Casper, WY 82602
(307)261-6529
Fax: (307)261-6530

Venture capital & financing companies

This section contains a listing of financing and loan companies in the United States and Canada. These listing are arranged alphabetically by country, then by state or province, then by city, then by organization name.

Canada

Alberta

Launchworks Inc.
1902J 11th St., S.E.
Calgary, AB, Canada T2G 3G2
(403)269-1119
Fax: (403)269-1141
Website: http://www.launchworks.com

Native Venture Capital Company, Inc.
21 Artist View Point, Box 7
Site 25, RR 12
Calgary, AB, Canada T3E 6W3
(903)208-5380

Miralta Capital Inc.
4445 Calgary Trail South
888 Terrace Plaza Alberta
Edmonton, AB, Canada T6H 5R7
(780)438-3535
Fax: (780)438-3129

Vencap Equities Alberta Ltd.
10180-101st St., Ste. 1980
Edmonton, AB, Canada T5J 3S4
(403)420-1171
Fax: (403)429-2541

British Columbia

Discovery Capital
5th Fl., 1199 West Hastings
Vancouver, BC, Canada V6E 3T5
(604)683-3000
Fax: (604)662-3457
E-mail: info@discoverycapital.com
Website: http://www.discoverycapital
.com

Greenstone Venture Partners
1177 West Hastings St.
Ste. 400
Vancouver, BC, Canada V6E 2K3
(604)717-1977
Fax: (604)717-1976
Website: http://www.greenstonevc.com

Growthworks Capital
2600-1055 West Georgia St.
Box 11170 Royal Centre

Vancouver, BC, Canada V6E 3R5
(604)895-7259
Fax: (604)669-7605
Website: http://www.wofund.com

**MDS Discovery Venture
Management, Inc.**
555 W. Eighth Ave., Ste. 305
Vancouver, BC, Canada V5Z 1C6
(604)872-8464
Fax: (604)872-2977
E-mail: info@mds-ventures.com

Ventures West Management Inc.
1285 W. Pender St., Ste. 280
Vancouver, BC, Canada V6E 4B1
(604)688-9495
Fax: (604)687-2145
Website: http://www.ventureswest.com

Nova Scotia

ACF Equity Atlantic Inc.
Purdy's Wharf Tower II
Ste. 2106
Halifax, NS, Canada B3J 3R7
(902)421-1965
Fax: (902)421-1808

Montgomerie, Huck & Co.
146 Bluenose Dr.
PO Box 538
Lunenburg, NS, Canada B0J 2C0
(902)634-7125
Fax: (902)634-7130

Ontario

IPS Industrial Promotion Services Ltd.
60 Columbia Way, Ste. 720
Markham, ON, Canada L3R 0C9
(905)475-9400
Fax: (905)475-5003

Betwin Investments Inc.
Box 23110
Sault Ste. Marie, ON, Canada P6A 6W6
(705)253-0744
Fax: (705)253-0744

Bailey & Company, Inc.
594 Spadina Ave.
Toronto, ON, Canada M5S 2H4
(416)921-6930
Fax: (416)925-4670

BCE Capital
200 Bay St.
South Tower, Ste. 3120
Toronto, ON, Canada M5J 2J2
(416)815-0078
Fax: (416)941-1073
Website: http://www.bcecapital.com

Castlehill Ventures
55 University Ave., Ste. 500
Toronto, ON, Canada M5J 2H7
(416)862-8574
Fax: (416)862-8875

CCFL Mezzanine Partners of Canada
70 University Ave.
Ste. 1450
Toronto, ON, Canada M5J 2M4
(416)977-1450
Fax: (416)977-6764
E-mail: info@ccfl.com
Website: http://www.ccfl.com

Celtic House International
100 Simcoe St., Ste. 100
Toronto, ON, Canada M5H 3G2
(416)542-2436
Fax: (416)542-2435
Website: http://www.celtic-house.com

Clairvest Group Inc.
22 St. Clair Ave. East
Ste. 1700
Toronto, ON, Canada M4T 2S3
(416)925-9270
Fax: (416)925-5753

Crosbie & Co., Inc.
One First Canadian Place
9th Fl.
PO Box 116
Toronto, ON, Canada M5X 1A4
(416)362-7726
Fax: (416)362-3447
E-mail: info@crosbieco.com
Website: http://www.crosbieco.com

Drug Royalty Corp.
Eight King St. East
Ste. 202
Toronto, ON, Canada M5C 1B5
(416)863-1865
Fax: (416)863-5161

Grieve, Horner, Brown & Asculai
8 King St. E, Ste. 1704
Toronto, ON, Canada M5C 1B5
(416)362-7668
Fax: (416)362-7660

Jefferson Partners
77 King St. West
Ste. 4010
PO Box 136
Toronto, ON, Canada M5K 1H1
(416)367-1533
Fax: (416)367-5827
Website: http://www.jefferson.com

J.L. Albright Venture Partners
Canada Trust Tower, 161 Bay St.
Ste. 4440
PO Box 215
Toronto, ON, Canada M5J 2S1
(416)367-2440
Fax: (416)367-4604
Website: http://www.jlaventures.com

McLean Watson Capital Inc.
One First Canadian Place
Ste. 1410
PO Box 129
Toronto, ON, Canada M5X 1A4
(416)363-2000
Fax: (416)363-2010
Website: http://www.mcleanwatson.com

Middlefield Capital Fund
One First Canadian Place
85th Fl.
PO Box 192
Toronto, ON, Canada M5X 1A6
(416)362-0714
Fax: (416)362-7925
Website: http://www.middlefield.com

Mosaic Venture Partners
24 Duncan St.
Ste. 300
Toronto, ON, Canada M5V 3M6
(416)597-8889
Fax: (416)597-2345

Onex Corp.
161 Bay St.
PO Box 700
Toronto, ON, Canada M5J 2S1
(416)362-7711
Fax: (416)362-5765

Penfund Partners Inc.
145 King St. West
Ste. 1920
Toronto, ON, Canada M5H 1J8
(416)865-0300
Fax: (416)364-6912
Website: http://www.penfund.com

Primaxis Technology Ventures Inc.
1 Richmond St. West, 8th Fl.
Toronto, ON, Canada M5H 3W4
(416)313-5210
Fax: (416)313-5218
Website: http://www.primaxis.com

Priveq Capital Funds
240 Duncan Mill Rd., Ste. 602
Toronto, ON, Canada M3B 3P1
(416)447-3330
Fax: (416)447-3331
E-mail: priveq@sympatico.ca

Roynat Ventures
40 King St. West, 26th Fl.
Toronto, ON, Canada M5H 1H1
(416)933-2667
Fax: (416)933-2783
Website: http://www.roynatcapital.com

Tera Capital Corp.
366 Adelaide St. East, Ste. 337
Toronto, ON, Canada M5A 3X9
(416)368-1024
Fax: (416)368-1427

Working Ventures Canadian Fund Inc.
250 Bloor St. East, Ste. 1600
Toronto, ON, Canada M4W 1E6
(416)934-7718
Fax: (416)929-0901
Website: http://www.workingventures.ca

Quebec

Altamira Capital Corp.
202 University
Niveau de Maisoneuve, Bur. 201
Montreal, QC, Canada H3A 2A5
(514)499-1656
Fax: (514)499-9570

Federal Business Development Bank
Venture Capital Division
Five Place Ville Marie, Ste. 600
Montreal, QC, Canada H3B 5E7
(514)283-1896
Fax: (514)283-5455

Hydro-Quebec Capitech Inc.
75 Boul, Rene Levesque Quest
Montreal, QC, Canada H2Z 1A4
(514)289-4783
Fax: (514)289-5420
Website: http://www.hqcapitech.com

Investissement Desjardins
2 complexe Desjardins
C.P. 760
Montreal, QC, Canada H5B 1B8
(514)281-7131
Fax: (514)281-7808
Website: http://www.desjardins.com/id

Marleau Lemire Inc.
One Place Ville-Marie, Ste. 3601
Montreal, QC, Canada H3B 3P2
(514)877-3800
Fax: (514)875-6415

Speirs Consultants Inc.
365 Stanstead
Montreal, QC, Canada H3R 1X5
(514)342-3858
Fax: (514)342-1977

Tecnocap Inc.
4028 Marlowe
Montreal, QC, Canada H4A 3M2
(514)483-6009
Fax: (514)483-6045
Website: http://www.technocap.com

Telsoft Ventures
1000, Rue de la Gauchetiere
Quest, 25eme Etage
Montreal, QC, Canada H3B 4W5
(514)397-8450
Fax: (514)397-8451

Saskatchewan

Saskatchewan Government Growth Fund
1801 Hamilton St., Ste. 1210
Canada Trust Tower
Regina, SK, Canada S4P 4B4
(306)787-2994
Fax: (306)787-2086

United states

Alabama

FHL Capital Corp.
600 20th Street North
Suite 350
Birmingham, AL 35203
(205)328-3098
Fax: (205)323-0001

Harbert Management Corp.
One Riverchase Pkwy. South
Birmingham, AL 35244
(205)987-5500
Fax: (205)987-5707
Website: http://www.harbert.net

Jefferson Capital Fund
PO Box 13129
Birmingham, AL 35213
(205)324-7709

Private Capital Corp.
100 Brookwood Pl., 4th Fl.
Birmingham, AL 35209
(205)879-2722
Fax: (205)879-5121

21st Century Health Ventures
One Health South Pkwy.
Birmingham, AL 35243
(256)268-6250
Fax: (256)970-8928

FJC Growth Capital Corp.
200 W. Side Sq., Ste. 340
Huntsville, AL 35801
(256)922-2918
Fax: (256)922-2909

Hickory Venture Capital Corp.
301 Washington St. NW
Suite 301
Huntsville, AL 35801
(256)539-1931
Fax: (256)539-5130
E-mail: hvcc@hvcc.com
Website: http://www.hvcc.com

Southeastern Technology Fund
7910 South Memorial Pkwy., Ste. F
Huntsville, AL 35802
(256)883-8711
Fax: (256)883-8558

Cordova Ventures
4121 Carmichael Rd., Ste. 301
Montgomery, AL 36106
(334)271-6011
Fax: (334)260-0120
Website: http://www.cordovaventures
.com

Small Business Clinic of Alabama/AG Bartholomew & Associates
PO Box 231074
Montgomery, AL 36123-1074
(334)284-3640

Arizona

Miller Capital Corp.
4909 E. McDowell Rd.
Phoenix, AZ 85008
(602)225-0504
Fax: (602)225-9024
Website: http://www.themillergroup.com

The Columbine Venture Funds
9449 North 90th St., Ste. 200
Scottsdale, AZ 85258
(602)661-9222
Fax: (602)661-6262

Koch Ventures
17767 N. Perimeter Dr., Ste. 101
Scottsdale, AZ 85255
(480)419-3600
Fax: (480)419-3606
Website: http://www.kochventures.com

McKee & Co.
7702 E. Doubletree Ranch Rd.
Suite 230
Scottsdale, AZ 85258
(480)368-0333
Fax: (480)607-7446

Merita Capital Ltd.
7350 E. Stetson Dr., Ste. 108-A
Scottsdale, AZ 85251
(480)947-8700
Fax: (480)947-8766

Valley Ventures / Arizona Growth Partners L.P.
6720 N. Scottsdale Rd., Ste. 208
Scottsdale, AZ 85253
(480)661-6600
Fax: (480)661-6262

Estreetcapital.com
660 South Mill Ave., Ste. 315
Tempe, AZ 85281
(480)968-8400
Fax: (480)968-8480
Website: http://www.estreetcapital.com

Coronado Venture Fund
PO Box 65420
Tucson, AZ 85728-5420
(520)577-3764
Fax: (520)299-8491

Arkansas

Arkansas Capital Corp.
225 South Pulaski St.
Little Rock, AR 72201
(501)374-9247
Fax: (501)374-9425
Website: http://www.arcapital.com

California

Sundance Venture Partners, L.P.
100 Clocktower Place, Ste. 130
Carmel, CA 93923
(831)625-6500
Fax: (831)625-6590

Westar Capital (Costa Mesa)
949 South Coast Dr., Ste. 650
Costa Mesa, CA 92626
(714)481-5160
Fax: (714)481-5166
E-mail: mailbox@westarcapital.com
Website: http://www.westarcapital.com

Alpine Technology Ventures
20300 Stevens Creek Boulevard, Ste. 495
Cupertino, CA 95014
(408)725-1810
Fax: (408)725-1207
Website: http://www.alpineventures.com

Bay Partners
10600 N. De Anza Blvd.
Cupertino, CA 95014-2031
(408)725-2444
Fax: (408)446-4502
Website: http://www.baypartners.com

Novus Ventures
20111 Stevens Creek Blvd., Ste. 130
Cupertino, CA 95014
(408)252-3900

Fax: (408)252-1713
Website: http://www.novusventures.com

Triune Capital
19925 Stevens Creek Blvd., Ste. 200
Cupertino, CA 95014
(310)284-6800
Fax: (310)284-3290

Acorn Ventures
268 Bush St., Ste. 2829
Daly City, CA 94014
(650)994-7801
Fax: (650)994-3305
Website: http://www.acornventures.com

Digital Media Campus
2221 Park Place
El Segundo, CA 90245
(310)426-8000
Fax: (310)426-8010
E-mail: info@thecampus.com
Website: http://
www.digitalmediacampus.com

**BankAmerica Ventures / BA Venture
Partners**
950 Tower Ln., Ste. 700
Foster City, CA 94404
(650)378-6000
Fax: (650)378-6040
Website: http://www.baventurepartners
.com

Starting Point Partners
666 Portofino Lane
Foster City, CA 94404
(650)722-1035
Website: http://
www.startingpointpartners.com

Opportunity Capital Partners
2201 Walnut Ave., Ste. 210
Fremont, CA 94538
(510)795-7000
Fax: (510)494-5439
Website: http://www.ocpcapital.com

Imperial Ventures Inc.
9920 S. La Cienega Boulevar, 14th Fl.
Inglewood, CA 90301
(310)417-5409
Fax: (310)338-6115

Ventana Global (Irvine)
18881 Von Karman Ave., Ste. 1150
Irvine, CA 92612
(949)476-2204
Fax: (949)752-0223
Website: http://www.ventanaglobal.com

Integrated Consortium Inc.
50 Ridgecrest Rd.
Kentfield, CA 94904

(415)925-0386
Fax: (415)461-2726

Enterprise Partners
979 Ivanhoe Ave., Ste. 550
La Jolla, CA 92037
(858)454-8833
Fax: (858)454-2489
Website: http://www.epvc.com

Domain Associates
28202 Cabot Rd., Ste. 200
Laguna Niguel, CA 92677
(949)347-2446
Fax: (949)347-9720
Website: http://www.domainvc.com

Cascade Communications Ventures
60 E. Sir Francis Drake Blvd., Ste. 300
Larkspur, CA 94939
(415)925-6500
Fax: (415)925-6501

Allegis Capital
One First St., Ste. Two
Los Altos, CA 94022
(650)917-5900
Fax: (650)917-5901
Website: http://www.allegiscapital.com

Aspen Ventures
1000 Fremont Ave., Ste. 200
Los Altos, CA 94024
(650)917-5670
Fax: (650)917-5677
Website: http://www.aspenventures.com

AVI Capital L.P.
1 First St., Ste. 2
Los Altos, CA 94022
(650)949-9862
Fax: (650)949-8510
Website: http://www.avicapital.com

Bastion Capital Corp.
1999 Avenue of the Stars, Ste. 2960
Los Angeles, CA 90067
(310)788-5700
Fax: (310)277-7582
E-mail: ga@bastioncapital.com
Website: http://www.bastioncapital.com

Davis Group
PO Box 69953
Los Angeles, CA 90069-0953
(310)659-6327
Fax: (310)659-6337

Developers Equity Corp.
1880 Century Park East, Ste. 211
Los Angeles, CA 90067
(213)277-0300

Far East Capital Corp.
350 S. Grand Ave., Ste. 4100
Los Angeles, CA 90071
(213)687-1361
Fax: (213)617-7939
E-mail: free@fareastnationalbank.com

Kline Hawkes & Co.
11726 San Vicente Blvd., Ste. 300
Los Angeles, CA 90049
(310)442-4700
Fax: (310)442-4707
Website: http://www.klinehawkes.com

Lawrence Financial Group
701 Teakwood
PO Box 491773
Los Angeles, CA 90049
(310)471-4060
Fax: (310)472-3155

Riordan Lewis & Haden
300 S. Grand Ave., 29th Fl.
Los Angeles, CA 90071
(213)229-8500
Fax: (213)229-8597

Union Venture Corp.
445 S. Figueroa St., 9th Fl.
Los Angeles, CA 90071
(213)236-4092
Fax: (213)236-6329

Wedbush Capital Partners
1000 Wilshire Blvd.
Los Angeles, CA 90017
(213)688-4545
Fax: (213)688-6642
Website: http://www.wedbush.com

Advent International Corp.
2180 Sand Hill Rd., Ste. 420
Menlo Park, CA 94025
(650)233-7500
Fax: (650)233-7515
Website: http://www.adventinternational
.com

Altos Ventures
2882 Sand Hill Rd., Ste. 100
Menlo Park, CA 94025
(650)234-9771
Fax: (650)233-9821
Website: http://www.altosvc.com

Applied Technology
1010 El Camino Real, Ste. 300
Menlo Park, CA 94025
(415)326-8622
Fax: (415)326-8163

APV Technology Partners
535 Middlefield, Ste. 150
Menlo Park, CA 94025

(650)327-7871
Fax: (650)327-7631
Website: http://www.apvtp.com

August Capital Management
2480 Sand Hill Rd., Ste. 101
Menlo Park, CA 94025
(650)234-9900
Fax: (650)234-9910
Website: http://www.augustcap.com

Baccharis Capital Inc.
2420 Sand Hill Rd., Ste. 100
Menlo Park, CA 94025
(650)324-6844
Fax: (650)854-3025

Benchmark Capital
2480 Sand Hill Rd., Ste. 200
Menlo Park, CA 94025
(650)854-8180
Fax: (650)854-8183
E-mail: info@benchmark.com
Website: http://www.benchmark.com

Bessemer Venture Partners (Menlo Park)
535 Middlefield Rd., Ste. 245
Menlo Park, CA 94025
(650)853-7000
Fax: (650)853-7001
Website: http://www.bvp.com

The Cambria Group
1600 El Camino Real Rd., Ste. 155
Menlo Park, CA 94025
(650)329-8600
Fax: (650)329-8601
Website: http://www.cambriagroup.com

Canaan Partners
2884 Sand Hill Rd., Ste. 115
Menlo Park, CA 94025
(650)854-8092
Fax: (650)854-8127
Website: http://www.canaan.com

Capstone Ventures
3000 Sand Hill Rd., Bldg. One, Ste. 290
Menlo Park, CA 94025
(650)854-2523
Fax: (650)854-9010
Website: http://www.capstonevc.com

Comdisco Venture Group (Silicon Valley)
3000 Sand Hill Rd., Bldg. 1, Ste. 155
Menlo Park, CA 94025
(650)854-9484
Fax: (650)854-4026

Commtech International
535 Middlefield Rd., Ste. 200
Menlo Park, CA 94025

(650)328-0190
Fax: (650)328-6442

Compass Technology Partners
1550 El Camino Real, Ste. 275
Menlo Park, CA 94025-4111
(650)322-7595
Fax: (650)322-0588
Website: http://www.compasstech
partners.com

Convergence Partners
3000 Sand Hill Rd., Ste. 235
Menlo Park, CA 94025
(650)854-3010
Fax: (650)854-3015
Website: http://www.convergence
partners.com

The Dakota Group
PO Box 1025
Menlo Park, CA 94025
(650)853-0600
Fax: (650)851-4899
E-mail: info@dakota.com

Delphi Ventures
3000 Sand Hill Rd.
Bldg. One, Ste. 135
Menlo Park, CA 94025
(650)854-9650
Fax: (650)854-2961
Website: http://www.delphiventures.com

El Dorado Ventures
2884 Sand Hill Rd., Ste. 121
Menlo Park, CA 94025
(650)854-1200
Fax: (650)854-1202
Website: http://www.eldorado
ventures.com

Glynn Ventures
3000 Sand Hill Rd., Bldg. 4, Ste. 235
Menlo Park, CA 94025
(650)854-2215

Indosuez Ventures
2180 Sand Hill Rd., Ste. 450
Menlo Park, CA 94025
(650)854-0587
Fax: (650)323-5561
Website: http://www.indosuezventures
.com

Institutional Venture Partners
3000 Sand Hill Rd., Bldg. 2, Ste. 290
Menlo Park, CA 94025
(650)854-0132
Fax: (650)854-5762
Website: http://www.ivp.com

Interwest Partners (Menlo Park)
3000 Sand Hill Rd., Bldg. 3, Ste. 255
Menlo Park, CA 94025-7112
(650)854-8585
Fax: (650)854-4706
Website: http://www.interwest.com

Kleiner Perkins Caufield & Byers (Menlo Park)
2750 Sand Hill Rd.
Menlo Park, CA 94025
(650)233-2750
Fax: (650)233-0300
Website: http://www.kpcb.com

Magic Venture Capital LLC
1010 El Camino Real, Ste. 300
Menlo Park, CA 94025
(650)325-4149

Matrix Partners
2500 Sand Hill Rd., Ste. 113
Menlo Park, CA 94025
(650)854-3131
Fax: (650)854-3296
Website: http://www.matrixpartners.com

Mayfield Fund
2800 Sand Hill Rd.
Menlo Park, CA 94025
(650)854-5560
Fax: (650)854-5712
Website: http://www.mayfield.com

McCown De Leeuw and Co. (Menlo Park)
3000 Sand Hill Rd., Bldg. 3, Ste. 290
Menlo Park, CA 94025-7111
(650)854-6000
Fax: (650)854-0853
Website: http://www.mdcpartners.com

Menlo Ventures
3000 Sand Hill Rd., Bldg. 4, Ste. 100
Menlo Park, CA 94025
(650)854-8540
Fax: (650)854-7059
Website: http://www.menloventures.com

Merrill Pickard Anderson & Eyre
2480 Sand Hill Rd., Ste. 200
Menlo Park, CA 94025
(650)854-8600
Fax: (650)854-0345

New Enterprise Associates (Menlo Park)
2490 Sand Hill Rd.
Menlo Park, CA 94025
(650)854-9499
Fax: (650)854-9397
Website: http://www.nea.com

Onset Ventures
2400 Sand Hill Rd., Ste. 150
Menlo Park, CA 94025
(650)529-0700
Fax: (650)529-0777
Website: http://www.onset.com

Paragon Venture Partners
3000 Sand Hill Rd., Bldg. 1, Ste. 275
Menlo Park, CA 94025
(650)854-8000
Fax: (650)854-7260

**Pathfinder Venture Capital Funds
(Menlo Park)**
3000 Sand Hill Rd., Bldg. 3, Ste. 255
Menlo Park, CA 94025
(650)854-0650
Fax: (650)854-4706

Rocket Ventures
3000 Sandhill Rd., Bldg. 1, Ste. 170
Menlo Park, CA 94025
(650)561-9100
Fax: (650)561-9183
Website: http://www.rocketventures.com

Sequoia Capital
3000 Sand Hill Rd., Bldg. 4, Ste. 280
Menlo Park, CA 94025
(650)854-3927
Fax: (650)854-2977
E-mail: sequoia@sequoiacap.com
Website: http://www.sequoiacap.com

Sierra Ventures
3000 Sand Hill Rd., Bldg. 4, Ste. 210
Menlo Park, CA 94025
(650)854-1000
Fax: (650)854-5593
Website: http://www.sierraventures.com

Sigma Partners
2884 Sand Hill Rd., Ste. 121
Menlo Park, CA 94025-7022
(650)853-1700
Fax: (650)853-1717
E-mail: info@sigmapartners.com
Website: http://www.sigmapartners.com

Sprout Group (Menlo Park)
3000 Sand Hill Rd.
Bldg. 3, Ste. 170
Menlo Park, CA 94025
(650)234-2700
Fax: (650)234-2779
Website: http://www.sproutgroup.com

TA Associates (Menlo Park)
70 Willow Rd., Ste. 100
Menlo Park, CA 94025
(650)328-1210

Fax: (650)326-4933
Website: http://www.ta.com

Thompson Clive & Partners Ltd.
3000 Sand Hill Rd., Bldg. 1, Ste. 185
Menlo Park, CA 94025-7102
(650)854-0314
Fax: (650)854-0670
E-mail: mail@tcvc.com
Website: http://www.tcvc.com

Trinity Ventures Ltd.
3000 Sand Hill Rd., Bldg. 1, Ste. 240
Menlo Park, CA 94025
(650)854-9500
Fax: (650)854-9501
Website: http://www.trinityventures.com

U.S. Venture Partners
2180 Sand Hill Rd., Ste. 300
Menlo Park, CA 94025
(650)854-9080
Fax: (650)854-3018
Website: http://www.usvp.com

USVP-Schlein Marketing Fund
2180 Sand Hill Rd., Ste. 300
Menlo Park, CA 94025
(415)854-9080
Fax: (415)854-3018
Website: http://www.usvp.com

Venrock Associates
2494 Sand Hill Rd., Ste. 200
Menlo Park, CA 94025
(650)561-9580
Fax: (650)561-9180
Website: http://www.venrock.com

Brad Peery Capital Inc.
145 Chapel Pkwy.
Mill Valley, CA 94941
(415)389-0625
Fax: (415)389-1336

Dot Edu Ventures
650 Castro St., Ste. 270
Mountain View, CA 94041
(650)575-5638
Fax: (650)325-5247
Website: http://www.doteduventures
.com

Forrest, Binkley & Brown
840 Newport Ctr. Dr., Ste. 480
Newport Beach, CA 92660
(949)729-3222
Fax: (949)729-3226
Website: http://www.fbbvc.com

Marwit Capital LLC
180 Newport Center Dr., Ste. 200
Newport Beach, CA 92660
(949)640-6234

Fax: (949)720-8077
Website: http://www.marwit.com

**Kaiser Permanente / National Venture
Development**
1800 Harrison St., 22nd Fl.
Oakland, CA 94612
(510)267-4010
Fax: (510)267-4036
Website: http://www.kpventures.com

Nu Capital Access Group, Ltd.
7677 Oakport St., Ste. 105
Oakland, CA 94621
(510)635-7345
Fax: (510)635-7068

Inman and Bowman
4 Orinda Way, Bldg. D, Ste. 150
Orinda, CA 94563
(510)253-1611
Fax: (510)253-9037

Accel Partners (San Francisco)
428 University Ave.
Palo Alto, CA 94301
(650)614-4800
Fax: (650)614-4880
Website: http://www.accel.com

Advanced Technology Ventures
485 Ramona St., Ste. 200
Palo Alto, CA 94301
(650)321-8601
Fax: (650)321-0934
Website: http://www.atvcapital.com

Anila Fund
400 Channing Ave.
Palo Alto, CA 94301
(650)833-5790
Fax: (650)833-0590
Website: http://www.anila.com

**Asset Management Company
Venture Capital**
2275 E. Bayshore, Ste. 150
Palo Alto, CA 94303
(650)494-7400
Fax: (650)856-1826
E-mail: postmaster@assetman.com
Website: http://www.assetman.com

**BancBoston Capital / BancBoston
Ventures**
435 Tasso St., Ste. 250
Palo Alto, CA 94305
(650)470-4100
Fax: (650)853-1425
Website: http://www.bancbostoncapital
.com

Charter Ventures
525 University Ave., Ste. 1400
Palo Alto, CA 94301
(650)325-6953
Fax: (650)325-4762
Website: http://www.charterventures
.com

Communications Ventures
505 Hamilton Avenue, Ste. 305
Palo Alto, CA 94301
(650)325-9600
Fax: (650)325-9608
Website: http://www.comven.com

HMS Group
2468 Embarcadero Way
Palo Alto, CA 94303-3313
(650)856-9862
Fax: (650)856-9864

Jafco America Ventures, Inc.
505 Hamilton Ste. 310
Palto Alto, CA 94301
(650)463-8800
Fax: (650)463-8801
Website: http://www.jafco.com

New Vista Capital
540 Cowper St., Ste. 200
Palo Alto, CA 94301
(650)329-9333
Fax: (650)328-9434
E-mail: fgreene@nvcap.com
Website: http://www.nvcap.com

Norwest Equity Partners (Palo Alto)
245 Lytton Ave., Ste. 250
Palo Alto, CA 94301-1426
(650)321-8000
Fax: (650)321-8010
Website: http://www.norwestvp.com

Oak Investment Partners
525 University Ave., Ste. 1300
Palo Alto, CA 94301
(650)614-3700
Fax: (650)328-6345
Website: http://www.oakinv.com

Patricof & Co. Ventures, Inc. (Palo Alto)
2100 Geng Rd., Ste. 150
Palo Alto, CA 94303
(650)494-9944
Fax: (650)494-6751
Website: http://www.patricof.com

RWI Group
835 Page Mill Rd.
Palo Alto, CA 94304
(650)251-1800

Fax: (650)213-8660
Website: http://www.rwigroup.com

Summit Partners (Palo Alto)
499 Hamilton Ave., Ste. 200
Palo Alto, CA 94301
(650)321-1166
Fax: (650)321-1188
Website: http://www.summitpartners
.com

Sutter Hill Ventures
755 Page Mill Rd., Ste. A-200
Palo Alto, CA 94304
(650)493-5600
Fax: (650)858-1854
E-mail: shv@shv.com

Vanguard Venture Partners
525 University Ave., Ste. 600
Palo Alto, CA 94301
(650)321-2900
Fax: (650)321-2902
Website: http://www.vanguardventures
.com

Venture Growth Associates
2479 East Bayshore St., Ste. 710
Palo Alto, CA 94303
(650)855-9100
Fax: (650)855-9104

Worldview Technology Partners
435 Tasso St., Ste. 120
Palo Alto, CA 94301
(650)322-3800
Fax: (650)322-3880
Website: http://www.worldview.com

Draper, Fisher, Jurvetson / Draper Associates
400 Seaport Ct., Ste.250
Redwood City, CA 94063
(415)599-9000
Fax: (415)599-9726
Website: http://www.dfj.com

Gabriel Venture Partners
350 Marine Pkwy., Ste. 200
Redwood Shores, CA 94065
(650)551-5000
Fax: (650)551-5001
Website: http://www.gabrielvp.com

Hallador Venture Partners, L.L.C.
740 University Ave., Ste. 110
Sacramento, CA 95825-6710
(916)920-0191
Fax: (916)920-5188
E-mail: chris@hallador.com

Emerald Venture Group
12396 World Trade Dr., Ste. 116
San Diego, CA 92128

(858)451-1001
Fax: (858)451-1003
Website: http://www.emeraldventure
.com

Forward Ventures
9255 Towne Centre Dr.
San Diego, CA 92121
(858)677-6077
Fax: (858)452-8799
E-mail: info@forwardventure.com
Website: http://www.forwardventure
.com

Idanta Partners Ltd.
4660 La Jolla Village Dr., Ste. 850
San Diego, CA 92122
(619)452-9690
Fax: (619)452-2013
Website: http://www.idanta.com

Kingsbury Associates
3655 Nobel Dr., Ste. 490
San Diego, CA 92122
(858)677-0600
Fax: (858)677-0800

Kyocera International Inc.
Corporate Development
8611 Balboa Ave.
San Diego, CA 92123
(858)576-2600
Fax: (858)492-1456

Sorrento Associates, Inc.
4370 LaJolla Village Dr., Ste. 1040
San Diego, CA 92122
(619)452-3100
Fax: (619)452-7607
Website: http://www.sorrentoventures
.com

Western States Investment Group
9191 Towne Ctr. Dr., Ste. 310
San Diego, CA 92122
(619)678-0800
Fax: (619)678-0900

Aberdare Ventures
One Embarcadero Center, Ste. 4000
San Francisco, CA 94111
(415)392-7442
Fax: (415)392-4264
Website: http://www.aberdare.com

Acacia Venture Partners
101 California St., Ste. 3160
San Francisco, CA 94111
(415)433-4200
Fax: (415)433-4250
Website: http://www.acaciavp.com

Access Venture Partners
319 Laidley St.
San Francisco, CA 94131
(415)586-0132
Fax: (415)392-6310
Website: http://www.accessventure
partners.com

Alta Partners
One Embarcadero Center, Ste. 4050
San Francisco, CA 94111
(415)362-4022
Fax: (415)362-6178
E-mail: alta@altapartners.com
Website: http://www.altapartners.com

Bangert Dawes Reade Davis & Thom
220 Montgomery St., Ste. 424
San Francisco, CA 94104
(415)954-9900
Fax: (415)954-9901
E-mail: bdrdt@pacbell.net

Berkeley International Capital Corp.
650 California St., Ste. 2800
San Francisco, CA 94108-2609
(415)249-0450
Fax: (415)392-3929
Website: http://www.berkeleyvc.com

Blueprint Ventures LLC
456 Montgomery St., 22nd Fl.
San Francisco, CA 94104
(415)901-4000
Fax: (415)901-4035
Website: http://www.blueprint
ventures.com

Blumberg Capital Ventures
580 Howard St., Ste. 401
San Francisco, CA 94105
(415)905-5007
Fax: (415)357-5027
Website: http://www.blumberg-
capital.com

Burr, Egan, Deleage, and Co. (San Francisco)
1 Embarcadero Center, Ste. 4050
San Francisco, CA 94111
(415)362-4022
Fax: (415)362-6178

Burrill & Company
120 Montgomery St., Ste. 1370
San Francisco, CA 94104
(415)743-3160
Fax: (415)743-3161
Website: http://www.burrillandco.com

CMEA Ventures
235 Montgomery St., Ste. 920
San Francisco, CA 94401

(415)352-1520
Fax: (415)352-1524
Website: http://www.cmeaventures.com

Crocker Capital
1 Post St., Ste. 2500
San Francisco, CA 94101
(415)956-5250
Fax: (415)959-5710

Dominion Ventures, Inc.
44 Montgomery St., Ste. 4200
San Francisco, CA 94104
(415)362-4890
Fax: (415)394-9245

Dorset Capital
Pier 1
Bay 2
San Francisco, CA 94111
(415)398-7101
Fax: (415)398-7141
Website: http://www.dorsetcapital.com

Gatx Capital
Four Embarcadero Center, Ste. 2200
San Francisco, CA 94904
(415)955-3200
Fax: (415)955-3449

IMinds
135 Main St., Ste. 1350
San Francisco, CA 94105
(415)547-0000
Fax: (415)227-0300
Website: http://www.iminds.com

LF International Inc.
360 Post St., Ste. 705
San Francisco, CA 94108
(415)399-0110
Fax: (415)399-9222
Website: http://www.lfvc.com

Newbury Ventures
535 Pacific Ave., 2nd Fl.
San Francisco, CA 94133
(415)296-7408
Fax: (415)296-7416
Website: http://www.newburyven.com

Quest Ventures (San Francisco)
333 Bush St., Ste. 1750
San Francisco, CA 94104
(415)782-1414
Fax: (415)782-1415

Robertson-Stephens Co.
555 California St., Ste. 2600
San Francisco, CA 94104
(415)781-9700

Fax: (415)781-2556
Website: http://www.omegaadventures
.com

Rosewood Capital, L.P.
One Maritime Plaza, Ste. 1330
San Francisco, CA 94111-3503
(415)362-5526
Fax: (415)362-1192
Website: http://www.rosewoodvc.com

Ticonderoga Capital Inc.
555 California St., No. 4950
San Francisco, CA 94104
(415)296-7900
Fax: (415)296-8956

21st Century Internet Venture Partners
Two South Park
2nd Floor
San Francisco, CA 94107
(415)512-1221
Fax: (415)512-2650
Website: http://www.21vc.com

VK Ventures
600 California St., Ste.1700
San Francisco, CA 94111
(415)391-5600
Fax: (415)397-2744

Walden Group of Venture Capital Funds
750 Battery St., Seventh Floor
San Francisco, CA 94111
(415)391-7225
Fax: (415)391-7262

Acer Technology Ventures
2641 Orchard Pkwy.
San Jose, CA 95134
(408)433-4945
Fax: (408)433-5230

Authosis
226 Airport Pkwy., Ste. 405
San Jose, CA 95110
(650)814-3603
Website: http://www.authosis.com

Western Technology Investment
2010 N. First St., Ste. 310
San Jose, CA 95131
(408)436-8577
Fax: (408)436-8625
E-mail: mktg@westerntech.com

Drysdale Enterprises
177 Bovet Rd., Ste. 600
San Mateo, CA 94402
(650)341-6336
Fax: (650)341-1329
E-mail: drysdale@aol.com

Greylock
2929 Campus Dr., Ste. 400
San Mateo, CA 94401
(650)493-5525
Fax: (650)493-5575
Website: http://www.greylock.com

Technology Funding
2000 Alameda de las Pulgas, Ste. 250
San Mateo, CA 94403
(415)345-2200
Fax: (415)345-1797

2M Invest Inc.
1875 S. Grant St.
Suite 750
San Mateo, CA 94402
(650)655-3765
Fax: (650)372-9107
E-mail: 2minfo@2minvest.com
Website: http://www.2minvest.com

Phoenix Growth Capital Corp.
2401 Kerner Blvd.
San Rafael, CA 94901
(415)485-4569
Fax: (415)485-4663

NextGen Partners LLC
1705 East Valley Rd.
Santa Barbara, CA 93108
(805)969-8540
Fax: (805)969-8542
Website: http://www.nextgenpartners.com

Denali Venture Capital
1925 Woodland Ave.
Santa Clara, CA 95050
(408)690-4838
Fax: (408)247-6979
E-mail: wael@denaliventurecapital.com
Website: http://www.denaliventurecapital.com

Dotcom Ventures LP
3945 Freedom Circle, Ste. 740
Santa Clara, CA 95045
(408)919-9855
Fax: (408)919-9857
Website: http://www.dotcomventuresatl.com

Silicon Valley Bank
3003 Tasman
Santa Clara, CA 95054
(408)654-7400
Fax: (408)727-8728

Al Shugart International
920 41st Ave.
Santa Cruz, CA 95062

(831)479-7852
Fax: (831)479-7852
Website: http://www.alshugart.com

Leonard Mautner Associates
1434 Sixth St.
Santa Monica, CA 90401
(213)393-9788
Fax: (310)459-9918

Palomar Ventures
100 Wilshire Blvd., Ste. 450
Santa Monica, CA 90401
(310)260-6050
Fax: (310)656-4150
Website: http://www.palomarventures.com

Medicus Venture Partners
12930 Saratoga Ave., Ste. D8
Saratoga, CA 95070
(408)447-8600
Fax: (408)447-8599
Website: http://www.medicusvc.com

Redleaf Venture Management
14395 Saratoga Ave., Ste. 130
Saratoga, CA 95070
(408)868-0800
Fax: (408)868-0810
E-mail: nancy@redleaf.com
Website: http://www.redleaf.com

Artemis Ventures
207 Second St., Ste. E
3rd Fl.
Sausalito, CA 94965
(415)289-2500
Fax: (415)289-1789
Website: http://www.artemisventures.com

Deucalion Venture Partners
19501 Brooklime
Sonoma, CA 95476
(707)938-4974
Fax: (707)938-8921

Windward Ventures
PO Box 7688
Thousand Oaks, CA 91359-7688
(805)497-3332
Fax: (805)497-9331

National Investment Management, Inc.
2601 Airport Dr., Ste.210
Torrance, CA 90505
(310)784-7600
Fax: (310)784-7605

Southern California Ventures
406 Amapola Ave. Ste. 125
Torrance, CA 90501

(310)787-4381
Fax: (310)787-4382

Sandton Financial Group
21550 Oxnard St., Ste. 300
Woodland Hills, CA 91367
(818)702-9283

Woodside Fund
850 Woodside Dr.
Woodside, CA 94062
(650)368-5545
Fax: (650)368-2416
Website: http://www.woodsidefund.com

Colorado

Colorado Venture Management
Ste. 300
Boulder, CO 80301
(303)440-4055
Fax: (303)440-4636

Dean & Associates
4362 Apple Way
Boulder, CO 80301
Fax: (303)473-9900

Roser Ventures LLC
1105 Spruce St.
Boulder, CO 80302
(303)443-6436
Fax: (303)443-1885
Website: http://www.roserventures.com

Sequel Venture Partners
4430 Arapahoe Ave., Ste. 220
Boulder, CO 80303
(303)546-0400
Fax: (303)546-9728
E-mail: tom@sequelvc.com
Website: http://www.sequelvc.com

New Venture Resources
445C E. Cheyenne Mtn. Blvd.
Colorado Springs, CO 80906-4570
(719)598-9272
Fax: (719)598-9272

The Centennial Funds
1428 15th St.
Denver, CO 80202-1318
(303)405-7500
Fax: (303)405-7575
Website: http://www.centennial.com

Rocky Mountain Capital Partners
1125 17th St., Ste. 2260
Denver, CO 80202
(303)291-5200
Fax: (303)291-5327

Sandlot Capital LLC
600 South Cherry St., Ste. 525
Denver, CO 80246
(303)893-3400
Fax: (303)893-3403
Website: http://www.sandlotcapital.com

Wolf Ventures
50 South Steele St., Ste. 777
Denver, CO 80209
(303)321-4800
Fax: (303)321-4848
E-mail: businessplan@wolfventures.com
Website: http://www.wolfventures.com

The Columbine Venture Funds
5460 S. Quebec St., Ste. 270
Englewood, CO 80111
(303)694-3222
Fax: (303)694-9007

Investment Securities of Colorado, Inc.
4605 Denice Dr.
Englewood, CO 80111
(303)796-9192

Kinship Partners
6300 S. Syracuse Way, Ste. 484
Englewood, CO 80111
(303)694-0268
Fax: (303)694-1707
E-mail: block@vailsys.com

Boranco Management, L.L.C.
1528 Hillside Dr.
Fort Collins, CO 80524-1969
(970)221-2297
Fax: (970)221-4787

Aweida Ventures
890 West Cherry St., Ste. 220
Louisville, CO 80027
(303)664-9520
Fax: (303)664-9530
Website: http://www.aweida.com

Access Venture Partners
8787 Turnpike Dr., Ste. 260
Westminster, CO 80030
(303)426-8899
Fax: (303)426-8828

Connecticut

Medmax Ventures, LP
1 Northwestern Dr., Ste. 203
Bloomfield, CT 06002
(860)286-2960
Fax: (860)286-9960

James B. Kobak & Co.
Four Mansfield Place
Darien, CT 06820

(203)656-3471
Fax: (203)655-2905

Orien Ventures
1 Post Rd.
Fairfield, CT 06430
(203)259-9933
Fax: (203)259-5288

ABP Acquisition Corporation
115 Maple Ave.
Greenwich, CT 06830
(203)625-8287
Fax: (203)447-6187

Catterton Partners
9 Greenwich Office Park
Greenwich, CT 06830
(203)629-4901
Fax: (203)629-4903
Website: http://www.cpequity.com

Consumer Venture Partners
3 Pickwick Plz.
Greenwich, CT 06830
(203)629-8800
Fax: (203)629-2019

Insurance Venture Partners
31 Brookside Dr., Ste. 211
Greenwich, CT 06830
(203)861-0030
Fax: (203)861-2745

The NTC Group
Three Pickwick Plaza
Ste. 200
Greenwich, CT 06830
(203)862-2800
Fax: (203)622-6538

Regulus International Capital Co., Inc.
140 Greenwich Ave.
Greenwich, CT 06830
(203)625-9700
Fax: (203)625-9706

Axiom Venture Partners
City Place II
185 Asylum St., 17th Fl.
Hartford, CT 06103
(860)548-7799
Fax: (860)548-7797
Website: http://www.axiomventures.com

Conning Capital Partners
City Place II
185 Asylum St.
Hartford, CT 06103-4105
(860)520-1289
Fax: (860)520-1299
E-mail: pe@conning.com
Website: http://www.conning.com

First New England Capital L.P.
100 Pearl St.
Hartford, CT 06103
(860)293-3333
Fax: (860)293-3338
E-mail: info@firstnewenglandcapital.com
Website: http://www.firstnewengland
capital.com

Northeast Ventures
One State St., Ste. 1720
Hartford, CT 06103
(860)547-1414
Fax: (860)246-8755

Windward Holdings
38 Sylvan Rd.
Madison, CT 06443
(203)245-6870
Fax: (203)245-6865

Advanced Materials Partners, Inc.
45 Pine St.
PO Box 1022
New Canaan, CT 06840
(203)966-6415
Fax: (203)966-8448
E-mail: wkb@amplink.com

RFE Investment Partners
36 Grove St.
New Canaan, CT 06840
(203)966-2800
Fax: (203)966-3109
Website: http://www.rfeip.com

Connecticut Innovations, Inc.
999 West St.
Rocky Hill, CT 06067
(860)563-5851
Fax: (860)563-4877
E-mail: pamela.hartley@ctinnovations. com
Website: http://www.ctinnovations.com

Canaan Partners
105 Rowayton Ave.
Rowayton, CT 06853
(203)855-0400
Fax: (203)854-9117
Website: http://www.canaan.com

Landmark Partners, Inc.
10 Mill Pond Ln.
Simsbury, CT 06070
(860)651-9760
Fax: (860)651-8890
Website: http://www.landmarkpartners. com

Sweeney & Company
PO Box 567
Southport, CT 06490
(203)255-0220
Fax: (203)255-0220
E-mail: sweeney@connix.com

Baxter Associates, Inc.
PO Box 1333
Stamford, CT 06904
(203)323-3143
Fax: (203)348-0622

Beacon Partners Inc.
6 Landmark Sq., 4th Fl.
Stamford, CT 06901-2792
(203)359-5776
Fax: (203)359-5876

Collinson, Howe, and Lennox, LLC
1055 Washington Blvd., 5th Fl.
Stamford, CT 06901
(203)324-7700
Fax: (203)324-3636
E-mail: info@chlmedical.com
Website: http://www.chlmedical.com

Prime Capital Management Co.
550 West Ave.
Stamford, CT 06902
(203)964-0642
Fax: (203)964-0862

Saugatuck Capital Co.
1 Canterbury Green
Stamford, CT 06901
(203)348-6669
Fax: (203)324-6995
Website: http://www.saugatuckcapital
.com

Soundview Financial Group Inc.
22 Gatehouse Rd.
Stamford, CT 06902
(203)462-7200
Fax: (203)462-7350
Website: http://www.sndv.com

TSG Ventures, L.L.C.
177 Broad St., 12th Fl.
Stamford, CT 06901
(203)406-1500
Fax: (203)406-1590

Whitney & Company
177 Broad St.
Stamford, CT 06901
(203)973-1400
Fax: (203)973-1422
Website: http://www.jhwhitney.com

**Cullinane & Donnelly Venture
Partners L.P.**
970 Farmington Ave.
West Hartford, CT 06107
(860)521-7811

**The Crestview Investment and
Financial Group**
431 Post Rd. E, Ste. 1
Westport, CT 06880-4403

(203)222-0333
Fax: (203)222-0000

**Marketcorp Venture Associates,
L.P. (MCV)**
274 Riverside Ave.
Westport, CT 06880
(203)222-3030
Fax: (203)222-3033

Oak Investment Partners (Westport)
1 Gorham Island
Westport, CT 06880
(203)226-8346
Fax: (203)227-0372
Website: http://www.oakinv.com

Oxford Bioscience Partners
315 Post Rd. W
Westport, CT 06880-5200
(203)341-3300
Fax: (203)341-3309
Website: http://www.oxbio.com

Prince Ventures (Westport)
25 Ford Rd.
Westport, CT 06880
(203)227-8332
Fax: (203)226-5302

LTI Venture Leasing Corp.
221 Danbury Rd.
Wilton, CT 06897
(203)563-1100
Fax: (203)563-1111
Website: http://www.ltileasing.com

Delaware

Blue Rock Capital
5803 Kennett Pike, Ste. A
Wilmington, DE 19807
(302)426-0981
Fax: (302)426-0982
Website: http://www.bluerockcapital
.com

District of Columbia

Allied Capital Corp.
1919 Pennsylvania Ave. NW
Washington, DC 20006-3434
(202)331-2444
Fax: (202)659-2053
Website: http://www.alliedcapital.com

Atlantic Coastal Ventures, L.P.
3101 South St. NW
Washington, DC 20007
(202)293-1166
Fax: (202)293-1181
Website: http://www.atlanticcv.com

Columbia Capital Group, Inc.
1660 L St. NW, Ste. 308
Washington, DC 20036
(202)775-8815
Fax: (202)223-0544

Core Capital Partners
901 15th St., NW
9th Fl.
Washington, DC 20005
(202)589-0090
Fax: (202)589-0091
Website: http://www.core-capital.com

Next Point Partners
701 Pennsylvania Ave. NW, Ste. 900
Washington, DC 20004
(202)661-8703
Fax: (202)434-7400
E-mail: mf@nextpoint.vc
Website: http://www.nextpointvc.com

**Telecommunications
Development Fund**
2020 K. St. NW
Ste. 375
Washington, DC 20006
(202)293-8840
Fax: (202)293-8850
Website: http://www.tdfund.com

Wachtel & Co., Inc.
1101 4th St. NW
Washington, DC 20005-5680
(202)898-1144

Winslow Partners LLC
1300 Connecticut Ave. NW
Washington, DC 20036-1703
(202)530-5000
Fax: (202)530-5010
E-mail: winslow@winslowpartners.com

Women's Growth Capital Fund
1054 31st St., NW
Ste. 110
Washington, DC 20007
(202)342-1431
Fax: (202)341-1203
Website: http://www.wgcf.com

Florida

Sigma Capital Corp.
22668 Caravelle Circle
Boca Raton, FL 33433
(561)368-9783

**North American Business
Development Co., L.L.C.**
111 East Las Olas Blvd.
Ft. Lauderdale, FL 33301
(305)463-0681

Fax: (305)527-0904
Website: http://www.northamerican
fund.com

Chartwell Capital Management Co. Inc.
1 Independent Dr., Ste. 3120
Jacksonville, FL 32202
(904)355-3519
Fax: (904)353-5833
E-mail: info@chartwellcap.com

CEO Advisors
1061 Maitland Center Commons
Ste. 209
Maitland, FL 32751
(407)660-9327
Fax: (407)660-2109

Henry & Co.
8201 Peters Rd., Ste. 1000
Plantation, FL 33324
(954)797-7400

Avery Business Development Services
2506 St. Michel Ct.
Ponte Vedra, FL 32082
(904)285-6033

New South Ventures
5053 Ocean Blvd.
Sarasota, FL 34242
(941)358-6000
Fax: (941)358-6078
Website: http://www.newsouth
ventures.com

Venture Capital Management Corp.
PO Box 2626
Satellite Beach, FL 32937
(407)777-1969

Florida Capital Venture Ltd.
325 Florida Bank Plaza
100 W. Kennedy Blvd.
Tampa, FL 33602
(813)229-2294
Fax: (813)229-2028

Quantum Capital Partners
339 South Plant Ave.
Tampa, FL 33606
(813)250-1999
Fax: (813)250-1998
Website: http://www.quantumcapital
partners.com

South Atlantic Venture Fund
614 W. Bay St.
Tampa, FL 33606-2704
(813)253-2500
Fax: (813)253-2360
E-mail: venture@southatlantic.com
Website: http://www.southatlantic.com

LM Capital Corp.
120 S. Olive, Ste. 400
West Palm Beach, FL 33401
(561)833-9700
Fax: (561)655-6587
Website: http://www.lmcapital
securities.com

Georgia

Venture First Associates
4811 Thornwood Dr.
Acworth, GA 30102
(770)928-3733
Fax: (770)928-6455

Alliance Technology Ventures
8995 Westside Pkwy., Ste. 200
Alpharetta, GA 30004
(678)336-2000
Fax: (678)336-2001
E-mail: info@atv.com
Website: http://www.atv.com

Cordova Ventures
2500 North Winds Pkwy., Ste. 475
Alpharetta, GA 30004
(678)942-0300
Fax: (678)942-0301
Website: http://www.cordovaventures
.com

Advanced Technology Development Fund
1000 Abernathy, Ste. 1420
Atlanta, GA 30328-5614
(404)668-2333
Fax: (404)668-2333

CGW Southeast Partners
12 Piedmont Center, Ste. 210
Atlanta, GA 30305
(404)816-3255
Fax: (404)816-3258
Website: http://www.cgwlp.com

Cyberstarts
1900 Emery St., NW
3rd Fl.
Atlanta, GA 30318
(404)267-5000
Fax: (404)267-5200
Website: http://www.cyberstarts.com

EGL Holdings, Inc.
10 Piedmont Center, Ste. 412
Atlanta, GA 30305
(404)949-8300
Fax: (404)949-8311

Equity South
1790 The Lenox Bldg.
3399 Peachtree Rd. NE

Atlanta, GA 30326
(404)237-6222
Fax: (404)261-1578

Five Paces
3400 Peachtree Rd., Ste. 200
Atlanta, GA 30326
(404)439-8300
Fax: (404)439-8301
Website: http://www.fivepaces.com

Frontline Capital, Inc.
3475 Lenox Rd., Ste. 400
Atlanta, GA 30326
(404)240-7280
Fax: (404)240-7281

Fuqua Ventures LLC
1201 W. Peachtree St. NW, Ste. 5000
Atlanta, GA 30309
(404)815-4500
Fax: (404)815-4528
Website: http://www.fuquaventures.com

Noro-Moseley Partners
4200 Northside Pkwy., Bldg. 9
Atlanta, GA 30327
(404)233-1966
Fax: (404)239-9280
Website: http://www.noro-moseley.com

Renaissance Capital Corp.
34 Peachtree St. NW, Ste. 2230
Atlanta, GA 30303
(404)658-9061
Fax: (404)658-9064

River Capital, Inc.
Two Midtown Plaza
1360 Peachtree St. NE, Ste. 1430
Atlanta, GA 30309
(404)873-2166
Fax: (404)873-2158

State Street Bank & Trust Co.
3414 Peachtree Rd. NE, Ste. 1010
Atlanta, GA 30326
(404)364-9500
Fax: (404)261-4469

UPS Strategic Enterprise Fund
55 Glenlake Pkwy. NE
Atlanta, GA 30328
(404)828-8814
Fax: (404)828-8088
E-mail: jcacyce@ups.com
Website: http://www.ups.com/sef/
sef_home

Wachovia
191 Peachtree St. NE, 26th Fl.
Atlanta, GA 30303
(404)332-1000

Fax: (404)332-1392
Website: http://www.wachovia.com/wca

Brainworks Ventures
4243 Dunwoody Club Dr.
Chamblee, GA 30341
(770)239-7447

First Growth Capital Inc.
Best Western Plaza, Ste. 105
PO Box 815
Forsyth, GA 31029
(912)781-7131

Financial Capital Resources, Inc.
21 Eastbrook Bend, Ste. 116
Peachtree City, GA 30269
(404)487-6650

Hawaii

HMS Hawaii Management Partners
Davies Pacific Center
841 Bishop St., Ste. 860
Honolulu, HI 96813
(808)545-3755
Fax: (808)531-2611

Idaho

Sun Valley Ventures
160 Second St.
Ketchum, ID 83340
(208)726-5005
Fax: (208)726-5094

Illinois

Open Prairie Ventures
115 N. Neil St., Ste. 209
Champaign, IL 61820
(217)351-7000
Fax: (217)351-7051
E-mail: inquire@openprairie.com
Website: http://www.openprairie.com

ABN AMRO Private Equity
208 S. La Salle St., 10th Fl.
Chicago, IL 60604
(312)855-7079
Fax: (312)553-6648
Website: http://www.abnequity.com

Alpha Capital Partners, Ltd.
122 S. Michigan Ave., Ste. 1700
Chicago, IL 60603
(312)322-9800
Fax: (312)322-9808
E-mail: acp@alphacapital.com

Ameritech Development Corp.
30 S. Wacker Dr., 37th Fl.
Chicago, IL 60606

(312)750-5083
Fax: (312)609-0244

Apex Investment Partners
225 W. Washington, Ste. 1450
Chicago, IL 60606
(312)857-2800
Fax: (312)857-1800
E-mail: apex@apexvc.com
Website: http://www.apexvc.com

Arch Venture Partners
8725 W. Higgins Rd., Ste. 290
Chicago, IL 60631
(773)380-6600
Fax: (773)380-6606
Website: http://www.archventure.com

The Bank Funds
208 South LaSalle St., Ste. 1680
Chicago, IL 60604
(312)855-6020
Fax: (312)855-8910

Batterson Venture Partners
303 W. Madison St., Ste. 1110
Chicago, IL 60606-3309
(312)269-0300
Fax: (312)269-0021
Website: http://www.battersonvp.com

William Blair Capital Partners, L.L.C.
222 W. Adams St., Ste. 1300
Chicago, IL 60606
(312)364-8250
Fax: (312)236-1042
E-mail: privateequity@wmblair.com
Website: http://www.wmblair.com

Bluestar Ventures
208 South LaSalle St., Ste. 1020
Chicago, IL 60604
(312)384-5000
Fax: (312)384-5005
Website: http://www.bluestarventures
.com

The Capital Strategy Management Co.
233 S. Wacker Dr.
Box 06334
Chicago, IL 60606
(312)444-1170

DN Partners
77 West Wacker Dr., Ste. 4550
Chicago, IL 60601
(312)332-7960
Fax: (312)332-7979

Dresner Capital Inc.
29 South LaSalle St., Ste. 310
Chicago, IL 60603
(312)726-3600
Fax: (312)726-7448

Eblast Ventures LLC
11 South LaSalle St., 5th Fl.
Chicago, IL 60603
(312)372-2600
Fax: (312)372-5621
Website: http://www.eblastventures.com

Essex Woodlands Health Ventures, L.P.
190 S. LaSalle St., Ste. 2800
Chicago, IL 60603
(312)444-6040
Fax: (312)444-6034
Website: http://www.essexwood
lands.com

First Analysis Venture Capital
233 S. Wacker Dr., Ste. 9500
Chicago, IL 60606
(312)258-1400
Fax: (312)258-0334
Website: http://www.firstanalysis.com

Frontenac Co.
135 S. LaSalle St., Ste.3800
Chicago, IL 60603
(312)368-0044
Fax: (312)368-9520
Website: http://www.frontenac.com

GTCR Golder Rauner, LLC
6100 Sears Tower
Chicago, IL 60606
(312)382-2200
Fax: (312)382-2201
Website: http://www.gtcr.com

High Street Capital LLC
311 South Wacker Dr., Ste. 4550
Chicago, IL 60606
(312)697-4990
Fax: (312)697-4994
Website: http://www.highstr.com

IEG Venture Management, Inc.
70 West Madison
Chicago, IL 60602
(312)644-0890
Fax: (312)454-0369
Website: http://www.iegventure.com

JK&B Capital
180 North Stetson, Ste. 4500
Chicago, IL 60601
(312)946-1200
Fax: (312)946-1103
E-mail: gspencer@jkbcapital.com
Website: http://www.jkbcapital.com

Kettle Partners L.P.
350 W. Hubbard, Ste. 350
Chicago, IL 60610
(312)329-9300

Fax: (312)527-4519
Website: http://www.kettlevc.com

Lake Shore Capital Partners
20 N. Wacker Dr., Ste. 2807
Chicago, IL 60606
(312)803-3536
Fax: (312)803-3534

LaSalle Capital Group Inc.
70 W. Madison St., Ste. 5710
Chicago, IL 60602
(312)236-7041
Fax: (312)236-0720

Linc Capital, Inc.
303 E. Wacker Pkwy., Ste. 1000
Chicago, IL 60601
(312)946-2670
Fax: (312)938-4290
E-mail: bdemars@linccap.com

Madison Dearborn Partners, Inc.
3 First National Plz., Ste. 3800
Chicago, IL 60602
(312)895-1000
Fax: (312)895-1001
E-mail: invest@mdcp.com
Website: http://www.mdcp.com

**Mesirow Private Equity
Investments Inc.**
350 N. Clark St.
Chicago, IL 60610
(312)595-6950
Fax: (312)595-6211
Website: http://www.meisrow
financial.com

Mosaix Ventures LLC
1822 North Mohawk
Chicago, IL 60614
(312)274-0988
Fax: (312)274-0989
Website: http://www.mosaixventures.
com

Nesbitt Burns
111 West Monroe St.
Chicago, IL 60603
(312)416-3855
Fax: (312)765-8000
Website: http://www.harrisbank.com

Polestar Capital, Inc.
180 N. Michigan Ave., Ste. 1905
Chicago, IL 60601
(312)984-9090
Fax: (312)984-9877
E-mail: wl@polestarvc.com
Website: http://www.polestarvc.com

Prince Ventures (Chicago)
10 S. Wacker Dr., Ste. 2575
Chicago, IL 60606-7407
(312)454-1408
Fax: (312)454-9125

Prism Capital
444 N. Michigan Ave.
Chicago, IL 60611
(312)464-7900
Fax: (312)464-7915
Website: http://www.prismfund.com

Third Coast Capital
900 N. Franklin St., Ste. 700
Chicago, IL 60610
(312)337-3303
Fax: (312)337-2567
E-mail: manic@earthlink.com
Website: http://www.thirdcoast
capital.com

Thoma Cressey Equity Partners
4460 Sears Tower, 92nd Fl.
233 S. Wacker Dr.
Chicago, IL 60606
(312)777-4444
Fax: (312)777-4445
Website: http://www.thomacressey.com

Tribune Ventures
435 N. Michigan Ave., Ste. 600
Chicago, IL 60611
(312)527-8797
Fax: (312)222-5993
Website: http://www.tribune
ventures.com

Wind Point Partners (Chicago)
676 N. Michigan Ave., Ste. 330
Chicago, IL 60611
(312)649-4000
Website: http://www.wppartners.com

Marquette Venture Partners
520 Lake Cook Rd., Ste. 450
Deerfield, IL 60015
(847)940-1700
Fax: (847)940-1724
Website: http://
www.marquetteventures.com

Duchossois Investments Limited, LLC
845 Larch Ave.
Elmhurst, IL 60126
(630)530-6105
Fax: (630)993-8644
Website: http://www.duchtec.com

Evanston Business Investment Corp.
1840 Oak Ave.
Evanston, IL 60201

(847)866-1840
Fax: (847)866-1808
E-mail: t-parkinson@nwu.com
Website: http://www.ebic.com

Inroads Capital Partners L.P.
1603 Orrington Ave., Ste. 2050
Evanston, IL 60201-3841
(847)864-2000
Fax: (847)864-9692

The Cerulean Fund/WGC Enterprises
1701 E. Lake Ave., Ste. 170
Glenview, IL 60025
(847)657-8002
Fax: (847)657-8168

Ventana Financial Resources, Inc.
249 Market Sq.
Lake Forest, IL 60045
(847)234-3434

Beecken, Petty & Co.
901 Warrenville Rd., Ste. 205
Lisle, IL 60532
(630)435-0300
Fax: (630)435-0370
E-mail: hep@bpcompany.com
Website: http://www.bpcompany.com

Allstate Private Equity
3075 Sanders Rd., Ste. G5D
Northbrook, IL 60062-7127
(847)402-8247
Fax: (847)402-0880

KB Partners
1101 Skokie Blvd., Ste. 260
Northbrook, IL 60062-2856
(847)714-0444
Fax: (847)714-0445
E-mail: keith@kbpartners.com
Website: http://www.kbpartners.com

Transcap Associates Inc.
900 Skokie Blvd., Ste. 210
Northbrook, IL 60062
(847)753-9600
Fax: (847)753-9090

**Graystone Venture Partners, L.L.C. /
Portage Venture Partners**
One Northfield Plaza, Ste. 530
Northfield, IL 60093
(847)446-9460
Fax: (847)446-9470
Website: http://www.portage
ventures.com

Motorola Inc.
1303 E. Algonquin Rd.
Schaumburg, IL 60196-1065
(847)576-4929

Fax: (847)538-2250
Website: http://www.mot.com/mne

Indiana

Irwin Ventures LLC
500 Washington St.
Columbus, IN 47202
(812)373-1434
Fax: (812)376-1709
Website: http://www.irwinventures.com

Cambridge Venture Partners
4181 East 96th St., Ste. 200
Indianapolis, IN 46240
(317)814-6192
Fax: (317)944-9815

CID Equity Partners
One American Square, Ste. 2850
Box 82074
Indianapolis, IN 46282
(317)269-2350
Fax: (317)269-2355
Website: http://www.cidequity.com

Gazelle Techventures
6325 Digital Way, Ste. 460
Indianapolis, IN 46278
(317)275-6800
Fax: (317)275-1101
Website: http://www.gazellevc.com

Monument Advisors Inc.
Bank One Center/Circle
111 Monument Circle, Ste. 600
Indianapolis, IN 46204-5172
(317)656-5065
Fax: (317)656-5060
Website: http://www.monumentadv.com

MWV Capital Partners
201 N. Illinois St., Ste. 300
Indianapolis, IN 46204
(317)237-2323
Fax: (317)237-2325
Website: http://www.mwvcapital.com

First Source Capital Corp.
100 North Michigan St.
PO Box 1602
South Bend, IN 46601
(219)235-2180
Fax: (219)235-2227

Iowa

Allsop Venture Partners
118 Third Ave. SE, Ste. 837
Cedar Rapids, IA 52401
(319)368-6675
Fax: (319)363-9515

InvestAmerica Investment Advisors, Inc.
101 2nd St. SE, Ste. 800
Cedar Rapids, IA 52401
(319)363-8249
Fax: (319)363-9683

Pappajohn Capital Resources
2116 Financial Center
Des Moines, IA 50309
(515)244-5746
Fax: (515)244-2346
Website: http://www.pappajohn.com

Berthel Fisher & Company Planning Inc.
701 Tama St.
PO Box 609
Marion, IA 52302
(319)497-5700
Fax: (319)497-4244

Kansas

Enterprise Merchant Bank
7400 West 110th St., Ste. 560
Overland Park, KS 66210
(913)327-8500
Fax: (913)327-8505

Kansas Venture Capital, Inc. (Overland Park)
6700 Antioch Plz., Ste. 460
Overland Park, KS 66204
(913)262-7117
Fax: (913)262-3509
E-mail: jdalton@kvci.com

Child Health Investment Corp.
6803 W. 64th St., Ste. 208
Shawnee Mission, KS 66202
(913)262-1436
Fax: (913)262-1575
Website: http://www.chca.com

Kansas Technology Enterprise Corp.
214 SW 6th, 1st Fl.
Topeka, KS 66603-3719
(785)296-5272
Fax: (785)296-1160
E-mail: ktec@ktec.com
Website: http://www.ktec.com

Kentucky

Kentucky Highlands Investment Corp.
362 Old Whitley Rd.
London, KY 40741
(606)864-5175
Fax: (606)864-5194
Website: http://www.khic.org

Chrysalis Ventures, L.L.C.
1850 National City Tower
Louisville, KY 40202
(502)583-7644
Fax: (502)583-7648
E-mail: bobsany@chrysalisventures.com
Website: http://www.chrysalisventures.com

Humana Venture Capital
500 West Main St.
Louisville, KY 40202
(502)580-3922
Fax: (502)580-2051
E-mail: gemont@humana.com
George Emont, Director

Summit Capital Group, Inc.
6510 Glenridge Park Pl., Ste. 8
Louisville, KY 40222
(502)332-2700

Louisiana

Bank One Equity Investors, Inc.
451 Florida St.
Baton Rouge, LA 70801
(504)332-4421
Fax: (504)332-7377

Advantage Capital Partners
LLE Tower
909 Poydras St., Ste. 2230
New Orleans, LA 70112
(504)522-4850
Fax: (504)522-4950
Website: http://www.advantagecap.com

Maine

CEI Ventures / Coastal Ventures LP
2 Portland Fish Pier, Ste. 201
Portland, ME 04101
(207)772-5356
Fax: (207)772-5503
Website: http://www.ceiventures.com

Commwealth Bioventures, Inc.
4 Milk St.
Portland, ME 04101
(207)780-0904
Fax: (207)780-0913

Maryland

Annapolis Ventures LLC
151 West St., Ste. 302
Annapolis, MD 21401
(443)482-9555
Fax: (443)482-9565
Website: http://www.annapolisventures.com

Delmag Ventures
220 Wardour Dr.
Annapolis, MD 21401
(410)267-8196
Fax: (410)267-8017
Website: http://www.delmagventures
.com

Abell Venture Fund
111 S. Calvert St., Ste. 2300
Baltimore, MD 21202
(410)547-1300
Fax: (410)539-6579
Website: http://www.abell.org

ABS Ventures (Baltimore)
1 South St., Ste. 2150
Baltimore, MD 21202
(410)895-3895
Fax: (410)895-3899
Website: http://www.absventures.com

Anthem Capital, L.P.
16 S. Calvert St., Ste. 800
Baltimore, MD 21202-1305
(410)625-1510
Fax: (410)625-1735
Website: http://www.anthemcapital.com

Catalyst Ventures
1119 St. Paul St.
Baltimore, MD 21202
(410)244-0123
Fax: (410)752-7721

Maryland Venture Capital Trust
217 E. Redwood St., Ste. 2200
Baltimore, MD 21202
(410)767-6361
Fax: (410)333-6931

New Enterprise Associates (Baltimore)
1119 St. Paul St.
Baltimore, MD 21202
(410)244-0115
Fax: (410)752-7721
Website: http://www.nea.com

T. Rowe Price Threshold Partnerships
100 E. Pratt St., 8th Fl.
Baltimore, MD 21202
(410)345-2000
Fax: (410)345-2800

Spring Capital Partners
16 W. Madison St.
Baltimore, MD 21201
(410)685-8000
Fax: (410)727-1436
E-mail: mailbox@springcap.com

Arete Corporation
3 Bethesda Metro Ctr., Ste. 770
Bethesda, MD 20814

(301)657-6268
Fax: (301)657-6254
Website: http://www.arete-microgen.com

Embryon Capital
7903 Sleaford Place
Bethesda, MD 20814
(301)656-6837
Fax: (301)656-8056

Potomac Ventures
7920 Norfolk Ave., Ste. 1100
Bethesda, MD 20814
(301)215-9240
Website: http://
www.potomacventures.com

Toucan Capital Corp.
3 Bethesda Metro Center, Ste. 700
Bethesda, MD 20814
(301)961-1970
Fax: (301)961-1969
Website: http://www.toucancapital.com

Kinetic Ventures LLC
2 Wisconsin Cir., Ste. 620
Chevy Chase, MD 20815
(301)652-8066
Fax: (301)652-8310
Website: http://
www.kineticventures.com

Boulder Ventures Ltd.
4750 Owings Mills Blvd.
Owings Mills, MD 21117
(410)998-3114
Fax: (410)356-5492
Website: http://
www.boulderventures.com

Grotech Capital Group
9690 Deereco Rd., Ste. 800
Timonium, MD 21093
(410)560-2000
Fax: (410)560-1910
Website: http://www.grotech.com

Massachusetts

Adams, Harkness & Hill, Inc.
60 State St.
Boston, MA 02109
(617)371-3900

Advent International
75 State St., 29th Fl.
Boston, MA 02109
(617)951-9400
Fax: (617)951-0566
Website: http://www.adventinernational
.com

American Research and Development
30 Federal St.
Boston, MA 02110-2508
(617)423-7500
Fax: (617)423-9655

Ascent Venture Partners
255 State St., 5th Fl.
Boston, MA 02109
(617)270-9400
Fax: (617)270-9401
E-mail: info@ascentvp.com
Website: http://www.ascentvp.com

Atlas Venture
222 Berkeley St.
Boston, MA 02116
(617)488-2200
Fax: (617)859-9292
Website: http://www.atlasventure.com

Axxon Capital
28 State St., 37th Fl.
Boston, MA 02109
(617)722-0980
Fax: (617)557-6014
Website: http://www.axxoncapital.com

BancBoston Capital/BancBoston Ventures
175 Federal St., 10th Fl.
Boston, MA 02110
(617)434-2509
Fax: (617)434-6175
Website: http://www.bancbostoncapital.
com

Boston Capital Ventures
Old City Hall
45 School St.
Boston, MA 02108
(617)227-6550
Fax: (617)227-3847
E-mail: info@bcv.com
Website: http://www.bcv.com

Boston Financial & Equity Corp.
20 Overland St.
PO Box 15071
Boston, MA 02215
(617)267-2900
Fax: (617)437-7601
E-mail: debbie@bfec.com

Boston Millennia Partners
30 Rowes Wharf
Boston, MA 02110
(617)428-5150
Fax: (617)428-5160
Website: http://www.millenniapartners
.com

Bristol Investment Trust
842A Beacon St.
Boston, MA 02215-3199
(617)566-5212
Fax: (617)267-0932

Brook Venture Management LLC
50 Federal St., 5th Fl.
Boston, MA 02110
(617)451-8989
Fax: (617)451-2369
Website: http://www.brookventure.com

Burr, Egan, Deleage, and Co. (Boston)
200 Clarendon St., Ste. 3800
Boston, MA 02116
(617)262-7770
Fax: (617)262-9779

Cambridge/Samsung Partners
One Exeter Plaza
Ninth Fl.
Boston, MA 02116
(617)262-4440
Fax: (617)262-5562

Chestnut Street Partners, Inc.
75 State St., Ste. 2500
Boston, MA 02109
(617)345-7220
Fax: (617)345-7201
E-mail: chestnut@chestnutp.com

Claflin Capital Management, Inc.
10 Liberty Sq., Ste. 300
Boston, MA 02109
(617)426-6505
Fax: (617)482-0016
Website: http://www.claflincapital.com

Copley Venture Partners
99 Summer St., Ste. 1720
Boston, MA 02110
(617)737-1253
Fax: (617)439-0699

Corning Capital / Corning Technology Ventures
121 High Street, Ste. 400
Boston, MA 02110
(617)338-2656
Fax: (617)261-3864
Website: http://www.corningventures
.com

Downer & Co.
211 Congress St.
Boston, MA 02110
(617)482-6200
Fax: (617)482-6201
E-mail: cdowner@downer.com
Website: http://www.downer.com

Fidelity Ventures
82 Devonshire St.
Boston, MA 02109
(617)563-6370
Fax: (617)476-9023
Website: http://www.fidelityventures.com

Greylock Management Corp. (Boston)
1 Federal St.
Boston, MA 02110-2065
(617)423-5525
Fax: (617)482-0059

Gryphon Ventures
222 Berkeley St., Ste.1600
Boston, MA 02116
(617)267-9191
Fax: (617)267-4293
E-mail: all@gryphoninc.com

Halpern, Denny & Co.
500 Boylston St.
Boston, MA 02116
(617)536-6602
Fax: (617)536-8535

Harbourvest Partners, LLC
1 Financial Center, 44th Fl.
Boston, MA 02111
(617)348-3707
Fax: (617)350-0305
Website: http://www.hvpllc.com

Highland Capital Partners
2 International Pl.
Boston, MA 02110
(617)981-1500
Fax: (617)531-1550
E-mail: info@hcp.com
Website: http://www.hcp.com

Lee Munder Venture Partners
John Hancock Tower T-53
200 Clarendon St.
Boston, MA 02103
(617)380-5600
Fax: (617)380-5601
Website: http://www.leemunder.com

M/C Venture Partners
75 State St., Ste. 2500
Boston, MA 02109
(617)345-7200
Fax: (617)345-7201
Website: http://www.mcventurepartners
.com

Massachusetts Capital Resources Co.
420 Boylston St.
Boston, MA 02116
(617)536-3900
Fax: (617)536-7930

Massachusetts Technology Development Corp. (MTDC)
148 State St.
Boston, MA 02109
(617)723-4920
Fax: (617)723-5983
E-mail: jhodgman@mtdc.com
Website: http://www.mtdc.com

New England Partners
One Boston Place, Ste. 2100
Boston, MA 02108
(617)624-8400
Fax: (617)624-8999
Website: http://www.nepartners.com

North Hill Ventures
Ten Post Office Square
11th Fl.
Boston, MA 02109
(617)788-2112
Fax: (617)788-2152
Website: http://www.northhillventures
.com

OneLiberty Ventures
150 Cambridge Park Dr.
Boston, MA 02140
(617)492-7280
Fax: (617)492-7290
Website: http://www.oneliberty.com

Schroder Ventures
Life Sciences
60 State St., Ste. 3650
Boston, MA 02109
(617)367-8100
Fax: (617)367-1590
Website: http://www.shroderventures.com

Shawmut Capital Partners
75 Federal St., 18th Fl.
Boston, MA 02110
(617)368-4900
Fax: (617)368-4910
Website: http://www.shawmutcapital.com

Solstice Capital LLC
15 Broad St., 3rd Fl.
Boston, MA 02109
(617)523-7733
Fax: (617)523-5827
E-mail: solticecapital@solcap.com

Spectrum Equity Investors
One International Pl., 29th Fl.
Boston, MA 02110
(617)464-4600
Fax: (617)464-4601
Website: http://www.spectrumequity.com

Spray Venture Partners
One Walnut St.
Boston, MA 02108
(617)305-4140
Fax: (617)305-4144
Website: http://www.sprayventure.com

The Still River Fund
100 Federal St., 29th Fl.
Boston, MA 02110
(617)348-2327
Fax: (617)348-2371
Website: http://www.stillriverfund.com

Summit Partners
600 Atlantic Ave., Ste. 2800
Boston, MA 02210-2227
(617)824-1000
Fax: (617)824-1159
Website: http://www.summitpartners.com

TA Associates, Inc. (Boston)
High Street Tower
125 High St., Ste. 2500
Boston, MA 02110
(617)574-6700
Fax: (617)574-6728
Website: http://www.ta.com

TVM Techno Venture Management
101 Arch St., Ste. 1950
Boston, MA 02110
(617)345-9320
Fax: (617)345-9377
E-mail: info@tvmvc.com
Website: http://www.tvmvc.com

UNC Ventures
64 Burough St.
Boston, MA 02130-4017
(617)482-7070
Fax: (617)522-2176

Venture Investment Management Company (VIMAC)
177 Milk St.
Boston, MA 02190-3410
(617)292-3300
Fax: (617)292-7979
E-mail: bzeisig@vimac.com
Website: http://www.vimac.com

MDT Advisers, Inc.
125 Cambridge Park Dr.
Cambridge, MA 02140-2314
(617)234-2200
Fax: (617)234-2210
Website: http://www.mdtai.com

TTC Ventures
One Main St., 6th Fl.
Cambridge, MA 02142

(617)528-3137
Fax: (617)577-1715
E-mail: info@ttcventures.com

Zero Stage Capital Co. Inc.
101 Main St., 17th Fl.
Cambridge, MA 02142
(617)876-5355
Fax: (617)876-1248
Website: http://www.zerostage.com

Atlantic Capital
164 Cushing Hwy.
Cohasset, MA 02025
(617)383-9449
Fax: (617)383-6040
E-mail: info@atlanticcap.com
Website: http://www.atlanticcap.com

Seacoast Capital Partners
55 Ferncroft Rd.
Danvers, MA 01923
(978)750-1300
Fax: (978)750-1301
E-mail: gdeli@seacoastcapital.com
Website: http://www.seacoastcapital.com

Sage Management Group
44 South Street
PO Box 2026
East Dennis, MA 02641
(508)385-7172
Fax: (508)385-7272
E-mail: sagemgt@capecod.net

Applied Technology
1 Cranberry Hill
Lexington, MA 02421-7397
(617)862-8622
Fax: (617)862-8367

Royalty Capital Management
5 Downing Rd.
Lexington, MA 02421-6918
(781)861-8490

Argo Global Capital
210 Broadway, Ste. 101
Lynnfield, MA 01940
(781)592-5250
Fax: (781)592-5230
Website: http://www.gsmcapital.com

Industry Ventures
6 Bayne Lane
Newburyport, MA 01950
(978)499-7606
Fax: (978)499-0686
Website: http://www.industryventures
.com

Softbank Capital Partners
10 Langley Rd., Ste. 202
Newton Center, MA 02459

(617)928-9300
Fax: (617)928-9305
E-mail: clax@bvc.com

Advanced Technology Ventures (Boston)
281 Winter St., Ste. 350
Waltham, MA 02451
(781)290-0707
Fax: (781)684-0045
E-mail: info@atvcapital.com
Website: http://www.atvcapital.com

Castile Ventures
890 Winter St., Ste. 140
Waltham, MA 02451
(781)890-0060
Fax: (781)890-0065
Website: http://www.castileventures.com

Charles River Ventures
1000 Winter St., Ste. 3300
Waltham, MA 02451
(781)487-7060
Fax: (781)487-7065
Website: http://www.crv.com

Comdisco Venture Group (Waltham)
Totton Pond Office Center
400-1 Totten Pond Rd.
Waltham, MA 02451
(617)672-0250
Fax: (617)398-8099

Marconi Ventures
890 Winter St., Ste. 310
Waltham, MA 02451
(781)839-7177
Fax: (781)522-7477
Website: http://www.marconi.com

Matrix Partners
Bay Colony Corporate Center
1000 Winter St., Ste.4500
Waltham, MA 02451
(781)890-2244
Fax: (781)890-2288
Website: http://www.matrixpartners.com

North Bridge Venture Partners
950 Winter St. Ste. 4600
Waltham, MA 02451
(781)290-0004
Fax: (781)290-0999
E-mail: eta@nbvp.com

Polaris Venture Partners
Bay Colony Corporate Ctr.
1000 Winter St., Ste. 3500
Waltham, MA 02451
(781)290-0770
Fax: (781)290-0880

E-mail: partners@polarisventures.com
Website: http://www.polarisventures
.com

Seaflower Ventures
Bay Colony Corporate Ctr.
1000 Winter St. Ste. 1000
Waltham, MA 02451
(781)466-9552
Fax: (781)466-9553
E-mail: moot@seaflower.com
Website: http://www.seaflower.com

Ampersand Ventures
55 William St., Ste. 240
Wellesley, MA 02481
(617)239-0700
Fax: (617)239-0824
E-mail: info@ampersandventures.com
Website: http://www.ampersandventures
.com

Battery Ventures (Boston)
20 William St., Ste. 200
Wellesley, MA 02481
(781)577-1000
Fax: (781)577-1001
Website: http://www.battery.com

Commonwealth Capital Ventures, L.P.
20 William St., Ste.225
Wellesley, MA 02481
(781)237-7373
Fax: (781)235-8627
Website: http://www.ccvlp.com

Fowler, Anthony & Company
20 Walnut St.
Wellesley, MA 02481
(781)237-4201
Fax: (781)237-7718

Gemini Investors
20 William St.
Wellesley, MA 02481
(781)237-7001
Fax: (781)237-7233

Grove Street Advisors Inc.
20 William St., Ste. 230
Wellesley, MA 02481
(781)263-6100
Fax: (781)263-6101
Website: http://www.grovestreetadvisors
.com

Mees Pierson Investeringsmaat B.V.
20 William St., Ste. 210
Wellesley, MA 02482
(781)239-7600
Fax: (781)239-0377

Norwest Equity Partners
40 William St., Ste. 305
Wellesley, MA 02481-3902
(781)237-5870
Fax: (781)237-6270
Website: http://www.norwestvp.com

**Bessemer Venture Partners
(Wellesley Hills)**
83 Walnut St.
Wellesley Hills, MA 02481
(781)237-6050
Fax: (781)235-7576
E-mail: travis@bvpny.com
Website: http://www.bvp.com

Venture Capital Fund of New England
20 Walnut St., Ste. 120
Wellesley Hills, MA 02481-2175
(781)239-8262
Fax: (781)239-8263

Prism Venture Partners
100 Lowder Brook Dr., Ste. 2500
Westwood, MA 02090
(781)302-4000
Fax: (781)302-4040
E-mail: dwbaum@prismventure.com

Palmer Partners LP
200 Unicorn Park Dr.
Woburn, MA 01801
(781)933-5445
Fax: (781)933-0698

Michigan

Arbor Partners, L.L.C.
130 South First St.
Ann Arbor, MI 48104
(734)668-9000
Fax: (734)669-4195
Website: http://www.arborpartners.com

EDF Ventures
425 N. Main St.
Ann Arbor, MI 48104
(734)663-3213
Fax: (734)663-7358
E-mail: edf@edfvc.com
Website: http://www.edfvc.com

White Pines Management, L.L.C.
2401 Plymouth Rd., Ste. B
Ann Arbor, MI 48105
(734)747-9401
Fax: (734)747-9704
E-mail: ibund@whitepines.com
Website: http://www.whitepines.com

Wellmax, Inc.
3541 Bendway Blvd., Ste. 100
Bloomfield Hills, MI 48301

(248)646-3554
Fax: (248)646-6220

Venture Funding, Ltd.
Fisher Bldg.
3011 West Grand Blvd., Ste. 321
Detroit, MI 48202
(313)871-3606
Fax: (313)873-4935

**Investcare Partners L.P. / GMA
Capital LLC**
32330 W. Twelve Mile Rd.
Farmington Hills, MI 48334
(248)489-9000
Fax: (248)489-8819
E-mail: gma@gmacapital.com
Website: http://www.gmacapital.com

Liberty Bidco Investment Corp.
30833 Northwestern Highway, Ste. 211
Farmington Hills, MI 48334
(248)626-6070
Fax: (248)626-6072

Seaflower Ventures
5170 Nicholson Rd.
PO Box 474
Fowlerville, MI 48836
(517)223-3335
Fax: (517)223-3337
E-mail: gibbons@seaflower.com
Website: http://www.seaflower.com

Ralph Wilson Equity Fund LLC
15400 E. Jefferson Ave.
Gross Pointe Park, MI 48230
(313)821-9122
Fax: (313)821-9101
Website: http://www.RalphWilsonEquity
Fund.com
J. Skip Simms, President

Minnesota

Development Corp. of Austin
1900 Eighth Ave., NW
Austin, MN 55912
(507)433-0346
Fax: (507)433-0361
E-mail: dca@smig.net
Website: http://www.spamtownusa.com

Northeast Ventures Corp.
802 Alworth Bldg.
Duluth, MN 55802
(218)722-9915
Fax: (218)722-9871

Medical Innovation Partners, Inc.
6450 City West Pkwy.
Eden Prairie, MN 55344-3245
(612)828-9616
Fax: (612)828-9596

St. Paul Venture Capital, Inc.
10400 Vicking Dr., Ste. 550
Eden Prairie, MN 55344
(612)995-7474
Fax: (612)995-7475
Website: http://www.stpaulvc.com

Cherry Tree Investments, Inc.
7601 France Ave. S, Ste. 150
Edina, MN 55435
(612)893-9012
Fax: (612)893-9036
Website: http://www.cherrytree.com

Shared Ventures, Inc.
6550 York Ave. S
Edina, MN 55435
(612)925-3411

Sherpa Partners LLC
5050 Lincoln Dr., Ste. 490
Edina, MN 55436
(952)942-1070
Fax: (952)942-1071
Website: http://www.sherpapartners.com

Affinity Capital Management
901 Marquette Ave., Ste. 1810
Minneapolis, MN 55402
(612)252-9900
Fax: (612)252-9911
Website: http://www.affinitycapital.com

Artesian Capital
1700 Foshay Tower
821 Marquette Ave.
Minneapolis, MN 55402
(612)334-5600
Fax: (612)334-5601
E-mail: artesian@artesian.com

Coral Ventures
60 S. 6th St., Ste. 3510
Minneapolis, MN 55402
(612)335-8666
Fax: (612)335-8668
Website: http://www.coralventures.com

Crescendo Venture Management, L.L.C.
800 LaSalle Ave., Ste. 2250
Minneapolis, MN 55402
(612)607-2800
Fax: (612)607-2801
Website: http://www.crescendoventures
.com

Gideon Hixon Venture
1900 Foshay Tower
821 Marquette Ave.
Minneapolis, MN 55402
(612)904-2314
Fax: (612)204-0913

Norwest Equity Partners
3600 IDS Center
80 S. 8th St.
Minneapolis, MN 55402
(612)215-1600
Fax: (612)215-1601
Website: http://www.norwestvp.com

Oak Investment Partners (Minneapolis)
4550 Norwest Center
90 S. 7th St.
Minneapolis, MN 55402
(612)339-9322
Fax: (612)337-8017
Website: http://www.oakinv.com

**Pathfinder Venture Capital Funds
(Minneapolis)**
7300 Metro Blvd., Ste. 585
Minneapolis, MN 55439
(612)835-1121
Fax: (612)835-8389
E-mail: jahrens620@aol.com

**U.S. Bancorp Piper Jaffray
Ventures, Inc.**
800 Nicollet Mall, Ste. 800
Minneapolis, MN 55402
(612)303-5686
Fax: (612)303-1350
Website: http://www.paperjaffrey
ventures.com

The Food Fund, Ltd. Partnership
5720 Smatana Dr., Ste. 300
Minnetonka, MN 55343
(612)939-3950
Fax: (612)939-8106

Mayo Medical Ventures
200 First St. SW
Rochester, MN 55905
(507)266-4586
Fax: (507)284-5410
Website: http://www.mayo.edu

Missouri

Bankers Capital Corp.
3100 Gillham Rd.
Kansas City, MO 64109
(816)531-1600
Fax: (816)531-1334

Capital for Business, Inc. (Kansas City)
1000 Walnut St., 18th Fl.
Kansas City, MO 64106
(816)234-2357
Fax: (816)234-2952
Website: http://www.capitalforbusiness
.com

De Vries & Co. Inc.
800 West 47th St.
Kansas City, MO 64112
(816)756-0055
Fax: (816)756-0061

**InvestAmerica Venture Group Inc.
(Kansas City)**
Commerce Tower
911 Main St., Ste. 2424
Kansas City, MO 64105
(816)842-0114
Fax: (816)471-7339

Kansas City Equity Partners
233 W. 47th St.
Kansas City, MO 64112
(816)960-1771
Fax: (816)960-1777
Website: http://www.kcep.com

Bome Investors, Inc.
8000 Maryland Ave., Ste. 1190
St. Louis, MO 63105
(314)721-5707
Fax: (314)721-5135
Website: http://www.gatewayventures.com

Capital for Business, Inc. (St. Louis)
11 S. Meramac St., Ste. 1430
St. Louis, MO 63105
(314)746-7427
Fax: (314)746-8739
Website: http://www.capitalforbusiness
.com

Crown Capital Corp.
540 Maryville Centre Dr., Ste. 120
Saint Louis, MO 63141
(314)576-1201
Fax: (314)576-1525
Website: http://www.crown- cap.com

Gateway Associates L.P.
8000 Maryland Ave., Ste. 1190
St. Louis, MO 63105
(314)721-5707
Fax: (314)721-5135

Harbison Corp.
8112 Maryland Ave., Ste. 250
Saint Louis, MO 63105
(314)727-8200
Fax: (314)727-0249

Nebraska

Heartland Capital Fund, Ltd.
PO Box 642117
Omaha, NE 68154
(402)778-5124
Fax: (402)445-2370
Website: http://www.heartlandcapital
fund.com

Odin Capital Group
1625 Farnam St., Ste. 700
Omaha, NE 68102
(402)346-6200
Fax: (402)342-9311
Website: http://www.odincapital.com

Nevada

Edge Capital Investment Co. LLC
1350 E. Flamingo Rd., Ste. 3000
Las Vegas, NV 89119
(702)438-3343
E-mail: info@edgecapital.net
Website: http://www.edgecapital.net

The Benefit Capital Companies Inc.
PO Box 542
Logandale, NV 89021
(702)398-3222
Fax: (702)398-3700

Millennium Three Venture Group LLC
6880 South McCarran Blvd., Ste. A-11
Reno, NV 89509
(775)954-2020
Fax: (775)954-2023
Website: http://www.m3vg.com

New Jersey

Alan I. Goldman & Associates
497 Ridgewood Ave.
Glen Ridge, NJ 07028
(973)857-5680
Fax: (973)509-8856

CS Capital Partners LLC
328 Second St., Ste. 200
Lakewood, NJ 08701
(732)901-1111
Fax: (212)202-5071
Website: http://www.cs-capital.com

Edison Venture Fund
1009 Lenox Dr., Ste. 4
Lawrenceville, NJ 08648
(609)896-1900
Fax: (609)896-0066
E-mail: info@edisonventure.com
Website: http://www.edisonventure.com

Tappan Zee Capital Corp. (New Jersey)
201 Lower Notch Rd.
PO Box 416
Little Falls, NJ 07424
(973)256-8280
Fax: (973)256-2841

The CIT Group/Venture Capital, Inc.
650 CIT Dr.
Livingston, NJ 07039
(973)740-5429

Fax: (973)740-5555
Website: http://www.cit.com

Capital Express, L.L.C.
1100 Valleybrook Ave.
Lyndhurst, NJ 07071
(201)438-8228
Fax: (201)438-5131
E-mail: niles@capitalexpress.com
Website: http://www.capitalexpress.com

Westford Technology Ventures, L.P.
17 Academy St.
Newark, NJ 07102
(973)624-2131
Fax: (973)624-2008

Accel Partners
1 Palmer Sq.
Princeton, NJ 08542
(609)683-4500
Fax: (609)683-4880
Website: http://www.accel.com

Cardinal Partners
221 Nassau St.
Princeton, NJ 08542
(609)924-6452
Fax: (609)683-0174
Website: http://www.cardinalhealth
partners.com

Domain Associates L.L.C.
One Palmer Sq., Ste. 515
Princeton, NJ 08542
(609)683-5656
Fax: (609)683-9789
Website: http://www.domainvc.com

Johnston Associates, Inc.
181 Cherry Valley Rd.
Princeton, NJ 08540
(609)924-3131
Fax: (609)683-7524
E-mail: jaincorp@aol.com

Kemper Ventures
Princeton Forrestal Village
155 Village Blvd.
Princeton, NJ 08540
(609)936-3035
Fax: (609)936-3051

Penny Lane Parnters
One Palmer Sq., Ste. 309
Princeton, NJ 08542
(609)497-4646
Fax: (609)497-0611

Early Stage Enterprises L.P.
995 Route 518
Skillman, NJ 08558
(609)921-8896

Fax: (609)921-8703
Website: http://www.esevc.com

MBW Management Inc.
1 Springfield Ave.
Summit, NJ 07901
(908)273-4060
Fax: (908)273-4430

BCI Advisors, Inc.
Glenpointe Center W.
Teaneck, NJ 07666
(201)836-3900
Fax: (201)836-6368
E-mail: info@bciadvisors.com
Website: http://www.bci partners.com

**Demuth, Folger & Wetherill / DFW
Capital Partners**
Glenpointe Center E., 5th Fl.
300 Frank W. Burr Blvd.
Teaneck, NJ 07666
(201)836-2233
Fax: (201)836-5666
Website: http://www.dfwcapital.com

First Princeton Capital Corp.
189 Berdan Ave., No. 131
Wayne, NJ 07470-3233
(973)278-3233
Fax: (973)278-4290
Website: http://www.lytellcatt.net

Edelson Technology Partners
300 Tice Blvd.
Woodcliff Lake, NJ 07675
(201)930-9898
Fax: (201)930-8899
Website: http://www.edelsontech.com

New Mexico

Bruce F. Glaspell & Associates
10400 Academy Rd. NE, Ste. 313
Albuquerque, NM 87111
(505)292-4505
Fax: (505)292-4258

High Desert Ventures, Inc.
6101 Imparata St. NE, Ste. 1721
Albuquerque, NM 87111
(505)797-3330
Fax: (505)338-5147

New Business Capital Fund, Ltd.
5805 Torreon NE
Albuquerque, NM 87109
(505)822-8445

SBC Ventures
10400 Academy Rd. NE, Ste. 313
Albuquerque, NM 87111

(505)292-4505
Fax: (505)292-4528

Technology Ventures Corp.
1155 University Blvd. SE
Albuquerque, NM 87106
(505)246-2882
Fax: (505)246-2891

New York

**Small Business Technology
Investment Fund**
99 Washington Ave., Ste. 1731
Albany, NY 12210
(518)473-9741
Fax: (518)473-6876

Rand Capital Corp.
2200 Rand Bldg.
Buffalo, NY 14203
(716)853-0802
Fax: (716)854-8480
Website: http://www.randcapital.com

Seed Capital Partners
620 Main St.
Buffalo, NY 14202
(716)845-7520
Fax: (716)845-7539
Website: http://www.seedcp.com

Coleman Venture Group
5909 Northern Blvd.
PO Box 224
East Norwich, NY 11732
(516)626-3642
Fax: (516)626-9722

Vega Capital Corp.
45 Knollwood Rd.
Elmsford, NY 10523
(914)345-9500
Fax: (914)345-9505

Herbert Young Securities, Inc.
98 Cuttermill Rd.
Great Neck, NY 11021
(516)487-8300
Fax: (516)487-8319

**Sterling/Carl Marks Capital,
Inc.**
175 Great Neck Rd., Ste. 408
Great Neck, NY 11021
(516)482-7374
Fax: (516)487-0781
E-mail: stercrlmar@aol.com
Website: http://www.serlingcarlmarks
.com

Impex Venture Management Co.
PO Box 1570
Green Island, NY 12183
(518)271-8008
Fax: (518)271-9101

Corporate Venture Partners L.P.
200 Sunset Park
Ithaca, NY 14850
(607)257-6323
Fax: (607)257-6128

Arthur P. Gould & Co.
One Wilshire Dr.
Lake Success, NY 11020
(516)773-3000
Fax: (516)773-3289

Dauphin Capital Partners
108 Forest Ave.
Locust Valley, NY 11560
(516)759-3339
Fax: (516)759-3322
Website: http://www.dauphincapital.com

550 Digital Media Ventures
555 Madison Ave., 10th Fl.
New York, NY 10022
Website: http://www.550dmv.com

Aberlyn Capital Management Co., Inc.
500 Fifth Ave.
New York, NY 10110
(212)391-7750
Fax: (212)391-7762

Adler & Company
342 Madison Ave., Ste. 807
New York, NY 10173
(212)599-2535
Fax: (212)599-2526

Alimansky Capital Group, Inc.
605 Madison Ave., Ste. 300
New York, NY 10022-1901
(212)832-7300
Fax: (212)832-7338

Allegra Partners
515 Madison Ave., 29th Fl.
New York, NY 10022
(212)826-9080
Fax: (212)759-2561

The Argentum Group
The Chyrsler Bldg.
405 Lexington Ave.
New York, NY 10174
(212)949-6262
Fax: (212)949-8294
Website: http://www.argentumgroup.com

Axavision Inc.
14 Wall St., 26th Fl.
New York, NY 10005
(212)619-4000
Fax: (212)619-7202

Bedford Capital Corp.
18 East 48th St., Ste. 1800
New York, NY 10017
(212)688-5700
Fax: (212)754-4699
E-mail: info@bedfordnyc.com
Website: http://www.bedfordnyc.com

Bloom & Co.
950 Third Ave.
New York, NY 10022
(212)838-1858
Fax: (212)838-1843

Bristol Capital Management
300 Park Ave., 17th Fl.
New York, NY 10022
(212)572-6306
Fax: (212)705-4292

**Citicorp Venture Capital Ltd.
(New York City)**
399 Park Ave., 14th Fl.
Zone 4
New York, NY 10043
(212)559-1127
Fax: (212)888-2940

CM Equity Partners
135 E. 57th St.
New York, NY 10022
(212)909-8428
Fax: (212)980-2630

Cohen & Co., L.L.C.
800 Third Ave.
New York, NY 10022
(212)317-2250
Fax: (212)317-2255
E-mail: nlcohen@aol.com

Cornerstone Equity Investors, L.L.C.
717 5th Ave., Ste. 1100
New York, NY 10022
(212)753-0901
Fax: (212)826-6798
Website: http://www.cornerstone-equity
.com

CW Group, Inc.
1041 3rd Ave., 2nd fl.
New York, NY 10021
(212)308-5266
Fax: (212)644-0354
Website: http://www.cwventures.com

DH Blair Investment Banking Corp.
44 Wall St., 2nd Fl.
New York, NY 10005
(212)495-5000
Fax: (212)269-1438

Dresdner Kleinwort Capital
75 Wall St.
New York, NY 10005
(212)429-3131
Fax: (212)429-3139
Website: http://www.dresdnerkb.com

East River Ventures, L.P.
645 Madison Ave., 22nd Fl.
New York, NY 10022
(212)644-2322
Fax: (212)644-5498

Easton Hunt Capital Partners
641 Lexington Ave., 21st Fl.
New York, NY 10017
(212)702-0950
Fax: (212)702-0952
Website: http://www.eastoncapital.com

Elk Associates Funding Corp.
747 3rd Ave., Ste. 4C
New York, NY 10017
(212)355-2449
Fax: (212)759-3338

EOS Partners, L.P.
320 Park Ave., 22nd Fl.
New York, NY 10022
(212)832-5800
Fax: (212)832-5815
E-mail: mfirst@eospartners.com
Website: http://www.eospartners.com

Euclid Partners
45 Rockefeller Plaza, Ste. 3240
New York, NY 10111
(212)218-6880
Fax: (212)218-6877
E-mail: graham@euclidpartners.com
Website: http://www.euclidpartners.com

Evergreen Capital Partners, Inc.
150 East 58th St.
New York, NY 10155
(212)813-0758
Fax: (212)813-0754

Exeter Capital L.P.
10 E. 53rd St.
New York, NY 10022
(212)872-1172
Fax: (212)872-1198
E-mail: exeter@usa.net

Financial Technology Research Corp.
518 Broadway
Penthouse

New York, NY 10012
(212)625-9100
Fax: (212)431-0300
E-mail: fintek@financier.com

4C Ventures
237 Park Ave., Ste. 801
New York, NY 10017
(212)692-3680
Fax: (212)692-3685
Website: http://www.4cventures.com

Fusient Ventures
99 Park Ave., 20th Fl.
New York, NY 10016
(212)972-8999
Fax: (212)972-9876
E-mail: info@fusient.com
Website: http://www.fusient.com

Generation Capital Partners
551 Fifth Ave., Ste. 3100
New York, NY 10176
(212)450-8507
Fax: (212)450-8550
Website: http://www.genpartners.com

Golub Associates, Inc.
555 Madison Ave.
New York, NY 10022
(212)750-6060
Fax: (212)750-5505

Hambro America Biosciences Inc.
650 Madison Ave., 21st Floor
New York, NY 10022
(212)223-7400
Fax: (212)223-0305

Hanover Capital Corp.
505 Park Ave., 15th Fl.
New York, NY 10022
(212)755-1222
Fax: (212)935-1787

Harvest Partners, Inc.
280 Park Ave, 33rd Fl.
New York, NY 10017
(212)559-6300
Fax: (212)812-0100
Website: http://www.harvpart.com

Holding Capital Group, Inc.
10 E. 53rd St., 30th Fl.
New York, NY 10022
(212)486-6670
Fax: (212)486-0843

Hudson Venture Partners
660 Madison Ave., 14th Fl.
New York, NY 10021-8405
(212)644-9797
Fax: (212)644-7430
Website: http://www.hudsonptr.com

IBJS Capital Corp.
1 State St., 9th Fl.
New York, NY 10004
(212)858-2018
Fax: (212)858-2768

InterEquity Capital Partners, L.P.
220 5th Ave.
New York, NY 10001
(212)779-2022
Fax: (212)779-2103
Website: http://www.interequity-capital
.com

The Jordan Edmiston Group Inc.
150 East 52nd St., 18th Fl.
New York, NY 10022
(212)754-0710
Fax: (212)754-0337

Josephberg, Grosz and Co., Inc.
633 3rd Ave., 13th Fl.
New York, NY 10017
(212)974-9926
Fax: (212)397-5832

J.P. Morgan Capital Corp.
60 Wall St.
New York, NY 10260-0060
(212)648-9000
Fax: (212)648-5002
Website: http://www.jpmorgan.com

The Lambda Funds
380 Lexington Ave., 54th Fl.
New York, NY 10168
(212)682-3454
Fax: (212)682-9231

Lepercq Capital Management Inc.
1675 Broadway
New York, NY 10019
(212)698-0795
Fax: (212)262-0155

Loeb Partners Corp.
61 Broadway, Ste. 2400
New York, NY 10006
(212)483-7000
Fax: (212)574-2001

Madison Investment Partners
660 Madison Ave.
New York, NY 10021
(212)223-2600
Fax: (212)223-8208

MC Capital Inc.
520 Madison Ave., 16th Fl.
New York, NY 10022
(212)644-0841
Fax: (212)644-2926

**McCown, De Leeuw and Co.
(New York)**
65 E. 55th St., 36th Fl.
New York, NY 10022
(212)355-5500
Fax: (212)355-6283
Website: http://www.mdcpartners.com

Morgan Stanley Venture Partners
1221 Avenue of the Americas, 33rd Fl.
New York, NY 10020
(212)762-7900
Fax: (212)762-8424
E-mail: msventures@ms.com
Website: http://www.msvp.com

Nazem and Co.
645 Madison Ave., 12th Fl.
New York, NY 10022
(212)371-7900
Fax: (212)371-2150

Needham Capital Management, L.L.C.
445 Park Ave.
New York, NY 10022
(212)371-8300
Fax: (212)705-0299
Website: http://www.needhamco.com

Norwood Venture Corp.
1430 Broadway, Ste. 1607
New York, NY 10018
(212)869-5075
Fax: (212)869-5331
E-mail: nvc@mail.idt.net
Website: http://www.norven.com

Noveltek Venture Corp.
521 Fifth Ave., Ste. 1700
New York, NY 10175
(212)286-1963

Paribas Principal, Inc.
787 7th Ave.
New York, NY 10019
(212)841-2005
Fax: (212)841-3558

**Patricof & Co. Ventures, Inc.
(New York)**
445 Park Ave.
New York, NY 10022
(212)753-6300
Fax: (212)319-6155
Website: http://www.patricof.com

The Platinum Group, Inc.
350 Fifth Ave, Ste. 7113
New York, NY 10118
(212)736-4300
Fax: (212)736-6086
Website: http://www.platinumgroup.com

Pomona Capital
780 Third Ave., 28th Fl.
New York, NY 10017
(212)593-3639
Fax: (212)593-3987
Website: http://www.pomonacapital.com

Prospect Street Ventures
10 East 40th St., 44th Fl.
New York, NY 10016
(212)448-0702
Fax: (212)448-9652
E-mail: wkohler@prospectstreet.com
Website: http://www.prospectstreet.com

Regent Capital Management
505 Park Ave., Ste. 1700
New York, NY 10022
(212)735-9900
Fax: (212)735-9908

Rothschild Ventures, Inc.
1251 Avenue of the Americas, 51st Fl.
New York, NY 10020
(212)403-3500
Fax: (212)403-3652
Website: http://www.nmrothschild.com

Sandler Capital Management
767 Fifth Ave., 45th Fl.
New York, NY 10153
(212)754-8100
Fax: (212)826-0280

Siguler Guff & Company
630 Fifth Ave., 16th Fl.
New York, NY 10111
(212)332-5100
Fax: (212)332-5120

Spencer Trask Ventures Inc.
535 Madison Ave.
New York, NY 10022
(212)355-5565
Fax: (212)751-3362
Website: http://www.spencertrask.com

Sprout Group (New York City)
277 Park Ave.
New York, NY 10172
(212)892-3600
Fax: (212)892-3444
E-mail: info@sproutgroup.com
Website: http://www.sproutgroup.com

US Trust Private Equity
114 W.47th St.
New York, NY 10036
(212)852-3949
Fax: (212)852-3759
Website: http://www.ustrust.com/
privateequity

Vencon Management Inc.
301 West 53rd St., Ste. 10F
New York, NY 10019
(212)581-8787
Fax: (212)397-4126
Website: http://www.venconinc.com

Venrock Associates
30 Rockefeller Plaza, Ste. 5508
New York, NY 10112
(212)649-5600
Fax: (212)649-5788
Website: http://www.venrock.com

Venture Capital Fund of America, Inc.
509 Madison Ave., Ste. 812
New York, NY 10022
(212)838-5577
Fax: (212)838-7614
E-mail: mail@vcfa.com
Website: http://www.vcfa.com

Venture Opportunities Corp.
150 E. 58th St.
New York, NY 10155
(212)832-3737
Fax: (212)980-6603

Warburg Pincus Ventures, Inc.
466 Lexington Ave., 11th Fl.
New York, NY 10017
(212)878-9309
Fax: (212)878-9200
Website: http://www.warburgpincus.com

Wasserstein, Perella & Co. Inc.
31 W. 52nd St., 27th Fl.
New York, NY 10019
(212)702-5691
Fax: (212)969-7879

Welsh, Carson, Anderson, & Stowe
320 Park Ave., Ste. 2500
New York, NY 10022-6815
(212)893-9500
Fax: (212)893-9575

Whitney and Co. (New York)
630 Fifth Ave. Ste. 3225
New York, NY 10111
(212)332-2400
Fax: (212)332-2422
Website: http://www.jhwitney.com

Winthrop Ventures
74 Trinity Place, Ste. 600
New York, NY 10006
(212)422-0100

The Pittsford Group
8 Lodge Pole Rd.
Pittsford, NY 14534
(716)223-3523

Genesee Funding
70 Linden Oaks, 3rd Fl.
Rochester, NY 14625
(716)383-5550
Fax: (716)383-5305

Gabelli Multimedia Partners
One Corporate Center
Rye, NY 10580
(914)921-5395
Fax: (914)921-5031

Stamford Financial
108 Main St.
Stamford, NY 12167
(607)652-3311
Fax: (607)652-6301
Website: http://www.stamfordfinancial
.com

Northwood Ventures LLC
485 Underhill Blvd., Ste. 205
Syosset, NY 11791
(516)364-5544
Fax: (516)364-0879
E-mail: northwood@northwood.com
Website: http://www.northwood
ventures.com

Exponential Business Development Co.
216 Walton St.
Syracuse, NY 13202-1227
(315)474-4500
Fax: (315)474-4682
E-mail: dirksonn@aol.com
Website: http://www.exponential-ny.com

Onondaga Venture Capital Fund Inc.
714 State Tower Bldg.
Syracuse, NY 13202
(315)478-0157
Fax: (315)478-0158

Bessemer Venture Partners (Westbury)
1400 Old Country Rd., Ste. 109
Westbury, NY 11590
(516)997-2300
Fax: (516)997-2371
E-mail: bob@bvpny.com
Website: http://www.bvp.com

Ovation Capital Partners
120 Bloomingdale Rd., 4th Fl.
White Plains, NY 10605
(914)258-0011
Fax: (914)684-0848
Website: http://www.ovationcapital.com

North Carolina

Carolinas Capital Investment Corp.
1408 Biltmore Dr.
Charlotte, NC 28207

(704)375-3888
Fax: (704)375-6226

First Union Capital Partners
1st Union Center, 12th Fl.
301 S. College St.
Charlotte, NC 28288-0732
(704)383-0000
Fax: (704)374-6711
Website: http://www.fucp.com

Frontier Capital LLC
525 North Tryon St., Ste. 1700
Charlotte, NC 28202
(704)414-2880
Fax: (704)414-2881
Website: http://www.frontierfunds.com

Kitty Hawk Capital
2700 Coltsgate Rd., Ste. 202
Charlotte, NC 28211
(704)362-3909
Fax: (704)362-2774
Website: http://www.kittyhawkcapital
.com

Piedmont Venture Partners
One Morrocroft Centre
6805 Morisson Blvd., Ste. 380
Charlotte, NC 28211
(704)731-5200
Fax: (704)365-9733
Website: http://www.piedmontvp.com

Ruddick Investment Co.
1800 Two First Union Center
Charlotte, NC 28282
(704)372-5404
Fax: (704)372-6409

The Shelton Companies Inc.
3600 One First Union Center
301 S. College St.
Charlotte, NC 28202
(704)348-2200
Fax: (704)348-2260

Wakefield Group
1110 E. Morehead St.
PO Box 36329
Charlotte, NC 28236
(704)372-0355
Fax: (704)372-8216
Website: http://www.wakefieldgroup
.com

Aurora Funds, Inc.
2525 Meridian Pkwy., Ste. 220
Durham, NC 27713
(919)484-0400
Fax: (919)484-0444
Website: http://www.aurora funds.com

Intersouth Partners
3211 Shannon Rd., Ste. 610
Durham, NC 27707
(919)493-6640
Fax: (919)493-6649
E-mail: info@intersouth.com
Website: http://www.intersouth.com

Geneva Merchant Banking Partners
PO Box 21962
Greensboro, NC 27420
(336)275-7002
Fax: (336)275-9155
Website: http://www.genevamerchant
bank.com

The North Carolina Enterprise Fund, L.P.
3600 Glenwood Ave., Ste. 107
Raleigh, NC 27612
(919)781-2691
Fax: (919)783-9195
Website: http://www.ncef.com

Ohio

Senmend Medical Ventures
4445 Lake Forest Dr., Ste. 600
Cincinnati, OH 45242
(513)563-3264
Fax: (513)563-3261

The Walnut Group
312 Walnut St., Ste. 1151
Cincinnati, OH 45202
(513)651-3300
Fax: (513)929-4441
Website: http://www.thewalnutgroup
.com

Brantley Venture Partners
20600 Chagrin Blvd., Ste. 1150
Cleveland, OH 44122
(216)283-4800
Fax: (216)283-5324

Clarion Capital Corp.
1801 E. 9th St., Ste. 1120
Cleveland, OH 44114
(216)687-1096
Fax: (216)694-3545

Crystal Internet Venture Fund, L.P.
1120 Chester Ave., Ste. 418
Cleveland, OH 44114
(216)263-5515
Fax: (216)263-5518
E-mail: jf@crystalventure.com
Website: http://www.crystalventure.com

Key Equity Capital Corp.
127 Public Sq., 28th Fl.
Cleveland, OH 44114

(216)689-3000
Fax: (216)689-3204
Website: http://www.keybank.com

Morgenthaler Ventures
Terminal Tower
50 Public Square, Ste. 2700
Cleveland, OH 44113
(216)416-7500
Fax: (216)416-7501
Website: http://www.morgenthaler.com

National City Equity Partners Inc.
1965 E. 6th St.
Cleveland, OH 44114
(216)575-2491
Fax: (216)575-9965
E-mail: nccap@aol.com
Website: http://www.nccapital.com

Primus Venture Partners, Inc.
5900 LanderBrook Dr., Ste. 2000
Cleveland, OH 44124-4020
(440)684-7300
Fax: (440)684-7342
E-mail: info@primusventure.com
Website: http://www.primusventure.com

Banc One Capital Partners (Columbus)
150 East Gay St., 24th Fl.
Columbus, OH 43215
(614)217-1100
Fax: (614)217-1217

Battelle Venture Partners
505 King Ave.
Columbus, OH 43201
(614)424-7005
Fax: (614)424-4874

Ohio Partners
62 E. Board St., 3rd Fl.
Columbus, OH 43215
(614)621-1210
Fax: (614)621-1240

Capital Technology Group, L.L.C.
400 Metro Place North, Ste. 300
Dublin, OH 43017
(614)792-6066
Fax: (614)792-6036
E-mail: info@capitaltech.com
Website: http://www.capitaltech.com

Northwest Ohio Venture Fund
4159 Holland-Sylvania R., Ste. 202
Toledo, OH 43623
(419)824-8144
Fax: (419)882-2035
E-mail: bwalsh@novf.com

Oklahoma

Moore & Associates
1000 W. Wilshire Blvd., Ste. 370
Oklahoma City, OK 73116
(405)842-3660
Fax: (405)842-3763

Chisholm Private Capital Partners
100 West 5th St., Ste. 805
Tulsa, OK 74103
(918)584-0440
Fax: (918)584-0441
Website: http://www.chisholmvc.com

Davis, Tuttle Venture Partners (Tulsa)
320 S. Boston, Ste. 1000
Tulsa, OK 74103-3703
(918)584-7272
Fax: (918)582-3404
Website: http://www.davistuttle.com

RBC Ventures
2627 E. 21st St.
Tulsa, OK 74114
(918)744-5607
Fax: (918)743-8630

Oregon

Utah Ventures II LP
10700 SW Beaverton-Hillsdale Hwy.,
Ste. 548
Beaverton, OR 97005
(503)574-4125
E-mail: adishlip@uven.com
Website: http://www.uven.com

Orien Ventures
14523 SW Westlake Dr.
Lake Oswego, OR 97035
(503)699-1680
Fax: (503)699-1681

OVP Venture Partners (Lake Oswego)
340 Oswego Pointe Dr., Ste. 200
Lake Oswego, OR 97034
(503)697-8766
Fax: (503)697-8863
E-mail: info@ovp.com
Website: http://www.ovp.com

Oregon Resource and Technology Development Fund
4370 NE Halsey St., Ste. 233
Portland, OR 97213-1566
(503)282-4462
Fax: (503)282-2976

Shaw Venture Partners
400 SW 6th Ave., Ste. 1100
Portland, OR 97204-1636
(503)228-4884

Fax: (503)227-2471
Website: http://www.shawventures.com

Pennsylvania

Mid-Atlantic Venture Funds
125 Goodman Dr.
Bethlehem, PA 18015
(610)865-6550
Fax: (610)865-6427
Website: http://www.mavf.com

Newspring Ventures
100 W. Elm St., Ste. 101
Conshohocken, PA 19428
(610)567-2380
Fax: (610)567-2388
Website: http://www.newsprint
ventures.com

Patricof & Co. Ventures, Inc.
455 S. Gulph Rd., Ste. 410
King of Prussia, PA 19406
(610)265-0286
Fax: (610)265-4959
Website: http://www.patricof.com

Loyalhanna Venture Fund
527 Cedar Way, Ste. 104
Oakmont, PA 15139
(412)820-7035
Fax: (412)820-7036

Innovest Group Inc.
2000 Market St., Ste. 1400
Philadelphia, PA 19103
(215)564-3960
Fax: (215)569-3272

Keystone Venture Capital Management Co.
1601 Market St., Ste. 2500
Philadelphia, PA 19103
(215)241-1200
Fax: (215)241-1211
Website: http://www.keystonevc.com

Liberty Venture Partners
2005 Market St., Ste. 200
Philadelphia, PA 19103
(215)282-4484
Fax: (215)282-4485
E-mail: info@libertyvp.com
Website: http://www.libertyvp.com

Penn Janney Fund, Inc.
1801 Market St., 11th Fl.
Philadelphia, PA 19103
(215)665-4447
Fax: (215)557-0820

Philadelphia Ventures, Inc.
The Bellevue
200 S. Broad St.

Organizations, Agencies, & Consultants

Philadelphia, PA 19102
(215)732-4445
Fax: (215)732-4644

Birchmere Ventures Inc.
2000 Technology Dr.
Pittsburgh, PA 15219-3109
(412)803-8000
Fax: (412)687-8139
Website: http://www.birchmerevc.com

CEO Venture Fund
2000 Technology Dr., Ste. 160
Pittsburgh, PA 15219-3109
(412)687-3451
Fax: (412)687-8139
E-mail: ceofund@aol.com
Website: http://www.ceoventurefund
.com

Innovation Works Inc.
2000 Technology Dr., Ste. 250
Pittsburgh, PA 15219
(412)681-1520
Fax: (412)681-2625
Website: http://www.innovation
works.org

Keystone Minority Capital Fund L.P.
1801 Centre Ave., Ste. 201
Williams Sq.
Pittsburgh, PA 15219
(412)338-2230
Fax: (412)338-2224

Mellon Ventures, Inc.
One Mellon Bank Ctr., Rm. 3500
Pittsburgh, PA 15258
(412)236-3594
Fax: (412)236-3593
Website: http://www.mellonventures
.com

Pennsylvania Growth Fund
5850 Ellsworth Ave., Ste. 303
Pittsburgh, PA 15232
(412)661-1000
Fax: (412)361-0676

Point Venture Partners
The Century Bldg.
130 Seventh St., 7th Fl.
Pittsburgh, PA 15222
(412)261-1966
Fax: (412)261-1718

Cross Atlantic Capital Partners
5 Radnor Corporate Center, Ste. 555
Radnor, PA 19087
(610)995-2650
Fax: (610)971-2062
Website: http://www.xacp.com

Meridian Venture Partners (Radnor)
The Radnor Court Bldg., Ste. 140
259 Radnor-Chester Rd.
Radnor, PA 19087
(610)254-2999
Fax: (610)254-2996
E-mail: mvpart@ix.netcom.com

TDH
919 Conestoga Rd., Bldg. 1, Ste. 301
Rosemont, PA 19010
(610)526-9970
Fax: (610)526-9971

Adams Capital Management
500 Blackburn Ave.
Sewickley, PA 15143
(412)749-9454
Fax: (412)749-9459
Website: http://www.acm.com

S.R. One, Ltd.
Four Tower Bridge
200 Barr Harbor Dr., Ste. 250
W. Conshohocken, PA 19428
(610)567-1000
Fax: (610)567-1039

Greater Philadelphia Venture Capital Corp.
351 East Conestoga Rd.
Wayne, PA 19087
(610)688-6829
Fax: (610)254-8958

PA Early Stage
435 Devon Park Dr., Bldg. 500, Ste. 510
Wayne, PA 19087
(610)293-4075
Fax: (610)254-4240
Website: http://www.paearlystage.com

The Sandhurst Venture Fund, L.P.
351 E. Constoga Rd.
Wayne, PA 19087
(610)254-8900
Fax: (610)254-8958

TL Ventures
700 Bldg.
435 Devon Park Dr.
Wayne, PA 19087-1990
(610)975-3765
Fax: (610)254-4210
Website: http://www.tlventures.com

Rockhill Ventures, Inc.
100 Front St., Ste. 1350
West Conshohocken, PA 19428
(610)940-0300
Fax: (610)940-0301

Puerto Rico

Advent-Morro Equity Partners
Banco Popular Bldg.
206 Tetuan St., Ste. 903
San Juan, PR 00902
(787)725-5285
Fax: (787)721-1735

North America Investment Corp.
Mercantil Plaza, Ste. 813
PO Box 191831
San Juan, PR 00919
(787)754-6178
Fax: (787)754-6181

Rhode Island

Manchester Humphreys, Inc.
40 Westminster St., Ste. 900
Providence, RI 02903
(401)454-0400
Fax: (401)454-0403

Navis Partners
50 Kennedy Plaza, 12th Fl.
Providence, RI 02903
(401)278-6770
Fax: (401)278-6387
Website: http://www.navispartners.com

South Carolina

Capital Insights, L.L.C.
PO Box 27162
Greenville, SC 29616-2162
(864)242-6832
Fax: (864)242-6755
E-mail: jwarner@capitalinsights.com
Website: http://www.capitalinsights.com

Transamerica Mezzanine Financing
7 N. Laurens St., Ste. 603
Greenville, SC 29601
(864)232-6198
Fax: (864)241-4444

Tennessee

Valley Capital Corp.
Krystal Bldg.
100 W. Martin Luther King Blvd.,
Ste. 212
Chattanooga, TN 37402
(423)265-1557
Fax: (423)265-1588

Coleman Swenson Booth Inc.
237 2nd Ave. S
Franklin, TN 37064-2649
(615)791-9462
Fax: (615)791-9636
Website: http://www.colemanswenson
.com

Capital Services & Resources, Inc.
5159 Wheelis Dr., Ste. 106
Memphis, TN 38117
(901)761-2156
Fax: (907)767-0060

Paradigm Capital Partners LLC
6410 Poplar Ave., Ste. 395
Memphis, TN 38119
(901)682-6060
Fax: (901)328-3061

SSM Ventures
845 Crossover Ln., Ste. 140
Memphis, TN 38117
(901)767-1131
Fax: (901)767-1135
Website: http://www.ssm ventures.com

Capital Across America L.P.
501 Union St., Ste. 201
Nashville, TN 37219
(615)254-1414
Fax: (615)254-1856
Website: http://www.capitalacross
america.com

Equitas L.P.
2000 Glen Echo Rd., Ste. 101
PO Box 158838
Nashville, TN 37215-8838
(615)383-8673
Fax: (615)383-8693

Massey Burch Capital Corp.
One Burton Hills Blvd., Ste. 350
Nashville, TN 37215
(615)665-3221
Fax: (615)665-3240
E-mail: tcalton@masseyburch.com
Website: http://www.masseyburch.com

Nelson Capital Corp.
3401 West End Ave., Ste. 300
Nashville, TN 37203
(615)292-8787
Fax: (615)385-3150

Texas

Phillips-Smith Specialty Retail Group
5080 Spectrum Dr., Ste. 805 W
Addison, TX 75001
(972)387-0725
Fax: (972)458-2560
E-mail: pssrg@aol.com
Website: http://www.phillips-smith.com

Austin Ventures, L.P.
701 Brazos St., Ste. 1400
Austin, TX 78701
(512)485-1900
Fax: (512)476-3952

E-mail: info@ausven.com
Website: http://www.austinventures.com

The Capital Network
3925 West Braker Lane, Ste. 406
Austin, TX 78759-5321
(512)305-0826
Fax: (512)305-0836

Techxas Ventures LLC
5000 Plaza on the Lake
Austin, TX 78746
(512)343-0118
Fax: (512)343-1879
E-mail: bruce@techxas.com
Website: http://www.techxas.com

Alliance Financial of Houston
218 Heather Ln.
Conroe, TX 77385-9013
(936)447-3300
Fax: (936)447-4222

Amerimark Capital Corp.
1111 W. Mockingbird, Ste. 1111
Dallas, TX 75247
(214)638-7878
Fax: (214)638-7612
E-mail: amerimark@amcapital.com
Website: http://www.amcapital.com

AMT Venture Partners / AMT Capital Ltd.
5220 Spring Valley Rd., Ste. 600
Dallas, TX 75240
(214)905-9757
Fax: (214)905-9761
Website: http://www.amtcapital.com

Arkoma Venture Partners
5950 Berkshire Lane, Ste. 1400
Dallas, TX 75225
(214)739-3515
Fax: (214)739-3572
E-mail: joelf@arkomavp.com

Capital Southwest Corp.
12900 Preston Rd., Ste. 700
Dallas, TX 75230
(972)233-8242
Fax: (972)233-7362
Website: http://www.capitalsouthwest
.com

Dali, Hook Partners
One Lincoln Center, Ste. 1550
5400 LBJ Freeway
Dallas, TX 75240
(972)991-5457
Fax: (972)991-5458
E-mail: dhook@hookpartners.com
Website: http://www.hookpartners.com

HO2 Partners
Two Galleria Tower
13455 Noel Rd., Ste. 1670
Dallas, TX 75240
(972)702-1144
Fax: (972)702-8234
Website: http://www.ho2.com

Interwest Partners (Dallas)
2 Galleria Tower
13455 Noel Rd., Ste. 1670
Dallas, TX 75240
(972)392-7279
Fax: (972)490-6348
Website: http://www.interwest.com

Kahala Investments, Inc.
8214 Westchester Dr., Ste. 715
Dallas, TX 75225
(214)987-0077
Fax: (214)987-2332

MESBIC Ventures Holding Co.
2435 North Central Expressway, Ste. 200
Dallas, TX 75080
(972)991-1597
Fax: (972)991-4770
Website: http://www.mvhc.com

North Texas MESBIC, Inc.
9500 Forest Lane, Ste. 430
Dallas, TX 75243
(214)221-3565
Fax: (214)221-3566

Richard Jaffe & Company, Inc,
7318 Royal Cir.
Dallas, TX 75230
(214)265-9397
Fax: (214)739-1845

Sevin Rosen Management Co.
13455 Noel Rd., Ste. 1670
Dallas, TX 75240
(972)702-1100
Fax: (972)702-1103
E-mail: info@srfunds.com
Website: http://www.srfunds.com

Stratford Capital Partners, L.P.
300 Crescent Ct., Ste. 500
Dallas, TX 75201
(214)740-7377
Fax: (214)720-7393
E-mail: stratcap@hmtf.com

Sunwestern Investment Group
12221 Merit Dr., Ste. 935
Dallas, TX 75251
(972)239-5650
Fax: (972)701-0024

Wingate Partners
750 N. St. Paul St., Ste. 1200
Dallas, TX 75201
(214)720-1313
Fax: (214)871-8799

Buena Venture Associates
201 Main St., 32nd Fl.
Fort Worth, TX 76102
(817)339-7400
Fax: (817)390-8408
Website: http://www.buenaventure.com

The Catalyst Group
3 Riverway, Ste. 770
Houston, TX 77056
(713)623-8133
Fax: (713)623-0473
E-mail: herman@thecatalystgroup.net
Website: http://www.thecatalyst
group.net

Cureton & Co., Inc.
1100 Louisiana, Ste. 3250
Houston, TX 77002
(713)658-9806
Fax: (713)658-0476

Davis, Tuttle Venture Partners (Dallas)
8 Greenway Plaza, Ste. 1020
Houston, TX 77046
(713)993-0440
Fax: (713)621-2297
Website: http://www.davistuttle.com

Houston Partners
401 Louisiana, 8th Fl.
Houston, TX 77002
(713)222-8600
Fax: (713)222-8932

Southwest Venture Group
10878 Westheimer, Ste. 178
Houston, TX 77042
(713)827-8947
(713)461-1470

AM Fund
4600 Post Oak Place, Ste. 100
Houston, TX 77027
(713)627-9111
Fax: (713)627-9119

Ventex Management, Inc.
3417 Milam St.
Houston, TX 77002-9531
(713)659-7870
Fax: (713)659-7855

MBA Venture Group
1004 Olde Town Rd., Ste. 102
Irving, TX 75061
(972)986-6703

First Capital Group Management Co.
750 East Mulberry St., Ste. 305
PO Box 15616
San Antonio, TX 78212
(210)736-4233
Fax: (210)736-5449

The Southwest Venture Partnerships
16414 San Pedro, Ste. 345
San Antonio, TX 78232
(210)402-1200
Fax: (210)402-1221
E-mail: swvp@aol.com

Medtech International Inc.
1742 Carriageway
Sugarland, TX 77478
(713)980-8474
Fax: (713)980-6343

Utah

First Security Business Investment Corp.
15 East 100 South, Ste. 100
Salt Lake City, UT 84111
(801)246-5737
Fax: (801)246-5740

Utah Ventures II, L.P.
423 Wakara Way, Ste. 206
Salt Lake City, UT 84108
(801)583-5922
Fax: (801)583-4105
Website: http://www.uven.com

Wasatch Venture Corp.
1 S. Main St., Ste. 1400
Salt Lake City, UT 84133
(801)524-8939
Fax: (801)524-8941
E-mail: mail@wasatchvc.com

Vermont

North Atlantic Capital Corp.
76 Saint Paul St., Ste. 600
Burlington, VT 05401
(802)658-7820
Fax: (802)658-5757
Website: http://www.northatlantic
capital.com

Green Mountain Advisors Inc.
PO Box 1230
Quechee, VT 05059
(802)296-7800
Fax: (802)296-6012
Website: http://www.gmtcap.com

Virginia

Oxford Financial Services Corp.
Alexandria, VA 22314
(703)519-4900
Fax: (703)519-4910
E-mail: oxford133@aol.com

Continental SBIC
4141 N. Henderson Rd.
Arlington, VA 22203
(703)527-5200
Fax: (703)527-3700

Novak Biddle Venture Partners
1750 Tysons Blvd., Ste. 1190
McLean, VA 22102
(703)847-3770
Fax: (703)847-3771
E-mail: roger@novakbiddle.com
Website: http://www.novakbiddle.com

Spacevest
11911 Freedom Dr., Ste. 500
Reston, VA 20190
(703)904-9800
Fax: (703)904-0571
E-mail: spacevest@spacevest.com
Website: http://www.spacevest.com

Virginia Capital
1801 Libbie Ave., Ste. 201
Richmond, VA 23226
(804)648-4802
Fax: (804)648-4809
E-mail: webmaster@vacapital.com
Website: http://www.vacapital.com

Calvert Social Venture Partners
402 Maple Ave. W
Vienna, VA 22180
(703)255-4930
Fax: (703)255-4931
E-mail: calven2000@aol.com

Fairfax Partners
8000 Towers Crescent Dr., Ste. 940
Vienna, VA 22182
(703)847-9486
Fax: (703)847-0911

Global Internet Ventures
8150 Leesburg Pike, Ste. 1210
Vienna, VA 22182
(703)442-3300
Fax: (703)442-3388
Website: http://www.givinc.com

Walnut Capital Corp. (Vienna)
8000 Towers Crescent Dr., Ste. 1070
Vienna, VA 22182
(703)448-3771
Fax: (703)448-7751

Washington

Encompass Ventures
777 108th Ave. NE, Ste. 2300
Bellevue, WA 98004
(425)486-3900
Fax: (425)486-3901
E-mail: info@evpartners.com
Website: http://www.encompass
ventures.com

Fluke Venture Partners
11400 SE Sixth St., Ste. 230
Bellevue, WA 98004
(425)453-4590
Fax: (425)453-4675
E-mail: gabelein@flukeventures.com
Website: http://www.flukeventures.com

**Pacific Northwest Partners
SBIC, L.P.**
15352 SE 53rd St.
Bellevue, WA 98006
(425)455-9967
Fax: (425)455-9404

Materia Venture Associates, L.P.
3435 Carillon Pointe
Kirkland, WA 98033-7354
(425)822-4100
Fax: (425)827-4086

OVP Venture Partners (Kirkland)
2420 Carillon Pt.
Kirkland, WA 98033
(425)889-9192
Fax: (425)889-0152
E-mail: info@ovp.com
Website: http://www.ovp.com

Digital Partners
999 3rd Ave., Ste. 1610
Seattle, WA 98104
(206)405-3607
Fax: (206)405-3617
Website: http://www.digitalpartners.com

Frazier & Company
601 Union St., Ste. 3300
Seattle, WA 98101
(206)621-7200
Fax: (206)621-1848
E-mail: jon@frazierco.com

Kirlan Venture Capital, Inc.
221 First Ave. W, Ste. 108
Seattle, WA 98119-4223
(206)281-8610
Fax: (206)285-3451
Website: http://www.kirlanventure.com

Phoenix Partners
1000 2nd Ave., Ste. 3600
Seattle, WA 98104
(206)624-8968
Fax: (206)624-1907

Voyager Capital
800 5th St., Ste. 4100
Seattle, WA 98103
(206)470-1180
Fax: (206)470-1185
E-mail: info@voyagercap.com
Website: http://www.voyagercap.com

Northwest Venture Associates
221 N. Wall St., Ste. 628
Spokane, WA 99201
(509)747-0728
Fax: (509)747-0758
Website: http://www.nwva.com

Wisconsin

**Venture Investors
Management, L.L.C.**
University Research Park
505 S. Rosa Rd.
Madison, WI 53719
(608)441-2700
Fax: (608)441-2727
E-mail: roger@ventureinvestors.com
Website: http://www.ventureinvesters
.com

Capital Investments, Inc.
1009 West Glen Oaks Lane, Ste. 103
Mequon, WI 53092
(414)241-0303
Fax: (414)241-8451
Website: http://www.capitalinvestment
sinc.com

Future Value Venture, Inc.
2745 N. Martin Luther King Dr., Ste. 204
Milwaukee, WI 53212-2300
(414)264-2252
Fax: (414)264-2253
E-mail: fvvventures@aol.com
William Beckett, President

Lubar and Co., Inc.
700 N. Water St., Ste. 1200
Milwaukee, WI 53202
(414)291-9000
Fax: (414)291-9061

GCI
20875 Crossroads Cir., Ste. 100
Waukesha, WI 53186
(262)798-5080
Fax: (262)798-5087

Glossary of Small Business Terms

Absolute liability
Liability that is incurred due to product defects or negligent actions. Manufacturers or retail establishments are held responsible, even though the defect or action may not have been intentional or negligent.

ACE
See Active Corps of Executives

Accident and health benefits
Benefits offered to employees and their families in order to offset the costs associated with accidental death, accidental injury, or sickness.

Account statement
A record of transactions, including payments, new debt, and deposits, incurred during a defined period of time.

Accounting system
System capturing the costs of all employees and/or machinery included in business expenses.

Accounts payable
See Trade credit

Accounts receivable
Unpaid accounts which arise from unsettled claims and transactions from the sale of a company's products or services to its customers.

Active Corps of Executives (ACE)
A group of volunteers for a management assistance program of the U.S. Small Business Administration; volunteers provide one-on-one counseling and teach workshops and seminars for small firms.

ADA
See Americans with Disabilities Act

Adaptation
The process whereby an invention is modified to meet the needs of users.

Adaptive engineering
The process whereby an invention is modified to meet the manufacturing and commercial requirements of a targeted market.

Adverse selection
The tendency for higher-risk individuals to purchase health care and more comprehensive plans, resulting in increased costs.

Advertising
A marketing tool used to capture public attention and influence purchasing decisions for a product or service. Utilizes various forms of media to generate consumer response, such as flyers, magazines, newspapers, radio, and television.

Age discrimination
The denial of the rights and privileges of employment based solely on the age of an individual.

Agency costs
Costs incurred to insure that the lender or investor maintains control over assets while allowing the borrower or entrepreneur to use them. Monitoring and information costs are the two major types of agency costs.

Agribusiness
The production and sale of commodities and products from the commercial farming industry.

Americans with Disabilities Act (ADA)
Law designed to ensure equal access and opportunity to handicapped persons.

Annual report
Yearly financial report prepared by a business that adheres to the requirements set forth by the Securities and Exchange Commission (SEC).

Antitrust immunity
Exemption from prosecution under antitrust laws. In the transportation industry, firms with antitrust immunity are permitted under certain conditions to set schedules and sometimes prices for the public benefit.

Applied research
Scientific study targeted for use in a product or process.

Assets
Anything of value owned by a company.

Audit
The verification of accounting records and business procedures conducted by an outside accounting service.

Average cost
Total production costs divided by the quantity produced.

Balance Sheet
A financial statement listing the total assets and liabilities of a company at a given time.

Bankruptcy
The condition in which a business cannot meet its debt obligations and petitions a federal district court either for reorganization of its debts (Chapter 11) or for liquidation of its assets (Chapter 7).

Basket clause
A provision specifying the amount of public pension funds that may be placed in investments not included on a state's legal list (see separate citation).

BDC
See Business development corporation

Benefit
Various services, such as health care, flextime, day care, insurance, and vacation, offered to employees as part of a hiring package. Typically subsidized in whole or in part by the business.

BIDCO
See Business and industrial development company

Billing cycle
A system designed to evenly distribute customer billing throughout the month, preventing clerical backlogs.

Blue chip security
A low-risk, low-yield security representing an interest in a very stable company.

Blue sky laws
A general term that denotes various states' laws regulating securities.

Bond
A written instrument executed by a bidder or contractor (the principal) and a second party (the surety or sureties) to assure fulfillment of the principal's obligations to a third party (the obligee or government) identified in the bond. If the principal's obligations are not met, the bond assures payment to the extent stipulated of any loss sustained by the obligee.

Bonding requirements
Terms contained in a bond (see separate citation).

Bonus
An amount of money paid to an employee as a reward for achieving certain business goals or objectives.

Brainstorming
A group session where employees contribute their ideas for solving a problem or meeting a company objective without fear of retribution or ridicule.

Brand name
The part of a brand, trademark, or service mark that can be spoken. It can be a word, letter, or group of words or letters.

Bridge financing
A short-term loan made in expectation of intermediateterm or long-term financing. Can be used when a company plans to go public in the near future.

Broker
One who matches resources available for innovation with those who need them.

Budget
An estimate of the spending necessary to complete a project or offer a service in comparison to cash-on-hand and expected earnings for the coming year, with an emphasis on cost control.

Business and industrial development company (BIDCO)
A private, for-profit financing corporation chartered by the state to provide both equity and long-term debt capital to small business owners (see separate citations for equity and debt capital).

Business birth
The formation of a new establishment or enterprise. The appearance of a new establishment or enterprise in the Small Business Data Base (see separate citation).

Business conditions
Outside factors that can affect the financial performance of a business.

Business contractions
The number of establishments that have decreased in employment during a specified time.

Business cycle
A period of economic recession and recovery. These cycles vary in duration.

Business death
The voluntary or involuntary closure of a firm or establishment. The disappearance of an establishment or enterprise from the Small Business Data Base (see separate citation).

Business development corporation (BDC)
A business financing agency, usually composed of the financial institutions in an area or state, organized to assist in financing businesses unable to obtain assistance through normal channels; the risk is spread among various members of the business development corporation, and interest rates may vary somewhat from those charged by member institutions. A venture capital firm in which shares of ownership are publicly held and to which the Investment Act of 1940 applies.

Business dissolution
For enumeration purposes, the absence of a business that was present in the prior time period from any current record.

Business entry
See Business birth

Business ethics
Moral values and principles espoused by members of the business community as a guide to fair and honest business practices.

Business exit
See Business death

Business expansions
The number of establishments that added employees during a specified time.

Business failure
Closure of a business causing a loss to at least one creditor.

Business format franchising
The purchase of the name, trademark, and an ongoing business plan of the parent corporation or franchisor by the franchisee.

Business license
A legal authorization issued by municipal and state governments and required for business operations.

Business name
Enterprises must register their business names with local governments usually on a "doing business as" (DBA) form. (This name is sometimes referred to as a "fictional name.") The procedure is part of the business licensing process and prevents any other business from using that same name for a similar business in the same locality.

Business norms
See Financial ratios

Business permit
See Business license

Business plan
A document that spells out a company's expected course of action for a specified period, usually including a detailed listing and analysis of risks and uncertainties. For the small business, it should examine the proposed products, the market, the industry, the management policies, the marketing policies, production needs, and financial needs. Frequently, it is used as a prospectus for potential investors and lenders.

Business proposal
See Business plan

Business service firm
An establishment primarily engaged in rendering services to other business organizations on a fee or contract basis.

Business start
For enumeration purposes, a business with a name or similar designation that did not exist in a prior time period.

Cafeteria plan
See Flexible benefit plan

Capacity
Level of a firm's, industry's, or nation's output corresponding to full practical utilization of available resources.

Capital
Assets less liabilities, representing the ownership interest in a business. A stock of accumulated goods, especially at a specified time and in contrast to income received during a specified time period. Accumulated goods devoted to production. Accumulated possessions calculated to bring income.

Capital expenditure
Expenses incurred by a business for improvements that will depreciate over time.

Capital gain
The monetary difference between the purchase price and the selling price of capital. Capital gains are taxed at a rate of 28% by the federal government.

Capital intensity
The relative importance of capital in the production process, usually expressed as the ratio of capital to labor but also sometimes as the ratio of capital to output.

Capital resource
The equipment, facilities and labor used to create products and services.

Catastrophic care
Medical and other services for acute and long-term illnesses that cost more than insurance coverage limits or that cost the amount most families may be expected to pay with their own resources.

CDC
See Certified development corporation

Certified development corporation (CDC)
A local area or statewide corporation or authority (for profit or nonprofit) that packages U.S. Small Business Administration (SBA), bank, state, and/or private money into financial assistance for existing business capital improvements. The SBA holds the second lien on its maximum share of 40 percent involvement. Each state has at least one certified development corporation. This program is called the SBA 504 Program.

Certified lenders
Banks that participate in the SBA guaranteed loan program (see separate citation). Such banks must have a good track record with the U.S. Small Business Administration (SBA) and must agree to certain conditions set forth by the agency. In return, the SBA agrees to process any guaranteed loan application within three business days.

Channel of distribution
The means used to transport merchandise from the manufacturer to the consumer.

Chapter 7 of the 1978 Bankruptcy Act
Provides for a court-appointed trustee who is responsible for liquidating a company's assets in order to settle outstanding debts.

Chapter 11 of the 1978 Bankruptcy Act
Allows the business owners to retain control of the company while working with their creditors to reorganize their finances and establish better business practices to prevent liquidation of assets.

Closely held corporation
A corporation in which the shares are held by a few persons, usually officers, employees, or others close to the management; these shares are rarely offered to the public.

Code of Federal Regulations
Codification of general and permanent rules of the federal government published in the Federal Register.

Code sharing
See Computer code sharing

Coinsurance
Upon meeting the deductible payment, health insurance participants may be required to make additional health care cost-sharing payments. Coinsurance is a payment of a fixed percentage of the cost of each service; copayment is usually a fixed amount to be paid with each service.

Collateral
Securities, evidence of deposit, or other property pledged by a borrower to secure repayment of a loan.

Collective ratemaking
The establishment of uniform charges for services by a group of businesses in the same industry.

Commercial insurance plan
See Underwriting

Commercial loans
Short-term renewable loans used to finance specific capital needs of a business.

Commercialization
The final stage of the innovation process, including production and distribution.

Common stock
The most frequently used instrument for purchasing ownership in private or public companies. Common stock generally carries the right to vote on certain corporate actions and may pay dividends, although it rarely does in venture investments. In liquidation, common stockholders are the last to share in the proceeds from the sale of a corporation's assets; bondholders and preferred shareholders have priority. Common stock is often used in firstround start-up financing.

Community development corporation
A corporation established to develop economic programs for a community and, in most cases, to provide financial support for such development.

Competitor
A business whose product or service is marketed for the same purpose/use and to the same consumer group as the product or service of another.

Consignment
A merchandising agreement, usually referring to secondhand shops, where the dealer pays the owner of an item a percentage of the profit when the item is sold.

Consortium
A coalition of organizations such as banks and corporations for ventures requiring large capital resources.

Consultant
An individual that is paid by a business to provide advice and expertise in a particular area.

Consumer price index
A measure of the fluctuation in prices between two points in time.

Consumer research
Research conducted by a business to obtain information about existing or potential consumer markets.

Continuation coverage
Health coverage offered for a specified period of time to employees who leave their jobs and to their widows, divorced spouses, or dependents.

Contractions
See Business contractions

Convertible preferred stock
A class of stock that pays a reasonable dividend and is convertible into common stock (see separate citation). Generally the convertible feature may only be exercised after being held for a stated period of time. This arrangement is usually considered second-round financing when a company needs equity to maintain its cash flow.

Convertible securities
A feature of certain bonds, debentures, or preferred stocks that allows them to be exchanged by the owner for another class of securities at a future date and in accordance with any other terms of the issue.

Copayment
See Coinsurance

Copyright
A legal form of protection available to creators and authors to safeguard their works from unlawful use or

claim of ownership by others. Copyrights may be acquired for works of art, sculpture, music, and published or unpublished manuscripts. All copyrights should be registered at the Copyright Office of the Library of Congress.

Corporate financial ratios
The relationship between key figures found in a company's financial statement expressed as a numeric value. Used to evaluate risk and company performance. Also known as Financial averages, Operating ratios, and Business ratios.

Corporation
A legal entity, chartered by a state or the federal government, recognized as a separate entity having its own rights, privileges, and liabilities distinct from those of its members.

Cost containment
Actions taken by employers and insurers to curtail rising health care costs; for example, increasing employee cost sharing (see separate citation), requiring second opinions, or preadmission screening.

Cost sharing
The requirement that health care consumers contribute to their own medical care costs through deductibles and coinsurance (see separate citations). Cost sharing does not include the amounts paid in premiums. It is used to control utilization of services; for example, requiring a fixed amount to be paid with each health care service.

Cottage industry
Businesses based in the home in which the family members are the labor force and family-owned equipment is used to process the goods.

Credit Rating
A letter or number calculated by an organization (such as Dun & Bradstreet) to represent the ability and disposition of a business to meet its financial obligations.

Customer service
Various techniques used to ensure the satisfaction of a customer.

Cyclical peak
The upper turning point in a business cycle.

Cyclical trough
The lower turning point in a business cycle.

DBA (Doing business as)
See Business name

Death
See Business death

Debenture
A certificate given as acknowledgment of a debt (see separate citation) secured by the general credit of the issuing corporation. A bond, usually without security, issued by a corporation and sometimes convertible to common stock.

Debt
Something owed by one person to another. Financing in which a company receives capital that must be repaid; no ownership is transferred.

Debt capital
Business financing that normally requires periodic interest payments and repayment of the principal within a specified time.

Debt financing
See Debt capital

Debt securities
Loans such as bonds and notes that provide a specified rate of return for a specified period of time.

Deductible
A set amount that an individual must pay before any benefits are received.

Demand shock absorbers
A term used to describe the role that some small firms play by expanding their output levels to accommodate a transient surge in demand.

Demographics
Statistics on various markets, including age, income, and education, used to target specific products or services to appropriate consumer groups.

Demonstration
Showing that a product or process has been modified sufficiently to meet the needs of users.

Deregulation
The lifting of government restrictions; for example, the lifting of government restrictions on the entry of new businesses, the expansion of services, and the setting of prices in particular industries.

Disaster loans
Various types of physical and economic assistance available to individuals and businesses through the U.S. Small Business Administration (SBA). This is the only SBA loan program available for residential purposes.

Discrimination
The denial of the rights and privileges of employment based on factors such as age, race, religion, or gender.

Diseconomies of scale
The condition in which the costs of production increase faster than the volume of production.

Dissolution
See Business dissolution

Distribution
Delivering a product or process to the user.

Distributor
One who delivers merchandise to the user.

Diversified company
A company whose products and services are used by several different markets.

Doing business as (DBA)
See Business name

Dow Jones
An information services company that publishes the Wall Street Journal and other sources of financial information.

Dow Jones Industrial Average
An indicator of stock market performance.

Earned income
A tax term that refers to wages and salaries earned by the recipient, as opposed to monies earned through interest and dividends.

Economic efficiency
The use of productive resources to the fullest practical extent in the provision of the set of goods and services that is most preferred by purchasers in the economy.

Economic indicators
Statistics used to express the state of the economy. These include the length of the average work week, the rate of unemployment, and stock prices.

Economically disadvantaged
See Socially and economically disadvantaged

Economies of scale
See Scale economies

EEOC
See Equal Employment Opportunity Commission

8(a) Program
A program authorized by the Small Business Act that directs federal contracts to small businesses owned and operated by socially and economically disadvantaged individuals.

Electronic mail (e-mail)
The electronic transmission of mail via phone lines.

E-mail
See Electronic mail

Employee leasing
A contract by which employers arrange to have their workers hired by a leasing company and then leased back to them for a management fee. The leasing company typically assumes the administrative burden of payroll and provides a benefit package to the workers.

Employee tenure
The length of time an employee works for a particular employer.

Employer identification number
The business equivalent of a social security number. Assigned by the U.S. Internal Revenue Service.

Enterprise
An aggregation of all establishments owned by a parent company. An enterprise may consist of a single, independent establishment or include subsidiaries and other branches under the same ownership and control.

Enterprise zone
A designated area, usually found in inner cities and other areas with significant unemployment, where businesses receive tax credits and other incentives to entice them to establish operations there.

Entrepreneur
A person who takes the risk of organizing and operating a new business venture.

Entry
See Business entry

Equal Employment Opportunity Commission (EEOC)
A federal agency that ensures nondiscrimination in the hiring and firing practices of a business.

Equal opportunity employer
An employer who adheres to the standards set by the Equal Employment Opportunity Commission (see separate citation).

Equity
The ownership interest. Financing in which partial or total ownership of a company is surrendered in exchange for capital. An investor's financial return comes from dividend payments and from growth in the net worth of the business.

Equity capital
See Equity; Equity midrisk venture capital

Equity financing
See Equity; Equity midrisk venture capital

Equity midrisk venture capital
An unsecured investment in a company. Usually a purchase of ownership interest in a company that occurs in the later stages of a company's development.

Equity partnership
A limited partnership arrangement for providing start-up and seed capital to businesses.

Equity securities
See Equity

Equity-type
Debt financing subordinated to conventional debt.

Establishment
A single-location business unit that may be independent (a single-establishment enterprise) or owned by a parent enterprise.

Establishment and Enterprise Microdata File
See U.S. Establishment and Enterprise Microdata File

Establishment birth
See Business birth

Establishment Longitudinal Microdata File
See U.S. Establishment Longitudinal Microdata File

Ethics
See Business ethics

Evaluation
Determining the potential success of translating an invention into a product or process.

Exit
See Business exit

Experience rating
See Underwriting

Export
A product sold outside of the country.

Export license
A general or specific license granted by the U.S. Department of Commerce required of anyone wishing to export goods. Some restricted articles need approval from the U.S. Departments of State, Defense, or Energy.

Failure
See Business failure

Fair share agreement
An agreement reached between a franchisor and a minority business organization to extend business ownership to minorities by either reducing the amount of capital required or by setting aside certain marketing areas for minority business owners.

Feasibility study
A study to determine the likelihood that a proposed product or development will fulfill the objectives of a particular investor.

Federal Trade Commission (FTC)
Federal agency that promotes free enterprise and competition within the U.S.

Federal Trade Mark Act of 1946
See Lanham Act

Fictional name
See Business name

Fiduciary
An individual or group that hold assets in trust for a beneficiary.

Financial analysis
The techniques used to determine money needs in a business. Techniques include ratio analysis, calculation of return on investment, guides for measuring profitability, and break-even analysis to determine ultimate success.

Financial intermediary
A financial institution that acts as the intermediary between borrowers and lenders. Banks, savings and loan associations, finance companies, and venture capital companies are major financial intermediaries in the United States.

Financial ratios
See Corporate financial ratios; Industry financial ratios

Financial statement
A written record of business finances, including balance sheets and profit and loss statements.

Financing
See First-stage financing; Second-stage financing; Thirdstage financing

First-stage financing
Financing provided to companies that have expended their initial capital, and require funds to start full-scale manufacturing and sales. Also known as First-round financing.

Fiscal year
Any twelve-month period used by businesses for accounting purposes.

504 Program
See Certified development corporation

Flexible benefit plan
A plan that offers a choice among cash and/or qualified benefits such as group term life insurance,

accident and health insurance, group legal services, dependent care assistance, and vacations.

FOB
See Free on board

Format franchising
See Business format franchising; Franchising

401(k) plan
A financial plan where employees contribute a percentage of their earnings to a fund that is invested in stocks, bonds, or money markets for the purpose of saving money for retirement.

Four Ps
Marketing terms referring to Product, Price, Place, and Promotion.

Franchising
A form of licensing by which the owner-the franchisor- distributes or markets a product, method, or service through affiliated dealers called franchisees. The product, method, or service being marketed is identified by a brand name, and the franchisor maintains control over the marketing methods employed. The franchisee is often given exclusive access to a defined geographic area.

Free on board (FOB)
A pricing term indicating that the quoted price includes the cost of loading goods into transport vessels at a specified place.

Frictional unemployment
See Unemployment

FTC
See Federal Trade Commission

Fulfillment
The systems necessary for accurate delivery of an ordered item, including subscriptions and direct marketing.

Full-time workers
Generally, those who work a regular schedule of more than 35 hours per week.

Garment registration number
A number that must appear on every garment sold in the U.S. to indicate the manufacturer of the garment,

which may or may not be the same as the label under which the garment is sold. The U.S. Federal Trade Commission assigns and regulates garment registration numbers.

Gatekeeper
A key contact point for entry into a network.

GDP
See Gross domestic product

General obligation bond
A municipal bond secured by the taxing power of the municipality. The Tax Reform Act of 1986 limits the purposes for which such bonds may be issued and establishes volume limits on the extent of their issuance.

GNP
See Gross national product

Good Housekeeping Seal
Seal appearing on products that signifies the fulfillment of the standards set by the Good Housekeeping Institute to protect consumer interests.

Goods sector
All businesses producing tangible goods, including agriculture, mining, construction, and manufacturing businesses.

GPO
See Gross product originating

Gross domestic product (GDP)
The part of the nation's gross national product (see separate citation) generated by private business using resources from within the country.

Gross national product (GNP)
The most comprehensive single measure of aggregate economic output. Represents the market value of the total output of goods and services produced by a nation's economy.

Gross product originating (GPO)
A measure of business output estimated from the income or production side using employee compensation, profit income, net interest, capital consumption, and indirect business taxes.

HAL
See Handicapped assistance loan program

Handicapped assistance loan program (HAL)
Low-interest direct loan program through the U.S. Small Business Administration (SBA) for handicapped persons. The SBA requires that these persons demonstrate that their disability is such that it is impossible for them to secure employment, thus making it necessary to go into their own business to make a living.

Health maintenance organization (HMO)
Organization of physicians and other health care professionals that provides health services to subscribers and their dependents on a prepaid basis.

Health provider
An individual or institution that gives medical care. Under Medicare, an institutional provider is a hospital, skilled nursing facility, home health agency, or provider of certain physical therapy services.

Hispanic
A person of Cuban, Mexican, Puerto Rican, Latin American (Central or South American), European Spanish, or other Spanish-speaking origin or ancestry.

HMO
See Health maintenance organization

Home-based business
A business with an operating address that is also a residential address (usually the residential address of the proprietor).

Hub-and-spoke system
A system in which flights of an airline from many different cities (the spokes) converge at a single airport (the hub). After allowing passengers sufficient time to make connections, planes then depart for different cities.

Human Resources Management
A business program designed to oversee recruiting, pay, benefits, and other issues related to the company's work force, including planning to determine the optimal use of labor to increase production, thereby increasing profit.

Idea
An original concept for a new product or process.

Import
Products produced outside the country in which they are consumed.

Income
Money or its equivalent, earned or accrued, resulting from the sale of goods and services.

Income statement
A financial statement that lists the profits and losses of a company at a given time.

Incorporation
The filing of a certificate of incorporation with a state's secretary of state, thereby limiting the business owner's liability.

Incubator
A facility designed to encourage entrepreneurship and minimize obstacles to new business formation and growth, particularly for high-technology firms, by housing a number of fledgling enterprises that share an array of services, such as meeting areas, secretarial services, accounting, research library, on-site financial and management counseling, and word processing facilities.

Independent contractor
An individual considered self-employed (see separate citation) and responsible for paying Social Security taxes and income taxes on earnings.

Indirect health coverage
Health insurance obtained through another individual's health care plan; for example, a spouse's employersponsored plan.

Industrial development authority
The financial arm of a state or other political subdivision established for the purpose of financing economic development in an area, usually through loans to nonprofit organizations, which in turn provide facilities for manufacturing and other industrial operations.

Industry financial ratios
Corporate financial ratios averaged for a specified industry. These are used for comparison purposes and reveal industry trends and identify differences between the performance of a specific company and the performance of its industry. Also known as Industrial averages, Industry ratios, Financial averages, and Business or Industrial norms.

Inflation
Increases in volume of currency and credit, generally resulting in a sharp and continuing rise in price levels.

Informal capital
Financing from informal, unorganized sources; includes informal debt capital such as trade credit or loans from friends and relatives and equity capital from informal investors.

Initial public offering (IPO)
A corporation's first offering of stock to the public.

Innovation
The introduction of a new idea into the marketplace in the form of a new product or service or an improvement in organization or process.

Intellectual property
Any idea or work that can be considered proprietary in nature and is thus protected from infringement by others.

Internal capital
Debt or equity financing obtained from the owner or through retained business earnings.

Internet
A government-designed computer network that contains large amounts of information and is accessible through various vendors for a fee.

Intrapreneurship
The state of employing entrepreneurial principles to nonentrepreneurial situations.

Invention
The tangible form of a technological idea, which could include a laboratory prototype, drawings, formulas, etc.

IPO
See Initial public offering

Job description
The duties and responsibilities required in a particular position.

Job tenure
A period of time during which an individual is continuously employed in the same job.

Joint marketing agreements
Agreements between regional and major airlines, often involving the coordination of flight schedules, fares, and baggage transfer. These agreements help regional carriers operate at lower cost.

Joint venture
Venture in which two or more people combine efforts in a particular business enterprise, usually a single transaction or a limited activity, and agree to share the profits and losses jointly or in proportion to their contributions.

Keogh plan
Designed for self-employed persons and unincorporated businesses as a tax-deferred pension account.

Labor force
Civilians considered eligible for employment who are also willing and able to work.

Labor force participation rate
The civilian labor force as a percentage of the civilian population.

Labor intensity
The relative importance of labor in the production process, usually measured as the capital-labor ratio; i.e., the ratio of units of capital (typically, dollars of tangible assets) to the number of employees. The higher the capital-labor ratio exhibited by a firm or industry, the lower the capital intensity of that firm or industry is said to be.

Labor surplus area
An area in which there exists a high unemployment rate. In procurement (see separate citation), extra points are given to firms in counties that are designated a labor surplus area; this information is requested on procurement bid sheets.

Labor union
An organization of similarly-skilled workers who collectively bargain with management over the conditions of employment.

Laboratory prototype
See Prototype

LAN
See Local Area Network

Lanham Act
Refers to the Federal Trade Mark Act of 1946. Protects registered trademarks, trade names, and other service marks used in commerce.

Large business-dominated industry
Industry in which a minimum of 60 percent of employment or sales is in firms with more than 500 workers.

LBO
See Leveraged buy-out

Leader pricing
A reduction in the price of a good or service in order to generate more sales of that good or service.

Legal list
A list of securities selected by a state in which certain institutions and fiduciaries (such as pension funds, insurance companies, and banks) may invest. Securities not on the list are not eligible for investment. Legal lists typically restrict investments to high quality securities meeting certain specifications. Generally, investment is limited to U.S. securities and investment-grade blue chip securities (see separate citation).

Leveraged buy-out (LBO)
The purchase of a business or a division of a corporation through a highly leveraged financing package.

Liability
An obligation or duty to perform a service or an act. Also defined as money owed.

License
A legal agreement granting to another the right to use a technological innovation.

Limited Liability Company
A hybrid type of legal structure that provides the limited liability features of a corporation and the tax efficiencies and operational flexibility of a partnership. Depending on the state, the members can consist of a single individual (one owner), two or more individuals, corporations or other LLCs.

Limited liability partnerships
A business organization that allows limited partners to enjoy limited personal liability while general partners have unlimited personal liability

Liquidity
The ability to convert a security into cash promptly.

Loans
See Commercial loans; Disaster loans; SBA direct loans; SBA guaranteed loans; SBA special lending institution categories Local Area Network (LAN) Computer networks contained within a single building or small area; used to facilitate the sharing of information.

Local development corporation
An organization, usually made up of local citizens of a community, designed to improve the economy of the area by inducing business and industry to locate and expand there. A local development corporation establishes a capability to finance local growth.

Long-haul rates
Rates charged by a transporter in which the distance traveled is more than 800 miles.

Long-term debt
An obligation that matures in a period that exceeds five years.

Low-grade bond
A corporate bond that is rated below investment grade by the major rating agencies (Standard and Poor's, Moody's).

Macro-efficiency
Efficiency as it pertains to the operation of markets and market systems.

Managed care
A cost-effective health care program initiated by employers whereby low-cost health care is made available to the employees in return for exclusive patronage to program doctors.

Management Assistance Programs
See SBA Management Assistance Programs

Management and technical assistance
A term used by many programs to mean business (as opposed to technological) assistance.

Mandated benefits
Specific treatments, providers, or individuals required by law to be included in commercial health plans.

Market evaluation
The use of market information to determine the sales potential of a specific product or process.

Market failure
The situation in which the workings of a competitive market do not produce the best results from the point of view of the entire society.

Market information
Data of any type that can be used for market evaluation, which could include demographic data, technology forecasting, regulatory changes, etc.

Market research
A systematic collection, analysis, and reporting of data about the market and its preferences, opinions, trends, and plans; used for corporate decision-making.

Market share
In a particular market, the percentage of sales of a specific product.

Marketing
Promotion of goods or services through various media.

Master Establishment List (MEL)
A list of firms in the United States developed by the U.S. Small Business Administration; firms can be selected by industry, region, state, standard metropolitan statistical area (see separate citation), county, and zip code.

Maturity
The date upon which the principal or stated value of a bond or other indebtedness becomes due and payable.

Medicaid (Title XIX)
A federally aided, state-operated and administered program that provides medical benefits for certain low income persons in need of health and medical care who are eligible for one of the government's welfare cash payment programs, including the aged, the blind, the disabled, and members of families with dependent children where one parent is absent, incapacitated, or unemployed.

Medicare (Title XVIII)
A nationwide health insurance program for disabled and aged persons. Health insurance is available to insured persons without regard to income. Monies from payroll taxes cover hospital insurance and monies from general revenues and beneficiary premiums pay for supplementary medical insurance.

MEL
See Master Establishment List

Merchant Status
The relationship between a company and a bank or credit card company allowing the company to accept credit card payments

MESBIC
See Minority enterprise small business investment corporation

MET
See Multiple employer trust

Metropolitan statistical area (MSA)
A means used by the government to define large population centers that may transverse different governmental jurisdictions. For example, the Washington, D.C. MSA includes the District of Columbia and contiguous parts of Maryland and Virginia because all of these geopolitical areas comprise one population and economic operating unit.

Mezzanine financing
See Third-stage financing

Micro-efficiency
Efficiency as it pertains to the operation of individual firms.

Microdata
Information on the characteristics of an individual business firm.

Microloan
An SBA loan program that helps entrepreneurs obtain loans from less than $100 to $25,000.

Mid-term debt
An obligation that matures within one to five years.

Midrisk venture capital
See Equity midrisk venture capital

Minimum premium plan
A combination approach to funding an insurance plan aimed primarily at premium tax savings. The employer self-funds a fixed percentage of estimated monthly claims and the insurance company insures the excess.

Minimum wage
The lowest hourly wage allowed by the federal government.

Minority Business Development Agency
Contracts with private firms throughout the nation to sponsor Minority Business Development Centers which provide minority firms with advice and technical assistance on a fee basis.

Minority Enterprise Small Business Investment Corporation (MESBIC)
A federally funded private venture capital firm licensed by the U.S. Small Business Administration to provide capital to minority-owned businesses (see separate citation).

Minority-owned business
Businesses owned by those who are socially or economically disadvantaged (see separate citation).

Mission statement
A short statement describing a company's function, markets and competitive advantages.

Mom and Pop business
A small store or enterprise having limited capital, principally employing family members.

Multi-employer plan
A health plan to which more than one employer is required to contribute and that may be maintained through a collective bargaining agreement and required to meet standards prescribed by the U.S. Department of Labor.

Multi-level marketing
A system of selling in which you sign up other people to assist you and they, in turn, recruit others to help them. Some entrepreneurs have built successful companies on this concept because the main focus of their activities is their product and product sales.

Multiple employer trust (MET)
A self-funded benefit plan generally geared toward small employers sharing a common interest.

NASDAQ
See National Association of Securities Dealers Automated Quotations

National Association of Securities Dealers Automated Quotations
Provides price quotes on over-the-counter securities as well as securities listed on the New York Stock Exchange.

National income
Aggregate earnings of labor and property arising from the production of goods and services in a nation's economy.

Net assets
See Net worth

Net income
The amount remaining from earnings and profits after all expenses and costs have been met or deducted. Also known as Net earnings.

Net profit
Money earned after production and overhead expenses (see separate citations) have been deducted.

Net worth
The difference between a company's total assets and its total liabilities.

Network
A chain of interconnected individuals or organizations sharing information and/or services.

New York Stock Exchange (NYSE)
The oldest stock exchange in the U.S. Allows for trading in stocks, bonds, warrants, options, and rights that meet listing requirements.

Niche
A career or business for which a person is well-suited. Also, a product which fulfills one need of a particular market segment, often with little or no competition.

Nodes
One workstation in a network, either local area or wide area (see separate citations).

Nonbank bank
A bank that either accepts deposits or makes loans, but not both. Used to create many new branch banks.

Noncompetitive awards
A method of contracting whereby the federal government negotiates with only one contractor to supply a product or service.

Nonmember bank
A state-regulated bank that does not belong to the federal bank system.

Nonprofit
An organization that has no shareholders, does not distribute profits, and is without federal and state tax liabilities.

Norms
See Financial ratios

North American Free Trade Agreement (NAFTA)
Passed in 1993, NAFTA eliminates trade barriers among businesses in the U.S., Canada, and Mexico.

NYSE
See New York Stock Exchange

Occupational Safety & Health Administration (OSHA)
Federal agency that regulates health and safety standards within the workplace.

Operating Expenses
Business expenditures not directly associated with the production of goods or services.

Optimal firm size
The business size at which the production cost per unit of output (average cost) is, in the long run, at its minimum.

Organizational chart
A hierarchical chart tracking the chain of command within an organization.

OSHA
See Occupational Safety & Health Administration

Overhead
Expenses, such as employee benefits and building utilities, incurred by a business that are unrelated to the actual product or service sold.

Glossary

Owner's capital
Debt or equity funds provided by the owner(s) of a business; sources of owner's capital are personal savings, sales of assets, or loans from financial institutions.

P & L
See Profit and loss statement

Part-time workers
Normally, those who work less than 35 hours per week. The Tax Reform Act indicated that part-time workers who work less than 17.5 hours per week may be excluded from health plans for purposes of complying with federal nondiscrimination rules.

Part-year workers
Those who work less than 50 weeks per year.

Partnership
Two or more parties who enter into a legal relationship to conduct business for profit. Defined by the U.S. Internal Revenue Code as joint ventures, syndicates, groups, pools, and other associations of two or more persons organized for profit that are not specifically classified in the IRS code as corporations or proprietorships.

Patent
A grant made by the government assuring an inventor the sole right to make, use, and sell an invention for a period of 17 years.

PC
See Professional corporation

Peak
See Cyclical peak

Pension
A series of payments made monthly, semiannually, annually, or at other specified intervals during the lifetime of the pensioner for distribution upon retirement. The term is sometimes used to denote the portion of the retirement allowance financed by the employer's contributions.

Pension fund
A fund established to provide for the payment of pension benefits; the collective contributions made by all of the parties to the pension plan.

Performance appraisal
An established set of objective criteria, based on job description and requirements, that is used to evaluate the performance of an employee in a specific job.

Permit
See Business license

Plan
See Business plan

Pooling
An arrangement for employers to achieve efficiencies and lower health costs by joining together to purchase group health insurance or self-insurance.

PPO
See Preferred provider organization

Preferred lenders program
See SBA special lending institution categories

Preferred provider organization (PPO)
A contractual arrangement with a health care services organization that agrees to discount its health care rates in return for faster payment and/or a patient base.

Premiums
The amount of money paid to an insurer for health insurance under a policy. The premium is generally paid periodically (e.g., monthly), and often is split between the employer and the employee. Unlike deductibles and coinsurance or copayments, premiums are paid for coverage whether or not benefits are actually used.

Prime-age workers
Employees 25 to 54 years of age.

Prime contract
A contract awarded directly by the U.S. Federal Government.

Private company
See Closely held corporation

Private placement
A method of raising capital by offering for sale an investment or business to a small group of investors (generally avoiding registration with the Securities and Exchange Commission or state securities registration agencies). Also known as Private financing or Private offering.

Pro forma

The use of hypothetical figures in financial statements to represent future expenditures, debts, and other potential financial expenses.

Proactive

Taking the initiative to solve problems and anticipate future events before they happen, instead of reacting to an already existing problem or waiting for a difficult situation to occur.

Procurement

A contract from an agency of the federal government for goods or services from a small business.

Product development

The stage of the innovation process where research is translated into a product or process through evaluation, adaptation, and demonstration.

Product franchising

An arrangement for a franchisee to use the name and to produce the product line of the franchisor or parent corporation.

Production

The manufacture of a product.

Production prototype

See Prototype

Productivity

A measurement of the number of goods produced during a specific amount of time.

Professional corporation (PC)

Organized by members of a profession such as medicine, dentistry, or law for the purpose of conducting their professional activities as a corporation. Liability of a member or shareholder is limited in the same manner as in a business corporation.

Profit and loss statement (P & L)

The summary of the incomes (total revenues) and costs of a company's operation during a specific period of time. Also known as Income and expense statement.

Proposal

See Business plan

Proprietorship

The most common legal form of business ownership; about 85 percent of all small businesses are proprietorships. The liability of the owner is unlimited in this form of ownership.

Prospective payment system

A cost-containment measure included in the Social Security Amendments of 1983 whereby Medicare payments to hospitals are based on established prices, rather than on cost reimbursement.

Prototype

A model that demonstrates the validity of the concept of an invention (laboratory prototype); a model that meets the needs of the manufacturing process and the user (production prototype).

Prudent investor rule or standard

A legal doctrine that requires fiduciaries to make investments using the prudence, diligence, and intelligence that would be used by a prudent person in making similar investments. Because fiduciaries make investments on behalf of third-party beneficiaries, the standard results in very conservative investments. Until recently, most state regulations required the fiduciary to apply this standard to each investment. Newer, more progressive regulations permit fiduciaries to apply this standard to the portfolio taken as a whole, thereby allowing a fiduciary to balance a portfolio with higher-yield, higher-risk investments. In states with more progressive regulations, practically every type of security is eligible for inclusion in the portfolio of investments made by a fiduciary, provided that the portfolio investments, in their totality, are those of a prudent person.

Public equity markets

Organized markets for trading in equity shares such as common stocks, preferred stocks, and warrants. Includes markets for both regularly traded and nonregularly traded securities.

Public offering

General solicitation for participation in an investment opportunity. Interstate public offerings are supervised by the U.S. Securities and Exchange Commission (see separate citation).

Quality control
The process by which a product is checked and tested to ensure consistent standards of high quality.

Rate of return
The yield obtained on a security or other investment based on its purchase price or its current market price. The total rate of return is current income plus or minus capital appreciation or depreciation.

Real property
Includes the land and all that is contained on it.

Realignment
See Resource realignment

Recession
Contraction of economic activity occurring between the peak and trough (see separate citations) of a business cycle.

Regulated market
A market in which the government controls the forces of supply and demand, such as who may enter and what price may be charged.

Regulation D
A vehicle by which small businesses make small offerings and private placements of securities with limited disclosure requirements. It was designed to ease the burdens imposed on small businesses utilizing this method of capital formation.

Regulatory Flexibility Act
An act requiring federal agencies to evaluate the impact of their regulations on small businesses before the regulations are issued and to consider less burdensome alternatives.

Research
The initial stage of the innovation process, which includes idea generation and invention.

Research and development financing
A tax-advantaged partnership set up to finance product development for start-ups as well as more mature companies.

Resource mobility
The ease with which labor and capital move from firm to firm or from industry to industry.

Resource realignment
The adjustment of productive resources to interindustry changes in demand.

Resources
The sources of support or help in the innovation process, including sources of financing, technical evaluation, market evaluation, management and business assistance, etc.

Retained business earnings
Business profits that are retained by the business rather than being distributed to the shareholders as dividends.

Return on investment
A profitability measure that evaluates the performance of a business by dividing net profit by net worth.

Revolving credit
An agreement with a lending institution for an amount of money, which cannot exceed a set maximum, over a specified period of time. Each time the borrower repays a portion of the loan, the amount of the repayment may be borrowed yet again.

Risk capital
See Venture capital

Risk management
The act of identifying potential sources of financial loss and taking action to minimize their negative impact.

Routing
The sequence of steps necessary to complete a product during production.

S corporations
See Sub chapter S corporations

SBA
See Small Business Administration

SBA direct loans
Loans made directly by the U.S. Small Business Administration (SBA); monies come from funds appropriated specifically for this purpose. In general, SBA direct loans carry interest rates slightly lower than those in the private financial markets and are available only to applicants unable to secure private financing or an SBA guaranteed loan.

SBA 504 Program
See Certified development corporation

SBA guaranteed loans
Loans made by lending institutions in which the U.S. Small Business Administration (SBA) will pay a prior agreed-upon percentage of the outstanding principal in the event the borrower of the loan defaults. The terms of the loan and the interest rate are negotiated between theborrower and the lending institution, within set parameters.

SBA loans
See Disaster loans; SBA direct loans; SBA guaranteed loans; SBA special lending institution categories

SBA Management Assistance Programs
Classes, workshops, counseling, and publications offered by the U.S. Small Business Administration.

SBA special lending institution categories
U.S. Small Business Administration (SBA) loan program in which the SBA promises certified banks a 72-hour turnaround period in giving its approval for a loan, and in which preferred lenders in a pilot program are allowed to write SBA loans without seeking prior SBA approval.

SBDB
See Small Business Data Base

SBDC
See Small business development centers

SBI
See Small business institutes program

SBIC
See Small business investment corporation

SBIR Program
See Small Business Innovation Development Act of 1982

Scale economies
The decline of the production cost per unit of output (average cost) as the volume of output increases.

Scale efficiency
The reduction in unit cost available to a firm when producing at a higher output volume.

SCORE
See Service Corps of Retired Executives

SEC
See Securities and Exchange Commission

SECA
See Self-Employment Contributions Act

Second-stage financing
Working capital for the initial expansion of a company that is producing, shipping, and has growing accounts receivable and inventories. Also known as Second-round financing.

Secondary market
A market established for the purchase and sale of outstanding securities following their initial distribution.

Secondary worker
Any worker in a family other than the person who is the primary source of income for the family.

Secondhand capital
Previously used and subsequently resold capital equipment (e.g., buildings and machinery).

Securities and Exchange Commission (SEC)
Federal agency charged with regulating the trade of securities to prevent unethical practices in the investor market.

Securitized debt
A marketing technique that converts long-term loans to marketable securities.

Seed capital
Venture financing provided in the early stages of the innovation process, usually during product development.

Self-employed person
One who works for a profit or fees in his or her own business, profession, or trade, or who operates a farm.

Self-Employment Contributions Act (SECA)
Federal law that governs the self-employment tax (see separate citation).

Self-employment income
Income covered by Social Security if a business earns a net income of at least $400.00 during the year. Taxes are paid on earnings that exceed $400.00.

Self-employment retirement plan
See Keogh plan

Self-employment tax
Required tax imposed on self-employed individuals for the provision of Social Security and Medicare. The tax must be paid quarterly with estimated income tax statements.

Self-funding
A health benefit plan in which a firm uses its own funds to pay claims, rather than transferring the financial risks of paying claims to an outside insurer in exchange for premium payments.

Service Corps of Retired Executives (SCORE)
Volunteers for the SBA Management Assistance Program who provide one-on-one counseling and teach workshops and seminars for small firms.

Service firm
See Business service firm

Service sector
Broadly defined, all U.S. industries that produce intangibles, including the five major industry divisions of transportation, communications, and utilities; wholesale trade; retail trade; finance, insurance, and real estate; and services.

Set asides
See Small business set asides

Short-haul service
A type of transportation service in which the transporter supplies service between cities where the maximum distance is no more than 200 miles.

Short-term debt
An obligation that matures in one year.

SIC codes
See Standard Industrial Classification codes

Single-establishment enterprise
See Establishment

Small business
An enterprise that is independently owned and operated, is not dominant in its field, and employs fewer than 500 people. For SBA purposes, the U.S. Small Business Administration (SBA) considers various other factors (such as gross annual sales) in determining size of a business.

Small Business Administration (SBA)
An independent federal agency that provides assistance with loans, management, and advocating interests before other federal agencies.

Small Business Data Base
A collection of microdata (see separate citation) files on individual firms developed and maintained by the U.S. Small Business Administration.

Small business development centers (SBDC)
Centers that provide support services to small businesses, such as individual counseling, SBA advice, seminars and conferences, and other learning center activities. Most services are free of charge, or available at minimal cost.

Small business development corporation
See Certified development corporation

Small business-dominated industry
Industry in which a minimum of 60 percent of employment or sales is in firms with fewer than 500 employees.

Small Business Innovation Development Act of 1982
Federal statute requiring federal agencies with large extramural research and development budgets to allocate a certain percentage of these funds to small research and development firms. The program, called the Small Business Innovation Research (SBIR) Program, is designed to stimulate technological innovation and make greater use of small businesses in meeting national innovation needs.

Small business institutes (SBI) program
Cooperative arrangements made by U.S. Small Business Administration district offices and local colleges and universities to provide small business firms with graduate students to counsel them without charge.

Small business investment corporation (SBIC)
A privately owned company licensed and funded through the U.S. Small Business Administration and private sector sources to provide equity or debt capital to small businesses.

Small business set asides
Procurement (see separate citation) opportunities required by law to be on all contracts under $10,000 or a certain percentage of an agency's total procurement expenditure.

Smaller firms
For U.S. Department of Commerce purposes, those firms not included in the Fortune 1000.

SMSA
See Metropolitan statistical area

Socially and economically disadvantaged
Individuals who have been subjected to racial or ethnic prejudice or cultural bias without regard to their qualities as individuals, and whose abilities to compete are impaired because of diminished opportunities to obtain capital and credit.

Sole proprietorship
An unincorporated, one-owner business, farm, or professional practice.

Special lending institution categories
See SBA special lending institution categories

Standard Industrial Classification (SIC) codes
Four-digit codes established by the U.S. Federal Government to categorize businesses by type of economic activity; the first two digits correspond to major groups such as construction and manufacturing, while the last two digits correspond to subgroups such as home construction or highway construction.

Start-up
A new business, at the earliest stages of development and financing.

Start-up costs
Costs incurred before a business can commence operations.

Start-up financing
Financing provided to companies that have either completed product development and initial marketing or have been in business for less than one year but have not yet sold their product commercially.

Stock
A certificate of equity ownership in a business.

Stop-loss coverage
Insurance for a self-insured plan that reimburses the company for any losses it might incur in its health claims beyond a specified amount.

Strategic planning
Projected growth and development of a business to establish a guiding direction for the future. Also used to determine which market segments to explore for optimal sales of products or services.

Structural unemployment
See Unemployment

Sub chapter S corporations
Corporations that are considered noncorporate for tax purposes but legally remain corporations.

Subcontract
A contract between a prime contractor and a subcontractor, or between subcontractors, to furnish supplies or services for performance of a prime contract (see separate citation) or a subcontract.

Surety bonds
Bonds providing reimbursement to an individual, company, or the government if a firm fails to complete a contract. The U.S. Small Business Administration guarantees surety bonds in a program much like the SBA guaranteed loan program (see separate citation).

Swing loan
See Bridge financing

Target market
The clients or customers sought for a business' product or service.

Targeted Jobs Tax Credit
Federal legislation enacted in 1978 that provides a tax credit to an employer who hires structurally unemployed individuals.

Tax number
A number assigned to a business by a state revenue department that enables the business to buy goods without paying sales tax.

Taxable bonds
An interest-bearing certificate of public or private indebtedness. Bonds are issued by public agencies to finance economic development.

GLOSSARY OF SMALL BUSINESS TERMS

Technical assistance
See Management and technical assistance

Technical evaluation
Assessment of technological feasibility.

Technology
The method in which a firm combines and utilizes labor and capital resources to produce goods or services; the application of science for commercial or industrial purposes.

Technology transfer
The movement of information about a technology or intellectual property from one party to another for use.

Tenure
See Employee tenure

Term
The length of time for which a loan is made.

Terms of a note
The conditions or limits of a note; includes the interest rate per annum, the due date, and transferability and convertibility features, if any.

Third-party administrator
An outside company responsible for handling claims and performing administrative tasks associated with health insurance plan maintenance.

Third-stage financing
Financing provided for the major expansion of a company whose sales volume is increasing and that is breaking even or profitable. These funds are used for further plant expansion, marketing, working capital, or development of an improved product. Also known as Third-round or Mezzanine financing.

Time management
Skills and scheduling techniques used to maximize productivity.

Trade credit
Credit extended by suppliers of raw materials or finished products. In an accounting statement, trade credit is referred to as "accounts payable."

Trade name
The name under which a company conducts business, or by which its business, goods, or services are

identified. It may or may not be registered as a trademark.

Trade periodical
A publication with a specific focus on one or more aspects of business and industry.

Trade secret
Competitive advantage gained by a business through the use of a unique manufacturing process or formula.

Trade show
An exhibition of goods or services used in a particular industry. Typically held in exhibition centers where exhibitors rent space to display their merchandise.

Trademark
A graphic symbol, device, or slogan that identifies a business. A business has property rights to its trademark from the inception of its use, but it is still prudent to register all trademarks with the Trademark Office of the U.S. Department of Commerce.

Trend
A statistical measurement used to track changes that occur over time.

Trough
See Cyclical trough

UCC
See Uniform Commercial Code

UL
See Underwriters Laboratories

Underwriters Laboratories (UL)
One of several private firms that tests products and processes to determine their safety. Although various firms can provide this kind of testing service, many local and insurance codes specify UL certification.

Underwriting
A process by which an insurer determines whether or not and on what basis it will accept an application for insurance. In an experience-rated plan, premiums are based on a firm's or group's past claims; factors other than prior claims are used for community-rated or manually rated plans.

Unfair competition

Refers to business practices, usually unethical, such as using unlicensed products, pirating merchandise, or misleading the public through false advertising, which give the offending business an unequitable advantage over others.

Unfunded accrued liability

The excess of total liabilities, both present and prospective, over present and prospective assets.

Unemployment

The joblessness of individuals who are willing to work, who are legally and physically able to work, and who are seeking work. Unemployment may represent the temporary joblessness of a worker between jobs (frictional unemployment) or the joblessness of a worker whose skills are not suitable for jobs available in the labor market (structural unemployment).

Uniform Commercial Code (UCC)

A code of laws governing commercial transactions across the U.S., except Louisiana. Their purpose is to bring uniformity to financial transactions.

Uniform product code (UPC symbol)

A computer-readable label comprised of ten digits and stripes that encodes what a product is and how much it costs. The first five digits are assigned by the Uniform Product Code Council, and the last five digits by the individual manufacturer.

Unit cost

See Average cost

UPC symbol

See Uniform product code

U.S. Establishment and Enterprise Microdata (USEEM) File

A cross-sectional database containing information on employment, sales, and location for individual enterprises and establishments with employees that have a Dun & Bradstreet credit rating.

U.S. Establishment Longitudinal Microdata (USELM) File

A database containing longitudinally linked sample microdata on establishments drawn from the U.S.

Establishment and Enterprise Microdata file (see separate citation).

U.S. Small Business Administration 504 Program

See Certified development corporation

USEEM

See U.S. Establishment and Enterprise Microdata File

USELM

See U.S. Establishment Longitudinal Microdata File

VCN

See Venture capital network

Venture capital

Money used to support new or unusual business ventures that exhibit above-average growth rates, significant potential for market expansion, and are in need of additional financing to sustain growth or further research and development; equity or equity-type financing traditionally provided at the commercialization stage, increasingly available prior to commercialization.

Venture capital company

A company organized to provide seed capital to a business in its formation stage, or in its first or second stage of expansion. Funding is obtained through public or private pension funds, commercial banks and bank holding companies, small business investment corporations licensed by the U.S. Small Business Administration, private venture capital firms, insurance companies, investment management companies, bank trust departments, industrial companies seeking to diversify their investment, and investment bankers acting as intermediaries for other investors or directly investing on their own behalf.

Venture capital limited partnerships

Designed for business development, these partnerships are an institutional mechanism for providing capital for young, technology-oriented businesses. The investors' money is pooled and invested in money market assets until venture investments have been selected. The general partners are experienced investment managers who select and invest the equity and debt securities of firms with high growth potential and the ability to go public in the near future.

Venture capital network (VCN)
A computer database that matches investors with entrepreneurs.

WAN
See Wide Area Network

Wide Area Network (WAN)
Computer networks linking systems throughout a state or around the world in order to facilitate the sharing of information.

Withholding
Federal, state, social security, and unemployment taxes withheld by the employer from employees' wages; employers are liable for these taxes and the corporate umbrella and bankruptcy will not exonerate an employer from paying back payroll withholding. Employers should escrow these funds in a separate account and disperse them quarterly to withholding authorities.

Workers' compensation
A state-mandated form of insurance covering workers injured in job-related accidents. In some states, the state is the insurer; in other states, insurance must be acquired from commercial insurance firms. Insurance rates are based on a number of factors, including salaries, firm history, and risk of occupation.

Working capital
Refers to a firm's short-term investment of current assets, including cash, short-term securities, accounts receivable, and inventories.

Yield
The rate of income returned on an investment, expressed as a percentage. Income yield is obtained by dividing the current dollar income by the current market price of the security. Net yield or yield to maturity is the current income yield minus any premium above par or plus any discount from par in purchase price, with the adjustment spread over the period from the date of purchase to the date of maturity.

Index

Listings in this index are arranged alphabetically by business plan type, then alphabetically by business plan name. Users are provided with the volume number in which the plan appears.

Index

Index